AF846452

Evolutionary Economics and Social Complexity Science

Volume 2

Editors-in-Chief
Takahiro Fujimoto, Tokyo, Japan
Yuji Aruka, Tokyo, Japan

Editorial Board
Satoshi Sechiyama, Kyoto, Japan
Yoshinori Shiozawa, Osaka, Japan
Kiichiro Yagi, Neyagawa, Japan
Kazuo Yoshida, Kyoto, Japan
Hideaki Aoyama, Kyoto, Japan
Hiroshi Deguchi, Yokohama, Japan
Makoto Nishibe, Sapporo, Japan
Takashi Hashimoto, Nomi, Japan
Masaaki Yoshida, Kawasaki, Japan
Tamotsu Onozaki, Tokyo, Japan
Shu-Heng Chen, Taipei, Taiwan
Dirk Helbing, Zurich, Switzerland

The Japanese Association for Evolutionary Economics (JAFEE) always has adhered to its original aim of taking an explicit "integrated" approach. This path has been followed steadfastly since the Association's establishment in 1997 and, as well, since the inauguration of our international journal in 2004. We have deployed an agenda encompassing a contemporary array of subjects including but not limited to: foundations of institutional and evolutionary economics, criticism of mainstream views in the social sciences, knowledge and learning in socio-economic life, development and innovation of technologies, transformation of industrial organizations and economic systems, experimental studies in economics, agent-based modeling of socio-economic systems, evolution of the governance structure of firms and other organizations, comparison of dynamically changing institutions of the world, and policy proposals in the transformational process of economic life. In short, our starting point is an "integrative science" of evolutionary and institutional views. Furthermore,we always endeavor to stay abreast of newly established methods such as agent-based modeling, socio/econo-physics, and network analysis as part of our integrative links.

More fundamentally, "evolution" in social science is interpreted as an essential key word, i.e., an integrative and/or communicative link to understand and re-domain various preceding dichotomies in the sciences: ontological or epistemological, subjective or objective, homogeneous or heterogeneous, natural or artificial, selfish or altruistic, individualistic or collective, rational or irrational, axiomatic or psychological-based, causal nexus or cyclic networked, optimal or adaptive, microor macroscopic, deterministic or stochastic, historical or theoretical, mathematical or computational, experimental or empirical, agent-based or socio/econo-physical, institutional or evolutionary, regional or global, and so on. The conventional meanings adhering to various traditional dichotomies may be more or less obsolete, to be replaced with more current ones vis-à-vis contemporary academic trends. Thus we are strongly encouraged to integrate some of the conventional dichotomies.

These attempts are not limited to the field of economic sciences, including management sciences, but also include social science in general. In that way, understanding the social profiles of complex science may then be within our reach. In the meantime, contemporary society appears to be evolving into a newly emerging phase, chiefly characterized by an information and communication technology (ICT) mode of production and a service network system replacing the earlier established factory system with a new one that is suited to actual observations. In the face of these changes we are urgently compelled to explore a set of new properties for a new socio/economic system by implementing new ideas. We thus are keen to look for "integrated principles" common to the above-mentioned dichotomies throughout our serial compilation of publications.We are also encouraged to create a new, broader spectrum for establishing a specific method positively integrated in our own original way.

More information about this series at http://www.springer.com/series/11930

Theodore Mariolis • Lefteris Tsoulfidis

Modern Classical Economics and Reality

A Spectral Analysis of the Theory of Value and Distribution

Springer

Theodore Mariolis
Department of Public Administration
Panteion University
Athens, Greece

Lefteris Tsoulfidis
Department of Economics
University of Macedonia
Thessaloniki, Greece

ISSN 2198-4204 ISSN 2198-4212 (electronic)
Evolutionary Economics and Social Complexity Science
ISBN 978-4-431-55003-7 ISBN 978-4-431-55004-4 (eBook)
DOI 10.1007/978-4-431-55004-4

Library of Congress Control Number: 2015955151

Springer Tokyo Heidelberg New York Dordrecht London
© Springer Japan 2016
This work is subject to copyright. All rights are reserved by the Publisher, whether the whole or part of the material is concerned, specifically the rights of translation, reprinting, reuse of illustrations, recitation, broadcasting, reproduction on microfilms or in any other physical way, and transmission or information storage and retrieval, electronic adaptation, computer software, or by similar or dissimilar methodology now known or hereafter developed.
The use of general descriptive names, registered names, trademarks, service marks, etc. in this publication does not imply, even in the absence of a specific statement, that such names are exempt from the relevant protective laws and regulations and therefore free for general use.
The publisher, the authors and the editors are safe to assume that the advice and information in this book are believed to be true and accurate at the date of publication. Neither the publisher nor the authors or the editors give a warranty, express or implied, with respect to the material contained herein or for any errors or omissions that may have been made.

Printed on acid-free paper

Springer Japan KK is part of Springer Science+Business Media (www.springer.com)

Preface

The salient feature of this book is to show the theoretical relevance and empirical significance of the classical theory of value and income distribution formulated by the old classical economists and Karl Marx and further advanced by the writings of Piero Sraffa as well as by modern followers of the classical tradition. The classical theory includes in its explanatory dataset the real wage(s) and the state of technology, which are both measurable variables and can be obtained through the available input–output and national income accounts data. As a consequence, by using data readily available in national or international organizations, one can estimate the uniform profit rate and the competitive ('long-period') relative prices for actual economies.

As is well-known, the classical approach had been "submerged and forgotten" since the advent of the neoclassical or marginalist theory, which was formulated in the last quarter of the nineteenth century and then begins to dominate economic thinking. The explanatory dataset of the neoclassical theory includes the preferences of consumers, the size and distribution of endowment of resources amongst individual agents, and the state of technology. The neoclassical theory is also capable of determining a set of commodity (and 'production factors') prices; however, the subjective character of components of its dataset casts doubt about the empirical reliability of the neoclassically-determined prices as predictors of relative commodity prices and distributive variables in actual economies. This theory has also been criticized for its logical inconsistency as this has been shown for both the theory of the perfectly competitive firm as early as the 1920s and the capital theory debates that started with Joan Robinson and culminated in the 1960s.

The present book deals with *linear* systems of production and two distributive variables, i.e. the wage and profit rates, and seeks to clarify and extend the classical theory of prices determined by physical quantities of labour, weighted with the compounded profit rate appropriate to their conceptual dates of application. The classical approach is subjected to empirical testing in an effort to show its representational and explanatory content with respect to observed phenomena and key economic policy issues related to various multiplier processes.

More specifically, we explore, both theoretically and empirically, the relative price effects of (i) income distribution changes; and (ii) total productivity shift ('Hicks-neutral technical change'), using data for a number of quite diverse actual economies and also across time for the same economy. This exploration has many important policy implications which arise, for instance, in cases where one examines the effects of changes in taxes or subsidies, changes in wages and in general strategic input costs on relative prices or purchasing power of consumers, and the effects of the currency devaluation in the international competitiveness of a national economy. At the same time, this exploration is a grand scale experiment for testing the consistency of the premises on which the two competing theories of value are resting. For example, do long-period relative prices move monotonically according to the capital-intensity of the industry relative to an average? Or do relative prices fluctuate displaying extreme points in the face of changes in the profit rate? The monotonicity of price paths is a condition *sine qua non* for the consistency of neoclassical theory, according to which prices reflect relative scarcities of 'goods and production factors', and, therefore, the presence of extreme points in the price paths contradicts the fundamental premises of that theory. These issues are treated in the six chapters that follow. It is important to emphasize that our analysis is mainly empirical in character, that is, we start with the main propositions of the classical theory which are tested empirically and the results of the empirical analysis illuminate certain theoretical aspects of the classical theory and enable its further development.

This book is structured as follows. Chapter 1 outlines the central relationships amongst classical, traditional neoclassical and modern classical theories of value, income distribution and capital. On the basis of both the latter theory and the modern, state variable representation of linear systems it also defines the basic premise of the book, that is, (i) the revelation of the essential properties of the static and dynamic behaviour of a linear production system as a whole; and, therefore, (ii) the determination of the extent to which these properties deviate from those predicted by the traditional theories.

Chapter 2 provides an overview and analysis of research on the relationships amongst long-period relative prices, physical outputs, interindustry structure of production, income distribution and growth in linear systems. Thus, it lays the groundwork for the propositions that follow in the other chapters. It is particularly pointed out that the functional expressions of those relationships admit lower and upper norm bounds, while their monotonicity could be connected to (i) the degree of deviation from the 'equal value compositions of capital' case; and (ii) the 'effective rank' of the matrix of 'vertically integrated' technical coefficients. Since nothing can be said a priori about these two factors in real-world economies, it follows that the examination of actual input–output data becomes necessary.

Chapter 3 estimates the proximities of labour values and production prices to market prices in real-world economies of single production, and explores in details the respective price-income distribution-technology relationships. The findings indicate that, although the actual economies deviate considerably from the equal value compositions of capital case, (i) their value-based approximations could be considered as accurate enough for 'realistic' values of the relative or normalized profit rate (i.e. the ratio of the uniform profit rate to the maximum one), as judged by alternative, 'traditional' and numeraire-free, measures; (ii) the directions of relative price-movements are, more often than not, consistent with the traditional theory's condition(s), that is, the 'capital-intensity effect' (direct or traditional effect) dominates the 'price effect' (indirect or Sraffian effect); and (iii) the effective ranks of the matrices of vertically integrated technical coefficients or, equivalently, the effective dimensions of these economies appear to be relatively low, that is to say, between two and three. Hence, a *spectral* analysis of actual economies becomes necessary.

Chapter 4 investigates the relationships between the traditional and the numeraire-free measures of production price-labour value deviation. It also provides an illustration of these relationships using actual input–output data. The main conclusion drawn in this chapter is that, for realistic values of the relative profit rate, all those measures of deviation tend to be close to each other and, at the same time, follow certain rankings, which we can explore starting from a two-industry economy.

Chapter 5 deals with the typical findings in many empirical studies that, within the economically relevant interval of the profit rate, actual single-product economies tend to behave as Samuelson-Hicks-Spaventa or 'corn-tractor' systems with respect to the shape of the wage-profit curve, and, at the same time, behave as three-industry systems with respect to the shape of the production price-profit rate curves. On the basis of spectral decompositions and reconstructions of the production price-wage-profit system this chapter shows that those typical findings could be connected to the fact that, across countries and over time, the moduli of the first non-dominant eigenvalues and the singular values of the system matrices fall markedly, whereas the rest constellate in much lower values forming a 'long tail'. The results finally indicate that there is room for using low-dimensional models as surrogates for actual single-product economies. It need hardly be stressed, however, that, in those models, the 'neoclassical parable relations' do not necessarily hold.

Chapter 6 tests empirically András Bródy's conjecture that, when the entries of the system matrix are identically and independently distributed, the ratio of the modulus of the subdominant eigenvalue to the dominant one tends to zero when the dimensions of the matrix tend to infinity and, therefore, the speed of convergence of the system to the equilibrium eigenvectors increases statistically with the dimensions of the system matrix. This conjecture seems to imply that a market economy of a large size converges to equilibrium more quickly than one of a smaller size. Our results do not support Bródy's conjecture suggesting that the actual input–output matrices do not share all the properties of random matrices. On the other hand, however, these same results (which are absolutely consistent with those exposed in Chap. 5) reveal that actual single-product economies can be represented in terms of a 'core' of only a few vertically integrated industries, or eigensectors, that conditions the motion of the aggregate economy in the case of (endogenous or exogenous) disturbances.

The modern classical research programme has given rise to some particularly encouraging results which, regrettably, are not yet widely known. Thus, although theoretical developments within the modern classical theory have been vigorous and the results supportive, this theory has not received (at least yet) the attention it deserves, despite being a viable and competitive alternative to the neoclassical approach. The present book would like to contribute even a little in the filling of the gap.

During the long gestation period of the book we have benefited from useful suggestions and constructive criticism on the part of many friends and colleagues. We wish to thank our – past and present – post-graduate and Ph.D. students Athanasios Angeloussis, Antonia Chistodoulaki, Heleni Groza, Fotoula Iliadi, Apostolis Katsinos, Dr. Dimitris Paitaridis, Aris Papageorgiou, Eleftheria Rodousaki, Eugenia Zouvela and, in particular, Dr. Nikolaos Rodousakis and Dr. George Soklis. They all worked with us in specific projects, and their input was invaluable. For criticisms, comments, hints and insightful discussions on the various materials that eventually became this book, we are indebted to Professors Paul Cockshott, Peter Flaschel, Saverio M. Fratini, Takao Fujimoto, Geoffrey C. Harcourt, Bart Los, Panayotis G. Michaelides, Sobei H. Oda, Carlo Panico, Bruce Philp, Ian Steedman, Judith Tomkins, Persefoni Tsaliki, Spyros Vassilakis, Roberto Veneziani and, in particular, Heinz D. Kurz, Neri Salvadori, Bertram Schefold, Anwar M. Shaikh and Robert M. Solow. We are also grateful to various publishers and editors for permission to draw freely on our published works. Last but not least we thank Professor Yuji Aruka who encouraged us to integrate our research by publishing the present book, and his help during this enterprise was invaluable. None of the above is in any way responsible for the analyses and views expressed by the authors.

Athens, Greece — Theodore Mariolis
Thessaloniki, Greece — Lefteris Tsoulfidis
June 2015

Contents

Chapter 1
Old and Modern Classical Economics

Abstract This introductory chapter outlines the central relationships amongst classical, traditional neoclassical and modern classical theories of value, distribution and capital. It then argues that the state variable representation of linear systems could be conceived of as an approach for revealing the essential properties of a linear system of production of commodities and positive profits by means of commodities and, therefore, determining the extent to which these properties deviate from those predicted by the traditional capital theories.

Keywords Capital theories • Classical and neoclassical systems • Diagonalizing transformation • State variable representation

1.1 Introduction

The term 'classical political economy' was originally coined by Karl Marx to characterize all economists beginning with William Petty in England and Pierre Le Pesant de Boisguilbert in France and ending with Ricardo in England and Simonde de Sismondi in France. According to Marx, the focus of classical economists was the determination of the surplus (value), defined as the difference between the value of total output produced and the value of (labour and nonlabour) inputs used in production.

The major problem that the classical theory of value and distribution was confronted with was the relation between the creation of surplus and the functioning of the system of commodity prices that allows the appearance of surplus in the forms of profit, rent, interest and taxes, whereas the real wage, that is, the basket of commodities that workers normally purchase, appears in the form of money wage. In the classical approach, the surplus is defined as the difference between the commodities produced and those that are required for the reproduction of society. Formally speaking, the surplus is equal to the vector of gross output minus the vector of intermediate inputs and real wages. This difference is called surplus because this is a quantity residually determined and it can, therefore, be consumed or invested. If all the surplus is consumed, then the society is in its stationary state or simple reproduction, which, however, can be conceived of only as an interesting theoretical case, rather than a realistic possibility, since capitalism is, by its very

© Springer Japan 2016

T. Mariolis, L. Tsoulfidis, *Modern Classical Economics and Reality*, Evolutionary Economics and Social Complexity Science 2, DOI 10.1007/978-4-431-55004-4_1

nature, an inherently growth-prone system. The more the surplus is devoted to net investment, the higher the economy's growth is, and if all surplus is invested, then the economy expands at its maximum growth rate or, in terms of reproduction, the economy attains its maximum expanded reproduction.

With this background in mind, when we investigate the quantification of surplus, we realize that we do not have to do with a homogenous quantity but rather with a vector of heterogeneous commodities from which we cannot refer to its specific forms. One way out that has been tried by David Ricardo (1815) is to theorize production as taking place in a single sector, where the same commodity serves as an input and produced output simultaneously. Corn, for instance, could be such a commodity, and the profit rate of the corn sector would be equal to the ratio of corn surplus to corn (seed corn and workers' real wages) inputs. Moreover, competition would ensure that the profit rate would equalize across the other sectors of the economy. Thus, given the uniform profit rate of the economy and the real wage rate, we could, in principle, at least, determine the actual commodity prices. The second way out is to express both inputs and outputs in terms of labour time ('pure labour theory of value'). However, as simple as it may be this alternative, there were a number of problems for which classical economists did not reach any satisfactory solution (particularly for those problems related to the interaction between income shares and commodity prices). The third way is to express the production of commodities as a system of n equations with n commodity prices (always assuming single-product industries). The problem with this treatment is the determination of the distributive variables, which already is not trivial by assuming only two social classes, i.e. capitalists and workers. Although the old classical economists were along this treatment, they could not arrive at a full solution because many of the necessary mathematical preliminaries had not yet been discovered (for instance, the Perron-Frobenius theorems for semi-positive matrices).

The assumption that free competition will tendentially equalize the interindustry profit rates to the economy's general one is of outmost importance for the classical analysis. The mechanism for this tendential equalization is the acceleration or deceleration of capital accumulation. For instance, if an industry makes a profit rate above the economy's general one, the accumulation of capital in this industry accelerates and the expansion of its output reduces the price to the level that gives the general profit rate. The converse is true for industries that make a lower profit rate. In this case, the deceleration of accumulation and the reduction of output raise the price of the product to a level where it incorporates the general profit rate. This position that the economic system gravitates towards whereby prices, outputs and profit rate are at their normal levels is called long-period equilibrium, and the analysis of such positions is called the long-period method. It should be stressed at the outset that the term 'long period' refers to the analytical time, which is required until the system attains its normal position.

This introductory chapter serves to outline the central relationships amongst classical, traditional neoclassical and modern classical theories of value, distribution and capital.[1] On the basis of both the latter theory and the modern, state variable representation of linear systems, it also defines the basic premise of the present book.

The remainder of the chapter is structured as follows. Section 1.2 exposes the relationships amongst the said theories and pinpoints the source of conceptual and analytical difficulties for the traditional ones. Section 1.3 sketches out the importance of state variable representation of linear production systems for capital theory. Finally, Sect. 1.4 concludes.

1.2 Classical Economics

Although none of the old classical economists specified the 'core' of their theory in any explicit way, it could be theorized, on both logical and textual grounds, that the classical contributions to the value and distribution theory share a common set of exogenously determined variables. This set includes only observable and measurable (or calculable) quantities and concerns (Kurz and Salvadori 1998, p. 8)[2]:

(i) The set of technical alternatives from which cost-minimizing producers can choose
(ii) The size and composition of the social product, reflecting, the needs and wants of the members of the different classes of society and the requirements of reproduction and capital accumulation
(iii) The ruling real wage rate(s)
(iv) The quantities of different qualities of land available and the known stocks of depletable resources (such as mineral deposits)

The said independent variables are sufficient to completely determine the system unknowns or dependent variables, i.e. the profit rate, the rent rates and the long-period relative commodity prices (or (re-) production prices).

Classical economists had all of the above implicit in their analyses, even though they did not have a single view. For example, Ricardos's theory of value was not the same with Marx's one, while there were also the pro-labour economists (e.g. Robert Owen, William Thompson and Thomas Hodgskin), who—inspired by the Ricardian labour theory of value—claimed that all the surplus should belong to the workers because the workers are the creators of the surplus; it follows, therefore, that the capitalist's profit and landlord's rent are direct deductions from the value of commodities. In short, the value of a commodity must be equal to the labour that went into its production, which is equivalent to saying that neither profits nor rents are incomes justified on moral grounds. The value of commodities is created by

[1] For a history-of-economic thought discussion of the structures of the classical and the neoclassical approaches, see Tsoulfidis (2010, Chaps. 6 and 7, 2011).

[2] Also consider Pasinetti (1959–1960, 1981), Eatwell (1983), Garegnani (1984) and Steedman (1979a, Chaps. 1–3, 1998).

labour alone and, therefore, all the value of a commodity should belong to the workers. This rather normative variant of the labour theory of value gave rise to an anticapitalist movement. A problem of this sort that was developed within the framework of the labour theory of value together with the inability of the proponents of the old classical economists to provide satisfactory answers to certain thorny questions (i.e. the role of demand, the quantity of capital employed, etc.) led to the 'disintegration of the Ricardian school' and with that of the classical thought. Gradually, many economists discarded the idea of price determined by systematic and, therefore, persistent market 'forces', and instead they ascribed to the idea that the commodity prices are determined by the ephemeral forces of supply and demand, that is, by competition. Marx characterized this approach 'vulgar' simply because it attributed the determination of market prices to the mere operation of competition and not to something more fundamental 'behind' the forces of demand and supply that could establish a causal relationship.

With this background, it does not come as a surprise that an increasing number of economists started drifting away from the classical thought, although not from many of the classical ideas, and even the labour theory of value remained for some time (especially with the British economists). What was really at stake was the causality, which for the old classical economists runs from the determination of cost through the quantity of labour time to equilibrium prices, whereas for the neoclassical economists, the 'arrow of causality' runs from demand that is determined by 'utility' (cardinal or ordinal). Supply (or cost of production), on the other hand, was determined by negative utility or disutility, and in doing so, neoclassical economists managed to express supply in terms of a common unit of measurement. For instance, wage is the compensation for the disutility that the workers suffer by offering part of their endowment of labour services. Similarly, profits and rents are the compensations for the disutility that the owners of capital and land, respectively, suffer by contributing their endowments to the production of goods and (other) services. Having expressed supply as disutility, neoclassical economists could put together demand and supply for the simultaneous determination of equilibrium price and quantity. For the determination of this equilibrium, individuals behave rationally, that is, they display optimizing behaviour. There is no doubt that this is an optimization problem, where the total gain is maximized since the marginal benefit (utility) is equal to the marginal sacrifice (disutility) (also see Eatwell 1983; Kurz and Salvadori 2015). It is interesting to note that in this new 'neoclassical or marginalist' theory, individualism-cum-subjectivism is the major characteristic of both demand and supply decisions. In this sense, neoclassical theory for it refers to the long period and acknowledges systematic forces that are underneath demand and supply schedules cannot be characterized as vulgar.

Clearly, the substantial difference between the old classical theory and the new theory was not fully grasped even by the leading proponents of the 'marginal revolution' of the 1870s (also consider Milgate and Stimson 2011, Chap. 13). For instance, Léon Walras ([1874–1877] 1954) stated that the classical system is, at best, underdetermined:

> We must now discuss the [English, i.e. classical] theory mathematically in order to sow how illusory it is. Let P be the aggregate price received for the products of an enterprise; let S, I, and F be respectively the wages, interest charges and rent laid out by the entrepreneurs, in the course of production, to pay for the services of personal faculties, capital and land. Let us recall now that, according to the English School, the selling price of products is determined by their costs of production, that is to say, it is equal to the cost of the productive services employed. Thus we have the equation
>
> $P = S + I + F$,
>
> And P is determined for us. It remains only to determine S, I, and F. Surely, if it is not the price of the products that determines the price of productive services, but the price of productive services that determines the price of the products, we must be told what determines the price of the services. That is precisely what the English economists try to do. To this end, they construct a theory of rent according to which rent is not included in the expenses of production, thus changing the above equation to
>
> $P = S + I$.
>
> Having done this, they determine S directly by the theory of wages. Then, finally, they tell us that "the amount of interest or profit is the excess of the aggregate price received for the products over the wages expended on their production", in other words, that it is determined by the equation
>
> $I = P - S$.
>
> It is clear now that the English economists are completely baffled by the problem of price determination; for it is impossible for I to determine P at the same time that P determines I. In the language of mathematics one equation cannot be used to determine two unknowns. This objection is raised without any reference to our position on the manner in which the English School eliminates rent before setting out to determine wages.[3] (pp. 424–425)

This crucial objection provides the starting point for the construction of a rather different determination system, known as the (traditional) neoclassical system, in which the exogenously determined variables are (Kurz and Salvadori 1998, p. 10):

(i) The set of technical alternatives from which cost-minimizing producers can choose
(ii) The preferences of consumers (which are *not* directly observable)
(iii) The initial endowments of the economy with all 'factors of production', *including* 'capital', and the distribution of property rights amongst individual agents

Within that system, both prices and distributive variables are explained simultaneously and symmetrically in terms of demand and supply for 'goods' and services of 'factors of production', respectively, and, thus, reflect the 'relative scarcities' of those 'goods and factors'.

Almost three decades later, Vladimir K. Dmitriev (1898), 'a romantic and shadowy figure, who founded Russian mathematical economics' (Samuelson 1975, p. 491), begun explicitly with Walras's objection and then demonstrated that in closed, *linear* production systems involving only single products, circulating capital and *two* distributive variables, i.e. the wage and profit rates, the classical (or,

---

[3] As Kurz (2014, p. 11) remarks, 'the same kind of criticism can be found also in most recent times' (and refers, as an example, two papers by Kenneth J. Arrow, published in 1972 and 1991).

more precisely, Ricardian) dataset suffices for a simultaneous determination of the profit rate and relative commodity prices (also see Kurz and Salvadori (2002)). In particular, he showed that:

(i) The relationship between the money wage rate and the profit rate is strictly decreasing irrespective of the numeraire chosen.
(ii) The profit rate is determined by the real wage rate and the technical conditions of production in the industries producing wage commodities and means of production used, directly or indirectly, in the production of wage commodities. According to Dmitriev (1898):

> Hardly anyone will dispute that the *only* process determining the level of profit at the *present time* is the [flow input-point output] process of production of the means of subsistence of the workers (*capitale alimento* [Achille Loria]). [...] [The] investigation of the conditions affecting the level of [the real wage rate] falls outside the scope (and competence) of political economy and within that of other disciplines [...]. [P]olitical economy should take [the real wage rate] to be given in its analysis.[4] (pp. 73–74)

(iii) The profit rate is positive iff surplus value (or surplus labour) is positive or, equivalently, iff the total input requirements of commodity i (i=1,2,$\cdots$,n) necessary to produce 1 unit of gross output of commodity i are less than 1.
(iv) Prices can be reduced to physical quantities of labour, weighted with the compounded profit rate appropriate to their conceptual dates of application. Hence, relative prices are independent of demand conditions.
(v) Prices are proportional to labour values only when either the profit rate is zero or the 'value composition of capital' (Marx) is uniform across all industries (we will return to all these issues in Chap. 2).
(vi) The neoclassical system is actually based on the extension of the 'principle of scarcity', which Ricardo (and other classical economists) had limited to natural resources only, to all 'goods and production factors' (also consider Mühlpfordt 1895, pp. 92–93 and 98–99).

Thus, Dmitriev (1898) finally concluded that

> To level at Ricardo's theory the hackneyed reproach that it 'defines price in terms of price' is to manifest a complete lack of understanding of the writings of this very great theoretical economist. (p. 61)

Modern classical economics are founded on the work of Piero Sraffa. As Garegnani (1998) emphasizes:

> The importance of [Sraffa's] work for today's economic theory appears to rest essentially on the following three elements: (1) his rediscovery of the theoretical approach characteristic of the classical economists; (2) his solution of some key analytical difficulties that they were not resolved by Ricardo and Marx; (3) his criticism of marginal theory. (p. 395)

[4] For criticisms of this statement, and way of closing the system, see, e.g. Samuelson (1975, p. 493) and Fan (1983).

The modern classical economics propositions that are particularly important for the present book can be summarized as follows[5]:

(i) Given the real wage rate, the relative commodity prices depend on the profit rate, and the profit rate depends on the relative commodity prices. Consequently, 'the distribution of the surplus must be determined through the same mechanism and at the same time as are the prices of commodities'. (Sraffa 1960, p. 6)

(ii) Even with unchanged production methods, changes in income distribution activate price-feedback effects, which imply that the directions of relative price movements are governed not only by the differences in the relevant capital intensities but also by the movements of the relevant capital intensities. Thus, the direction of relative price movements cannot be known a priori.

(iii) The 'capital intensity' of the production techniques need not decrease (increase) as the profit (the wage) rate rises.

(iv) The said propositions imply that the traditional neoclassical or Austrian school attempts to start from a given 'quantity of capital' or an 'average period of production' in order to determine the profit or interest rate is ill-founded. They also undermine the neoclassical analysis of demand and supply for 'capital' and labour and, thus, the explanation of the distributive variables as the service prices of the 'production factors' that reflect their 'scarcities'. In effect, all statements and relationships derived from an aggregate production function or average production period framework cannot, in general, be extended beyond a world where (a) there are no produced means of production; or (b) there are produced means of production, while the profit rate on the value of those means of production is zero (also see Samuelson 1953–1954, pp. 17–19); or, finally, (c) that profit rate is positive, while the economy produces one and only one, single or composite, commodity (also see Steedman 1994). In that world, there also exist traditional classical and Marxian statements that are necessarily valid. Burmeister (1975) has noted:

> There is no doubt that economics would be an easier subject if God had imposed the restriction 'equal organic [value] composition of capital' on the world, a *technological* restriction of nature as immutable as the laws of physics. (p. 456)

It can, therefore, be concluded that the conceptual and analytical difficulties of the traditional theories of value and distribution arise from the existence of complex interindustry linkages in the realistic case of production of commodities and *positive* profits by means of commodities.

---

[5] See Bhaduri (1966), Pasinetti (1966), Garegnani (1970), Steedman (1979a, b), Kurz and Salvadori (1995) and the references therein. In modern classical economics system, the real wage rate(s) is not necessarily an exogenously given variable. That system determines relations between, on the one hand, distributive variables and commodity prices and, on the other hand, growth, physical outputs and labour allocations. Thus, there are alternative ways of closing it (consider, for instance, the 'monetary theory of distribution', i.e. the possible determination of the profit rate by the money interest rate; Sraffa 1960, p. 33, Panico 1988, Pivetti 1991).

1.3 State Variable Representation and Capital Theory

It is well known that an important class of linear systems can be represented axiomatically by[6]

$$\boldsymbol{\psi}_{t+1} = \gamma_t \boldsymbol{\beta} + \boldsymbol{\psi}_t \mathbf{A}, \quad t = 0, 1, \ldots \tag{1.1}$$

$$\varepsilon_t = \boldsymbol{\psi}_t \boldsymbol{\delta}^{\mathrm{T}} \tag{1.2}$$

where $\boldsymbol{\psi}_t$ denotes the real $1 \times n$ 'state' vector, i.e. the vector that captures the state of the system with n nodes at time t; $\mathbf{A}$ the real, constant, $n \times n$ system matrix (also known as the plant coefficient matrix), which describes the *interaction* strengths between the system components; γ_t the input of the system, which constitutes a scalar function of time (also known as the one-dimensional control vector); $\boldsymbol{\beta}$ the real, constant, $1 \times n$ input vector (it may identify the nodes controlled by an outside controller who imposes γ_t); $\boldsymbol{\delta}^{\mathrm{T}}$ the real, constant, $n \times 1$ output vector; ε_t the output of the system (also known as the measurement variable); and Eqs. 1.1 and 1.2 are the dynamical equations of the system. The analogue of these equations in continuous time is

$$d\boldsymbol{\psi}(t)/dt = \gamma(t)\boldsymbol{\beta} + \boldsymbol{\psi}(t)[\mathbf{A} - \mathbf{I}] \tag{1.1a}$$

$$\varepsilon(t) = \boldsymbol{\psi}(t)\boldsymbol{\delta}^{\mathrm{T}} \tag{1.2a}$$

It should be noticed that the so-called traditional representation of linear systems is based on the 'transfer function' (a proper rational function of degree no greater than n) rather than the difference Eqs. 1.1 and 1.2 or the differential Eqs. 1.1a and 1.2a. This function, however, does not necessarily contain all the information which characterizes the behaviour of the system (we will return to this issue in Sect. 2.2.2).

This axiomatic representation is based on Newton's laws of mechanics:

> Macroscopic physical phenomena are commonly described in terms of cause-and-effect relationships. This is the 'Principle of Causality'. The idea involved here is at least as old as Newtonian mechanics. According to the latter, the motion of a system of particles is fully determined for all future time by the present positions and momenta of the particles and by the present and future forces acting on the system. How the particles actually attained their present positions and momenta is immaterial. Future forces can have no effect on what happens at present. In modern terminology, we say that the numbers which specify the instantaneous position and momentum of each particle represent the *state* of the system. The state is to be regarded always as an abstract quantity.[7] (Kalman 1963, p. 154)

---

[6] Matrices (and vectors) are delineated in boldface letters. The transpose of a $1 \times n$ vector $\boldsymbol{\psi} \equiv [\psi_j]$ is denoted by $\boldsymbol{\psi}^{\mathrm{T}}$. The diagonal matrix formed from the elements of $\boldsymbol{\psi}$ will be denoted by $\hat{\boldsymbol{\psi}}$, and $\mathbf{I}$ will denote the $n \times n$ identity matrix.

[7] By definition, this axiomatization is incomplete for systems that include agents' expectations about the future. In that case, 'the future influences the present just as much as the past' (Friedrich Nietzsche) and, therefore, the concept of *futurität* (futurity) becomes indispensable (see, e.g. Willke 1993, Chap. 4).

Thus, the state of a system is a mathematical structure containing the n variables ψ_{jt}, i.e. the so-called state variables. The initial values, ψ_{j0}, of these variables and the input, γ_t, are sufficient for uniquely determining the system behaviour for any $t \geq 0$. The state variables need not be observable and measurable quantities; they may be purely mathematical, abstract quantities. On the contrary, the input and output of the system are directly observable and measurable quantities, that is, quantities which have a concrete meaning (e.g. physical or economic). It may be said that the inputs are the forces acting on the particles. State space is the n-dimensional space, in which the components of the state vector represent its coordinate axes. The choice of state variables, i.e. the choice of the smallest possible set of variables for uniquely determining the future behaviour of the system, is not unique. Nevertheless, a uniquely determined state corresponds to each choice of the said variables.

Two representations $[\mathbf{A},\boldsymbol{\beta},\boldsymbol{\delta}^{\mathrm{T}}]$ and $[\mathbf{A}^*,\boldsymbol{\beta}^*,\boldsymbol{\delta}^{*\mathrm{T}}]$ of the same system are said to be strictly equivalent when their state vectors, $\boldsymbol{\psi}_t$ and $\boldsymbol{\psi}^*_t$, respectively, are related for all t as follows:

$$\boldsymbol{\psi}_t^* = \boldsymbol{\psi}_t \mathbf{T} \tag{1.3}$$

where $\mathbf{T}$ denotes a constant non-singular matrix. From Eqs. 1.1, 1.2 and 1.3, it follows that strict equivalence implies the following relationships (and vice versa):

$$\mathbf{A}^* = \mathbf{T}^{-1}\mathbf{A}\mathbf{T}$$
$$\boldsymbol{\beta}^* = \boldsymbol{\beta}\mathbf{T}$$
$$\boldsymbol{\delta}^* = \mathbf{T}^{-1}\boldsymbol{\delta}^{\mathrm{T}}$$

These relationships define a similarity transformation by the matrix $\mathbf{T}$ or, in other words, a change of the coordinate system in the state space.

If $\mathbf{A}$ has a complete set of n linearly independent eigenvectors ('diagonalizable matrix'), then system (1.1) is strictly equivalent to the system

$$\widetilde{\boldsymbol{\psi}}_{t+1} = \gamma_t \widetilde{\boldsymbol{\beta}} + \widetilde{\boldsymbol{\psi}}_t \hat{\boldsymbol{\lambda}}_{\mathrm{A}} \tag{1.4}$$

where $\hat{\boldsymbol{\lambda}}_{\mathrm{A}} = \mathbf{X}_{\mathbf{A}}^{-1}\mathbf{A}\mathbf{X}_{\mathbf{A}}$ denotes the diagonal matrix formed from the eigenvalues of $\mathbf{A}$, $\mathbf{X}_{\mathbf{A}}$ $\left(\mathbf{X}_{\mathbf{A}}^{-1}\right)$ the matrix formed from the right (left) eigenvectors of $\mathbf{A}$, known as the modal matrix, $\widetilde{\boldsymbol{\psi}}_t \equiv \boldsymbol{\psi}_t \mathbf{X}_{\mathbf{A}}$ and $\widetilde{\boldsymbol{\beta}} \equiv \boldsymbol{\beta}\mathbf{X}_{\mathbf{A}}$. Thus, the modal matrix defines a new coordinate system ('normal coordinates') in which the system matrix is represented by its diagonal eigenvalue matrix and, therefore, the system is decomposed into a set of *uncoupled* first-order sub-systems, where each of them is associated with a particular system eigenvalue.[8]

[8] If there is not a complete set of eigenvectors, matrix $\mathbf{A}$ cannot be reduced to a diagonal form by a similarity transformation and, therefore, the original system cannot be decomposed into a set of

Finally, assume that the system input is constant, i.e.

$$\boldsymbol{\psi}_{t+1} = \gamma\boldsymbol{\beta} + \boldsymbol{\psi}_t\mathbf{A} \tag{1.5}$$

An equilibrium point, $\overline{\boldsymbol{\psi}}$, of system (1.5) must satisfy the equation

$$\overline{\boldsymbol{\psi}} = \gamma\boldsymbol{\beta} + \overline{\boldsymbol{\psi}}\mathbf{A} \tag{1.6}$$

Provided that matrix $[\mathbf{I}-\mathbf{A}]$ is non-singular or, equivalently, that 1 is not an eigenvalue of $\mathbf{A}$, there is a unique solution

$$\overline{\boldsymbol{\psi}} = \gamma\boldsymbol{\beta}[\mathbf{I} - \mathbf{A}]^{-1}$$

In the opposite case, either there is no equilibrium point (the system (1.6) is inconsistent) or there is an infinity of such points. From Eqs. 1.5 and 1.6, it follows that

$$\boldsymbol{\psi}_{t+1} - \overline{\boldsymbol{\psi}} = (\boldsymbol{\psi}_t - \overline{\boldsymbol{\psi}})\mathbf{A}$$

or

$$\boldsymbol{\psi}_{t+1} - \overline{\boldsymbol{\psi}} = (\boldsymbol{\psi}_0 - \overline{\boldsymbol{\psi}})\mathbf{A}^{t+1}$$

or, since $\mathbf{A} = \mathbf{X}_{\mathbf{A}}\hat{\boldsymbol{\lambda}}_{\mathbf{A}}\mathbf{X}_{\mathbf{A}}^{-1}$ (see Eq. 1.4),

$$(\boldsymbol{\psi}_{t+1} - \overline{\boldsymbol{\psi}})\mathbf{X}_{\mathbf{A}} = (\boldsymbol{\psi}_0 - \overline{\boldsymbol{\psi}})\mathbf{X}_{\mathbf{A}}\left[\hat{\boldsymbol{\lambda}}_{\mathbf{A}}\right]^{t+1}$$

or

$$\tilde{\boldsymbol{\psi}}_{t+1} - \tilde{\overline{\boldsymbol{\psi}}} = \left(\tilde{\boldsymbol{\psi}}_0 - \tilde{\overline{\boldsymbol{\psi}}}\right)\left[\hat{\boldsymbol{\lambda}}_{\mathbf{A}}\right]^{t+1}$$

where $\tilde{\overline{\boldsymbol{\psi}}} \equiv \overline{\boldsymbol{\psi}}\mathbf{X}_{\mathbf{A}}$. It can, therefore, be stated that the equilibrium point is 'asymptotically stable', i.e. for any initial condition, $\boldsymbol{\psi}_0$, the state vector tends to the equilibrium point as time increases, iff the eigenvalues of $\mathbf{A}$ all have moduli less than 1.[9]

uncoupled first-order sub-systems (we will return to this issue in Chap. 2). It is always possible, however, to find a basis in which **A** is almost diagonal ('Jordan normal form'; see, e.g. Meyer 2001, Sects. 7.8 and 7.9). In that case, the transformed system (also) contains 'chains' of first-order sub-systems (associated with a particular system eigenvalue), where the output of one is the input of another.

[9] In that case, the eigenvalues of [**A**–**I**] all have negative real part (and vice versa); thus, the equilibrium point of system (1.1a), with $\gamma(t)=\gamma$, is asymptotically stable.

Luenberger (1979) emphasizes the importance of the diagonalizing transformation as follows:

> [T]he role of the diagonalization process is at least as much conceptual as it is computational. Although calculation of the state-transition matrix $\left[\mathbf{A}^t = \mathbf{X}_\mathbf{A}\left[\hat{\boldsymbol{\lambda}}_\mathbf{A}\right]^t\mathbf{X}_\mathbf{A}^{-1}\right]$ can be facilitated if the eigenvectors are known, the problem of computing the eigenvalues and eigenvectors for a large system is itself a formidable task. Often this form of detailed analysis is not justified by the scope of the motivating study. Indeed, when restricted to numerical methods it is usually simplest to evaluate a few particular solutions directly by recursion. A full collection of eigenvectors in numerical form is not always very illuminating. On the other hand, from a conceptual viewpoint, the diagonalization process is invaluable, for it reveals an underlying simplicity of linear systems. Armed with this concept, we know, when faced with what appears to be a complex interconnected system, that there is a way to look at it, through a kind of distorted lenses which changes variables, so that it appears simply as a collection of first-order systems. Even if we never find the diagonalizing transformation, the knowledge that one exists profoundly influences our perception of a system and enriches our analysis methodology. (pp. 141–142)

Consider, then, a closed, linear system of production involving only single products, 'basic' commodities (in the sense of Sraffa 1960, pp. 7–8) and circulating capital; thus, $\mathbf{A}$ ($\geq\mathbf{0}$), $\boldsymbol{\beta}$ ($>\mathbf{0}$) now denote the matrix of 'direct technical coefficients' and the vector of 'direct labour coefficients', respectively. The case where $\boldsymbol{\beta}$ is an eigenvector of $\mathbf{A}$, i.e. $\boldsymbol{\beta}\mathbf{A}=\lambda\boldsymbol{\beta}$, corresponds, as is well-known, to the 'equal value compositions of capital' case. In that (extreme) case and for $\boldsymbol{\psi}_0=\mathbf{0}$, $\boldsymbol{\psi}_{t+1}$ and $\boldsymbol{\beta}$ are linearly dependent irrespective of the input sequence, γ_t, i.e.

$$\boldsymbol{\psi}_{t+1} = \left(\gamma_0\lambda^t + \gamma_1\lambda^{t-1} + \ldots + \gamma_{t-1}\lambda + \gamma_t\right)\boldsymbol{\beta}$$

The application of the diagonalizing transformation to a linear system of production $[\mathbf{A}, \boldsymbol{\beta}]$ leads to n uncoupled one-commodity worlds that can be adequately analysed in terms of the traditional capital theories:

> It is to be understood that we take this to be in the 'as if' sense, that is, we can reckon in such a way that is as if wages, materials, and profits were actually being paid in own products. It is of course a fiction; the linear transformation is an accounting system but there is no corresponding reality. Therefore we have a universal Ricardian *Corn* Economy with all the clarity it embodies. The *i*th corn is produced by the *i*th corn, by labour that is paid in the *i*th corn, which leaves a profit in *i*th corn. In this sense it seems to share the simplicity and intelligibility of Marshall's supply and demand analysis, whilst avoiding its grave defect (that is, it takes full account of interdependence and employs no *ceteris paribus*). An *awkward* aspect of this device is that it will ordinarily involve negative and complex quantities, so that it is difficult to give common sense interpretations to the analysis. Of course, in transforming *back*, these complex and negative quantities disappear. The great advantage of the transformation is that it *separates* value from distribution and allocation from growth. (Goodwin 1976, pp. 131–133; emphasis added)

The fundamental trouble is not so much that those sub-systems or eigensectors are 'fictitious', but rather that they have no economic meaning since, in the general case, the eigenvalues of the system matrix are not all semi-positive. Hence, putting aside extreme (and trivial) cases as well as the possible existence of other, unknown so far, transformations leading to a meaningful universe of Ricardian corn economies, the inevitability of the non-semi-positivity problem further corroborates the Sraffa-based critique of the traditional theories. Nevertheless, the diagonalizing transformation could be conceived of as an approach for (i) revealing the *essential* properties of the static and dynamic behaviour of a linear production system as a whole and, therefore, (ii) determining the *extent* to which these properties deviate from those predicted by the traditional theories. The basic premise of the present book is that the said issues can be intensively investigated both theoretically and empirically.

1.4 Concluding Remarks

Capitalist economies do not behave like the parable of a one-commodity world of the traditional neoclassical theory, which theorize the relative scarcities of 'goods and production factors' as the fundamental determinants of relative commodity prices. By contrast, the modern classical theory, which makes the intersectoral structure of production and the way in which net output is distributed amongst its claimants the fundamental determinants of price magnitudes, provides an open-ended framework for dealing with price effects arising from changes in income distribution or/and technical production conditions. In particular, it seems that the integration of this theory with the state variable representation of linear systems could further operationalize the Sraffa-based critique of the traditional capital theories, by shedding new empirical *and* theoretical light on the price-income distribution-technology relationships.

References

Bhaduri, A. (1966). The concept of the marginal productivity of capital and the Wicksell effect. *Oxford Economic Papers, 18*(3), 284–288.

Burmeister, E. (1975). A comment on "This age of Leontief ... and who?". *Journal of Economic Literature, 13*(2), 454–457.

Dmitriev, V. K. (1898). The theory of value of David Ricardo: An attempt at a rigorous analysis. In V. K. Dmitriev (Ed.) ([1904] 1974), *Economic essays on value, competition and utility* (pp. 37–95). Edited with an introduction by D. M. Nuti, London: Cambridge University Press.

Eatwell, J. (1983). Theories of value, output and employment. In J. Eatwell & M. Milgate (Eds.), *Keynes's economics and the theory of value and distribution* (pp. 93–128). London: Duckworth.

Fan, Y.-K. (1983). On the rate of profit in the Ricardo-Dmitriev-Sraffa models. *Atlantic Economic Journal, 11*(2), 97.

Garegnani, P. (1970). Heterogeneous capital, the production function and the theory of distribution. *The Review of Economic Studies, 37*(3), 407–436.

Garegnani, P. (1984). Value and distribution in the classical economists and Marx. *Oxford Economic Papers, 36*(2), 291–325.

Garegnani, P. (1998). Sraffa, Piero. In H. D. Kurz & N. Salvadori (Eds.), *The Elgar companion to classical economics L-Z* (pp. 391–399). Cheltenham: Edward Elgar.

Goodwin, R. M. (1976). Use of normalized general co-ordinates in linear value and distribution theory. In K. R. Polenske & J. V. Skolka (Eds.), *Advances in input-output analysis* (pp. 581–602). Cambridge, MA: Ballinger.

Kalman, R. E. (1963). Mathematical description of linear dynamical systems. *Journal of the Society for Industrial and Applied Mathematics on Control, 1*(2), 152–192.

Kurz, H. D. (2014). The 'standpoint of the old classical economists'. In *Heterodoxy in economics: From history to pluralism. Festschrift in honour of John King*. http://www.vu.edu.au/sites/default/files/cses/pdfs/kurz-paper.pdf. Accessed 12 Dec 2014.

Kurz, H. D., & Salvadori, N. (1995). *Theory of production. A long-period analysis*. Cambridge: Cambridge University Press.

Kurz, H. D., & Salvadori, N. (1998). *Understanding 'classical' economics. Studies in long-period theory*. London: Routledge.

Kurz, H. D., & Salvadori, N. (2002). One theory or two? Walras's critique of Ricardo. In H. D. Kurz & N. Salvadori (Eds.) (2007), *Interpreting classical economics. Studies in long-period analysis* (pp. 53–78). London: Routledge.

Kurz, H. D., & Salvadori, N. (2015). *Classical economics after Sraffa*. Paper presented at the 19th European Society for the History of Economic Thought Conference, 14–16 May 2015, Roma Tre University, Italy.

Luenberger, D. G. (1979). *Introduction to dynamic systems. Theory, models, and applications*. New York: Wiley.

Meyer, C. D. (2001). *Matrix analysis and applied linear algebra*. New York: Society for Industrial and Applied Mathematics.

Milgate, M., & Stimson, S. C. (2011). *After Adam Smith: A century of transformation in politics and political economy*. Princeton: Princeton University Press.

Mühlpfordt, W. (1895). Karl Marx und die durchschnittsprofitrate. *Jahrbücher für Nationalökonomie und Statistik, 10*(65), 92–99.

Panico, C. (1988). *Interest and profit in the theories of value and distribution*. London: Macmillan.

Pasinetti, L. L. (1959–1960). A mathematical formulation of the Ricardian system. *The Review of Economic Studies, 27*(2), 78–98.

Pasinetti, L. L. (1966). Changes in the rate of profit and switches of techniques. *The Quarterly Journal of Economics, 80*(4), 503–517.

Pasinetti, L. L. (1981). On the Ricardian theory of value: A note. *The Review of Economic Studies, 48*(4), 673–675.

Pivetti, M. (1991). *An essay on money and distribution*. Basingstoke: Macmillan.

Ricardo, D. (1815). *An essay on the influence of a low price of corn on the profits of stock, with remarks on Mr Malthus' two last publications*. London: John Murray.

Samuelson, P. A. (1953–1954). Prices of factors and goods in general equilibrium. *The Review of Economic Studies, 21*(1), 1–20.

Samuelson, P. A. (1975). Review of V.K. Dmitriev's Economic essays on value, competition and utility. *Journal of Economic Literature, 13*(2), 491–495.

Sraffa, P. (1960). *Production of commodities by means of commodities. Prelude to a critique of economic theory*. Cambridge: Cambridge University Press.

Steedman, I. (1979a). *Trade amongst growing economies*. Cambridge: Cambridge University Press.

Steedman, I. (Ed.). (1979b). *Fundamental issues in trade theory*. London: Macmillan.

Steedman, I. (1994). 'Perverse' behaviour in a 'one commodity' model. *Cambridge Journal of Economics, 18*(3), 299–311.

Steedman, I. (1998). Classical economics and marginalism. In H. D. Kurz & N. Salvadori (Eds.), *The Elgar companion to classical economics A-K* (pp. 117–121). Cheltenham: Edward Elgar.

Tsoulfidis, L. (2010). *Competing schools of economic thought*. Heidelberg: Springer.

Tsoulfidis, L. (2011). Economic theory in historical perspective. *Journal of Economic Analysis, 2* (1), 32–45.
Walras, L. ([1874–1877] 1954). *Elements of pure economics* (trans: Jaffé, W). London: Allen and Unwin.
Willke, H. (1993). *Systemtheorie. Eine Einführung in die Grundprobleme der Theorie sozialer Systeme*. Stuttgart: Gustav Fischer Verlag.

Chapter 2
Modern Classical Theory of Prices and Outputs

Abstract This chapter investigates the relationships amongst long-period relative prices, outputs, interindustry structure of production, income distribution and growth in linear systems. It is particularly pointed out that the functional expressions of those relationships admit lower and upper norm bounds, while their monotonicity could be connected to (i) the degree of deviation from the 'equal value compositions of capital' case and (ii) the 'effective rank' of the matrix of vertically integrated technical coefficients.

Keywords Effective matrix rank • Income distribution • Growth • Norm bounds • Price effects

2.1 Introduction

Modern classical theory is concerned with both price and quantity sides of systems of production of commodities by means of themselves. This chapter provides an overview and analysis of research on the relationships amongst long-period relative prices, physical outputs, interindustry structure of production, income distribution and growth in linear systems. Thus, it forms the analytical basis for the propositions derived in this book.

The remainder of the chapter is structured as follows. Section 2.2 presents the necessary preliminaries by focusing on the determination of relative prices and outputs by the technical conditions of production and one of the distributive variables (i.e. the real wage rate or, alternatively, the profit rate). Section 2.3 gives lower and upper bounds, which are expressed in terms of the 'maximum column sum matrix norm', for the wage-price-profit rate curves. Section 2.4 explores the relative price effects of (i) income distribution changes and (ii) total productivity shift. Finally, Sect. 2.5 concludes.

© Springer Japan 2016

T. Mariolis, L. Tsoulfidis, *Modern Classical Economics and Reality*, Evolutionary Economics and Social Complexity Science 2, DOI 10.1007/978-4-431-55004-4_2

2.2 Preliminaries

2.2.1 *The System of Stationary Production Prices*

Consider a closed, linear system involving only single products, basic commodities and circulating capital. Assume that (i) the input-output coefficients are fixed; (ii) the system is strictly 'profitable' or, equivalently, 'viable', i.e. the Perron-Frobenius (P-F hereafter) eigenvalue of the irreducible $n \times n$ matrix of direct technical coefficients, $\mathbf{A}$, is less than 1,[1] and diagonalizable[2]; (iii) the price of a commodity obtained as an output at the end of the production period is the same as the price of that commodity used as an input at the beginning of that period ('stationary' prices); (iv) the net product is distributed to profits and wages that are paid at the end (unless it is stated otherwise) of the common production period (for the general case, see Steedman 1977, pp. 103–105, and Harris 1981), and there are no savings out of this income; (v) labour is not an input to the household sector and may be treated as homogeneous because relative wage rates are invariant (Sraffa 1960, p. 10; Kurz and Salvadori 1995, pp. 322–325); and (vi) the profit (or interest) rate, r, is uniform.

2.2.1.1 Relative Prices, Income Distribution and Growth

On the basis of these assumptions, the price side of the system can be described by

$$\mathbf{p} = w\mathbf{l} + (1 + r)\,\mathbf{pA} \tag{2.1}$$

where $\mathbf{p}$ denotes a $1 \times n$ vector of production prices, w the money wage rate, and $\mathbf{l}\,(> \mathbf{0})$ the $1 \times n$ vector of direct labour coefficients. At $r = -1$, we obtain $\mathbf{p} = w\mathbf{l}$, i.e. the vector of prices is proportional to the vector of direct labour coefficients. At $r = 0$ we obtain $\mathbf{p} = w\mathbf{l} + \mathbf{pA}$ or, solving for $\mathbf{p}$, $\mathbf{p} = w\mathbf{v}$, where $\mathbf{v} \equiv \mathbf{l}[\mathbf{I} - \mathbf{A}]^{-1}\,(> \mathbf{0})$ denotes the vector of 'vertically integrated' (Pasinetti 1973, 1988) labour coefficients or 'labour values'. That is, prices are proportional to labour values. At $w = 0$, we obtain $\mathbf{p} = (1 + r)\,\mathbf{pA}$, i.e. prices are proportional to the cost of means of production. Since a non-positive price vector is economically insignificant, it follows that $(1 + r)^{-1}$ is the P-F eigenvalue of $\mathbf{A}$, or $r = R \equiv \lambda_{\mathbf{A}1}^{-1} - 1$, and $\mathbf{p}$ is the corresponding left eigenvector. Iff $-1 \leq r < R$, then

---

[1] The symbol $\mathbf{A}_j$ will denote the jth column of a semi-positive $n \times n$ matrix $\mathbf{A} \equiv [a_{ij}]$, $\lambda_{\mathbf{A}1}$ the P-F eigenvalue of $\mathbf{A}$ and $(\mathbf{x}_{\mathbf{A}1}^{\mathrm{T}}, \mathbf{y}_{\mathbf{A}1})$ the corresponding eigenvectors, while $\lambda_{\mathbf{A}k}$, $k = 2,\ldots n$ and $|\lambda_{\mathbf{A}2}| \geq |\lambda_{\mathbf{A}3}| \geq \ldots \geq |\lambda_{\mathbf{A}n}|$, will denote the non-dominant eigenvalues and $(\mathbf{x}_{\mathbf{A}k}^{\mathrm{T}}, \mathbf{y}_{\mathbf{A}k})$ the corresponding eigenvectors. Finally, $\mathbf{e}$ will denote the summation vector, i.e. $\mathbf{e} \equiv [1,1,\ldots,1]$, $\mathbf{e}_j$ the jth unit vector and $\|\bullet\|$ the maximum column sum matrix norm.

[2] Given any $\mathbf{A}$ and an arbitrary $\varepsilon \neq 0$, it is possible to perturb the entries of $\mathbf{A}$ by an amount less than $|\varepsilon|$ so that the resulting matrix is diagonalizable (see, e.g. Aruka 1991, pp. 74–76).

$$\mathbf{p} = w\mathbf{l}[\mathbf{I} - (1 + r)\mathbf{A}]^{-1}$$

or

$$\mathbf{p} = w\left[\mathbf{l} + (1 + r)\mathbf{lA} + (1 + r)^2\mathbf{lA}^2 + \ldots\right] \quad (2.2)$$

This formula is the reduction of prices to physical quantities of labour, weighted with the compounded profit rate appropriate to their conceptual dates of application or to 'dated quantities of direct labour' (Sraffa 1960, pp. 34–35).[3] If $\mathbf{l}$ is the P-F eigenvector of $\mathbf{A}$, then Eq. 2.2 reduces to

$$\mathbf{p} = w\mathbf{l}(1 + R)(R - r)^{-1} = w\mathbf{v}R(R - r)^{-1}$$

i.e. the vector of prices is proportional to the vector of direct labour coefficients and, at the same time, to the vector of labour values. This corresponds to Marx's (1959, Chaps. 9 and 10) and Samuelson's (1962) 'equal value compositions of capital' case. In any other case, the *entire* price vector cannot be proportional to that of labour values at a positive level of r (Sraffa 1960, Chap. 3; Mainwaring 1974, pp. 93–101). Thus, it can be stated that $r = 0$ or $\mathbf{lA} = \lambda_{\mathbf{A}1}\mathbf{l}$ implies that the 'pure labour theory of value' holds true and $w = 0$ implies that the 'pure capital theory of value' holds true, while the 'capital-labour theory of value' (Gilibert 1998a) applies to all other cases.[4] Finally, multiplying Eq. 2.1 by p_j^{-1} (> 0), $j = 1,2,\ldots,n$, gives

$$\mathbf{p}p_j^{-1} = \left(wp_j^{-1}\right)\mathbf{l} + (1 + r)\left(\mathbf{p}p_j^{-1}\right)\mathbf{A}$$

where wp_j^{-1} represents the wage rate in terms of commodity j. It then follows that if $\lambda_{\mathbf{A}1}$ tends to 1, then R tends to 0 and, therefore, r tends to 0 irrespective of the magnitude of $\left(wp_j^{-1}\right)\mathbf{l}$. This corresponds to Marx's (1959, Chaps. 13, 14, and 15) 'law of the tendency of the profit rate to fall' (also see Okishio 1961, 1987).

Now let $\mathbf{b}^{\mathrm{T}}$ $(\geq \mathbf{0}^{\mathrm{T}})$ be the $n \times 1$ commodity vector representing the real wage rate. Substituting $w = \mathbf{p}\mathbf{b}^{\mathrm{T}}$ in Eq. 2.1 yields

---

[3] The series is finite iff no commodity enters, directly or indirectly, into its own production ('Austrian'-type models). In that case, $\mathbf{A}$ is strictly triangular and, therefore, nilpotent, i.e. there exists a positive integer number $\kappa < n$, such that $\mathbf{A}^{\kappa} = \mathbf{0}$ and the system of production can be represented by a single flow input-point output process of finite duration. For the main attributes and the economic meaning of those models, see Sraffa (1960, pp. 93–94), Burmeister (1974), and Howard (1980).

[4] Prices are proportional to labour values also when the vector of profits per unit activity level is proportional to the vector of direct labour coefficients. In that case, however, the profit rates differ between industries (also see, e.g. Okishio 1963, pp. 289–291; Foley 1982, pp. 39–40).

$$\mathbf{p} = \mathbf{p}\mathbf{b}^{\mathrm{T}}\mathbf{l} + (1+r)\,\mathbf{p}\mathbf{A} \tag{2.3}$$

Postmultiplying Eq. 2.3 by $\mathbf{b}^{\mathrm{T}}$, and rearranging terms, gives

$$\left(1 - \mathbf{l}\mathbf{b}^{\mathrm{T}}\right)\mathbf{p}\mathbf{b}^{\mathrm{T}} = (1+r)\,\mathbf{p}\mathbf{A}\mathbf{b}^{\mathrm{T}}$$

which implies that $[\mathbf{p} > \mathbf{0},\ 1+r > 0]$ iff $\mathbf{l}\mathbf{b}^{\mathrm{T}} < 1$. If $\mathbf{l}\mathbf{b}^{\mathrm{T}} < 1$, then Eq. 2.3 can be rewritten as

$$\mathbf{p} = (1+r)\,\mathbf{p}\boldsymbol{\Gamma} \tag{2.4}$$

where

$$\boldsymbol{\Gamma} \equiv \mathbf{A}\left[\mathbf{I} - \mathbf{b}^{\mathrm{T}}\mathbf{l}\right]^{-1} = \mathbf{A}\left[\mathbf{I} + \left(1 - \mathbf{l}\mathbf{b}^{\mathrm{T}}\right)^{-1}\mathbf{b}^{\mathrm{T}}\mathbf{l}\right]$$

(by applying the Sherman-Morrison formula).[5] Consequently, $(1+r)^{-1}$ is the P-F eigenvalue of $\boldsymbol{\Gamma}$ ($r < R$, since $\boldsymbol{\Gamma} \geq \mathbf{A}$), $r > 0$ iff $\lambda_{\Gamma 1} < 1$ and $\mathbf{p}$ is the corresponding left eigenvector. Alternatively, Eq. 2.3 can be written as

$$\mathbf{p} = \mathbf{p}\mathbf{C} + r\,\mathbf{p}\mathbf{A} \tag{2.5}$$

where $\mathbf{C} \equiv \mathbf{b}^{\mathrm{T}}\mathbf{l} + \mathbf{A}$ denotes the matrix of the 'augmented' input coefficients, i.e. each coefficient represents the sum of the respective material and wage commodity input per unit of gross output, and $\lambda_{\mathbf{C}1} > \lambda_{\mathbf{A}1}$. Postmultiplying Eq. 2.5 by $\mathbf{x}_{\mathbf{C}1}^{\mathrm{T}}$, and rearranging terms, gives

$$(1 - \lambda_{\mathbf{C}1})\,\mathbf{p}\mathbf{x}_{\mathbf{C}1}^{\mathrm{T}} = r\,\mathbf{p}\mathbf{A}\mathbf{x}_{\mathbf{C}1}^{\mathrm{T}}$$

which implies that $[\mathbf{p} > \mathbf{0}, \mathrm{r} > 0]$ iff $\lambda_{\mathbf{C}1} < 1$. If $\lambda_{\mathbf{C}1} < 1$, then Eq. 2.5 can be rewritten as

$$\mathbf{p} = r\,\mathbf{p}\mathbf{A}[\mathbf{I} - \mathbf{C}]^{-1}$$

Consequently, r^{-1} is the P-F eigenvalue of $\mathbf{A}[\mathbf{I} - \mathbf{C}]^{-1}$.

---

[5] Let $\boldsymbol{\chi}$, $\boldsymbol{\psi}$ be arbitrary n – vectors. Then

$$\det\left[\mathbf{I} - \boldsymbol{\chi}^{\mathrm{T}}\boldsymbol{\psi}\right] = 1 - \boldsymbol{\psi}\boldsymbol{\chi}^{\mathrm{T}}$$

and

$$\left[\mathbf{I} - \boldsymbol{\chi}^{\mathrm{T}}\boldsymbol{\psi}\right]^{-1} = \mathbf{I} + \left(1 - \boldsymbol{\psi}\boldsymbol{\chi}^{\mathrm{T}}\right)^{-1}\boldsymbol{\chi}^{\mathrm{T}}\boldsymbol{\psi}$$

iff $\boldsymbol{\psi}\boldsymbol{\chi}^{\mathrm{T}} \neq 1$ (see, e.g. Meyer 2001, p. 124).

If wages are paid *ex ante*, then

$$\mathbf{p} = (1 + r)\,\mathbf{pC} \tag{2.6}$$

or, if $\lambda_{\mathbf{C}1} < 1$,

$$\mathbf{p} = r\,\mathbf{pC}[\mathbf{I} - \mathbf{C}]^{-1}$$

Consequently, r^{-1} is the P-F eigenvalue of $\mathbf{C}[\mathbf{I} - \mathbf{C}]^{-1}\left(\geq \mathbf{C}[\mathbf{I} - \mathbf{A}]^{-1}\right)$ and, therefore, the profit rate is less than that corresponding to *ex post* payment of wages. Assuming that all profits are reinvested, the quantity side of the system can be described by

$$\mathbf{Ix} = (1 + g)\mathbf{Cx} \tag{2.7}$$

where $\mathbf{x}^{\mathrm{T}}$ denotes the $n \times 1$ vector of activity levels, $\mathbf{Ix}^{\mathrm{T}}$ $(=\mathbf{x}^{\mathrm{T}})$ the gross output vector and g the uniform growth rate. Equations 2.6 and 2.7 imply that $g = r = \lambda_{\mathbf{C}1}^{-1} - 1$ and $\mathbf{x}^{\mathrm{T}}$ is the corresponding right eigenvector (von Charasoff 1910; von Neumann 1937 growth path or 'ray').[6]

Following Dmitriev's (1898), Eq. 2.6 can be restated as[7]

$$\mathbf{p} = (1 + r)(p_i\mathbf{c}(i) + \mathbf{pC}(i)), i = 1, 2, \ldots, n \tag{2.8}$$

or, iff $-1 \leq r < \lambda_{\mathbf{C}(i)1}^{-1} - 1$,

$$\mathbf{p} = (1 + r)\,p_i\mathbf{c}(i)[\mathbf{I} - (1 + r)\mathbf{C}(i)]^{-1} = (1 + r)\,p_i\mathbf{c}(i)\sum_{h=0}^{+\infty}[(1 + r)\mathbf{C}(i)]^{h}$$

or

[6] System (2.6) corresponds to the seminal contributions of Isnard (1781), Torrens (1821) and Mühlpfordt (1893, 1895) as well as to the more recent contributions of Leontief (1928) and Remak (1929, 1933) (see, e.g. Gilibert 1998a, b). In the periods 1911–1914 and 1935–1942, Maurice Potron constructed and investigated generalized models (see Abraham-Frois and Lendjel 2004; Mori 2008; Bidard and Erreygers 2010). Some of the 'endogenous (or new) growth models', developed in the 1980s and 1990s, contain 'a "core" of capital goods that can be produced without the direct or indirect contribution of nonreproducible factors' (King and Rebelo 1990, p. 127; also see Rebelo 1991, p. 515) and, therefore, have the same analytical structure as the classical model of Eqs. 2.6 and 2.7. Both models depict (implicitly or explicitly, respectively) the process of reproduction of 'labour', and, hence, the profit rate and commodity prices are determined by technology alone, while the growth rate is determined by the saving-investment mechanism (Kurz and Salvadori 1998, Chap. 4, 2000; also consider Cesaratto 2010).

[7] We shall set aside the fact that, for the determination of positive-profit prices, Dmitriev (1898) normally uses an Austrian-type model in which **A** is nilpotent (see footnote 3 in this chapter). For a possible explanation of that choice, see Mariolis (2005).

$$\mathbf{p} = (1+r)p_i\left[\mathbf{d}(i) + r\mathbf{c}(i)\left[\mathbf{C}(i) + (2+r)\mathbf{C}(i)^2 + \ldots\right]\right] \tag{2.9}$$

where $\mathbf{c}(i)$ denotes the ith row of $\mathbf{C}$, $\mathbf{C}(i)$ the matrix derived from $\mathbf{C}$ by replacing all the elements on its ith row by zeroes, $[\mathbf{I} - (1+r)\mathbf{C}(i)]^{-1} \geq \mathbf{0}$ and $\mathbf{d}(i) \equiv \mathbf{c}(i)[\mathbf{I} - \mathbf{C}(i)]^{-1}$ $(> \mathbf{0})$ the vector of 'commodity i values', i.e. of the direct and indirect input requirements of commodity i necessary to produce one unit of gross output of commodity j (also see Gintis and Bowles 1981, pp. 18–21, and Roemer 1986, pp. 24–26). Equation 2.9 may be interpreted as the 'reduction of the production costs to the production cost of the commodity i' (Dmitriev 1898, pp. 59–64) or, using Sraffa's terminology, the 'reduction of prices to dated quantities of commodity i'. Postmultiplying Eq. 2.9 by $\mathbf{e}_i^{\mathrm{T}}$ gives

$$1 = (1+r)d(i)_i + (1+r)r\mathbf{c}(i)\left[\mathbf{C}(i) + (2+r)\mathbf{C}(i)^2 + \ldots\right]\mathbf{e}_i^{\mathrm{T}} \tag{2.10}$$

where $d(i)_i \equiv \mathbf{d}(i)\mathbf{e}_i^{\mathrm{T}}$. The right-hand side of Eq. 2.10 is known to be a strictly increasing and convex function of r, tending to plus infinity as r approaches $\lambda_{\mathbf{C}(i)1}^{-1}$ -1 from below (see, e.g. Kurz and Salvadori 1995, p. 116). Thus, Eq. 2.10 determines a unique, positive, finite value of r, provided that $d(i)_i < 1$ or, in the words of Dmitriev (1898),

> we can obtain a *larger* quantity of the same product [...] as a result of the production process. (p. 62)

In that case, $\max_i\{d(i)_i\} < \lambda_{\mathbf{C}1}$, since $(1+r)^{-1} = \lambda_{\mathbf{C}1}$ (see Eqs. 2.6 and 2.10). It then follows that the conditions

$$0 < r < \min_i\left\{d(i)_i^{-1} - 1\right\},\ \max_i\left\{d(i)_i\right\} < \lambda_{\mathbf{C}1} < 1,\ 0 < d(i)_i < 1 \tag{2.11}$$

are all equivalent. Postmultiplying Eq. 2.9 by $\mathbf{e}_j^{\mathrm{T}}, j \neq i$, gives

$$p_j = p_i d(i,r)_j,\ d(i,r)_j \equiv (1+r)\mathbf{c}(i)[\mathbf{I} - (1+r)\mathbf{C}(i)]^{-1}\mathbf{e}_j^{\mathrm{T}} \tag{2.12}$$

while from the reduction to dated quantities of commodity j, we get

$$p_i = p_j d(j,r)_i,\ d(j,r)_i \equiv (1+r)\mathbf{c}(j)[\mathbf{I} - (1+r)\mathbf{C}(j)]^{-1}\mathbf{e}_i^{\mathrm{T}} \tag{2.13}$$

Since $p_i d(i)_j$ ($p_j d(j)_i$) can be defined as the 'pure forward linkage' of industry i (of industry j) to industry j (to industry i), the right-hand side of Eq. 2.12

(of Eq. 2.13) may be considered as the 'r – pure forward linkage' of industry i (of industry j).[8] Thus, when conditions (2.11) hold,

$$d(i)_j < p_j p_i^{-1} < d(j)_i^{-1}$$

namely, p_j (p_i) is greater than the pure forward linkage of industry i (of industry j).

Analogously, Eq. 2.6 can be solved as (also consider Eq. 2.2)

$$\mathbf{p} = (1+r)\left(\mathbf{pb}^{\mathrm{T}}\right)\mathbf{l}[\mathbf{I} - (1+r)\mathbf{A}]^{-1} = (1+r)\left(\mathbf{pb}^{\mathrm{T}}\right)\mathbf{l}\sum_{h=0}^{+\infty}[(1+r)\mathbf{A}]^{h} \tag{2.14}$$

Postmultiplying Eq. 2.14 by $\mathbf{b}^{\mathrm{T}}$ gives

$$1 = (1+r)\mathbf{vb}^{\mathrm{T}} + (1+r)r\mathbf{l}\left[\mathbf{A} + (2+r)\mathbf{A}^2 + \ldots\right]\mathbf{b}^{\mathrm{T}} \tag{2.15}$$

Equation 2.15 determines a unique, positive, finite value of r, provided that $\mathbf{vb}^{\mathrm{T}} < 1$ (Dmitriev 1898, p. 62), where $\mathbf{vb}^{\mathrm{T}}$ represents the direct and indirect input requirements of labour necessary to produce one unit of labour or, using Marx's (1954, Chap. 6) terminology, the unit 'value of labour power' (1 represents the unit 'value of labour' and $\left(\mathbf{vb}^{\mathrm{T}}\right)^{-1} - 1$ the 'rate of surplus labour (or of exploitation)'). This is the 'fundamental Marxian theorem',[9] while it follows that, in *non*-fully automated systems, $\mathbf{l} \neq 0$, conditions (2.11) and

$$\left\{0 < \mathbf{vb}^{\mathrm{T}} < 1,\ 0 < r < \left(\mathbf{vb}^{\mathrm{T}}\right)^{-1} - 1\right\}$$

are all equivalent ('generalized commodity exploitation theorem'; for recent exchanges on this topic, see Fujimoto and Fujita 2008; Matsuo 2009; Veneziani and Yoshihara 2010; Yoshihara 2014).

Consequently, Eqs. 2.6 (or Eq. 2.4), 2.10 and 2.15 provide equivalent, although *different*, forms of the classical-Marxian determination of the profit rate (and the prices) by the technical conditions of production and the real wage rate.

---

[8] This concept of 'pure forward linkage' (see Sonis et al. 1995 and, for example, Cai and Leung 2004) is based on the 'hypothetical extraction method' (Paelinck et al. 1965; Miller 1966; Strassert 1968), which is one of the modern methods for the measurement of intersectoral linkages. For the connections between Dmitriev's (1898) contribution to value and profit theory and that method, see Mariolis and Rodousaki (2011).

[9] See Okishio (1955, pp. 75–78), Morishima and Seton (1961, pp. 207–209) and Fujimori (1982). For alternative interpretations of the Marxian theory of profits, which are based on the concept of 'abstract social labour', see Duménil (1980), Krause (1980, 1982), Foley (1982, 2000), Reuten and Williams (1989) and Mariolis (2006a, b). For an alternative microeconomic theory inspired by the 'heterodox surplus approach', see Lee (2012).

2.2.1.2 Vertical Integration

The similarity transformation of the system matrix into a stochastic one and the statistical distribution of its eigenvalues are crucial to the arguments of this book. Hence, it is both convenient and appropriate to focus on the normalized vertically integrated representation of the system. After rearrangement, Eq. 2.1 becomes

$$\mathbf{p} = w\mathbf{v} + r\,\mathbf{pH}$$

or

$$\mathbf{p} = w\mathbf{v} + \rho\,\mathbf{pJ} \tag{2.16}$$

or, iff $0 \leq \rho < 1$,

$$\mathbf{p} = w\mathbf{v}[\mathbf{I} - \rho\mathbf{J}]^{-1} = w\mathbf{v}\sum_{h=0}^{+\infty} (\rho\mathbf{J})^{h} \tag{2.17}$$

where $\mathbf{H} \equiv \mathbf{A}[\mathbf{I} - \mathbf{A}]^{-1}$ $(> \mathbf{0})$ denotes the vertically integrated technical coefficients matrix, $\rho \equiv rR^{-1}$ the 'relative (or normalized) profit rate' and $\mathbf{J} \equiv R\mathbf{H}$ the normalized vertically integrated technical coefficients matrix, with $\lambda_{\mathbf{J}1} = R\lambda_{\mathbf{H}1} = 1$ (since $R = \lambda_{\mathbf{H}1}^{-1}$). Finally, the moduli of the normalized non-dominant eigenvalues of system (2.16) are less than those of system (2.1): If $\lambda_{\mathbf{A}k}$ is positive, then $\lambda_{\mathbf{A}k} < \lambda_{\mathbf{A}1}$. If it is negative or complex, then $|\lambda_{\mathbf{A}k}| \leq \lambda_{\mathbf{A}1}$ (the equality holds iff $\mathbf{A}$ is 'imprimitive', i.e. has more than one eigenvalue on its spectral circle)[10] and $|1 - \lambda_{\mathbf{A}k}| > 1 - |\lambda_{\mathbf{A}k}|$. Hence,

$$|\lambda_{\mathbf{J}k}| = R|\lambda_{\mathbf{A}k}||1 - \lambda_{\mathbf{A}k}|^{-1} < \left(|\lambda_{\mathbf{A}k}|\lambda_{\mathbf{A}1}^{-1}\right)(1 - \lambda_{\mathbf{A}1})(1 - |\lambda_{\mathbf{A}k}|)^{-1} \leq |\lambda_{\mathbf{A}k}|\lambda_{\mathbf{A}1}^{-1}$$

or $|\lambda_{\mathbf{J}k}| < |\lambda_{\mathbf{A}k}|\lambda_{\mathbf{A}1}^{-1}$ holds for all k.

Equation 2.17 represents the 'reduction to dated quantities of *embodied* labour' (Kurz and Salvadori 1995, p. 175) and implies that each element in the vector of 'labour-commanded' (Smith 1937, p. 30) prices, $\mathbf{p}_w \equiv w^{-1}\,\mathbf{p}$, is a strictly increasing and convex function of ρ, tending to plus infinity as ρ approaches 1 from below:

$$\dot{\mathbf{p}}_w \equiv d\,\mathbf{p}_w/d\rho = \mathbf{p}_w\mathbf{J}[\mathbf{I} - \rho\mathbf{J}]^{-1}$$

(also see Sraffa 1960, pp. 38–39). The matrix $[\mathbf{I} - \rho\mathbf{J}]^{-1}$ could be conceived of as a linear operator that 'transforms' labour values into production prices (Pasinetti 1973; also see Reati 1986). In this sense, the linear operator

---

[10] Matrix $\mathbf{A}$ is primitive iff $\mathbf{A}^{n^2-2n+2} > \mathbf{0}$ or, equivalently, iff it is 'acyclic' (see, e.g. Solow 1952; Meyer 2001, pp. 674–680).

$\left[\mathbf{I} - r\mathbf{C}(i)[\mathbf{I} - \mathbf{C}(i)]^{-1}\right]^{-1}$ (derived from Eq. 2.8) 'transforms' commodity i values into production prices (Mariolis 2001).

Substituting $w = \mathbf{pb}^{\mathrm{T}}$ in Eq. 2.16 yields

$$\mathbf{p} = \mathbf{pb}^{\mathrm{T}}\mathbf{v} + \rho\,\mathbf{pJ} \tag{2.18}$$

Postmultiplying Eq. 2.18 by $\mathbf{b}^{\mathrm{T}}$, and rearranging terms, gives

$$\left(1 - \mathbf{vb}^{\mathrm{T}}\right)\mathbf{pb}^{\mathrm{T}} = \rho\,\mathbf{pJb}^{\mathrm{T}}$$

which implies that $[\mathbf{p} > \mathbf{0},\ \rho > 0]$ iff $\mathbf{vb}^{\mathrm{T}} < 1$. If $\mathbf{vb}^{\mathrm{T}} < 1$, then Eq. 2.18 can be rewritten as

$$\mathbf{p} = \rho\,\mathbf{pK} \tag{2.19}$$

where

$$\mathbf{K} \equiv \mathbf{J}\left[\mathbf{I} - \mathbf{b}^{\mathrm{T}}\mathbf{v}\right]^{-1} = \mathbf{J}\left[\mathbf{I} + \left(1 - \mathbf{vb}^{\mathrm{T}}\right)^{-1}\mathbf{b}^{\mathrm{T}}\mathbf{v}\right]$$

Consequently, ρ^{-1} is the P-F eigenvalue of $\mathbf{K}$ ($\rho < 1$, since $\mathbf{K} \geq \mathbf{J}$) and $\mathbf{p}$ is the corresponding left eigenvector.[11]

2.2.1.3 The Wage-Relative Profit Rate Curve

If commodity $\mathbf{z}^{\mathrm{T}}$, with $\mathbf{vz}^{\mathrm{T}} = 1$, is chosen as the standard of value or numeraire, i.e. $\mathbf{pz}^{\mathrm{T}} = 1$, then Eqs. 2.16, 2.17 imply

---

[11] If there are m types of labour ('heterogeneous labour case'), then Eq. 2.18 becomes

$$\mathbf{p} = \mathbf{pb}_m\mathbf{v}_m + \rho\,\mathbf{pJ} \tag{2.18a}$$

where $\mathbf{b}_m$ denotes the $n \times m$ matrix of real wage rates, $\mathbf{v}_m = \mathbf{l}_m[\mathbf{I} - \mathbf{A}]^{-1}$ the $m \times n$ matrix of labour values and $\mathbf{l}_m$ the $m \times n$ matrix of direct labour coefficients. Post-multiplying Eq. 2.18a by $\mathbf{b}_m\mathbf{l}_m\mathbf{x}^{\mathrm{T}}$, and rearranging terms, gives

$$\mathbf{pb}_m\mathbf{S}_m^{\mathrm{T}} = \rho\,\mathbf{pJb}_m\mathbf{l}_m\mathbf{x}^{\mathrm{T}}$$

where $\mathbf{S}_m^{\mathrm{T}} \equiv \mathbf{l}_m\mathbf{x}^{\mathrm{T}} - \mathbf{v}_m\mathbf{b}_m\mathbf{l}_m\mathbf{x}^{\mathrm{T}}$ denotes the $m \times 1$ vector of surplus labours (Bowles and Gintis 1977, p. 186) and $\mathbf{b}_m\mathbf{S}_m^{\mathrm{T}}$ equals the surplus product of the vertically integrated industry producing the total real wages. It then follows that $\mathbf{S}_m^{\mathrm{T}} \geq \mathbf{0}^{\mathrm{T}}$ is a sufficient but not necessary condition for $\mathbf{b}_m\mathbf{S}_m^{\mathrm{T}} \geq \mathbf{0}^{\mathrm{T}}$ and, therefore, for $[\mathbf{p} > \mathbf{0},\ \rho > 0]$ (Rosinger 1996; Mariolis 2006a, p. 5; also consider the numerical examples provided by Morishima 1978, pp. 306–307, and Krause 1981, p. 65).

$$w = W - \rho k_{\mathbf{z}} = 1 - \rho k_{\mathbf{z}} \tag{2.20}$$

and, respectively,

$$w = \left(\mathbf{v}[\mathbf{I} - \rho\mathbf{J}]^{-1}\mathbf{z}^{\mathrm{T}}\right)^{-1} = \det[\mathbf{I} - \rho\mathbf{J}]\left(\mathbf{v}\mathrm{adj}[\mathbf{I} - \rho\mathbf{J}]\mathbf{z}^{\mathrm{T}}\right)^{-1}$$

or

$$w = \left[\prod_{j=1}^{n}\left(1 - \rho\lambda_{\mathbf{J}j}\right)\right]\left(\mathbf{v}\mathrm{adj}[\mathbf{I} - \rho\mathbf{J}]\mathbf{z}^{\mathrm{T}}\right)^{-1} \tag{2.21}$$

where $W \equiv \mathbf{pz}^{\mathrm{T}}(\mathbf{vz}^{\mathrm{T}})^{-1} = 1$ and

$$k_{\mathbf{z}} \equiv \mathbf{pJz}^{\mathrm{T}}\left(\mathbf{vz}^{\mathrm{T}}\right)^{-1} = \mathbf{pJz}^{\mathrm{T}} \tag{2.22}$$

Postmultiplying Eq. 2.16 by Sraffa's (1960, Chap. 4) Standard commodity (SSC), i.e. $\mathbf{s}^{\mathrm{T}} \equiv [\mathbf{I} - \mathbf{A}]\mathbf{x}_{\mathbf{A}1}^{\mathrm{T}}$, with $\mathbf{lx}_{\mathbf{A}1}^{\mathrm{T}} = 1$, and rearranging terms, gives

$$w = (1 - \rho)\,\mathbf{ps}^{\mathrm{T}} \tag{2.23}$$

where $\mathbf{ps}^{\mathrm{T}}$ equals the price of net output (measured in terms of $\mathbf{z}^{\mathrm{T}}$) of the Sraffian Standard system (SSS). It then follows that $\rho\ \left(= 1 - w(\mathbf{ps}^{\mathrm{T}})^{-1}\right)$ and R equal the share of profits and the net output-capital ratio in the SSS, respectively. Thus, $k_{\mathbf{z}}$ (see Eq. 2.22) equals the ratio of the capital-net output ratio in the vertically integrated industry (or 'sub-system'; Sraffa 1960, Appendix A), producing the numeraire commodity to the capital-net output ratio in the SSS. From Eq. 2.23 it follows that the profit-wage ratio, $\rho(1 - \rho)^{-1}$, in the SSS equals the elasticity of $\mathbf{p}_w\mathbf{s}^{\mathrm{T}}$ with respect to ρ or, alternatively, the percentage deviation of $\mathbf{p}_w\mathbf{s}^{\mathrm{T}}$ from $\mathbf{vs}^{\mathrm{T}} = 1$. At, say, $\rho = 30$ %, an increase in ρ by 1 percentage point, $\Delta\rho = 1$ %, leads to a percentage change in $\mathbf{p}_w\mathbf{s}^{\mathrm{T}}$ of 1.45 %, while at, say, $\rho = 90$ %, it leads to a percentage change of 11.11 % (consider 'Ricardo's (1951, pp. 33–36) 1 % rule' or '93 % labour theory of value'; Stigler 1958). Moreover, writing Eq. 2.23 as

$$\mathbf{p}_w\mathbf{s}^{\mathrm{T}} = (1 - \rho)^{-1} = 1 + \rho + \rho^2 + \ldots$$

it follows that, at $\rho = 30$ % ($\rho = 90$ %), about 6 (87) terms are needed to approximate $\mathbf{p}_w\mathbf{s}^{\mathrm{T}}$ with an accuracy of 10^{-3}.

Equation 2.21 gives a trade-off between w and ρ, known as the 'wage-relative profit rate curve' (WPC):

(i) Equations 2.20 and 2.23 imply

$$\dot{w} = -\left(k_{\mathbf{z}} + \rho \dot{k_{\mathbf{z}}}\right) \tag{2.24}$$

and

$$\dot{w} = -\mathbf{p}\mathbf{s}^{\mathrm{T}} + (1-\rho)\,\dot{\mathbf{p}}\mathbf{s}^{\mathrm{T}} \tag{2.25}$$

respectively.

(ii) At $\rho = 0$ we obtain $w(0) = 1$, $\mathbf{p}(0) = \mathbf{v}$, $k_{\mathbf{z}}(0) = \mathbf{vJz}^{\mathrm{T}}$ and

$$\dot{w}(0) = -k_{\mathbf{z}}(0)\left(= -1 + \dot{\mathbf{p}}(0)\mathbf{s}^{\mathrm{T}}\right) \tag{2.26}$$

In the other extreme case, i.e. at $\rho = 1$, we obtain $w(1) = 0$, $\mathbf{p}(1) = \mathbf{y}_{\mathbf{J}1}$ (with $\mathbf{y}_{\mathbf{J}1}\mathbf{z}^{\mathrm{T}} = 1$), $k_{\mathbf{z}}\,(1) = 1$ and

$$\dot{w}(1) = -\mathbf{p}(1)\mathbf{s}^{\mathrm{T}}\left(= -\left(1 + \dot{k_{\mathbf{z}}}(1)\right)\right) \tag{2.27}$$

That is, the slope, $-\dot{w}R^{-1}$, of the $w - r$ curve at $\rho = 0$ (at $\rho = 1$) represents the capital-labour ratio in the vertically integrated industry producing the numeraire commodity (in the SSS). At any other value of the profit rate, this slope no longer represents a capital-labour ratio (except by a fluke).

(iii) If $\mathbf{v}$ ($\mathbf{l}$) is the P-F eigenvector of $\mathbf{J}$ (of $\mathbf{A}$) or if SSC is chosen as the numeraire, then $k_{\mathbf{z}} = \mathbf{p}\mathbf{s}^{\mathrm{T}} = 1$ and

$$w = w^{\mathrm{S}} \equiv 1 - \rho \tag{2.28}$$

i.e. the WPC is linear, as in a one-commodity world.[12] In the *general* case, the WPC is a ratio between a polynomial of the nth degree and one of the $(n-1)$th degree in ρ (see Eq. 2.21) and, therefore, may admit up to $3n - 6$ inflection points (though we cannot be sure that they will all occur for $0 \leq \rho \leq 1$; Garegnani 1970, p. 419). The relative commodity prices are ratios of polynomials of degree $(n-1)$ in ρ (consider Eq. 2.17) and, therefore, may admit up to $2n - 4$ extreme points, which implies that, for $n \geq 3$, $k_{\mathbf{z}}$ (and $\mathbf{p}\mathbf{s}^{\mathrm{T}}$) can change in a complicated way as ρ changes. It then follows that the slope of the WPC does not necessarily equal 1 (see Eq. 2.23 or 2.25), and, in contrast with what is normally expected in the traditional neoclassical theory, $k_{\mathbf{z}}$ is not necessarily a non-increasing function of ρ (for instance, see Fig. 2.1).[13]

---

[12] If wages are paid *ex ante*, then $k_{\mathbf{z}} = Rw + \mathbf{pJz}^{\mathrm{T}}$, $(1+r)w^{\mathrm{S}} = (1-\rho)$ or

$$w^{\mathrm{S}} = (1 + R\rho)^{-1}(1-\rho)$$

and ρ is no greater than the share of profits in the SSS.

[13] Because of Eqs. 2.20 and 2.22, $\tan\alpha = 1$ gives (i) $k_{\mathbf{z}}$ at $\rho = \rho_2$ and $\rho = 1$ and (ii) $\mathbf{p}\mathbf{s}^{\mathrm{T}}$ at $\rho = 0$ and $\rho = \rho_2$, respectively.

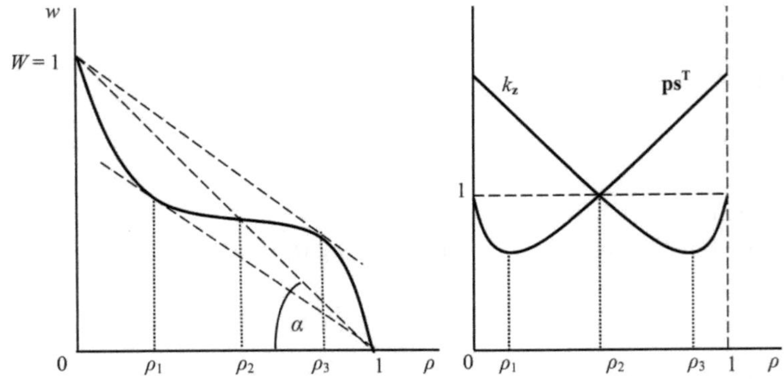

Fig. 2.1 A WPC, with an inflection point, and its alternative components as functions of the relative profit rate

(iv) The phenomenon in which $\dot{k}_{\mathbf{z}} > 0$ for some ρ, known as 'negative price Wicksell effect' (Robinson 1953, p. 95), can occur in the simplest two-industry system, i.e. reducible and without 'self-reproducing non-basics' (in the sense of Sraffa 1960, Appendix B). This system corresponds to the Samuelson-Hicks-Spaventa or 'corn-tractor' model (see Spaventa 1970). Indeed, with $n = 2, a_{21} = a_{22} = 0$ and $p_2 = v_2 \equiv l_1 a_{12}(1 - a_{11})^{-1} + l_2$ (normalization condition), we get

$$k_{\mathbf{z}} = [\mathrm{E} - \rho(\mathrm{E} - 1)]^{-1} \tag{2.29}$$

and, invoking Eq. 2.28,

$$w = w^{\mathrm{S}}[1 + \rho(\mathrm{E}^{-1} - 1)]^{-1} \tag{2.30}$$

where $\mathrm{E} \equiv a_{11}(l_2 - \Delta)(a_{12}l_1)^{-1}, \Delta \equiv a_{11}l_2 - a_{12}l_1, l_2 > \Delta$ (since $a_{11} < 1$; viability condition) and $\mathrm{E} > 1$ iff $\Delta > 0$, i.e. the capital-commodity industry is more capital intensive than the consumption-commodity (numeraire) industry. Differentiating Eqs. 2.29 and 2.30 with respect to ρ gives $\dot{k}_{\mathbf{z}} > 0$ and $\ddot{w} < 0$ iff $\Delta > 0$.[14] If both commodities are basic, and $p_2 = v_2$, then $\dot{p}_1 > 0$, $\dot{k}_{\mathbf{z}} > 0$ and $\ddot{w} < 0$ iff

[14] When there is more than one production technique available, the phenomenon of 'reswitching' (i.e. a technique is cost-minimizing at two disconnected ranges of the profit rate and not so in between these ranges; Sraffa 1960, Chap. 12) can also occur. For systematic investigations of the possibility of switching and the probability of reswitching, see Egidi (1977), Salvadori and Steedman (1988), Woods (1988), Aruka (2000), Mainwaring and Steedman (2000) and Petri (2011) and consider the computer-simulation results reported by Zambelli (2004, pp. 107–115).

$$(l_1 a_{11} + l_2 a_{21}) l_1^{-1} > (l_1 a_{12} + l_2 a_{22}) l_2^{-1}$$

or, equivalently,

$$(p_1 a_{11} + v_2 a_{21}) l_1^{-1} > (p_1 a_{12} + v_2 a_{22}) l_2^{-1}$$

i.e. the industry producing commodity 1 is more capital intensive than the industry producing commodity 2 (Mainwaring 1974, Chap. 2). It should finally be added that iff $n \geq 3$, non-monotonic movements of $p_i p_j^{-1}$ need not imply 'capital-intensity reversal' for the relevant industries (see the numerical examples provided by Mainwaring 1978, pp. 16–17, and Shaikh 1998, pp. 229–230, in which SSC is used as the numeraire; the latter example also presents a 'price-labour value reversal', i.e. a reversal in the sign of the difference: $p_j - v_j$).

2.2.1.4 The Consumption-Relative Growth Rate Curve

The quantity side of the system can be described by

$$\mathbf{Ix}^{\mathrm{T}} = c\mathbf{f}^{\mathrm{T}} + (1+g)\mathbf{Ax}^{\mathrm{T}}, \ \ \mathbf{l}(\mathbf{Ix}^{\mathrm{T}}) = 1 \tag{2.31}$$

where $\mathbf{Ix}^{\mathrm{T}}$ now denotes the $n \times 1$ vector of gross outputs per unit of labour employed, $\mathbf{f}^{\mathrm{T}}$ the $n \times 1$ commodity vector that serves as the unit of consumption and c the level of consumption per unit of labour employed. Equation 2.31 implies

$$\mathbf{u}^{\mathrm{T}} = c\mathbf{f}^{\mathrm{T}} + \gamma\mathbf{Ju}^{\mathrm{T}}, \ \ \mathbf{vu}^{\mathrm{T}} = 1 \tag{2.32}$$

and, therefore, the 'consumption-relative growth rate curve' (CGC) is given by

$$c = \left(\mathbf{v}[\mathbf{I} - \gamma\mathbf{J}]^{-1}\mathbf{f}^{\mathrm{T}}\right)^{-1} \tag{2.33}$$

where $\mathbf{u}^{\mathrm{T}} \equiv [\mathbf{I} - \mathbf{A}]\mathbf{x}^{\mathrm{T}}$ denotes the vector of net outputs per unit of labour employed, $\gamma \equiv gG^{-1}$ the 'relative growth rate' and $G\ (= R)$ the maximum uniform growth rate, i.e. the growth rate corresponding to $\left[c = 0, \mathbf{x}^{\mathrm{T}} > \mathbf{0}^{\mathrm{T}}\right]$.[15] Since the CGC is formally equivalent to the WPC ('duality'; Bruno 1969), it follows that the previous analysis also applies to the quantity side.

[15] For an extension of system (2.31) that allows estimations of the maximum attainable number of persons not employed per person employed or maximum attainable 'economic dependency ratio', see Mariolis et al. (2012). It is also noted that if $\mathbf{f}^{\mathrm{T}}$ is a function of prices, then the quantity and price sides cannot, in general, be separated; see, e.g. Kurz and Salvadori (1995, pp. 102–104) and Franke (1998).

In steady, equilibrium growth, investment adjusts to savings (classical viewpoint) or savings adjust to investment (post-Keynesian viewpoint). Hence, $\gamma = s\rho$ or $\rho = s^{-1}\gamma$, respectively, where s, $0 \leq s \leq 1$, denotes the saving ratio out of profits, and this equation provides the link between the two sides (for further analysis on this point, see Kurz and Salvadori 1995, Chap. 15).

2.2.2 A Dynamic System

Consider the linear, time-invariant, dynamic price system described by (see Sect. 1.3)

$$\mathbf{p}_{t+1} = w_{t+1}\mathbf{v} + \overline{\rho}\,\mathbf{p}_t\mathbf{J}, \quad t = 0, 1, \ldots \tag{2.34}$$

$$q_t = \mathbf{p}_t\mathbf{z}^{\mathrm{T}} \tag{2.35}$$

where $\overline{\rho}$ denotes the exogenously given nominal relative profit rate, q_t the so-called measurement variable and $\mathbf{p}_0 = \mathbf{0}$, $w_0 = 0$ (see Solow 1959). The system $[\mathbf{J}, \mathbf{v}]$ is said to be completely controllable if the initial state $\mathbf{p}_0$ can be transferred, by application of w_t, to any state, in some finite time. It is completely controllable iff the Krylov controllability matrix

$$\left[\mathbf{v}^{\mathrm{T}}, \mathbf{J}^{\mathrm{T}}\mathbf{v}^{\mathrm{T}}, \ldots, \left[\mathbf{J}^{\mathrm{T}}\right]^{n-1}\mathbf{v}^{\mathrm{T}}\right]^{\mathrm{T}}$$

has rank n or, equivalently, iff no right eigenvector of $\mathbf{J}$ is orthogonal to $\mathbf{v}$. In that case, there is a real vector $\boldsymbol{\eta}^{\mathrm{T}}$ ('feedback gain') such that the matrix, $\mathbf{J}^{+} = \mathbf{J} + \boldsymbol{\eta}^{\mathrm{T}}\mathbf{v}$, of the closed-loop system

$$\mathbf{p}_{t+1} = \tilde{w}_{t+1}\mathbf{v} + \overline{\rho}\,\mathbf{p}_t\mathbf{J}, \quad \tilde{w}_{t+1} \equiv w_{t+1} + \overline{\rho}\,\mathbf{p}_t\boldsymbol{\eta}^{\mathrm{T}}$$

has any desired set of eigenvalues ('eigenvalue assignment theorem'; Wonhman 1967).[16] The system $[\mathbf{J}, \mathbf{z}^{\mathrm{T}}]$ is said to be completely observable if the knowledge of q_t, over a finite interval of time, is sufficient to determine the initial state $\mathbf{p}_0$. It is completely observable iff the Krylov observability matrix

$$\left[\mathbf{z}^{\mathrm{T}}, \mathbf{J}\mathbf{z}^{\mathrm{T}}, \ldots, \mathbf{J}^{n-1}\mathbf{z}^{\mathrm{T}}\right]$$

has rank n or, equivalently, iff no left eigenvector of $\mathbf{J}$ is orthogonal to $\mathbf{z}^{\mathrm{T}}$.

---

[16] The matrix Γ ($\mathbf{K}$) in Eq. 2.4 (in Eq. 2.19) is also a rank-one, but necessarily semi-positive, perturbation of $\mathbf{A}$ ($\mathbf{J}$).

Let ζ be a complex variable and let

$$y \equiv \sum_{t=0}^{+\infty} y_t \zeta^{-t} \tag{2.36}$$

be the 'unilateral ζ-transform' of a given sequence of numbers y_t.[17] Application of the ζ-transform, with $\zeta = \overline{\rho}\rho^{-1}$, to Eqs. 2.34 and 2.35 yields

$$\mathbf{p} = w\mathbf{v}[\mathbf{I} - \rho\mathbf{J}]^{-1} \tag{2.37}$$

$$qw^{-1} = \mathbf{v}[\mathbf{I} - \rho\mathbf{J}]^{-1}\mathbf{z}^{\mathrm{T}} \tag{2.38}$$

where Eq. 2.38 gives the 'transfer function' of the system. Equations 2.17, 2.21, 2.37, 2.38 imply that the vertically integrated system of production prices constitutes the '$\overline{\rho}\rho^{-1}$-transformed' dynamic system and that the reciprocal of the WPC of the former constitutes the transfer function of the latter.

Iff the system $[\mathbf{J}, \mathbf{v}, \mathbf{z}^{\mathrm{T}}]$ is both 'completely controllable' and 'completely observable', then the transfer function (2.38) contains all the information which characterizes its dynamic behaviour or, equivalently, the knowledge of the transfer function is sufficient for the unique determination of the dynamic Eqs. 2.34 and 2.35. In the opposite case, the transfer function represents only the completely controllable and completely observable parts of the system (Kalman 1961, 1963; also consider Gilbert 1963, while for the non-diagonalizable case, see Chen and Desoer 1968). The concepts of 'controllability-observability' and 'regularity' are algebraically equivalent (Mariolis 2003). The latter concept has been introduced by Schefold (1971, 1976) and refers to the production price system and/or to the commodity output system. The system (2.16) (the system (2.32)) is said to be 'regular' if the commodity price (output) vector varies in such a way with the profit (growth) rate that it assumes n linearly independent values at any n different levels of the profit (growth) rate (furthermore, see Kurz and Salvadori 1995, Chap. 6). For instance, if the WPC is linear (see Eq. 2.28), then the system is irregular and, at the same time, uncontrollable and/or unobservable (the relevant Krylov matrix has rank 1; also consider Miyao 1977; Baldone 1980).[18]

[17] The 'ζ-transform' is the discrete-time counterpart of the 'Laplace transform'. Provided that the series (2.36) converges, y can be regarded, from an economic viewpoint, as the 'present value' of the sequence y_t (ζ^{-t} is the 'discount factor'; see Grubbström and Yinzhong 1989). It is also noted that if the sequence y_t has the ζ-transform y, then the unit advanced sequence y_{t+1} has the transform $\zeta y - \zeta y_0$ (see, e.g. Aseltine 1958, Chap. 16).

[18] Schefold (1976, pp. 26–30, 1978, pp. 268–269) argues that non-diagonalizable and irregular systems are of measure zero in the set of all systems and, thus, not generic (also see Aruka 1990, pp. 9–14).

2.2.3 *Differential Profit Rates, Fixed Capital and Joint Production*

Consider the case of differential profit rates and fixed capital. In terms of the 'Leontief-Bródy approach', Eq. 2.1 becomes

$$\mathbf{p} = w\mathbf{l} + \mathbf{p}(\mathbf{A} + \mathbf{A}^{\mathrm{D}}) + \mathbf{p}\mathbf{A}^{\mathrm{C}}\hat{\mathbf{r}} \tag{2.1a}$$

where $\mathbf{p}$ now denotes a vector of 'disequilibrium prices', $\mathbf{A}^{\mathrm{D}}$ the matrix of depreciation coefficients, $\mathbf{A}^{\mathrm{c}}$ the matrix of capital stock coefficients and $\hat{\mathbf{r}}$ the diagonal matrix of the sectoral profit rates, r_j. Provided that r_j exhibit a stable structure in relative terms, which implies that $\hat{\mathbf{r}}$ can be written as $r\hat{\bar{\mathbf{r}}}$, where $\hat{\bar{\mathbf{r}}}$ represents the relative magnitudes of the profit rates in different sectors and r now represents the 'overall level' of the profit rates, Eq. 2.1a can be rewritten as

$$\mathbf{p} = w\mathbf{v} + \rho\,\mathbf{p}\mathbf{J}^{+} \tag{2.16a}$$

where the vector of labour values, $\mathbf{v}$, now equals $\mathbf{l}[\mathbf{I} - \mathbf{A}^{+}]^{-1}$, $\mathbf{A}^{+} \equiv \mathbf{A} + \mathbf{A}^{\mathrm{D}}$, $\mathbf{J}^{+} \equiv R^{+}\mathbf{H}^{+}$, $\mathbf{H}^{+} \equiv \mathbf{A}^{\mathrm{C}}\hat{\bar{\mathbf{r}}}[\mathbf{I} - \mathbf{A}^{+}]^{-1}$, $R^{+} \equiv \lambda_{\mathbf{H}^{+}}^{-1}$ and ρ now equals $r(R^{+})^{-1}$.[19] Since Eq. 2.16a is formally equivalent to Eq. 2.16, our analysis remains valid for this case. This is not necessarily true for the joint production case, where Eq. 2.1 becomes

$$\mathbf{p}\mathbf{B} = w\mathbf{l} + (1 + r)\,\mathbf{p}\mathbf{A} \tag{2.1b}$$

and $\mathbf{B}$ denotes the $n \times n$ output matrix, which allows both for pure joint products and utilized fixed capital commodities (Sraffa-von Neumann approach). Provided that $[\mathbf{B} - \mathbf{A}]$ is non-singular, Eq. 2.1b can be rewritten as

$$\mathbf{p} = w\mathbf{v}_{\mathbf{B}} + r\,\mathbf{p}\mathbf{H}_{\mathbf{B}} \tag{2.16b}$$

where $\mathbf{v}_{\mathbf{B}} \equiv \mathbf{l}[\mathbf{B} - \mathbf{A}]^{-1}$ $(= \mathbf{p}_w(0))$ denotes the vector of 'additive labour values' (Steedman 1975, 1976), i.e. of direct and indirect labour requirements per unit of net output for each commodity, and $\mathbf{H}_{\mathbf{B}} \equiv \mathbf{A}[\mathbf{B} - \mathbf{A}]^{-1}$. Thus, $\mathbf{v}_{\mathbf{B}}$ does not represent

[19] For the Leontief-Bródy approach, see Leontief (1953), Bródy (1970), Mathur (1977), Semmler (1984, Part 3) and Flaschel (2010, Chap. 8). For instance, r could be the average or the minimum profit rate of the system (Steedman 1977, pp. 180–181, and Reati 1986, pp. 159–160). For more recent, alternative modellings of disequilibrium prices and quantities, see Benetti et al. (2007, 2008) and Oda (2007). For the excess capacity case, and the interactions between the real wage, labour employment, capacity utilization, profit and capital accumulation rates, see Bhaduri and Marglin (1990), Dutt (1990), Kurz (1990), Hein (2008), Mariolis (2013) and the references therein.

the 'labour costs' of commodities but rather 'employment multipliers' (*à la* Kahn 1931).[20] As Sraffa (1960) stresses:

> [I]n the case of joint-products there is no obvious criterion for apportioning the labour among individual products, and indeed it seems doubtful whether it makes any sense to speak of a *separate* quantity of labour as having gone to produce one of a number of *jointly* produced commodities. (p. 56)

A commodity is said to be 'separately producible' in system $[\mathbf{B}, \mathbf{A}]$ if it is possible to produce a net output consisting of a unit of that commodity alone with a nonnegative intensity vector. A system of production is called 'all-productive' if all commodities are separately producible in it. Thus, if $[\mathbf{B}, \mathbf{A}]$ is 'all-productive', then $[\mathbf{B} - \mathbf{A}]^{-1} \geq \mathbf{0}$. Furthermore, a process is 'indispensable' within a system of production if it has to be activated whatever net output is to be produced. An 'all-productive system' whose processes are all indispensable is called 'all-engaging'. Thus, if $[\mathbf{B}, \mathbf{A}]$ is 'all-engaging', then $[\mathbf{B} - \mathbf{A}]^{-1} > \mathbf{0}$. These two types of systems retain all the essential properties of single-product systems (Schefold 1971, 1978). Hence, the main difference introduced here is that $\mathbf{v_B}$ and/or $\mathbf{H_B}$ can contain one or more negative elements:

(i) Some additive labour values are negative if a nonnegative linear combination of some processes yields a greater net output per unit of labour employed than a nonnegative linear combination of the remaining ones (Filippini and Filippini 1982).
(ii) $\mathbf{v_B}\mathbf{b}^{\mathrm{T}} < 1$ is neither a necessary nor a sufficient condition for $[\mathbf{p} > \mathbf{0},\ r > 0]$ (Steedman 1975, 1977, Chaps. 11 and 12; also see Fujimoto and Krause 1988).
(iii) Each element in the vector of labour-commanded prices is not necessarily a strictly increasing function of the profit rate and, therefore, the monotonicity of the WPC is a priori unknown and can depend on the numeraire chosen (Sraffa 1960, Chap. 9; also see Steedman 1982; d' Autume 1988).

When $r > g$ (non-'golden rule' steady state), the possible existence of positive additive labour values with an interval of r in which $[\mathbf{B} - (1 + r)\mathbf{A}]^{-1} > \mathbf{0}$,

$$[\mathbf{I} - r\mathbf{H_B}]^{-1}\left(= [\mathbf{B} - \mathbf{A}][\mathbf{B} - (1 + r)\mathbf{A}]^{-1}\right) > \mathbf{0}$$

and the relative commodity supply curve is downward-sloping cannot be ruled out (see Saucier 1984, pp. 168–173, and Mariolis 2004a, pp. 453–454; compare with Samuelson 1999, 2000).

[20] For alternative definitions of labour values and their differences, both qualitative and quantitative, in the joint production case, see Fujimori (1982, Chaps. 3 and 4). For an attempt to determine labour costs, which is based on the 'industry technology assumption' and the 'market or sales value method' (and, therefore, involves a conversion of the original system into a *single* production system), see Flaschel (1980, pp. 121–126, 1983, pp. 443–450).

Finally, if an *ad valorem* tax is imposed on a number of commodities, then Eq. 2.1b should be replaced by

$$\mathbf{p}\left[\mathbf{I}+\hat{\mathbf{T}}\right]^{-1}\mathbf{B} = w\mathbf{l} + (1+r)\,\mathbf{pA}$$

or, in the case of differential profit rates,

$$\mathbf{p}\left[\mathbf{I}+\hat{\mathbf{T}}\right]^{-1}\mathbf{B} = w\mathbf{l} + \mathbf{pA}[\mathbf{I}+\hat{\mathbf{r}}] \tag{2.1c}$$

where $\hat{\mathbf{T}} \equiv [t_i]$ denotes the diagonal matrix of tax rates and t_i the tax rate imposed on commodity i.[21]

2.2.4 *Open Economy*

Consider an open system involving only single products and circulating capital. Assume that (i) there are no competitive imports; (ii) the foreign currency prices of the imported commodities are independent of the volume of the economy's imports, while the economy's exports are exogenously given; and (iii) production imports are paid at the beginning of the production period (for the construction and study of this model, see Metcalfe and Steedman 1981; for its extension to the joint production case, see Mariolis 2008a). The system can be described by

$$\begin{aligned}\mathbf{p} &= w\mathbf{l} + (1+r)\left(\mathbf{pA} + \varepsilon\,\mathbf{p}^{\mathrm{M}}\mathbf{A}^{\mathrm{M}}\right) \\ \mathbf{x}^{\mathrm{T}} &= c\left(\mathbf{l}\mathbf{x}^{\mathrm{T}}\right)\mathbf{f}_1^{\mathrm{T}} + (1+g)\mathbf{A}\mathbf{x}^{\mathrm{T}} + \mathbf{E}^{\mathrm{T}}\end{aligned} \tag{2.1d}$$

where $\mathbf{p}$ now denotes the price vector of domestically produced commodities, ε the nominal exchange rate, $\mathbf{p}^{\mathrm{M}}$ the $1 \times m$ vector of foreign currency prices of the imported commodities, $\mathbf{A}^{\mathrm{M}}$ the $m \times n$ matrix of imported input-output coefficients (for a pure consumption import, the corresponding row of $\mathbf{A}^{\mathrm{M}}$ is null), $\mathbf{f}^{\mathrm{T}} \equiv [\mathbf{f}_1, \mathbf{f}_2]^{\mathrm{T}}$ the commodity vector that serves as the unit of consumption ($\mathbf{f}_1^{\mathrm{T}}$ corresponds to domestically produced commodities, and $\mathbf{f}_2^{\mathrm{T}}$ corresponds to imported commodities) and $\mathbf{E}^{\mathrm{T}}$ the $n \times 1$ vector of commodities exported. If we adopt the unit of consumption as the numeraire, i.e. $\mathbf{p}\mathbf{f}_1^{\mathrm{T}} + \varepsilon\,\mathbf{p}^{\mathrm{M}}\mathbf{f}_2^{\mathrm{T}} = 1$, then Eq. 2.1d implies

[21] For general treatments of joint production, see Schefold (1989), Bidard (1991) and Kurz and Salvadori (1995, Chaps. 7, 8 and 9). For the physiocratic, classical, Marxian and Sraffian theories of taxation, see Metcalfe and Steedman (1971), Semmler (1983), Tsoulfidis (1989, 1993) and Gehrke and Lager (1995); for alternative types of indirect taxation and their price effects, see Erreygers (1989).

$$w\mathbf{l}[\mathbf{I}-(1+r)\mathbf{A}]^{-1}\mathbf{f}_1^{\mathrm{T}}+\varepsilon\mathbf{p}^{\mathrm{M}}\left[(1+r)\mathbf{A}^{\mathrm{M}}[\mathbf{I}-(1+r)\mathbf{A}]^{-1}\mathbf{f}_1^{\mathrm{T}}+\mathbf{f}_2^{\mathrm{T}}\right]=1$$

which defines a '$w-\varepsilon-r$ curve' for this open economy, in which each variable is inversely related to each of the others. The main differences introduced here are that (i) when trade is unbalanced, the CGC is no longer dual to the WPC (Mainwaring 1979; Steedman and Metcalfe 1981, pp. 134–137), and (ii) even when trade is balanced and $m=1$, both absolute and relative labour values of domestically produced commodities (defined by the labour-commanded prices corresponding to zero profits) depend on the terms of trade (Steedman and Metcalfe 1981, pp. 140–141, Steedman 1999a, pp. 267–268, 2008, pp. 168–173, and Mariolis and Soklis 2007, pp. 252–254; compare with Okishio and Nakatani 1985, pp. 62–63).

2.3 Norm Bounds

Although the specific shapes of the wage-production price-profit rate curves have crucial implications for the so-called capital controversy (see Garegnani 1970; Harcourt 1972, Chaps. 1 and 4), it is widely recognized that very little a priori can be said about them (also consider Mas-Colell 1989). Before exploring those shapes, it is worth to show that they admit lower and upper norm bounds.

2.3.1 *Bounds for the Wage-Relative Profit Rate Curve*

Consider the matrix $\mathbf{M}\equiv\hat{\mathbf{y}}_{\mathbf{J}1}\mathbf{J}\hat{\mathbf{y}}_{\mathbf{J}1}^{-1}$, the elements of which are independent of the choice of physical measurement units and the normalization of $\mathbf{y}_{\mathbf{J}1}$.[22] This matrix can be conceived of as a matrix of the relative shares of the capital commodities in the cost of outputs, evaluated at $\rho=1$, or, alternatively, as derived from $\mathbf{J}$ by changing the units in which the various commodity quantities are measured (see Ara 1963; Fisher 1965). Since $\mathbf{eM}=\mathbf{y}_{\mathbf{J}1}\hat{\mathbf{y}}_{\mathbf{J}1}^{-1}=\mathbf{e}$, $\mathbf{M}$ is a column *stochastic* matrix. Substituting $\mathbf{J}=\hat{\mathbf{y}}_{\mathbf{J}1}^{-1}\mathbf{M}\hat{\mathbf{y}}_{\mathbf{J}1}$ in Eq. 2.16 yields

$$\boldsymbol{\pi}=w\boldsymbol{\omega}+\rho\boldsymbol{\pi}\mathbf{M} \tag{2.39}$$

where $\pi\equiv\mathbf{p}\hat{\mathbf{y}}_{\mathbf{J}1}^{-1}$, $\omega\equiv\mathbf{v}\hat{\mathbf{y}}_{\mathbf{J}1}^{-1}$ are the *transformed* vectors of prices and labour

[22] What follows draw on Mariolis (2015) and use, in turn, two ideas provided by Mariolis (2010) and Kurz and Salvadori (1995, pp. 100–101).

values, respectively. Since $\boldsymbol{\pi}\boldsymbol{\zeta}^{\mathrm{T}} = 1$, where $\boldsymbol{\zeta}^{\mathrm{T}} \equiv \hat{\mathbf{y}}_{\mathbf{J}1}\mathbf{z}^{\mathrm{T}}$, the price system (2.39) can be rewritten as

$$\boldsymbol{\pi} = w\left(\boldsymbol{\pi}\boldsymbol{\zeta}^{\mathrm{T}}\right)\boldsymbol{\omega} + \rho\boldsymbol{\pi}\mathbf{M}$$

or, since $\left[\mathbf{I} - w\boldsymbol{\zeta}^{\mathrm{T}}\boldsymbol{\omega}\right]^{-1} = \mathbf{I} + \left(1 - w\boldsymbol{\omega}\boldsymbol{\zeta}^{\mathrm{T}}\right)^{-1} w\boldsymbol{\zeta}^{\mathrm{T}}\boldsymbol{\omega}$, provided that $w\omega\zeta^{\mathrm{T}} \ (= w) < 1 \ (= W)$,

$$\boldsymbol{\pi} = \rho\boldsymbol{\pi}\boldsymbol{\Xi} \tag{2.40}$$

where

$$\boldsymbol{\Xi} \equiv \mathbf{M}\left[\mathbf{I} + (1 - w)^{-1} w\boldsymbol{\zeta}^{\mathrm{T}}\boldsymbol{\omega}\right] \tag{2.41}$$

From Eq. 2.40 it follows that

$$\rho^{-1} = \lambda_{\Xi 1} \tag{2.42}$$

and $\boldsymbol{\pi}$ is the corresponding left eigenvector. For $\lambda_{\Xi 1}$ it holds that ('Frobenius bounds'; see, e.g. Meyer 2001, p. 668)

$$\min_{1 \le j \le n} \{\mathbf{e}\boldsymbol{\Xi}_j\} = \left(\left\|\hat{\boldsymbol{\xi}}^{-1}\right\|\right)^{-1} \le \lambda_{\Xi 1} \le \max_{1 \le j \le n} \{\mathbf{e}\boldsymbol{\Xi}_j\} = \|\boldsymbol{\xi}\| \tag{2.43}$$

where $\boldsymbol{\xi} \equiv \mathbf{e}\boldsymbol{\Xi}$. Taking norms of Eq. 2.41, and invoking $\|\mathbf{M}\| = 1$, we obtain

$$\|\boldsymbol{\xi}\| = \|\boldsymbol{\Xi}\| = 1 + (1 - w)^{-1} w\Phi \tag{2.44}$$

and

$$\left(\left\|\hat{\boldsymbol{\xi}}^{-1}\right\|\right)^{-1} = 1 + (1 - w)^{-1} w\phi \tag{2.45}$$

where $\Phi \equiv \| \omega \| \| \zeta^{\mathrm{T}} \| \ge \| \omega\zeta^{\mathrm{T}} \| = 1$, $\ \phi \equiv (\| \hat{\omega}^{-1} \|)^{-1} \| \zeta^{\mathrm{T}} \| \le 1$,

$$\Omega \equiv \Phi\phi^{-1} = \|\boldsymbol{\omega}\|\left\|\hat{\boldsymbol{\omega}}^{-1}\right\| = \left(\max_j \{\omega_j\}\right)\left(\min_j \{\omega_j\}\right)^{-1}$$

is the antilogarithm of the 'Hilbert distance (or projective metric)' between $\mathbf{v}$ and $\mathbf{y}_{\mathbf{J}1}$, which is numeraire-free (and unit-free), and[23]

---

[23] Bidard and Krause (1996) prove that, for a fixed profit rate $r^* \ (\le R)$, the Hilbert distance between two price vectors $\mathbf{p}(r)$ and $\mathbf{p}(r^*)$ decreases as $r \ (\ge -1)$ increases towards r^* (also see Bidard and Ehrbar 2007, pp. 183–188).

$$\Omega \leq \left(\max_j \left\{ l_j y_{\mathbf{J}1j}^{-1} \right\} \right) \left(\min_j \left\{ l_j y_{\mathbf{J}1j}^{-1} \right\} \right)^{-1}$$

Equations 2.42, 2.43, 2.44, and 2.45 imply

$$\left[1 + (1 - w)^{-1} w \Phi \right]^{-1} \leq \rho \leq \left[1 + (1 - w)^{-1} w \phi \right]^{-1}$$

or, solving for w and invoking Eq. 2.28, i.e. $w^{\mathrm{S}} \equiv 1 - \rho$,

$$L \equiv w^{\mathrm{S}} [1 + \rho(\Phi - 1)]^{-1} \leq w \leq U \equiv w^{\mathrm{S}} [1 + \rho(\phi - 1)]^{-1} \tag{2.46}$$

It then follows that relations (2.46) give lower, L, and upper, U, bounds for w, which have exactly the same algebraic form as the WPC for the corn-tractor model (see Eq. 2.30):[24]

(i) $L(0) = U(0) = 1, \; L(1) = U(1) = 0.$
(ii) $\dot{L} < 0, \; \dot{U} < 0, \; \ddot{L} > 0, \; \ddot{U} < 0.$
(iii) If Φ (ϕ) tends to 1, then L (U) tends to w^{S}, while if Φ (ϕ) tends to $+\infty$ (to 0), then L (U) tends to 0 (to 1).
(iv) If $\mathbf{z}^{\mathrm{T}} = \mathbf{e}_m^{\mathrm{T}}$, where $\omega_m = \min_j \{\omega_j\}$, then Φ and ϕ take their largest values, i.e. $\Phi = \Omega$ and $\phi = 1$, while if $\mathbf{z}^{\mathrm{T}} = \mathbf{e}_M^{\mathrm{T}}$, where $\omega_M = \max_j \{\omega_j\}$, then Φ and ϕ take their smallest values, i.e. $\Phi = 1$ and $\phi = \Omega^{-1}$.

Finally, the area $S(\phi)$ between the bound curves, U and L, on the interval $0 \leq \rho \leq 1$ depends on the choice of numeraire and takes its smallest value at $\phi = \Omega^{-1}$ and $\phi = 1$, i.e.

$$S_{\mathrm{sm}} \equiv S(\Omega^{-1}) = S(1) = -\left(1 - \Omega^2 + 2\Omega \ln \Omega\right) \left[2(\Omega - 1)^2 \right]^{-1} \tag{2.47}$$

and its maximum value at $\phi = \Omega^{-0.5}$, i.e.

$$S_{\max} \equiv S(\Omega^{-0.5}) = \left[\left(1 - \Omega - \Omega^{0.5} + \Omega^{1.5}\right) - \left(\Omega - \Omega^{0.5}\right) \ln \Omega \right] \left(\Omega^{0.5} - 1\right)^{-3} \tag{2.48}$$

where S_{sm} tends to 0 (to 2^{-1}) as Ω tends to 1 (to $+\infty$), while $S_{\max}$ tends to 0 (to 1) as Ω tends to 1 (to $+\infty$). For instance, see Fig. 2.2, where $\Omega = 10$ or 20 and, therefore, $S_{\mathrm{sm}} \cong 0.327$ or 0.387, and $S_{\max} \cong 0.368$ or 0.465 at $\phi \cong 0.316$ or 0.224, respectively.

[24] It seems that the bounds may be improved by using generalized 'Geršgorin regions' (instead of relations (2.43)), especially when $\mathbf{M}$ (and, therefore, Ξ) is a large sparse matrix (see Melman 2013). Those matrices usually arise from actual input-output data on fixed capital stocks.

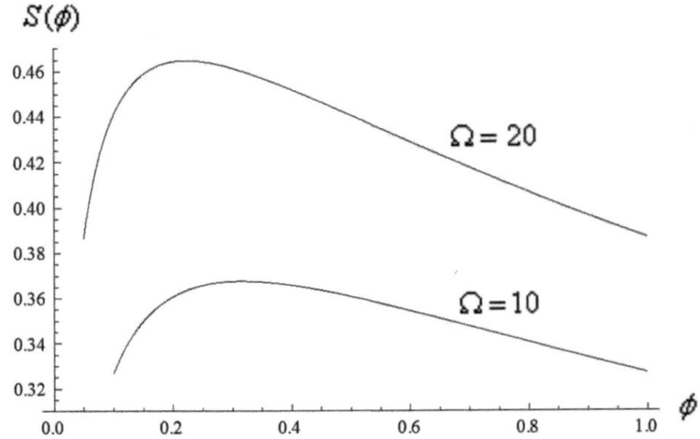

Fig. 2.2 The area between the bound curves as a function of the composition of the numeraire

2.3.2 *Bounds for the Price-Relative Profit Rate Curves*

If SSC is chosen as the numeraire, then Eqs. 2.1, 2.2 and 2.28 imply

$$\mathbf{p} = \left(1 - rR^{-1}\right)\mathbf{l} + (1 + r)\,\mathbf{pA}$$

and, since at $r = -1$, $\mathbf{p}$ equals $\left(1 + R^{-1}\right)\mathbf{l}$,

$$\mathbf{p} = \left(1 + R^{-1}\right)^{-1}\mathbf{p}(-1)\sum_{h=0}^{+\infty}\left(1 - rR^{-1}\right)[(1 + r)\mathbf{A}]^h \tag{2.49}$$

Equation 2.49 is the reduction to dated quantities of direct labour in terms of SSC, where (i) the term $\left(1 - rR^{-1}\right)(1 + r)^h, h \geq 1$, takes its maximum value of $(1 + R)^{h+1}R^{-1}h^h(h + 1)^{-1-h}$ ($\rightarrow +\infty$, i.e. tends to plus infinity as h tends to infinity) at $r = (Rh - 1)(h + 1)^{-1}(\rightarrow R)$ and, therefore, (ii) the terms for which $hR \leq 1$ decrease as r increases from 0 to R (Sraffa 1960, pp. 35–37).[25]

We now return to the normalized vertically integrated representation of the system. Equations 2.16, 2.17 and 2.28 imply

$$\mathbf{p} = (1 - \rho)\mathbf{v} + \rho\,\mathbf{pJ} \tag{2.50}$$

and, since $\mathbf{p}(0) = \mathbf{v}$,

[25] For the correction, by Harry G. Johnson and his students, of a slip in the first edition of Sraffa's book, and Sraffa's response to it, see Kurz and Salvadori (2003, pp. 209–215).

$$\mathbf{p} = \mathbf{p}(0)\sum_{h=0}^{+\infty}(1-\rho)(\rho\mathbf{J})^h \tag{2.51}$$

Equation 2.50 indicates that p_j is a convex combination of v_j and $\mathbf{pJ}_j$, where the latter equals the ratio of means of production in the vertically integrated industry producing commodity j to means of production in the SSS. Equation 2.51 is the reduction to dated quantities of embodied labour in terms of SSC, where (Steedman 1999b, pp. 315–316):

(i) The sum of all the terms $(1-\rho)\rho^h$ equals 1.
(ii) There is only one strictly decreasing term (that for $h=0$).
(iii) The term $(1-\rho)\rho^h,\ \ h \geq 2$ takes its maximum value of $h^h(h+1)^{-h-1}(\rightarrow 0)$ at $\rho = h(h+1)^{-1}$, and its 'inflection value' of $2(h-1)^h(h+1)^{-h-1}(\rightarrow 0)$ at $\rho = (h-1)(h+1)^{-1}\big)$.
(iv) The ratio of the inflection value to the maximum value tends to $2e^{-1} \cong 0.736$.
(v) The first term is greater than the sum of all the remaining terms for $\rho < 2^{-1} = 0.5$, while the sum of the first two (first m) terms is greater than the sum of all the remaining terms for $\rho < 2^{-0.5} \cong 0.707$ (for $\rho < 2^{-m^{-1}}$).

It can therefore be stated that the integrated reduction (2.51) presents certain advantages over the direct reduction (2.49). The former generates a much simpler pattern of monotonically falling terms and non-monotonic terms, while the value of R is irrelevant to the distinction between them and, at the same time, requires far fewer terms to give an acceptable approximation of the production prices, provided that one is interested only in relatively *low* values of ρ. Nevertheless, as Steedman (1999b) also remarks, in the integrated reduction (2.51)

> [I]t is not, of course, only the $(1-\rho)\,\rho^h$ terms which influence relative prices and the fact that those terms decrease rapidly as h increases (for small ρ) would be less significant if the labour vectors which they multiply – the $\mathbf{vJ}^h$ – were to increase rapidly in magnitude as h increases. Hence the *norm* of matrix $\mathbf{J}$ is important here. By the definition of $\mathbf{J}$, its Perron-Frobenius root is unity. If, by chance, $\mathbf{H}$ and hence $\mathbf{J}$ should happen to be normal matrices [i.e. $\mathbf{HH}^{\mathrm{T}} = \mathbf{H}^{\mathrm{T}}\mathbf{H}$; also see Bidard and Steedman (1996)] (whether diagonal or otherwise), it would then follow at once that $\left(\mathbf{vJ}^h\left[\mathbf{J}^h\right]^{\mathrm{T}}\mathbf{v}^{\mathrm{T}}\right) \leq (\mathbf{vv}^{\mathrm{T}})$ [...]. Hence *no* vector $\mathbf{vJ}^h$, for $h=1,2,\ldots$,would be of greater Euclidean length than $\mathbf{v}$ and the decrease in $(1-\rho)\,\rho^h$ with h would certainly not be counteracted by any tendency for the vectors $\mathbf{vJ}^h$ to increase in magnitude with h. More generally, we can of course say that there will be no such tendency provided that every matrix $\mathbf{J}^h$ has a norm of unity or less – but this is merely true by definition and we shall not attempt here to characterize the conditions on $\mathbf{H}$ under which this requirement will be met. (p. 316; using our symbols)

Thus, it seems useful to deal with the transformed price system (2.39), where the system matrix is stochastic. Substituting $w^{\mathrm{S}} \equiv 1-\rho$ in that system yields

$$\boldsymbol{\pi} = (1 - \rho)\boldsymbol{\omega} + \rho\boldsymbol{\pi}\mathbf{M} \tag{2.52}$$

or

$$\boldsymbol{\pi} = \boldsymbol{\omega}[\mathbf{N}(\rho)]^{-1} \tag{2.53}$$

where $\mathbf{N}(\rho) \equiv (1 - \rho)^{-1}[\mathbf{I} - \rho\mathbf{M}]$ and $[\mathbf{N}(\rho)]^{-1}$ is a column stochastic matrix, since $[\mathbf{N}(\rho)]^{-1} \geq \mathbf{0}$ and

$$\mathbf{e}[\mathbf{N}(\rho)]^{-1} = (1 - \rho)(1 - \rho)^{-1}\mathbf{e} = \mathbf{e}$$

From Eqs. 2.52, 2.53 and $\mathbf{y}_{\mathbf{J}1}[\mathbf{I} - \mathbf{A}]\mathbf{x}_{\mathbf{J}1}^{\mathrm{T}} = 1$ we derive the following:

(i) $\boldsymbol{\pi} = \boldsymbol{\omega}$ at $\rho = 0$, and $\boldsymbol{\pi} = \mathbf{e}$ at $\rho = 1$. In the equal value compositions of capital case, $\boldsymbol{\omega} = \mathbf{e} = \boldsymbol{\pi}$. Furthermore, since $(\boldsymbol{\pi} - \boldsymbol{\omega})(\hat{\mathbf{y}}_{\mathbf{J}1}\mathbf{x}_{\mathbf{J}1}) = 0$ for each ρ, it follows that $(\mathbf{e} - \boldsymbol{\omega})(\hat{\mathbf{y}}_{\mathbf{J}1}\mathbf{x}_{\mathbf{J}1}) = 0$, which in its turn implies

$$\min_j \{\omega_j\} \leq 1 \leq \max_j \{\omega_j\} \tag{2.54}$$

(if $\boldsymbol{\omega} \neq \mathbf{e}$, then both inequalities in relations (2.54) are strict).

(ii) Equation 2.53 implies that π_j is a convex combination of the elements of $\boldsymbol{\omega}$. Thus, we can write

$$\min_j \{\omega_j\} \leq \pi_j \leq \max_j \{\omega_j\}$$

or

$$\|\boldsymbol{\pi}\| \leq \|\boldsymbol{\omega}\| \tag{2.55}$$

and

$$\left(\|\hat{\boldsymbol{\omega}}^{-1}\|\right)^{-1} \leq \left(\|\hat{\boldsymbol{\pi}}^{-1}\|\right)^{-1} \tag{2.56}$$

(iii) Equation 2.52 can be restated as

$$(1 - \rho)\boldsymbol{\omega} = \boldsymbol{\pi}[\mathbf{I} - \rho\mathbf{M}] \tag{2.57}$$

Taking norms of Eq. 2.57, we obtain

$$(1-\rho)\|\boldsymbol{\omega}\| \leq \|\boldsymbol{\pi}\|\left(\max_j\left\{1-\rho m_{jj}+\sum_{\substack{i=1\\ i\neq j}}^{n}\rho m_{ij}\right\}\right) \tag{2.58}$$

or, given that $\sum_{\substack{i=1\\ i\neq j}}^{n} m_{ij} = 1 - m_{jj}$,

$$(1-\rho)\|\boldsymbol{\omega}\| \leq \|\boldsymbol{\pi}\|\left(\max_j\left\{1+\rho\left(1-2m_{jj}\right)\right\}\right)$$

or

$$(1-\rho)\|\boldsymbol{\omega}\| \leq \|\boldsymbol{\pi}\|[1+\rho(1-2m)]$$

or

$$f(\rho) \leq \|\boldsymbol{\pi}\|(\|\boldsymbol{\omega}\|)^{-1} \tag{2.59}$$

where $m \equiv \min_j\left\{m_{jj}\right\}, 0 < m < 1$ and $f(\rho) \equiv (1-\rho)[1+\rho(1-2m)]^{-1}, 0 < f(\rho) \leq 1$, a strictly decreasing function of ρ, which is strictly convex to the origin for $m < 0.5$, and tends to 1 as m tends to 1. The 'condition number' (see, e.g. Meyer (2001), pp. 127–128) of $\mathbf{N}(\rho)$, defined as $\|\mathbf{N}(\rho)\|\left\|[\mathbf{N}(\rho)]^{-1}\right\|$, equals $(f(\rho))^{-1}$. This number is a measure of the sensitivity of $\boldsymbol{\pi}$ to perturbations in $\mathbf{N}(\rho)$.

(iv) Postmultiplying Eq. 2.52 by $\hat{\boldsymbol{\omega}}^{-1}\hat{\boldsymbol{\pi}}^{-1}\left(=\hat{\boldsymbol{\pi}}^{-1}\hat{\boldsymbol{\omega}}^{-1}\right)$ gives

$$\mathbf{e}\hat{\boldsymbol{\omega}}^{-1} = (1-\rho)\mathbf{e}\hat{\boldsymbol{\pi}}^{-1} + \rho\boldsymbol{\pi}\mathbf{M}\hat{\boldsymbol{\omega}}^{-1}\hat{\boldsymbol{\pi}}^{-1}$$

Taking norms, and invoking $\|\mathbf{M}\| = 1$, we obtain

$$\left\|\hat{\boldsymbol{\omega}}^{-1}\right\| \leq (1-\rho)\left\|\hat{\boldsymbol{\pi}}^{-1}\right\| + \rho\|\boldsymbol{\pi}\|\left\|\hat{\boldsymbol{\omega}}^{-1}\right\|\left\|\hat{\boldsymbol{\pi}}^{-1}\right\|$$

or, dividing both sides by $\left\|\hat{\boldsymbol{\pi}}^{-1}\right\|$ and invoking relation (2.55),

$$\left\|\hat{\boldsymbol{\omega}}^{-1}\right\|\left(\left\|\hat{\boldsymbol{\pi}}^{-1}\right\|\right)^{-1} \leq g(\rho) \leq h(\rho) \tag{2.60}$$

where

$$g(\rho) \equiv 1 + \rho\left(\|\boldsymbol{\pi}\|\left\|\hat{\boldsymbol{\omega}}^{-1}\right\| - 1\right)(\geq 1)$$
$$g(1) = \|\boldsymbol{\pi}(1)\|\left\|\hat{\boldsymbol{\omega}}^{-1}\right\| = \left(\left\|\hat{\boldsymbol{\pi}}^{-1}(1)\right\|\right)^{-1}\left\|\hat{\boldsymbol{\omega}}^{-1}\right\| = \left\|\hat{\boldsymbol{\omega}}^{-1}\right\|$$

(since at $\rho = 1$, $\boldsymbol{\pi} = \mathbf{e}$), the monotonicity of $g(\rho)$ is a priori unknown, and

$$1 \leq h(\rho) \equiv 1 + \rho\left(\|\boldsymbol{\omega}\|\left\|\hat{\boldsymbol{\omega}}^{-1}\right\| - 1\right) = 1 + \rho(\Omega - 1) \leq \Omega$$

Combining relations (2.55) and (2.59) gives

$$f(\rho) \leq \|\boldsymbol{\pi}\|(\|\boldsymbol{\omega}\|)^{-1} \leq 1 \tag{2.61}$$

while combining relations (2.56) and (2.60) gives

$$1 \leq \left\|\hat{\boldsymbol{\omega}}^{-1}\right\|\left(\left\|\hat{\boldsymbol{\pi}}^{-1}\right\|\right)^{-1} \leq h(\rho) \tag{2.62}$$

Hence, the upper (lower) bound for $\|\boldsymbol{\pi}\|(\|\boldsymbol{\omega}\|)^{-1}$ (for $\left\|\hat{\boldsymbol{\omega}}^{-1}\right\|\left(\left\|\hat{\boldsymbol{\pi}}^{-1}\right\|\right)^{-1}$) equals 1 and the lower (upper) bound decreases (increases) with increasing ρ.

It has, therefore, been shown that, when the system matrix can be transformed into a stochastic one, both the wage rate (measured in terms of any numeraire) and the transformed price vector (measured in terms of SSC) admit lower and upper norm bounds. Furthermore, this analysis can be applied to (i) *some* systems of pure joint production (Mariolis 2010, pp. 563–564), (ii) systems with many primary inputs (such as labour of different kinds, land of different qualities and noncompetitive imports; consider Metcalfe and Steedman 1972, pp. 156–157, 1981, pp. 9–10; Montani 1975) and (iii) the physical quantity system (Rodousakis and Soklis 2010; Mariolis et al. 2012, Appendix 3). Finally, it may be considered as an alternative approach to the 'problem of the transformation' of labour values into prices (also consider Roemer 1981, Chap. 8; Nakatani and Okishio 1995) and can be reformulated in terms of alternative value bases, i.e. of commodity i values (Mariolis 2010, pp. 562–563).

2.4 Relative Price Effects

Central theorems of the traditional analysis of single-product economies (either closed or open) reduce, in essence, to the existence of an unambiguous relationship between the movement of the relative price of two commodities, on the one hand, and the ratios of relative capital intensities (or, equivalently, of relative labour shares) to growth rates of total productivity in the industries producing these commodities, on the other. Since Sraffa's (1960, Chaps. 3 and 6) contribution, it has been gradually recognized, however, that such a relationship does not necessarily exist.[26] In what follows, we explore, in turn, the relative price effects of (i) income distribution changes and (ii) total productivity shift ('Hicks-neutral technical change').[27]

2.4.1 Price Effects of Income Distribution Changes

The question of price movements arising from changes in income distribution starts with the works of classical economists and continues in Marx (1959, Chaps. 11 and 12). Ricardo's (1951) answer is neatly summarized, by himself, as follows:

> [I]t may be proper to observe, that Adam Smith, and all the writers who have followed him, have, without one exception that I know of, maintained that a rise in the price of labour would be uniformly followed by a rise in the price of all commodities. I hope I have succeeded in showing, that there are no grounds for such an opinion, and that only those commodities would rise which had less fixed capital employed upon them than the *medium* in which price was *estimated*, and that all those which had more, would positively fall in price when wages rose. On the contrary, if wages fell, those commodities only would fall, which had a less proportion of fixed capital employed on them, than the medium in which price was estimated; all those which had more, would positively rise in price. (p. 46; emphasis added)

Sraffa (1960) remarked that the directions of relative price movements are governed not only by the differences in the relevant capital intensities but also by the movements of the relevant capital intensities arising from changes in relative commodity prices:

> [T]he means of production of an industry are themselves the product of one or more industries which may in their turn employ a still lower proportion of labour to means of production (and the same may be the case with these latter means of production; and so on). (pp. 14–15)

Thus, he pointed out that

> [A]s the wages fall the price of the product of a low-proportion [. . .] industry may rise or it may fall, or it may even alternate in rising and falling, relative to its means of production (p. 15). [. . .] The reversals in the direction of the movement of relative prices, in the face of unchanged methods of production, cannot be reconciled with *any* notion of capital as measurable quantity independent of distribution and prices. (p. 38)

Sraffa's analysis was extended by Pasinetti (1977, pp. 82–84) who showed that the relative price movement can be decomposed into a 'capital-intensity effect'

---

[26] For the closed economies, see Kurz and Salvadori (1995, Chaps. 4, 5 and 14) and Steedman (2000); for the open ones, see Parrinello (1970), Steedman (1979), Mariolis (2008b) and the references therein. Some aspects of the analysis of changes within the labour process (see Steedman 1977, Chap. 6) and of variable returns to scale (see Howard 1981) are relevant.

[27] This exploration draws on Mariolis and Tsoulfidis (2009) and Mariolis (2008b), Mariolis et al. (2015), respectively. The Austrian (Böhm-Bawerkian) approach to the former issue is summarized in the Appendix at the end of this chapter and draws on Mariolis et al. (2013).

(direct or traditional effect) and a ‘price effect’ (indirect or Sraffian effect), where the former reflects differences in the relevant capital intensities, while the latter depends on the entire economic system and, therefore, is not predictable at the level of any *single* industry. Moreover, he claimed that, more often than not, the direct effect dominates the indirect one, although there are cases where the latter is so strong that it can reverse the former. Pasinetti’s contribution can be formulated in vertically integrated terms as follows.[28] Substituting Eq. 2.20 in Eq. 2.16 yields

$$\mathbf{p} = (1 - \rho k_{\mathbf{z}})\mathbf{v} + \rho\,\mathbf{pJ}$$

Postmultiplying by $\hat{\mathbf{v}}^{-1}$, and rearranging terms, gives

$$\mathbf{p}\hat{\mathbf{v}}^{-1} = \mathbf{e} + \rho R\left(\mathbf{pH}\hat{\mathbf{v}}^{-1} - \kappa_{\mathbf{z}}\right)$$

or, in terms of an industry j,

$$p_j v_j^{-1} = 1 + \rho R\left(\kappa_j - \kappa_{\mathbf{z}}\right) \tag{2.63}$$

where $\kappa_j \equiv \mathbf{pH}_j v_j^{-1}$ denotes the capital intensity of the vertically integrated industry producing commodity j and $\kappa_{\mathbf{z}} \equiv R^{-1} k_{\mathbf{z}}$ equals the capital intensity of the vertically integrated industry producing the numeraire commodity. Differentiation of Eq. 2.63 with respect to ρ gives

$$\dot{p}_j v_j^{-1} = R\left[\left(\kappa_j - \kappa_{\mathbf{z}}\right) - \rho\left(\dot{\kappa}_{\mathbf{z}} - \dot{\kappa}_j\right)\right] \tag{2.64}$$

where, using Pasinetti’s (1977) terminology, $(\kappa j - \kappa_{\mathbf{z}})$ represents the ‘capital-intensity effect’ and $\left(\dot{\kappa}_{\mathbf{z}} - \dot{\kappa}_j\right)$ represents the ‘price effect’. It then follows that, iff $n \geq 3$ (see Sect. 2.2.1.3, point iv), the ‘traditional condition’

[28] This formulation is associated with that proposed by Parys (1982). For other, alternative formulations, see Caravale and Tosato (1980, pp. 85–87), Bidard (1991, pp. 56–58) and Kurz and Salvadori (1995, pp. 99–100). More recently, C. Bidard, H. G. Ehrbar, U. Krause and I. Steedman have detected some ‘monotonicity (theoretical) laws’ for the relative prices (see Bidard 1998, and Bidard and Ehrbar 2007, and the references therein).

$$\kappa_j > (<)\kappa_{\mathbf{z}} \Leftrightarrow \dot{p}_j > (<)0 \tag{2.65}$$

does not necessarily hold true.[29] When $(\kappa j - \kappa_z)$ and $\left(\dot{\kappa}_{\mathbf{z}} - \dot{\kappa}_j\right)$ have opposite signs, the two effects work in the same direction; when they have the same sign, condition (2.65) may be violated. If SSC is chosen as the numeraire, then the price movement can be 'observed as in a vacuum' (Sraffa 1960, p. 18): $\kappa_{\mathbf{z}}$ $(=R^{-1})$ is independent of prices and distribution and, therefore, Eqs. 2.63 and 2.64 reduce to

$$p_j v_j^{-1} = 1 + \rho R\left(\kappa_j - R^{-1}\right) \tag{2.66}$$

and

$$\dot{p}_j v_j^{-1} = Rk_j\left(\eta_{\kappa j} - D_j\right) \tag{2.67}$$

where $\eta_{\kappa j} \equiv \dot{\kappa}_j \rho \kappa_j^{-1}$ denotes the elasticity of κ_j with respect to ρ and $D_j \equiv \left(R\kappa_j\right)^{-1} -1$ the percentage deviation of the capital intensity of the SSS from κ_j. At $\rho = 0$, Eq. 2.67 gives

$$\dot{p}_j(0) v_j^{-1} = R\left(\kappa_j(0) - R^{-1}\right) \tag{2.68}$$

where $\kappa_j(0) \equiv \mathbf{vH}_j v_j^{-1}$ and at $\rho = 1$, Eq. 2.66 gives

$$p_j(1) v_j^{-1} = R\kappa_j(1) \tag{2.69}$$

where $\kappa_j(1) \equiv \mathbf{p}(1)\mathbf{H}_j v_j^{-1}$.

From Eqs. 2.66, 2.67, 2.68, and 2.69, we derive the following conclusions:

(i) The deviations of prices from labour values are determined by the signs of D_j, i.e. $p_j v_j^{-1} > 1$ iff $D_j < 0$, and may change in complicated ways as ρ gets to its maximum level.

(ii) Setting aside the equal value compositions of capital case, there is no value of ρ at which the kth derivative of the price vector is zero: Consider the case $k = 1$. Equations $\dot{\mathbf{p}} = \mathbf{0}$ imply $\dot{\kappa}_j = 0$ for all j. Thus, for $\rho > 0$, Eq. 2.67 implies $\kappa_j = R^{-1}$. Substituting $\kappa_j = R^{-1}$ in Eq. 2.66 yields $\mathbf{p} = \mathbf{v}$. At $\rho = 0$, $\dot{\mathbf{p}} = \mathbf{0}$ and

29 It may be recalled that the counterpart of the Stolper and Samuelson (1941) condition for $n \times n$ systems is

$$\kappa_j > (<)\ \kappa_{\mathbf{z}} \Leftrightarrow \widehat{r} > \widehat{p}_j > 0 > \widehat{w}\ \ (\widehat{w} > \widehat{p}_j > 0 > \widehat{r})$$

where $\widehat{y}$ denotes the logarithmic derivative for any positive variable y (also see Metcalfe and Steedman 1979; Mariolis 2004b).

Eq. 2.68 imply $\kappa_j(0) = R^{-1}$, that is, $\mathbf{vH} = R\mathbf{v}$. Hence, for $\rho \geq 0$, there is a contradiction (the case $k > 1$ can be treated in the same way).

(iii) At $\rho = 0$, the movement of the jth price-labour value ratio is determined by the sign of D_j. However, for $\rho > 0$, this is not necessarily true. More specifically, for each ρ the capital intensity of a vertically integrated industry can be less (more) than R^{-1}, i.e. $D_j > (<)\ 0$, but as ρ increases, its price-labour value ratio may rise (fall) due to the fact that $\eta_{\kappa j} > (<)\ 0$. Thus, it follows that the necessary condition for the violation of the traditional condition

$$D_j < (>)\ 0 \Leftrightarrow \dot{p}_j v_j^{-1} > (<)\ 0 \tag{2.70}$$

is the existence of a value of ρ, such that $\eta_{\kappa j}$ and D_j have the same sign, while the sufficient condition is $\eta_{\kappa j} < (>)\ D_j < (>)\ 0$ or, alternatively,

$$\eta_{\kappa j} D_j^{-1} = \dot{\kappa}_j \rho \left(R^{-1} - \kappa_j\right)^{-1} > 1 \tag{2.71}$$

Relation (2.71) signifies that the violation of relation (2.70) is 'more unlikely' the smaller is the value of the relative profit rate and/or the greater is the difference between the capital intensity of the SSS and the capital intensity of the vertically integrated industry under consideration.

(iv) Multiplying Eq. 2.67 by D_j^{-1}, and invoking Eq. 2.66, gives

$$\dot{p}_j v_j^{-1} = -\left(p_j v_j^{-1} - 1\right)\left(D_j \rho\right)^{-1}\left(\eta_{\kappa j} - D_j\right)$$

or

$$\eta_{dj} = 1 - \eta_{\kappa j} D_j^{-1} \tag{2.72}$$

where η_{dj} denotes the elasticity of the percentage deviation $\left(p_j v_j^{-1} - 1\right)$ with respect to ρ. From Eq. 2.72 it follows that $\eta_{dj} > 1$ iff $\eta_{\kappa j}$ and D_j have opposite signs, i.e. iff the two effects work in the same direction.

(v) A vertically integrated industry can be in the 'beginning', i.e. for low values of ρ, capital (labour)-intensive relative to the SSS, but as ρ increases, it may be transformed to a labour (capital)-intensive industry (price-labour value reversal). The presence of such a transformation leads to the violation of condition (2.70): Let $\widetilde{\rho}_j$ be the critical positive value of ρ, in which we observe the transformation, that is, $D_j(\widetilde{\rho}_j) = 0$. Consequently, in the interval $(0, \widetilde{\rho}_j)$ there is at least one change in the direction of the movement of $p_j v_j^{-1}$, whereas the sign of D_j is invariable by assumption.

(vi) Multiplying Eq. 2.66 by $(1 - \rho)^{-1}$, and rearranging terms, gives

$$(1-\rho)^{-1}p_jv_j^{-1} = (1-\rho)^{-1}R\kappa_{j\rho} + 1 \tag{2.73}$$

From Eq. 2.73 and the fact that each element, $(1-\rho)^{-1}p_j$, in the vector of labour-commanded prices is a strictly increasing function of ρ, it follows that $(1-\rho)^{-1}\kappa_{j\rho}$ is a strictly increasing function of ρ, which in its turn implies

$$\kappa_j + (1-\rho)\dot{\kappa}_{j\rho} > 0$$

or

$$\eta_{\kappa j} > -(1-\rho)^{-1}$$

That is, $-(1-\rho)^{-1}$ represents a lower bound for a falling κ_j.

This research can be further developed by considering, for a given value of the relative profit rate, $0 < \rho < 1$, the following iterative procedure associated with the price system (2.50):

$$\mathbf{p}^{(m)} = \mathbf{v}' + \mathbf{p}^{(m-1)}\mathbf{J}', \quad m = 1, 2, \ldots \tag{2.74}$$

where $\mathbf{v}' \equiv (1-\rho)\mathbf{v}$ and $\mathbf{J}' \equiv \rho\mathbf{J}$. Given that the P-F eigenvalue of the iteration matrix $\mathbf{J}'$ equals ρ, the procedure converges to the solution of the price system for each $\mathbf{p}^{(0)}$. The application of the Lyusternik's method for solving linear systems (see, e.g. Forsythe 1953, pp. 307–308), with $\mathbf{p}^{(0)} = \mathbf{v}'$, gives

$$\begin{aligned}\mathbf{p} &= \mathbf{v}'[\mathbf{I} - \mathbf{J}']^{-1} = \mathbf{v}'[\mathbf{I} + \mathbf{J}' + \mathbf{J}'^2 + \ldots] \\ &\approx \mathbf{p}^{(m)} + \rho(1-\rho)^{-1}(\mathbf{p}^{(m)} - \mathbf{p}^{(m-1)})\end{aligned}$$

or

$$\mathbf{p} \approx \mathbf{v}'\left[\mathbf{I} + \rho\mathbf{J} + (\rho\mathbf{J})^2 + \ldots + (\rho\mathbf{J})^m\right] + \rho^{m+1}\mathbf{v}\mathbf{J}^m \tag{2.75}$$

where the accuracy of approximation (2.75) depends on the term

$$\mathbf{d} \equiv \rho^{m+1}\mathbf{v}\mathbf{J}^m - \mathbf{v}'\sum_{h=m+1}^{+\infty}(\rho\mathbf{J})^h$$

For any semi-positive $n-$ vector $\mathbf{y}$, $\mathbf{yJ}^h$ tends to the left P-F eigenvector of $\mathbf{J}$ as h tends to infinity,[30] i.e.

$$\mathbf{yJ}^h \rightarrow \left(\mathbf{yx}_{\mathbf{J}1}^{\mathrm{T}}\right)\left(\mathbf{p}(1)\mathbf{x}_{\mathbf{J}1}^{\mathrm{T}}\right)^{-1}\mathbf{p}(1) \tag{2.76}$$

Therefore, for a sufficiently large value of m such that

$$\mathbf{vJ}^m \approx \mathbf{vJ}^{m+1} \approx \ldots \approx \mathbf{p}(1) \tag{2.77}$$

it holds $\mathbf{d} \approx \mathbf{0}$, and approximation (2.75) can be written as

$$\mathbf{p} \approx \mathbf{v} + \left[\sum_{h=1}^{m-1} \rho^h\left(\mathbf{vJ}^h - \mathbf{vJ}^{h-1}\right)\right] + \rho^m\left(\mathbf{p}(1) - \mathbf{vJ}^{m-1}\right) \tag{2.78}$$

---

[30] The 'power method or iteration' implies that, under certain conditions (see, e.g. Faddeev and Faddeeva 1963, Chap. 5, and Dietzenbacher 1993), if an arbitrary $n-$ vector, $\mathbf{y}_0$, is repeatedly multiplied by the matrix of input-output coefficients, $\mathbf{A}$, then the result converges to the P-F eigenvector of $\mathbf{A}$, i.e.

$$\lim_{h\rightarrow+\infty} \mathbf{y}_0\left(\lambda_{\mathbf{A}1}^{-1}\mathbf{A}\right)^h = \left(\mathbf{y}_0\mathbf{x}_{\mathbf{A}1}^{\mathrm{T}}\right)\left(\mathbf{y}_{\mathbf{A}1}\mathbf{x}_{\mathbf{A}1}^{\mathrm{T}}\right)^{-1}\mathbf{y}_{\mathbf{A}1}$$

and

$$\lim_{h\rightarrow+\infty} \left(\mathbf{y}_0\mathbf{A}^{h+1}\mathbf{x}_0^{\mathrm{T}}\right)\left(\mathbf{y}_0\mathbf{A}^h\mathbf{x}_0^{\mathrm{T}}\right)^{-1} = \lambda_{\mathbf{A}1}$$

provided that $\mathbf{y}_0\mathbf{x}_{\mathbf{A}1}^{\mathrm{T}} \neq 0$ and $\mathbf{y}_{\mathbf{A}1}\mathbf{x}_0^{\mathrm{T}} \neq 0$, where $\mathbf{x}_0$ is an arbitrary $n-$ vector. The speed of convergence depends on the ratio of the modulus of the subdominant eigenvalue to the dominant one, $|\lambda_{\mathbf{A}2}|\lambda_{\mathbf{A}1}^{-1}$, since

$$\mathbf{y}_0\left(\lambda_{\mathbf{A}1}^{-1}\mathbf{A}\right)^h = \alpha_1\mathbf{y}_{\mathbf{A}1} + \sum_{k=2}^{n}\left(\lambda_{\mathbf{A}k}\lambda_{\mathbf{A}1}^{-1}\right)^h \alpha_k\mathbf{y}_{\mathbf{A}k}$$

where $[\alpha_1, \alpha_k]$ denotes the coordinates of $\mathbf{y}_0$ in terms of the left eigenbasis $[\mathbf{y}_{\mathbf{A}1}^{\mathrm{T}}, \mathbf{y}_{\mathbf{A}k}^{\mathrm{T}}]^{\mathrm{T}}$. More precisely, the closer to zero $|\lambda_{\mathbf{A}2}|\lambda_{\mathbf{A}1}^{-1}$ is, the faster is the convergence to the P-F eigenvector, i.e. the convergence is asymptotically exponential, at a rate at *least* as fast as $\log\left(|\lambda_{\mathbf{A}2}|^{-1}\lambda_{\mathbf{A}1}\right)$. The number $|\lambda_{\mathbf{A}2}|^{-1}\lambda_{\mathbf{A}1}$ is called the 'damping ratio', in population dynamics theory, and can be considered as a measure of the intrinsic resilience of the state vector to disturbance (for critical remarks on this and alternative measures, see Keyfitz and Caswell 2005, pp. 165–175, and Stott et al. 2011, pp. 960–961). The power method has been introduced by Richard von Mises and Hilda Pollaczek-Geiringer in 1929 (see, e.g. Golub and van der Vorst 2000). For recently developed variations of this method that enable the determination of multiple extremal eigenpairs of a matrix, while the convergence to the dominant one is accelerated as it is controlled by $|\lambda_{\mathbf{A}3}|^{-1}\lambda_{\mathbf{A}1}$, see Gubernatis and Booth (2008).

Relation (2.78) is an approximate formula for the price vector, which is exact at the extreme, economically significant, values of ρ. Differentiation of relation (2.78) with respect to ρ, and invoking Eq. 2.69, gives the following approximation of Eq. 2.67:

$$\dot{p}_j v_j^{-1} \approx R\left(\kappa_j(0) - R^{-1}\right) + B + m\rho^{m-1} R\left(\kappa_j(1) - \mathbf{v}\mathbf{J}^{m-2}\mathbf{H}_j v_j^{-1}\right) \tag{2.79}$$

where the first term on the right-hand side equals the first derivative of $p_j v_j^{-1}$ at $\rho = 0$ (see Eq. 2.68) and

$$B \equiv R\sum_{h=2}^{m-1} h\rho^{h-1}\left(\mathbf{v}\mathbf{J}^{h-1}\mathbf{H}_j v_j^{-1} - \mathbf{v}\mathbf{J}^{h-2}\mathbf{H}_j v_j^{-1}\right)$$

or

$$B \equiv \sum_{h=2}^{m-1} R^h h\rho^{h-1}\left(\mathbf{v}\mathbf{H}^{h-2}\mathbf{H}_j v_j^{-1}\right)\left[\mathbf{v}\mathbf{H}^{h-1}\mathbf{H}_j\left(\mathbf{v}\mathbf{H}^{h-2}\mathbf{H}_j\right)^{-1} - R^{-1}\right]$$

The sign of the hth term in B is positive (negative) when the capital intensity, in terms of labour values, of the vertically integrated industry producing the composite commodity $\mathbf{H}^{h-2}\mathbf{H}_j$ is greater (less) than R^{-1}. Setting $m = 1$, relation (2.78) reduces to the linear formula

$$\mathbf{p} \approx \mathbf{v} + \rho(\mathbf{p}(1) - \mathbf{v})$$

or

$$\mathbf{p} \approx \mathbf{p}(0) + \rho(\mathbf{p}(1) - \mathbf{p}(0)) \tag{2.80}$$

and substituting approximation (2.80) in $\kappa_j = \mathbf{p}\mathbf{H}_j\left(p_j(0)\right)^{-1}$ yields $\kappa_j \approx \kappa_j(0)$, since $\mathbf{p}(0)\mathbf{J} \approx \mathbf{p}(1)$, i.e. the approximate $\kappa_j - \rho$ relationships are constant. Setting $m = 2$, approximation (2.78) reduces to the quadratic formula

$$\mathbf{p} \approx \mathbf{p}(0) + \rho(\mathbf{p}(0)\mathbf{J} - \mathbf{p}(0)) + \rho^2(\mathbf{p}(1) - \mathbf{p}(0)\mathbf{J}) \tag{2.81}$$

which implies that the approximate $P_j - \rho$ curves have at most one extreme point, at

$$\rho_j^* = 2^{-1}\left(p_j(0) - \mathbf{p}(0)\mathbf{J}_j\right)\left(p_j(1) - \mathbf{p}(0)\mathbf{J}_j\right)^{-1}$$

or

$$\rho_j^* = 2^{-1}\left(R^{-1} - \kappa_j(0)\right)\left(\kappa_j(1) - \kappa_j(0)\right)^{-1} \tag{2.82}$$

where $0 \leq \rho_j^* \leq 1$ does not necessarily hold true. Substituting approximation (2.81) in $\kappa_j = \mathbf{pH}_j\left(p_j(0)\right)^{-1}$ yields

$$\kappa_j \approx \kappa_j(0) + \rho\left(\kappa_j(1) - \kappa_j(0)\right) \tag{2.83}$$

that is, the approximate $\kappa_j - \rho$ curves are linear. Equations $D_j(\widetilde{\rho}_j) = 0$, 2.82 and relation (2.83) imply that $\widetilde{\rho}_j = 2\rho_j^*$.

The accuracy of approximation (2.77) and, therefore, the accuracy of an *m*th order approximation is directly related to the rate of convergence in relation (2.76), which in its turn is directly related to the magnitudes of $|\lambda_{\mathbf{J}k}|^{-1}$. The Hopf-Ostrowski and Deutsch upper bounds (or 'coefficients of ergodicity'; Seneta 2006, pp. 63–64) imply that

$$|\lambda_{\mathbf{J}2}| \leq 2^{-1} \max_{i,\ j}\left\{\sum_{f=1}^{n}\left|m_{fi} - m_{fj}\right|\right\} \leq (v-1)(v+1)^{-1} \leq (\mathrm{M}-\mu)(\mathrm{M}+\mu)^{-1}$$
$$< 1$$

where

$$v \equiv \max_{i,\ j,\ g,\ l}\left\{\sqrt{m_{ij}m_{gl}\left(m_{il}m_{gj}\right)^{-1}}\right\}$$

$\left|m_{ij}m_{gl}\left(m_{il}m_{gj}\right)^{-1} - 1\right|m_{il}m_{gj}$ equals 0 or the absolute value of the determinant of a 2×2 submatrix of $\mathbf{M} \equiv \left[m_{ij}\right]$ (see Eq. 2.39) and M(μ) represents the largest (smallest) element of $\mathbf{M}$ (see Ostrowski 1963; Maitre 1970; Rothblum and Tan 1985). Thus, we may conclude that when the columns of $\mathbf{M}$ tend to be close to each other, i.e. its '*effective* rank' is low, a low-order approximation works pretty well. In the extreme case where $\mathbf{J}$ has rank 1, i.e.

$$\mathbf{J} = \left(\mathbf{p}(1)\mathbf{x}_{\mathbf{J}1}^{\mathrm{T}}\right)^{-1}\left(\mathbf{x}_{\mathbf{J}1}^{\mathrm{T}}\mathbf{p}(1)\right) = \left(\mathbf{p}(0)\mathbf{x}_{\mathbf{J}1}^{\mathrm{T}}\right)^{-1}\left(\mathbf{x}_{\mathbf{J}1}^{\mathrm{T}}\mathbf{p}(1)\right)$$

it follows that $\mathbf{p}(0)\mathbf{J} = \mathbf{p}(1)$, $|\lambda_{\mathbf{J}2}| = 0$, all the columns of $\mathbf{M}$ are equal to each other and the linear approximation (2.80) becomes exact for all ρ. In that case or iff $\mathbf{v}$ (or $\mathbf{b}^{\mathrm{T}}$) is the P-F eigenvector of $\mathbf{J}$, then[31]

[31] See Eq. 2.19 and consider the following theorem (e.g. Ding and Zhou 2007, p. 1224): Let $\mathbf{Q}$ be a *n x n* matrix, with eigenvalues $\{\lambda_1, \lambda_2, \ldots, \lambda_n\}$, counting algebraic multiplicity. Then the eigenvalues of $\mathbf{Q} + \mathbf{x}^{\mathrm{T}}\mathbf{y}$, where either $\mathbf{y}$ or $\mathbf{x}^{\mathrm{T}}$ are eigenvectors of $\mathbf{Q}$ associated with λ_1, are $\{\lambda_1 + \mathbf{x}^{\mathrm{T}}\mathbf{y}, \lambda_2, \ldots, \lambda_n\}$, counting algebraic multiplicity.

$$\lambda_{\mathbf{K}1} = 1 + \left(1 - \mathbf{v}\mathbf{b}^{\mathrm{T}}\right)^{-1}\mathbf{v}\mathbf{J}\mathbf{b}^{\mathrm{T}}, \lambda_{\mathbf{K}k} = \lambda_{\mathbf{J}k}$$

In the general case, however, it does not necessarily hold true that $|\lambda_{\mathbf{K}k}|\lambda_{\mathbf{K}1}^{-1} \leq |\lambda_{\mathbf{J}k}|$ (consider, e.g. the numerical example provided by Faddeev and Faddeeva 1963, p. 231). It should also be added that if for a given *system* [**J**, **v**] there exists a positive integer number κ such that $\mathbf{v}\mathbf{J}^{\kappa-1} \neq \mathbf{p}(1)$ and $\mathbf{v}\mathbf{J}^{\kappa} = \mathbf{p}(1)$, then $\det[\mathbf{J}] = 0$ (since $\left(\mathbf{v}\mathbf{J}^{\kappa-1} - \mathbf{p}(1)\right)\mathbf{J} = \mathbf{0}$). In that case, borrowing Morishima's (1973, pp. 77–78, 1974, pp. 630–632) terminology, the vertically integrated industries are 'linearly dependent on each other at degree κ'.

Using Eq. 2.51 and relations (2.77), Bienenfeld (1988) first derived the approximation formula (2.78). On this basis, an approximation to the WPC (2.21) can also be constructed: If $p_{\mathbf{z}}^{\mathrm{S}}$ denotes the price of commodity $\mathbf{z}^{\mathrm{T}}(\mathbf{v}\mathbf{z}^{\mathrm{T}} = 1)$ in terms of SSC, and w the money wage rate corresponding to the normalization equation $\mathbf{p}\mathbf{z}^{\mathrm{T}} = 1$, then

$$\mathbf{p}\mathbf{z}^{\mathrm{T}}w^{-1} = p_{\mathbf{z}}^{\mathrm{S}}\left(w^{\mathrm{S}}\right)^{-1}$$

or

$$w = w^{\mathrm{S}}\left(p_{\mathbf{z}}^{\mathrm{S}}\right)^{-1}$$

Thus, invoking approximation (2.78), we obtain

$$w \approx w^{\mathrm{S}}\left\{1 + \left[\sum_{h=1}^{m-1}\rho^{h}\left(\mathbf{v}\mathbf{J}^{h} - \mathbf{v}\mathbf{J}^{h-1}\right)\right]\mathbf{z}^{\mathrm{T}} + \rho^{m}\left(\mathbf{p}^{\mathrm{S}}(1) - \mathbf{v}\mathbf{J}^{m-1}\right)\mathbf{z}^{\mathrm{T}}\right\}^{-1} \tag{2.78a}$$

Setting, for instance, $m = 1$, approximation (2.78a) reduces to the 'homographic' formula

$$w \approx w^{\mathrm{S}}\left[1 + \rho\left(p_{\mathbf{z}}^{\mathrm{S}}(1) - 1\right)\right]^{-1} \tag{2.80a}$$

which has exactly the same algebraic form as the WPC for the corn-tractor model (see Eq. 2.30).

Finally, consider the Bródy (1970, pp. 88–91) and Okishio (1972) iterative procedure associated with the production price system (2.6)

$$\begin{aligned}\mathbf{p}^{(m)} &= \left(1 + r^{(m-1)}\right)\mathbf{p}^{(m-1)}\mathbf{C},\ \ 1 + r^{(m-1)} \\ &= \left(\mathbf{p}^{(m-1)}\mathbf{x}^{\mathrm{T}}\right)\left(\mathbf{p}^{(m-1)}\mathbf{C}\mathbf{x}^{\mathrm{T}}\right)^{-1},\ \ \mathbf{p}^{(0)} = \mathbf{v}\end{aligned} \tag{2.84}$$

where $\mathbf{x}^{\mathrm{T}}$ is an arbitrary gross output vector. The power method ensures that Eq. 2.84 converges to the long-run equilibrium price vector and profit rate, i.e.

$$\mathbf{p}^{(m)} \to \mathbf{y}_{\mathbf{C}1}, \quad 1 + r^{(m-1)} \to \lambda_{\mathbf{C}1}^{-1}$$

while Marx's 'first equality' (total price equals total labour value), $\mathbf{p}^{(m)}\mathbf{x}^{\mathrm{T}} = \mathbf{v}\mathbf{x}^{\mathrm{T}}$, holds for all m. Only for $\mathbf{x}^{\mathrm{T}} = \mathbf{x}_{\mathbf{C}1}^{\mathrm{T}}$ (see Eq. 2.7), which implies that the profit rate, $1 + r^{(m-1)} = 1 + g = \lambda_{\mathbf{C}1}^{-1}$, is independent of prices, Marx's 'second equality' (total profits equal total surplus labour) also holds true.[32] Iff, however, $rank[\mathbf{C}] = 1$, then Marx's (1959, Chap. 9) price vector, i.e. the second term, $\mathbf{p}^{(1)}$, of the price sequence generated by Eq. 2.84, necessarily equals the true production price vector. The key idea of the power method can be detected, although in less rigorous terms, in Charasoff's (1910) contribution to price-quantity theory, who concluded:

> Marx wished [...] to start from the [labour] values of the commodities: but this is absolutely inessential for the theory of prices as such. The starting prices can be arbitrary. (cited in Egidi and Gilibert 1989, p. 72)

Furthermore, Abraham-Frois and Berrebi (1997) remark:

> For the transformation process complemented by Marx to work actually, there must be a central (planning) office which calculate the rate of profit $r^{(0)}$ on the basis of the system of [labour] values and then $r^{(1)}, r^{(2)}, \ldots, r^{(m)}$ and indicates their levels to capitalists so that they can set their production prices. (p. 165; using our symbols)

It should also be noted that, in joint-production systems, the iterative procedure (2.84) may be quantitatively misleading, since (i) a given value of the real wage rate may be associated with more than one, economically significant, value of $[\mathbf{p}, r]$ or (ii) the P-F eigenpair is not necessarily the economically relevant solution of the system (consider the numerical examples provided by Steedman 1992; Bidard 1997; Mariolis 2004a).

2.4.2 Price Effects of Total Productivity Shift

The price system (2.1) can be written as

$$\mathbf{p}\hat{\boldsymbol{\tau}} = w\mathbf{l} + (1 + \overline{r})\,\mathbf{p}\mathbf{A} \tag{2.85}$$

where $\hat{\boldsymbol{\tau}}$ $(= \mathbf{I})$ denotes the diagonal matrix of the sectoral productivity shifters and $\overline{r}$ the exogenously given value of the profit rate $(-1 < \overline{r} < R)$. Let $\boldsymbol{\Theta}$ denote the matrix of the relative shares of the capital commodities in the cost of outputs, i.e.

[32] For relevant iterative procedures and the (in-)compatibility of Marx's equalities, see Shaikh ([1973] 1977), Morishima (1974), Morishima and Catephores (1978, pp. 160–166) and Parys (1986).

$$\mathbf{\Theta} \equiv [\theta_{ij}], \theta_{ij} \equiv p_i a_{ij}(1+\bar{r})p_j^{-1}$$

and let $\mathbf{\theta}_L$ denote the vector of the relative shares of labour, i.e.

$$\mathbf{\theta}_{\mathrm{L}} \equiv [\theta_{\mathrm{L}j}], \theta_{\mathrm{L}j} \equiv w l_j p_j^{-1}$$

Thus, we can write

$$\theta_{\mathrm{L}i} > (<)\ \theta_{\mathrm{L}j} \Leftrightarrow \kappa_i^*(\bar{r}) < (>)\ \kappa_j^*(\bar{r})$$

where $\kappa_m^*(\bar{r}) \equiv (p_1 a_{1m} + \cdots + p_n a_{nm})(1+\bar{r})l_m^{-1}$, $m = i, j$, represents the 'r – *direct* capital intensity' of the industry producing commodity m.[33] Moreover, $\mathbf{e} = \mathbf{e}\ \mathbf{\Theta} + \mathbf{\theta}_{\mathrm{L}}$ or

$$\mathbf{e} = \mathbf{\theta}_{\mathrm{L}}[\mathbf{I} - \mathbf{\Theta}]^{-1} \tag{2.86}$$

where $[\mathbf{I} - \mathbf{\Theta}]^{-1}$ is positive, since $(1+\bar{r})\mathbf{A}$ and $\mathbf{\Theta}$ are similar matrices $(\mathbf{\Theta} = \hat{\mathbf{p}}\,[(1+\bar{r})\mathbf{A}]\,\hat{\mathbf{p}}^{-1})$ and $0 < D \equiv \det[\mathbf{I} - \mathbf{\Theta}] < 1$ (Holley 1951; $D = 1$ iff $\mathbf{A}$ is strictly triangular and, therefore, nilpotent).

Now consider a rise in the sectoral productivity shifters. Differentiation of Eq. 2.85 gives

$$\overset{\frown}{\mathbf{p}} = \overset{\frown}{w}\mathbf{\theta}_{\mathrm{L}} + \overset{\frown}{\mathbf{p}}\mathbf{\Theta} - \overset{\frown}{\mathbf{\tau}}$$

or, solving for $\overset{\frown}{\mathbf{p}}$ and invoking Eq. 2.86,[34]

$$\overset{\frown}{\mathbf{p}} = \overset{\frown}{w}\mathbf{e} - \overset{\frown}{\mathbf{\tau}}\,[\mathbf{I} - \mathbf{\Theta}]^{-1} \tag{2.87}$$

From Eq. 2.87 (which also holds true in the case of constant returns to scale production functions; see Mariolis 2008b, pp. 239–241), it follows that the movement of the relative price of two arbitrary commodities, i and j, is given by

$$\overset{\frown}{\mathbf{p}}\left(\mathbf{e}_i^{\mathrm{T}} - \mathbf{e}_j^{\mathrm{T}}\right) = \left(\overset{\frown}{w}\mathbf{e} - \overset{\frown}{\mathbf{\tau}}\,[\mathbf{I} - \mathbf{\Theta}]^{-1}\right)\left(\mathbf{e}_i^{\mathrm{T}} - \mathbf{e}_j^{\mathrm{T}}\right)$$

or, since $\mathbf{e}\left(\mathbf{e}_i^{\mathrm{T}} - \mathbf{e}_j^{\mathrm{T}}\right) = 0$,

[33] It is noted that the differences in direct and integrated capital intensities may have opposite signs (Parys 1982; Steedman 2004).

[34] In the joint production case, $\overset{\frown}{\mathbf{\tau}} \geq \mathbf{0}$ does not necessarily imply $\overset{\frown}{w}\mathbf{e} > \overset{\frown}{\mathbf{p}}$, i.e. productivity growth does not necessarily lead to an increase in the real wage rate (see Steedman 1985).

$$\widehat{p}_i - \widehat{p}_j = -\widehat{\boldsymbol{\tau}}[\mathbf{I} - \boldsymbol{\Theta}]^{-1}\left(\mathbf{e}_i^{\mathrm{T}} - \mathbf{e}_j^{\mathrm{T}}\right) \tag{2.88}$$

In the (extreme) case of a uniform rate of productivity change, i.e. $\widehat{\boldsymbol{\tau}} = \tau\mathbf{e}$, Eq. 2.88 takes the form

$$\widehat{p}_i - \widehat{p}_j = -\tau\mathbf{e}[\mathbf{I} - \boldsymbol{\Theta}]^{-1}\left(\mathbf{e}_i^{\mathrm{T}} - \mathbf{e}_j^{\mathrm{T}}\right) \tag{2.89}$$

or, since $[\mathbf{I} - \boldsymbol{\Theta}]^{-1} = \mathbf{I} + \sum_{h=1}^{+\infty} \boldsymbol{\Theta}^h, \mathbf{e}\boldsymbol{\Theta}^h = (\mathbf{e} - \boldsymbol{\theta}_{\mathrm{L}})\boldsymbol{\Theta}^{h-1}$ (see Eq. 2.86),

$$\widehat{p}_i - \widehat{p}_j = \tau\left(E_{i-j}^{\mathrm{I}} - E_{i-j}^{\mathrm{II}}\right) \tag{2.90}$$

where

$$E_{i-j}^{\mathrm{I}} \equiv \theta_{\mathrm{L}i} - \theta_{\mathrm{L}j}$$

$$E_{i-j}^{\mathrm{II}} \equiv (\mathbf{e} - \boldsymbol{\theta}_{\mathrm{L}})\left[\left(\sum_{h=1}^{+\infty} \boldsymbol{\Theta}^h\right)\left(\mathbf{e}_i^{\mathrm{T}} - \mathbf{e}_j^{\mathrm{T}}\right)\right]$$

represent the 'direct' and 'indirect' effects, respectively. It then follows that the direction of the relative price movement is not necessarily governed by E_{i-j}^{I} or, in other words, that the traditional condition

$$E_{i-j}^{\mathrm{I}} > (<)\ 0 \Leftrightarrow \widehat{p}_i > (<)\ \widehat{p}_j \tag{2.91}$$

does not necessarily hold true. That direction is rather governed by the range of relative shares of labour in the industries producing these commodities, in the industries producing the means of production of these commodities, in the industries producing the means of production of the aforesaid means of production and so on, ad infinitum. When E_{i-j}^{I} and E_{i-j}^{II} have opposite signs, the two effects work in the same direction; when they have the same sign, condition (2.91) may be violated. The point can be further illustrated by considering the following two cases:

(i) When $n = 2$, Eqs. 2.89 and 2.90 imply

$$\widehat{p}_1 - \widehat{p}_2 = \tau D^{-1} E_{1-2}^{\mathrm{I}}, E_{1-2}^{\mathrm{II}} = \left(1 - D^{-1}\right) E_{1-2}^{\mathrm{I}}$$

Since $0 < D < 1$, condition (2.91) is necessarily true. If $\widehat{\boldsymbol{\tau}} \neq \tau\mathbf{e}$, then Eq. 2.88 implies

$$\widehat{p}_1 - \widehat{p}_2 = D^{-1}\left(\widehat{\tau}_2\theta_{L1} - \widehat{\tau}_1\theta_{L2}\right)$$

or

$$\theta_{L1}\,\widehat{\tau}_1^{-1} > (<)\theta_{L2}\,\widehat{\tau}_2^{-1} \Leftrightarrow \widehat{p}_1 > (<)\widehat{p}_2 \tag{2.92}$$

which is the basic condition for the validity of the 'Harrod (1933, Chap. 4), Balassa (1964) and Samuelson (1964) hypothesis'. Obstfeld and Rogoff (1998, pp. 204–209 and 214–216) quite rightly note the direct analytical relationships between that hypothesis, the Stolper and Samuelson (1941) theorem and the 'factor price' equalization theorem (Samuelson 1948). It should be remarked, however, that the labour-intensity difference depends, in general, on the ratio of sectoral productivities. Therefore, when, for instance, $\theta_{L1} > \theta_{L2}$ holds *initially*, and $\widehat{\tau}_2 > \widehat{\tau}_1$, a reversal of the range of the sectoral labour intensities may take place, which will bring a change in the sign of $\widehat{p}_1 - \widehat{p}_2$. Finally, if $a_{21} = a_{22} = 0$ (corn-tractor model), and commodity 2 is the numeraire, then

$$\widehat{w} = \widehat{\tau}_1(1 - \theta_{L2})\theta_{L1}^{-1} + \widehat{\tau}_2$$
$$\widehat{p}_1 = \widehat{\tau}_2 - \widehat{\tau}_1\theta_{L2}\theta_{L1}^{-1}$$

And if commodities are produced by unassisted labour alone (as in the textbook 'Ricardian' theory and in Balassa 1964), then

$$\widehat{p}_1 = \widehat{\tau}_2 - \widehat{\tau}_1$$

This last equation is often used for the analysis of real phenomena (see, e.g. De Grauwe 2000, Chaps. 1 and 2).

(ii) When $n = 3$ and, for instance, $\widehat{\tau}_1 \neq \widehat{\tau}_2 = \widehat{\tau}_3$, Eq. 2.88 implies

$$\widehat{p}_1 - \widehat{p}_2 = D^{-1}\left[(1-\theta_{33})\left(\widehat{\tau}_2\theta_{L1} - \widehat{\tau}_1\theta_{L2}\right) + \theta_{32}\left(\widehat{\tau}_2\theta_{L1} - \widehat{\tau}_1\theta_{L3}\right) + \widehat{\tau}_2\theta_{31}(\theta_{L3} - \theta_{L2})\right]$$
$$\widehat{p}_1 - \widehat{p}_3 = D^{-1}\left[(1-\theta_{22})\left(\widehat{\tau}_2\theta_{L1} - \widehat{\tau}_1\theta_{L3}\right) + \theta_{23}\left(\widehat{\tau}_2\theta_{L1} - \widehat{\tau}_1\theta_{L2}\right) + \widehat{\tau}_2\theta_{21}(\theta_{L2} - \theta_{L3})\right]$$
$$\widehat{p}_2 - \widehat{p}_3 = D^{-1}\left[\theta_{12}\left(\widehat{\tau}_2\theta_{L1} - \widehat{\tau}_1\theta_{L3}\right) + \theta_{13}\left(\widehat{\tau}_1\theta_{L2} - \widehat{\tau}_2\theta_{L1}\right) + \widehat{\tau}_2(1-\theta_{11})(\theta_{L2} - \theta_{L3})\right]$$

Assume that $\theta_{L1} \geq (\theta_{L2}, \theta_{L3})$ and $\widehat{\tau}_2 > \widehat{\tau}_1$. If $\theta_{L1} = \theta_{L2} = \theta_{L3}$, then $\widehat{p}_1 > \widehat{p}_2$ and $\widehat{p}_1 > \widehat{p}_3$, while the sign of $\widehat{p}_2 - \widehat{p}_3$ is the same as that of $\theta_{12} - \theta_{13}$. If $\theta_{L2} > (<)\theta_{L3}$, then $\widehat{p}_1 > \widehat{p}_3$ (then $\widehat{p}_1 > \widehat{p}_2$), while the signs of $\widehat{p}_1 - \widehat{p}_2$ (of $\widehat{p}_1 - \widehat{p}_3$) and $\widehat{p}_2 - \widehat{p}_3$ are not known a priori. Now assume that $\widehat{\boldsymbol{\tau}} = \tau\mathbf{e}$ and $\theta_{L1} = \theta_{L2}$ $(E_{1-3}^{I} = E_{2-3}^{I})$. It then follows that

$$\widehat{p}_1 - \widehat{p}_2 = -\tau E^{\mathrm{II}}_{1-2} = \tau D^{-1} E^{\mathrm{I}}_{1-3}(\theta_{32} - \theta_{31})$$
$$\widehat{p}_2 - \widehat{p}_3 = \tau D^{-1} E^{\mathrm{I}}_{2-3}(1 - \theta_{11} + \theta_{12})$$

Thus, it is concluded that the traditional conditions (2.91) and (2.92) cannot, in general, be extended beyond a two-commodity world.

It need hardly be emphasized that the issue at hand is formally equivalent to that of price movements arising from changes in the uniform profit rate or from nonuniform changes in the sectoral profit (or in the tax) rates (consider Eqs. 2.1a and 2.1c, with $\mathbf{B} = \mathbf{I}$; also see Steedman 1990). The former case corresponds to $\widehat{\boldsymbol{\tau}} = \tau\mathbf{e}$, while the latter to $\widehat{\boldsymbol{\tau}} \neq \tau\mathbf{e}$.

2.5 Concluding Remarks

In a world of fixed input-output coefficients and at least three commodities, long-period relative prices can change in a complicated way as income distribution or total productivity changes. This fact has critical implications for the traditional analysis of both closed and open economies. It has been shown, however, that the price functions are subject to lower and upper norm bounds and their monotonicity could be connected to (i) the degree of deviation from the equal value compositions of capital case and (ii) the magnitudes of the normalized non-dominant eigenvalues or, equivalently, the effective rank of the matrix of vertically integrated technical coefficients. Since nothing can be said a priori about these two factors in *real*-world economies, the examination of actual input-output data becomes necessary.

Appendix: The Böhm-Bawerkian Approach

Böhm-Bawerk's ([1889] 1959, vol. 2, pp. 86 and 356–358) theory is based on the concept of the 'average period of production' as a distribution-free measure of capital intensity. The construction is subject to the following assumptions: (i) there are only single production and circulating capital (see Hicks 1973, p. 8), (ii) there is only a single 'original factor of production', and (iii) profits accrue on the basis of simple interest. Closer scrutiny shows, however, that when profits accrue on the basis of compound interest, which is compatible with free competition and optimizing behaviour, the average period of production fails to reflect capital intensity.

It then follows that the argument cannot be sustained even when the simplifying assumptions (i) and (ii) are met.[35]

Assuming that wages are paid *ex ante* (which is compatible with the Austrian theory; see Burmeister 1974, pp. 416–418), Eq. 2.2 is written as

$$\mathbf{p} = w\left[(1+r)\mathbf{l} + (1+r)^2\mathbf{lA} + (1+r)^3\mathbf{lA}^2 + \ldots\right] \tag{2.93}$$

which implies that the relative price of two arbitrary commodities, *j* and *i*, is given by

$$p_{ji} \equiv p_j p_i^{-1} = \left(\mathbf{l}\boldsymbol{\Delta}_j(r)\right)\left(\mathbf{l}\boldsymbol{\Delta}_i(r)\right)^{-1} \tag{2.94}$$

where $\boldsymbol{\Delta}(r) \equiv [\mathbf{I} - (1+r)\mathbf{A}]^{-1}$. Since

$$\dot{\boldsymbol{\Delta}}(r) = \boldsymbol{\Delta}(r)\mathbf{A}\boldsymbol{\Delta}(r)$$

differentiation of Eq. 2.94 with respect to r implies

$$\widetilde{\kappa}_j(r) > (<)\ \widetilde{\kappa}_i(r) \Leftrightarrow \dot{\mathrm{p}}_{ji} > (<)\ 0 \tag{2.95}$$

where $\widetilde{\kappa}_\mu(r) \equiv \left(\mathbf{pA}\boldsymbol{\Delta}_\mu(r)\right)\left(\mathbf{l}\boldsymbol{\Delta}_\mu(r)\right)^{-1}, \mu = i, j,$ is, in the general case, a non-monotonic function of the profit rate, which can be interpreted as the ratio of means of production to labour in vertically integrated industry producing commodity μ that grows at the constant rate r, i.e. in the 'μth golden sub-system' (Salvadori and Steedman 1985, p. 84; Bidard 1991, p. 57). Since

[35] For a thorough survey and analysis of the issue, see Orosel (1979), who notes that 'Böhm-Bawerk repeatedly mentions compound interest (as opposed to simple interest) and explicitly points out that *only for simplicity* he uses the principle of simple interest in his numerical examples' (pp. 5–6, footnote 5; on this point, also see Shibata 1935, p. 119). For the close relationships between average period of production and Marx's value composition of capital or, on the other hand, Jevons's 'average time of investment', see von Weizsäcker (1977) and Steedman (1972), respectively. For a recent examination of the various conceptions of capital in the Austrian tradition, which are not necessarily related to the Böhm-Bawerkian average period of production, see Endres and Harper (2011). Finally, for the theoretical and historical relationships between (traditional and modern) Austrian and Sraffa's capital theories, see Burmeister (1974, 1980, Chap. 4), Faber (1980), Howard (1980), Kurz and Salvadori (1995, pp. 176–178, 213–214 and Chap. 14), Lager (2000), Gehrke and Kurz (2009), and Matsuo (2010), *inter alia*.

$$\mathbf{I} + (1 + r)\mathbf{A}\boldsymbol{\Delta}(r) = \boldsymbol{\Delta}(r)$$

and

$$\boldsymbol{\zeta} \equiv \sum_{h=1}^{+\infty} h\mathbf{l}\mathbf{A}^{h-1} = \mathbf{v}\boldsymbol{\Delta}(0)$$

represents the sum of the dated quantities of labour weighted by 'the time in which they remain in production',

$$T_\mu(0) \equiv \left(w + \widetilde{\kappa}_\mu(0)\right)w^{-1} = \mathbf{v}\boldsymbol{\Delta}_\mu(0)\mathbf{v}_\mu^{-1} = \zeta_\mu \mathbf{v}_\mu^{-1}$$

equals the Böhm-Bawerkian average period of production of the flow input-point output process producing commodity μ. Consequently,

$$T_\mu(r) \equiv \left(w + \widetilde{\kappa}_\mu(r)\right)w^{-1} = \zeta_\mu(r)\left(\mathbf{v}_\mu(r)\right)^{-1}$$

where $\mathbf{v}(r) \equiv \mathbf{l}\boldsymbol{\Delta}(r)$ and $\boldsymbol{\zeta}(r) \equiv \mathbf{v}(r)\boldsymbol{\Delta}(r)$ may be called 'r – average period of production' and condition (2.95) can be written as

$$\Delta T_j(r) \equiv T_j(r) - T_i(r) > (<)\ 0 \Leftrightarrow \dot{\mathrm{p}}_{ji} > (<)\ 0 \tag{2.96}$$

As is easily checked, $T_\mu(r)$ (i) corresponds to Macaulay (1938, pp. 47–51) 'average maturity of a stream of payments' and Hicks (1939, p. 186) and von Weizsäcker (1971, pp. 41–43, 1974, pp. 742–743) average period of production and (ii) equals the elasticity of the labour-commanded price of commodity μ with respect to the profit factor, $1 + r$.[36] Moreover, if SSC is chosen as the numeraire, then $T_i(r)$ should be replaced by

$$T_\mathrm{S}(r) \equiv 1 + \left(w^\mathrm{S}\right)^{-1}\left[\left(\mathbf{p}\mathbf{A}\boldsymbol{\Delta}(r)\mathbf{s}^\mathrm{T}\right)\left(\mathbf{l}\boldsymbol{\Delta}(r)\mathbf{s}^\mathrm{T}\right)^{-1}\right] = 1 + \left(w^\mathrm{S}R\right)^{-1}$$

or, since $w^\mathrm{S} = (1 + r)^{-1}\left(1 - rR^{-1}\right)$,

$$T_\mathrm{S}(r) = (1 + R)(R - r)^{-1}$$

Condition (2.96) implies that, at $r = 0$, the direction of the movement of the relative prices is governed by the differences in the relevant average periods of production, while for $r > 0$, this is not necessarily true.

[36] Therefore, in the joint production case (see Sect. 2.2.3), $T_\mu(r)$ may be negative for certain economically significant intervals of r (also see von Weizsäcker 1971, p. 72).

Now consider Böhm-Bawerk's theory as a linear approximation of Eq. 2.93, based on the formula $(1+r)^h \approx 1+hr$ ('rule of simple interest'). Thus, Eq. 2.93 reduces to

$$\mathbf{p} \approx w\left[(1+r)\mathbf{l} + (1+2r)\mathbf{lA} + (1+3r)\mathbf{lA}^2 + \ldots\right]$$

or, recalling the definition equations of $\mathbf{v}$ and $\boldsymbol{\zeta}$, and ignoring the error,

$$\mathbf{p}_{\mathrm{A}} = w\mathbf{v}\left(\mathbf{I} + r\hat{\mathbf{T}}(0)\right) \tag{2.97}$$

where $\mathbf{p}_{\mathrm{A}}$ denotes a vector of Austrian (Böhm-Bawerkian) production prices and $\hat{\mathbf{T}}(0) \equiv \hat{\mathbf{v}}^{-1}\hat{\boldsymbol{\zeta}}$ a diagonal matrix that has the Böhm-Bawerkian average periods of production of the different processes on its main diagonal. Equation 2.97 implies that

$$\Delta T_j(0) > (<)\ 0 \Leftrightarrow \dot{p}_{\mathrm{A}ji} > (<)\ 0 \tag{2.98}$$

which is no more than a special case of condition (2.96). Marx's (1959, Chaps. 11 and 12) relevant condition is

$$\mathbf{vH}_j v_j^{-1} > (<)\ \mathbf{vH}_i v_i^{-1} \Leftrightarrow \dot{p}_{ji} > (<)\ 0 \tag{2.99}$$

(consider Eq. 2.64 at $\rho = 0$), which is equivalent to condition (2.98), since $\zeta_j = \mathbf{vH}_j + v_j$.

References

Abraham-Frois, G., & Berrebi, E. (1997). *Price, profits and rhythms of accumulation*. Cambridge: Cambridge University Press.

Abraham-Frois, G., & Lendjel, E. (Eds.). (2004). *Les œuvres économiques de l'Abbé Potron*. Paris: L'Harmattan.

Ara, K. (1963). A note on input-output matrices. *Hitotsubashi Journal of Economics, 3*(2), 68–70.

Aruka, Y. (1990). Perturbation theorems on the linear production model and some properties of eigenprices. The Australian National University, Faculty of Economics, Working Papers in Economics and Econometrics, Working Paper No. 203.

Aruka, Y. (1991). Generalized Goodwin's theorems on general coordinates. *Structural Change and Economic Dynamics, 2*(1), 69–91. Reprinted in Y. Aruka (Ed.), (2011). *Complexities of production and interacting human behaviour* (pp. 39–66). Heidelberg: Physica-Verlag.

Aruka, Y. (2000). Possibility theorems on reswitching of techniques and the related issues of price variations. *Bulletin of the Institute of Economic Research*, Chuo University, *30,* 79–119. Reprinted in Y. Aruka (Ed.), (2011). *Complexities of production and interacting human behaviour* (pp. 67–111). Heidelberg: Physica-Verlag.

Aseltine, J. A. (1958). *Transform method in linear system analysis*. New York: McGraw-Hill).

Balassa, B. (1964). The purchasing power parity doctrine: A reappraisal. *Journal of Political Economy, 72*(6), 584–596.

Baldone, S. (1980). Misure invariabili del valore e merce tipo. *Ricerche Economiche, 34*(3–4), 272–283.
Benetti, C., Bidard, C., & Klimovsky, E. (2007). Classical dynamics of disequilibrium. *Cambridge Journal of Economics, 31*(1), 41–54.
Benetti, C., Bidard, C., & Klimovsky, E. (2008). A classical model of equilibrium and disequilibrium. *Bulletin of Political Economy, 2*(1), 25–41.
Bhaduri, A., & Marglin, S. (1990). Unemployment and the real wage rate: The economic basis for contesting political ideologies. *Cambridge Journal of Economics, 14*(4), 375–393.
Bidard, C. (1991). *Prix, reproduction, rareté*. Paris: Dunod.
Bidard, C. (1997). Pure joint production. *Cambridge Journal of Economics, 21*(6), 685–701.
Bidard, C. (1998). Laws on long-term prices. *The Manchester School, 66*(4), 453–465.
Bidard, C., & Ehrbar, H. G. (2007). Relative prices in the classical theory: Facts and figures. *Bulletin of Political Economy, 1*(2), 161–211.
Bidard, C., & Erreygers, G. (2010). *The analysis of linear economic systems. Father Maurice Potron's pioneering works*. Abingdon: Routledge.
Bidard, C., & Krause, U. (1996). A monotonicity law for relative prices. *Economic Theory, 7*(1), 51–61.
Bidard, C., & Steedman, I. (1996). Monotonic movement of price vectors. *Economic Issues, 1*(2), 41–44.
Bienenfeld, M. (1988). Regularity in price changes as an effect of changes in distribution. *Cambridge Journal of Economics, 12*(2), 247–255.
Böhm-Bawerk, E. V. ([1889] 1959). *Capital and interest*. South Holland: Libertarian Press.
Bowles, S., & Gintis, H. (1977). The Marxian theory of value and heterogeneous labour: A critique and reformulation. *Cambridge Journal of Economics, 1*(2), 173–192.
Bródy, A. (1970). *Proportions, prices and planning. A mathematical restatement of the labor theory of value*. Budapest: Akadémiai Kiadó. Amsterdam: North-Holland.
Bruno, M. (1969). Fundamental duality relations in the pure theory of capital and growth. *The Review of Economic Studies, 36*(1), 39–53.
Burmeister, E. (1974). Synthesizing the Neo-Austrian and alternative approaches to capital theory: A survey. *Journal of Economic Literature, 12*(2), 413–456.
Burmeister, E. (1980). *Capital theory and dynamics*. Cambridge: Cambridge University Press.
Cai, J., & Leung, P. (2004). Linkage measures: A revisit and a suggested alternative. *Economic Systems Research, 16*(1), 65–85.
Caravale, G., & Tosato, D. (1980). *Ricardo and the theory of value and distribution*. London: Routledge.
Cesaratto, S. (2010). Endogenous growth theory twenty years on: A critical assessment. *Bulletin of Political Economy, 4*(1), 1–30.
Charasoff, G. V. (1910). *Das system des Marxismus: Darstellung und kritik*. Berlin: H. Bondy.
Chen, C.-T., & Desoer, C. A. (1968). Proof of controllability of Jordan form state equations. *The Institute of Electrical and Electronics Engineers Transactions on Automatic Control, 13*(2), 195–196.
d'Autume, A. (1988). La production jointe: Le point de vue de la théorie de l'équilibre général. *Revue Économique, 39*(2), 325–347.
De Grauwe, P. (2000). *Economics of monetary union* (4th ed.). Oxford: Oxford University Press.
Dietzenbacher, E. (1993). A limiting property for the powers of a non-negative, reducible matrix. *Structural Change and Economic Dynamics, 4*(2), 353–366.
Ding, J., & Zhou, A. (2007). Eigenvalues of rank-one updated matrices with some applications. *Applied Mathematics Letters, 20*(12), 1223–1226.
Dmitriev, V. K. (1898). *The theory of value of David Ricardo: An attempt at a rigorous analysis*. In V. K. Dmitriev ([1904] 1974), *Economic essays on value, competition and utility* (pp. 37–95). Edited with an introduction by D.M. Nuti, London: Cambridge University Press.
Duménil, G. (1980). *De la valeur aux prix de production*. Paris: Economica.

Dutt, A. K. (1990). *Growth, distribution and uneven development*. Cambridge: Cambridge University Press.

Egidi, M. (1977). The conditions for the reswitching of techniques. *Economia Internazionale, 30*(4), 434–449.

Egidi, M., & Gilibert, G. (1989). The objective theory of prices. *Political Economy: Studies in the Surplus Approach, 5*(1), 59–74.

Endres, A. M., & Harper, D. A. (2011). Carl Menger and his followers in the Austrian tradition on the nature of capital and its structure. *Journal of the History of Economic Thought, 33*(3), 357–384.

Erreygers, G. (1989). On indirect taxation and weakly basic commodities. *Journal of Economics, 50*(2), 139–156.

Faber, M. (1980). Relationships between modern Austrian and Sraffa's capital theory. *Zeitschrift für die gesamte Staatswissenschaft/Journal of Institutional and Theoretical Economics, 136*(4), 617–629.

Faddeev, D. K., & Faddeeva, V. N. (1963). *Computational methods of linear algebra*. San Francisco: W. H. Freeman and Company.

Filippini, C., & Filippini, L. (1982). Two theorems on joint production. *The Economic Journal, 92*(366), 386–390.

Fisher, F. M. (1965). Choice of units, column sums, and stability in linear dynamic systems with nonnegative square matrices. *Econometrica, 33*(2), 445–450.

Flaschel, P. (1980). The derivation and comparison of employment multipliers and labour productivity indexes using monetary and physical input-output tables. *Economics of Planning, 16*(3), 118–129.

Flaschel, P. (1983). Actual labor values in a general model of production. *Econometrica, 51*(2), 435–454.

Flaschel, P. (2010). *Topics in classical micro- and macroeconomics. Elements of a critique of Neoricadian theory*. Heidelberg: Springer.

Foley, D. K. (1982). The value of money, the value of labor power and the Marxian transformation problem. *Review of Radical Political Economics, 14*(2), 37–47.

Foley, D. K. (2000). Recent developments in the labor theory of value. *Review of Radical Political Economics, 32*(1), 1–39.

Forsythe, G. E. (1953). Solving linear algebraic equations can be interesting. *Bulletin of the American Mathematical Society, 59*(4), 299–329.

Franke, R. (1998). Quantities and prices. In H. D. Kurz & N. Salvadori (Eds.), *The Elgar companion to classical economics L-Z* (pp. 236–238). Cheltenham: Edward Elgar.

Fujimori, Y. (1982). *Modern analysis of value theory*. Berlin: Springer.

Fujimoto, T., & Fujita, Y. (2008). A refutation of the commodity exploitation theorem. *Metroeconomica, 59*(3), 530–540.

Fujimoto, T., & Krause, U. (1988). More theorems on joint production. *Journal of Economics, 48*(2), 189–196.

Garegnani, P. (1970). Heterogeneous capital, the production function and the theory of distribution. *The Review of Economic Studies, 37*(3), 407–436.

Gehrke, C., & Kurz, H. D. (2009). Hicks's neo-Austrian theory and Böhm-Bawerk's Austrian theory of capital. In H. Hagemann & R. Scazzieri (Eds.), *Capital, time and transitional dynamics* (pp. 72–95). London: Routledge.

Gehrke, C., & Lager, C. (1995). Environmental taxes, relative prices and choice of technique in a linear model of production. *Metroeconomica, 46*(2), 127–145.

Gilbert, E. G. (1963). Controllability and observability in multivariable control systems. *Journal of the Society for Industrial and Applied Mathematics on Control, 1*(2), 128–151.

Gilibert, G. (1998a). Necessary price. In H. D. Kurz & N. Salvadori (Eds.), *The Elgar companion to classical economics L-Z* (pp. 166–176). Cheltenham: Edward Elgar.

Gilibert, G. (1998b). Leontief, Wassily. In H. D. Kurz & N. Salvadori (Eds.), *The Elgar companion to classical economics L-Z* (pp. 40–45). Cheltenham: Edward Elgar.

Gintis, H., & Bowles, S. (1981). Structure and practice in the labor theory of value. *Review of Radical Political Economics, 12*(4), 1–26.

Golub, G. H., & van der Vorst, H. A. (2000). Eigenvalue computation in the in the 20th century. *Journal of Computational and Applied Mathematics, 123*(1–2), 35–65.

Grubbström, R. W., & Yinzhong, J. (1989). A survey and analysis of the application of the Laplace transform to present value problems. *Rivista di Matematica per le Scienze Economiche e Sociale/Decisions in Economics and Finance, 12*(1), 43–62.

Gubernatis, J. E., & Booth, T. E. (2008). Multiple extremal eigenpairs by the power method. *Journal of Computational Physics, 227*(19), 8508–8522.

Harcourt, G. C. (1972). *Some Cambridge controversies in the theory of capital*. Cambridge: Cambridge University Press.

Harris, D. J. (1981). On the timing of wage payments. *Cambridge Journal of Economics, 5*(4), 369–381.

Harrod, R. F. (1933). *International economics*. London: James Nisbet.

Hein, E. (2008). *Money, distribution and capital accumulation. Contributions to 'monetary analysis'*. Basingstoke: Palgrave MacMillan.

Hicks, J. R. (1939). *Value and capital*. Oxford: Clarendon.

Hicks, J. R. (1973). *Capital and time: A neo-Austrian theory*. Oxford: Oxford University Press.

Holley, J. L. (1951). Note on the inversion of the Leontief Matrix. *Econometrica, 19*(3), 317–320.

Howard, M. C. (1980). Austrian capital theory: An evaluation in terms of Piero Sraffa's *Production of commodities by means of commodities. Metroeconomica, 32*(1), 1–23.

Howard, M. C. (1981). Ricardo's analysis of profit: An evaluation in terms of Piero Sraffa's *Production of commodities by means of commodities. Metroeconomica, 33*(1-2-3), 105–128.

Isnard, A.-N. (1781). *Traité des richesses*. Londres: F. Grasset & Company.

Kahn, R. (1931). The relation of home investment to unemployment. *The Economic Journal, 41* (162), 173–198.

Kalman, R. E. (1961). On the general theory of control systems. In *Proceedings of the First International Congress on Automatic Control* (Vol. 1, pp. 481–492). London: Butterworths.

Kalman, R. E. (1963). Mathematical description of linear dynamical systems. *Journal of the Society for Industrial and Applied Mathematics on Control, 1*(2), 152–192.

Keyfitz, N., & Caswell, H. (2005). *Applied mathematical demography* (3rd ed.). New York: Springer.

King, R. G., & Rebelo, S. (1990). Public policy and economic growth: Developing neoclassical implications. *Journal of Political Economy, 98*(5), 126–150.

Krause, U. (1980). Abstract labour in general joint systems. *Metroeconomica, 32*(2–3), 115–135.

Krause, U. (1981). Marxian inequalities in a von Neumann setting. *Journal of Economics, 41*(1–2), 59–67.

Krause, U. (1982). *Money and abstract labour. On the analytical foundations of political economy*. London: New Left Books.

Kurz, H. D. (1990). Technical change, growth and distribution: A steady-state approach to 'unsteady' growth. In H. D. Kurz (Ed.), *Capital, distribution and effective demand. Studies in the 'classical' approach to economic theory* (pp. 211–239). Cambridge: Polity Press.

Kurz, H. D., & Salvadori, N. (1995). *Theory of production. A long-period analysis*. Cambridge: Cambridge University Press.

Kurz, H. D., & Salvadori, N. (1998). *Understanding 'classical' economics. Studies in long-period theory*. London: Routledge.

Kurz, H. D., & Salvadori, N. (2000). The dynamic Leontief model and the theory of endogenous growth. *Economic Systems Research, 12*(2), 255–265.

Kurz, H. D., & Salvadori, N. (2003). *Classical economics and modern theory. Studies in long-period analysis*. London: Routledge.

Lager, C. (2000). Production, prices and time: A comparison of some alternative concepts. *Economic Systems Research, 12*(2), 231–253.

Lee, F. S. (2012). Heterodox surplus approach: Production, prices, and value theory. *Bulletin of Political Economy, 6*(2), 65–105.

Leontief, W. (1928). Die Wirtschaft als Kreislauf. *Archiv für Sozialwissenschaft und Sozialpolitik, 60*(3), 577–623.

Leontief, W. (1953). *Studies in the structure of the American economy*. New York: Oxford University Press.

Macaulay, F. R. (1938). *Some theoretical problems suggested by the movements of interest rates, bond yields, and stock prices in the United States since 1856*. New York: Columbia University Press.

Mainwaring, L. (1974). *A neo-Ricardian analysis of trade* (Ph.D. Thesis, University of Manchester, Manchester).

Mainwaring, L. (1978). The interest rate equalisation theorem with non-traded goods. *Journal of International Economics, 8*(1), 11–19. Reprinted in I. Steedman (Ed.), (1979). *Fundamental issues in trade theory* (pp. 90–98). London: Macmillan.

Mainwaring, L. (1979). Exchange rate changes and the choice of technique. In I. Steedman (Ed.), *Fundamental issues in trade theory* (pp. 188–200). London: Macmillan.

Mainwaring, L., & Steedman, I. (2000). On the probability of re-switching and capital reversing in a two-sector Sraffian model. In H. D. Kurz (Ed.), *Critical essays on Piero Sraffa's legacy in economics* (pp. 323–354). Cambridge: Cambridge University Press.

Maitre, J. F. (1970). Sur la séparation des valeurs propres d'une matrice positive. *Revue Française d'Informatique and et de recherche opérationnel, 4*(3), 118–124. Série Rouge.

Mariolis, T. (2001). On V.K. Dmitriev's contribution to the so-called «transformation problem» and to the profit theory. *Political Economy. Review of Political Economy and Social Sciences, 9*(1), 45–60.

Mariolis, T. (2003). Controllability, observability, regularity, and the so-called problem of transforming values into prices of production. *Asian African Journal of Economics, and Econometrics, 3*(2), 113–127.

Mariolis, T. (2004a). Pure joint production and international trade: A note. *Cambridge Journal of Economics, 28*(3), 449–456.

Mariolis, T. (2004b). A Sraffian approach to the Stolper-Samuelson theorem. *Asian African Journal of Economics and Econometrics, 4*(1), 1–11.

Mariolis, T. (2005). On an 'enigma' in V. K. Dmitriev's essay on the Ricardian theory of value. In T. Mariolis (2010). *Essays on the logical history of political economy* (in Greek) (pp. 77–94). Athens: Matura.

Mariolis, T. (2006a). A critical note on Marx's theory of profits. *Asian African Journal of Economics and Econometrics, 6*(1), 1–11.

Mariolis, T. (2006b). A critique of the 'New Approach' to the transformation problem and a proposal. *Indian Development Review. An International Journal of Development Economics, 4* (1), 23–37. Reprinted in T. Mariolis & L. Tsoulfidis (Eds.), (2006). *Distribution, development and prices. Critical perspectives* (pp. 23–37). New Delhi: Serials.

Mariolis, T. (2008a). Pure joint production, income distribution, employment and the exchange rate. *Metroeconomica, 59*(4), 656–665.

Mariolis, T. (2008b). Heterogeneous capital goods and the Harrod-Balassa-Samuelson effect. *Metroeconomica, 59*(2), 238–248.

Mariolis, T. (2010). Norm bounds for a transformed price vector in Sraffian systems. *Applied Mathematical Sciences, 4*(9–12), 551–574.

Mariolis, T. (2013). Goodwin's growth cycle model with the Bhaduri-Marglin accumulation function. *Evolutionary and Institutional Economics Review, 10*(1), 131–144.

Mariolis, T. (2015). Norm bounds and a homographic approximation for the wage-profit curve. *Metroeconomica, 66*(2), 263–283.

Mariolis, T., & Rodousaki, E. (2011). Total requirements for gross output and intersectoral linkages: A note on Dmitriev's contribution to the theory of profits. *Contributions to Political Economy, 30*(1), 67–75.

Mariolis, T., & Soklis, G. (2007). On the empirical validity of the labour theory of value. In T. Mariolis (2010), *Essays on the logical history of political economy* (in Greek) (pp. 231–260). Athens: Matura.

Mariolis, T., & Tsoulfidis, L. (2009). Decomposing the changes in production prices into 'capital-intensity' and 'price' effects: Theory and evidence from the Chinese economy. *Contributions to Political Economy, 28*(1), 1–22.

Mariolis, T., Soklis, G., & Groza, E. (2012). Estimation of the maximum attainable economic dependency ratio: Evidence from the symmetric input-output tables of four European economies. *Journal of Economic Analysis, 3*(1), 52–71.

Mariolis, T., Soklis, G., & Zouvela, E. (2013). Testing Böhm-Bawerk's theory of capital: Some evidence from the Finnish economy. *The Review of Austrian Economics, 26*(2), 207–220.

Mariolis, T., Rodousakis, N., & Christodoulaki, A. (2015). Input-output evidence on the relative price effects of total productivity shift. *International Review of Applied Economics, 29*(2), 150–163.

Marx, K. (1954). *Capital* (Vol. 1). Moscow: Progress Publisher.

Marx, K. (1959). *Capital* (Vol. 3). Moscow: Progress Publisher.

Mas-Colell, A. (1989). Capital theory paradoxes: Anything goes. In G. Feiwel (Ed.), *Joan Robinson and modern economic theory* (pp. 505–520). London: Macmillan.

Mathur, P. N. (1977). A study of sectoral prices and their movements in the British economy in an input-output framework. In W. Leontief (Ed.), *Structure, system and economic policy* (pp. 29–47). Cambridge: Cambridge University Press.

Matsuo, T. (2009). Generalized commodity exploitation theorem and the net-production concept. *Bulletin of Political Economy, 3*(1), 1–13.

Matsuo, T. (2010). Average period of production in circulating input-output structure. *Applied Mathematical Sciences, 4*(46), 2293–2313.

Melman, A. (2013). Upper and lower bounds for the Perron root of a nonnegative matrix. *Linear and Multilinear Algebra, 61*(2), 171–181.

Metcalfe, J. S., & Steedman, I. (1971). Some effects of taxation in a linear model of production. *The Manchester School, 39*(3), 171–185.

Metcalfe, J. S., & Steedman, I. (1972). Reswitching and primary input use. *The Economic Journal, 82*(325), 140–157.

Metcalfe, J. S., & Steedman, I. (1979). Heterogeneous capital and the Heckscher-Ohlin-Samuelson theory of trade. In I. Steedman (Ed.), *Fundamental issues in trade theory* (pp. 64–76). London: Macmillan.

Metcalfe, J. S., & Steedman, I. (1981). Some long-run theory of employment, income distribution and the exchange rate. *The Manchester School, 49*(1), 1–20.

Meyer, C. D. (2001). *Matrix analysis and applied linear algebra*. New York: SIAM.

Miller, R. E. (1966). Interregional feedback effects in input-output models: Some preliminary results. *Papers of the Regional Science Association, 17*(1), 105–125.

Miyao, T. (1977). A generalization of Sraffa's standard commodity and its complete characterization. *International Economic Review, 18*(1), 151–162.

Montani, G. (1975). Scarce natural resources and income distribution. *Metroeconomica, 27*(1), 68–101.

Mori, K. (2008). Maurice Potron's linear economic model: A de facto proof of 'fundamental Marxian theorem'. *Metroeconomica, 59*(3), 511–529.

Morishima, M. (1973). *Marx's economics. A dual theory of value and growth*. Cambridge: Cambridge University Press.

Morishima, M. (1974). Marx in the light of modern economic theory. *Econometrica, 42*(4), 611–632.

Morishima, M. (1978). S. Bowles and H. Gintis on the Marxian theory of value and heterogeneous labour. *Cambridge Journal of Economics, 2*(3), 305–309.

Morishima, M., & Catephores, G. (1978). *Value, exploitation and growth: Marx in the light of modern economic theory*. London: McGraw-Hill.

Morishima, M., & Seton, F. (1961). Aggregation in Leontief matrices and the labour theory of value. *Econometrica, 29*(2), 203–220.

Mühlpfordt, W. (1893). *Preis und Einkommen in der privatkapitalistischen Gesellschaft*. Königsberg: Hartungsche Buchdruckerei.

Mühlpfordt, W. (1895). Karl Marx und die durchschnittsprofitrate. *Jahrbücher für Nationalökonomie und Statistik, 10*(65), 92–99.

Nakatani, T., & Okishio, N. (1995). The permissible range of relative prices in the light of labor values. *Kobe University Economic Review, 41*, 1–14.

Neumann, J. V. (1937). Über ein ökonomisches Gleichungssystem und eine Verallgemeinerung des Brouwerschen Fixpunktsatzes. In K. Menger (Ed.), *Ergebnisse eines Mathematischen Kolloquiums* (Vol. 8, pp. 73–83). Leipzig: Deuticke.

Obstfeld, M., & Rogoff, K. (1998). *Foundations of international macroeconomics*. Cambridge MA: MIT Press.

Oda, S. H. (2007). Formulating non-proportionally growing economies: A generalisation of Pasinetti's analysis. *Bulletin of Political Economy, 1*(2), 128–159.

Okishio, N. (1955). Monopoly and the rates of profit. *Kobe University Economic Review, 1*, 71–88. Reprinted in M. Krüger & P. Flaschel (Eds.), (1993). *Nobuo Okishio. Essays on political economy* (pp. 381–398). Frankfurt am Main: Peter Lang.

Okishio, N. (1961). Technical changes and the rate of profit. *Kobe University Economic Review, 7*, 85–99. Reprinted in M. Krüger & P. Flaschel (Eds.), (1993). *Nobuo Okishio. Essays on political economy* (pp. 359–373). Frankfurt am Main: Peter Lang.

Okishio, N. (1963). A mathematical note on Marxian theorems. *Weltwirtschaftliches Archiv*, *91*, 287–299. Reprinted in M. Krüger & P. Flaschel (Eds.), (1993). *Nobuo Okishio. Essays on political economy* (pp. 27–39). Frankfurt am Main: Peter Lang.

Okishio, N. (1972). On Marx's production prices (in Japanese). *Keizaigaku-Kenkyu, 19*, 38–63. Reprinted in M. Krüger & P. Flaschel (Eds.), (1993). *Nobuo Okishio. Essays on political economy* (pp. 41–59). Frankfurt am Main: Peter Lang.

Okishio, N. (1987). Constant and variable capital. In J. Eatwell, M. Milgate, & P. Newman (Eds.), *The new Palgrave. A dictionary of economics* (pp. 581–584). London: Macmillan. Volume 1.

Okishio, N., & Nakatani, T. (1985). A measurement of the rate of surplus value in Japan: The 1980 case. *Kobe University Economic Review, 31*, 1–13. Reprinted in M. Krüger & P. Flaschel (Eds.), (1993). *Nobuo Okishio. Essays on political economy* (pp. 61–73). Frankfurt am Main: Peter Lang.

Orosel, G. O. (1979). A reformulation of the Austrian theory of capital and its application to the debate on reswitching and related paradoxa. *Journal of Economics, 39*(1–2), 1–31.

Ostrowski, A. M. (1963). On positive matrices. *Mathematische Annalen, 150*(3), 276–284.

Paelinck, J., Caevel, J. D., & Degueldre, J. (1965). Analyse quantitative de certains phénomènes du développement régional polarisé: Essai de simulation statique d'itinéraires de propagation. In *Problèmes de conversion économique: Analyses théorétiques et études appliquées. Bibliothèque de l'Institut de Science Économique*, No. 7 (pp. 341–387). Paris: M.-Th. Génin.

Parrinello, S. (1970). Introduzione ad una teoria neoricardiana del commercio internazionale. *Studi Economici, 25*(3–4), 267–321.

Parys, W. (1982). The deviation of prices from labor values. *The American Economic Review, 72* (5), 1208–1212.

Parys, W. (1986). Standard commodities and the transformation problem. *Economie Appliquee, 39* (1), 181–190.

Pasinetti, L. L. (1973). The notion of vertical integration in economic analysis. *Metroeconomica, 25*(1), 1–29.

Pasinetti, L. L. (1977). *Lectures on the theory of production*. New York: Columbia University Press.

Pasinetti, L. L. (1988). Growing subsystems, vertically hyper-integrated sectors and the labour theory of value. *Cambridge Journal of Economics, 12*(1), 125–134.

Petri, F. (2011). On the likelihood and relevance of reswitching and reverse capital deepening. In N. Salvadori & C. Gehrke (Eds.), *Keynes, Sraffa and the criticisms of neoclassical theory. Essays in honour of Heinz Kurz* (pp. 380–418). London: Routledge.
Reati, A. (1986). La Transformation des valeurs en prix non concurrentiels. *Economie Appliquee, 39*(1), 157–179.
Rebelo, S. (1991). Long-run policy analysis and long-run growth. *Journal of Political Economy, 99*(3), 500–521.
Remak, R. (1929). Kann die Volkswirtschaftslehre eine exakte Wissenschaft werden? *Jahrbücher für Nationalökonomie und Statistik, 76*(131), 703–735.
Remak, R. (1933). Können superponierte Preissysteme praktisch berechnet werden? *Jahrbücher für Nationalökonomie und Statistik, 83*(138), 839–842.
Reuten, G., & Williams, M. (1989). *Value-form and the state*. London: Routledge.
Ricardo, D. (1951). *The works and correspondence of David Ricardo*, Vol. 1. Edited by P. Sraffa with the collaboration of M.H. Dobb, Cambridge: Cambridge University Press.
Robinson, J. V. (1953). The production function and the theory of capital. *The Review of Economic Studies, 21*(2), 81–106.
Rodousakis, N., & Soklis, G. (2010). Norm bounds for a transformed activity level vector in Sraffian systems: A 'dual' exercise'. *Applied Mathematical Sciences, 4*(60), 2955–2961.
Roemer, J. E. (1981). *Analytical foundations of Marxian economic theory*. Cambridge: Cambridge University Press.
Roemer, J. E. (1986). *Value, exploitation and class*. Chur: Harwood Academic Publishers.
Rosinger, J.-L. (1996). An elementary proof of the Bowles-Gintis-Morishima fundamental Marxian theorem with heterogeneous labour. *Cambridge Journal of Economics, 20*(6), 779–782.
Rothblum, U. G., & Tan, C. P. (1985). Upper bounds on the maximum modulus of subdominant eigenvalues of nonnegative matrices. *Linear Algebra and its Applications, 66*, 45–86.
Salvadori, N., & Stedman, I. (1985). Cost functions and produced means of production: Duality and capital theory. *Contributions to Political Economy, 4*(1), 79–90.
Salvadori, N., & Steedman, I. (1988). No reswitching? No switching! *Cambridge Journal of Economics, 12*(4), 481–486.
Samuelson, P. A. (1948). International trade and the equalisation of factor prices. *The Economic Journal, 58*(230), 163–184.
Samuelson, P. A. (1962). Parable and realism in capital theory: The surrogate production function. *The Review of Economic Studies, 29*(3), 193–206.
Samuelson, P. A. (1964). Theoretical notes on trade problems. *The Review of Economics and Statistics, 46*(2), 145–154.
Samuelson, P. A. (1999). The special thing I learned from Sraffa. In G. Mongiovi & F. Petri (Eds.), *Value distribution and capital. Essays in honour of Pierangelo Garegnani* (pp. 210–217). London: Routledge.
Samuelson, P. A. (2000). Revisionist findings on Sraffa. In H. D. Kurz (Ed.), *Critical essays on Piero Sraffa's legacy in economics* (pp. 25–45). Cambridge: Cambridge University Press.
Saucier, P. (1984). La production jointe en situation de concurrence. In C. Bidard (Ed.), *La production jointe: Nouveaux débats* (pp. 155–174). Paris: Economica.
Schefold, B. (1971). *Mr. Sraffa on joint production* (Ph.D. Thesis, University of Basle, Basle).
Schefold, B. (1976). Relative prices as a function of the profit rate: A mathematical note. *Journal of Economics, 36*(1–2), 21–48. Reprinted in B. Schefold (1997). *Normal prices, technical change and accumulation* (pp. 46–75). London: Macmillan.
Schefold, B. (1978). On counting equations. *Journal of Economics, 38*(3–4), 253–285.
Schefold, B. (1989). *Mr. Sraffa on joint production and other essays*. London: Unwin Hyman.
Semmler, W. (1983). On the classical theory of taxation. An analysis of tax incidence in a linear production model. *Metroeconomica, 35*(1–2), 129–146.
Semmler, W. (1984). *Competition, monopoly, and differential profit rates. On the relevance of the Classical and Marxian theories of production prices for modern industrial and corporate pricing*. New York: Columbia University Press.

Seneta, R. E. (2006). *Non-negative matrices and Markov chains*. New York: Springer.
Shaikh, A. M. (1998). The empirical strength of the labour theory of value. In R. Bellofiore (Ed.), *Marxian economics: A reappraisal* (pp. 225–251). New York: St. Martin's Press. Volume 2.
Shaikh, A. M. ([1973] 1977). Marx's theory of value and the transformation problem. In J. Schwartz (Ed.), (1977). *The subtle anatomy of capitalism* (pp. 106–139). Santa Monica: Goodyear Publishing.
Shibata, K. (1935). On Böhm-Bawerk's theory of interest-rate. *Kyoto University Economic Review, 10*(1), 107–127.
Smith, A. (1937). *The wealth of nations*. New York: Random House.
Solow, R. (1952). On the structure of linear models. *Econometrica, 20*(1), 29–46.
Solow, R. M. (1959). Competitive valuation in a dynamic input-output system. *Econometrica, 27* (1), 30–53.
Sonis, M., Guilhoto, J. J. M., Hewings, G. J. D., & Martins, E. B. (1995). Linkages, key sectors, and structural change: Some new perspectives. *The Developing Economies, 33*(3), 233–270.
Spaventa, L. (1970). Rate of profit, rate of growth, and capital intensity in a simple production model. *Oxford Economic Papers, 22*(2), 129–147.
Sraffa, P. (1960). *Production of commodities by means of commodities. Prelude to a critique of economic theory*. Cambridge: Cambridge University Press.
Steedman, I. (1972). Jevons's theory of capital and interest. *The Manchester School, 40*(1), 31–52.
Steedman, I. (1975). Positive profits with negative surplus value. *The Economic Journal, 85*(337), 114–123.
Steedman, I. (1976). Positive profits with negative surplus value: A reply. *The Economic Journal, 86*(343), 604–608.
Steedman, I. (1977). *Marx after Sraffa*. London: New Left Books.
Steedman, I. (Ed.). (1979). *Fundamental issues in trade theory*. London: Macmillan.
Steedman, I. (1982). Joint production and the wage-rent frontier. *The Economic Journal, 92*(366), 377–385.
Steedman, I. (1985). Joint production and technical progress. *Political Economy. Studies in the Surplus Approach, 1*(1), 127–138.
Steedman, I. (1990). Changements dans la répartition et changements dans les prix relatifs des marchandises. In R. Arena & J. L. Ravix (Eds.), *Sraffa trente ans après* (pp. 67–74). Paris: Presses Universitaires de France.
Steedman, I. (1992). Joint production and the 'New Solution' to the transformation problem. *Indian Economic Review*, 27, Special Number in Memory of Sukhamoy Chakravarty, 123–127.
Steedman, I. (1999a). *Production of commodities by means of commodities* and the open economy. *Metroeconomica, 50*(3), 260–276.
Steedman, I. (1999b). Vertical integration and 'reduction to dated quantities of labour'. In G. Mongiovi & F. Petri (Eds.), *Value distribution and capital. Essays in honour of Pierangelo Garegnani* (pp. 314–318). London: Routledge.
Steedman, I. (2000). Hicks-Neutral technical progress and relative price change. *Structural Change and Economic Dynamics, 11*(1), 181–184.
Steedman, I. (2004). Vertical integration in the changing economy. In R. Arena & N. Salvadori (Eds.), *Money, credit and the role of the state. Essays in honour of Augusto Graziani* (pp. 361–370). Aldershot: Ashgate.
Steedman, I. (2008). Marx after Sraffa and the open economy. *Bulletin of Political Economy, 2*(2), 165–174.
Steedman, I., & Metcalfe, J. S. (1981). On duality and basic commodities in an open economy. *Australian Economic Papers, 20*(36), 133–141.
Stigler, G. J. (1958). Ricardo and the 93% labor theory of value. *The American Economic Review, 48*(3), 357–367.
Stolper, W. F., & Samuelson, P. A. (1941). Protection and real wages. *The Review of Economic Studies, 9*(1), 58–73.

Stott, I., Townley, S., & Hodgson, D. J. (2011). A framework for studying transient dynamics of population projection matrix models. *Ecology Letters, 14*(9), 959–970.

Strassert, G. (1968). Zur bestimmung strategischer sektoren mit hilfe von input-output modellen. *Jahrbücher für Nationalökonomie und Statistik, 182*(30), 211–215.

Torrens, R. (1821). *An essay on the production of wealth.* London: Longman, Hurst, Rees, Orme, and Brown.

Tsoulfidis, L. (1989). The physiocratic theory of tax incidence. *Scottish Journal of Political Economy, 36*(3), 301–310.

Tsoulfidis, L. (1993). On the Ricardian theory of taxation and neutrality of money. *Spoudai, 43*(2), 111–127.

Veneziani, R., & Yoshihara, N. (2010). Exploitation and productiveness: The generalised commodity exploitation theorem once again. *Bulletin of Political Economy, 4*(1), 45–58.

Weizsäcker, C. C. V. (1971). *Steady state capital theory*. Berlin: Springer Verlag.

Weizsäcker, C. C. V. (1974). Substitution along the time axis. *Kyklos, 27*(4), 732–756.

Weizsäcker, C. C. V. (1977). Organic composition of capital and average period of production. *Revue d'Economie Politique, 87*(2), 198–231.

Wonhman, W. M. (1967). On pole assignment in multi-input controllable linear systems. *The Institute of Electrical and Electronics Engineers Transactions on Automatic Control, 12*(6), 660–665.

Woods, J. E. (1988). On switching of techniques in two-sector models. *Scottish Journal of Political Economy, 35*(1), 84–91.

Yoshihara, N. (2014). A progressive report on Marxian economic theory: On the controversies in exploitation theory since Okishio (1963). Institute of Economic Research, Hitotsubashi University, Discussion Paper Series A No. 607. http://hermes-ir.lib.hit-u.ac.jp/rs/bitstream/10086/26615/1/DP607.pdf. Accessed 12 Dec 2014.

Zambelli, S. (2004). The 40% neoclassical aggregate theory of production. *Cambridge Journal of Economics, 28*(1), 99–120.

Chapter 3
Values, Prices and Income Distribution in Actual Economies

Abstract This chapter estimates the proximities of labour values and production prices to market prices in real-world economies and explores at length the respective relationships amongst production prices, interindustry structure of production and changes in income distribution. The results finally suggest that value-based approximations of actual single-product economies could be considered as accurate enough, and the effective dimensions of those economies appear to be relatively low, that is to say, between two and three.

Keywords Actual economies • Capital intensities • Direct prices • Market prices • Wage-production price-profit rate curves

3.1 Introduction

This chapter zeroes in on *actual* economies by dealing with (i) the question of proximity of 'direct prices' and 'actual production prices' to market prices and (ii) the relationships amongst production prices, interindustry structure of production and income distribution. It is important to clarify at the outset that the term 'direct price' is used to indicate the monetary expression of direct and indirect labour requirements per unit of output; in other words, 'direct prices' are money prices proportional to labour values. And the term 'actual production prices' is used to signify production prices that correspond to the 'actual' real wage rate (estimated on the basis of the available input-output data). For these purposes, we use linear models of production and input-output data from a number of quite diverse economies or from the same economy over the years. Also we take into account findings from other empirical studies.

The remainder of the chapter is structured as follows. Section 3.2 presents a simple but realistic example of input-output relations of the US economy, for the year 1990, aggregated into three sectors. It shows the applicability of the classical theory of value to actual economies and tests its quantitative accuracy. Section 3.3 deals with the deviations of direct and actual production prices from market prices using input-output data from a number of countries. Section 3.4 tests Steedman's (1999) polynomial approximation of actual production prices through direct prices and highlights the importance of the relative profit rate in this approximation.

© Springer Japan 2016

T. Mariolis, L. Tsoulfidis, *Modern Classical Economics and Reality*, Evolutionary Economics and Social Complexity Science 2, DOI 10.1007/978-4-431-55004-4_3

Section 3.5 focuses on the intertemporal comparison of those prices. Section 3.6 correlates actual production price-direct price differences with actual capital-intensity differences. Section 3.7 provides an empirical illustration of the norm bounds for the production price-relative profit rate curves. Section 3.8 deals with the monotonicity of those curves. Section 3.9 provides empirical illustrations of the wage-relative profit rate curve. Finally, Sect. 3.10 concludes.[1]

3.2 A Numerical Example of the US Input-Output Table

For the better understanding of the preceding analysis, let us take a simple but realistic symmetric input-output table (SIOT) of the US economy, for the year 1990, aggregated into three sectors (agriculture, industry and services).

We use input-output data from the OECD STAN data base (http://www.oecd.org/trade/input-outputtables.htm), which are constructed using the same methodology and industry detail for a number of OECD countries. Furthermore, the US input-output tables are supplemented by respective capital flow tables, which make the estimation of the matrices of depreciation coefficients as well as the matrices of capital stock coefficients possible. Thus, the analysis can be extended from a circulating capital model to a more realistic one.

The three-by-three input-output table, the result of an aggregation of the larger 32 industry-detail input-output table of the year 1990, is presented in Table 3.1.[2]

The market prices of all products are taken to be equal to 1; that is to say, the physical unit of measurement of each product is that unit which is worth of a monetary unit. Thus, the matrix of direct technical coefficients, $\mathbf{A}$, is obtained by dividing element-by-element the inputs of each industry by its gross output. The employment coefficients, adjusted for skills of the workers, are estimated by dividing the total wages (adjusted for the self-employed) of each industry by the average workers' compensation. So we finally get

$$\mathbf{A} \cong \begin{pmatrix} 0.198 & 0.080 & 0.004 \\ 0.178 & 0.376 & 0.087 \\ 0.145 & 0.152 & 0.231 \end{pmatrix}, \quad \mathbf{l} \cong [0.005, \ 0.007, \ 0.011]$$

where $\mathbf{l}$ denotes the vector of direct labour coefficients. The matrix of depreciation coefficients is estimated on the basis of the symmetric capital flow table (investment matrix) of the same year. The next step is to create a matrix of shares of capital flows (investment matrix) by dividing the column vector of capital flows of each

[1] This chapter draws on Mariolis et al. (2006, 2013), Tsoulfidis and Rieu (2006), Tsoulfidis and Mariolis (2007), Tsoulfidis (2008), Mariolis and Tsoulfidis (2009), Tsoulfidis and Paitaridis (2009) and Mariolis (2010a, 2015).

[2] For the aggregation, we applied the method suggested by Miller and Blair (2009, pp. 160–164).

Table 3.1 Aggregated input-output table; USA, 1990, millions of dollars

Outputs Inputs	Agriculture	Industry	Services	Total output
Agriculture	81,663.0	288,063.0	163,098.0	412,481.0
Industry	73,595.0	1,346,368.0	320,222.0	3,584,560.0
Services	59,722.0	544,120.0	849,714.0	3,671,139.0
Wages	75,850.4	922,850.3	1,461,812.1	
Total output	412,481.0	3,584,560.0	3,671,139.0	7,668,180.0

industry by the sum of its capital flows, and we get the matrix of investment shares. The latter multiplied by the respective depreciation of each industry gives us the matrix of depreciation. The depreciation matrix is in turn divided by the respective element of the vector of gross output, and we derive the matrix of depreciation coefficients. In our case, we get

$$\mathbf{A}^{\mathrm{D}} \cong \begin{pmatrix} 0.0010 & 0.0003 & 0.0000 \\ 0.1033 & 0.0478 & 0.0819 \\ 0.0266 & 0.0069 & 0.0148 \end{pmatrix}$$

3.2.1 Labour Values and Direct Prices

If we symbolize the vector of values of produced commodities by $\mathbf{v}$, then we will have (see Sect. 2.2.3):

$$\mathbf{v} = \mathbf{l} + \mathbf{vA} + \mathbf{vA}^{\mathrm{D}}$$

or, solving for $\mathbf{v}$,

$$\mathbf{v} = \mathbf{l}[\mathbf{I} - \mathbf{A}^{+}]^{-1}$$

Using the above input-output numerical example, together with the corresponding matrix of depreciation coefficients and the vector of the labour input coefficients, we get

$$\mathbf{v} \cong [0.018,\ \ 0.020,\ \ 0.019]$$

The vector $\mathbf{v}$ gives the quantity of homogenized labour 'embodied or crystallized' in the output of each industry. Subsequently, we transform the above quantities of labour time to direct prices, $\overline{\mathbf{v}}$, by means of the normalization condition

$$\overline{\mathbf{v}} \equiv \left[\left(\mathbf{e}\overline{\mathbf{x}}^{\mathrm{T}}\right)\left(\mathbf{v}\overline{\mathbf{x}}^{\mathrm{T}}\right)^{-1}\right]\mathbf{v} \tag{3.1}$$

where $\bar{\mathbf{x}}^{\mathrm{T}}$ equals the actual gross output vector, while the vector of market prices is identified with the summation vector $\mathbf{e}$. The idea of this normalization is that it equates the gross output in value terms with that of market prices, i.e.

$$\bar{\mathbf{v}}\bar{\mathbf{x}}^{\mathrm{T}} = \mathbf{e}\bar{\mathbf{x}}^{\mathrm{T}}$$

So we get

$$\bar{\mathbf{v}} \cong [0.897,\ \ 1.028,\ \ 0.984]$$

and, thus, observe that the vector of direct prices is close to the vector of market prices (or, indirectly, that the absolute difference between the vector of profits per unit activity level proportional to the vector of direct labour coefficients and the vector of market profits per unit activity level is relatively low).[3] This can be judged by various statistics or measures of deviation,[4] with first the mean absolute deviation (MAD), i.e.

$$\mathrm{MAD} \equiv n^{-1}\sum_{j=1}^{n}\left|\bar{v}_j e_j^{-1} - 1\right| \cong 0.049$$

The mean absolute weighted deviation (MAWD) is another measure, whose difference from the MAD is that the row vector of absolute deviations is multiplied by the column vector of each industry's share in total gross output, i.e.

$$\mathrm{MAWD} \equiv \sum_{j=1}^{n}\left|\bar{v}_j e_j^{-1} - 1\right|\bar{x}_j\left(\mathbf{e}\bar{\mathbf{x}}^{\mathrm{T}}\right)^{-1} \cong 0.026$$

These measures of deviation are independent of the choice of physical measurement units. However, they are *not* numeraire-free. Thus, there is a good reason for preferring the 'd – distance' (Steedman and Tomkins 1998; also see Mariolis and Soklis 2011): Consider two price vectors, $\boldsymbol{\chi}$ and $\boldsymbol{\psi}$, corresponding to the same production technique. The Euclidean angle, θ, between $\mathbf{X} \equiv \boldsymbol{\chi}\hat{\boldsymbol{\psi}}^{-1}$ and $\boldsymbol{\Psi} \equiv \boldsymbol{\psi}\hat{\boldsymbol{\psi}}^{-1} = \mathbf{e}$, is determined by

$$\cos\theta = \left(\|\mathbf{X}\|_2\|\mathbf{e}\|_2\right)^{-1}\left(\mathbf{X}\mathbf{e}^{\mathrm{T}}\right)$$

where $\|\bullet\|_2$ denotes the Euclidean norm of $\bullet$. Now, let d be the Euclidean distance between the unit vectors $\mathbf{X}' \equiv \left(\|\mathbf{X}\|_2\right)^{-1}\mathbf{X}$ and $\boldsymbol{\Psi}' \equiv \left(\|\boldsymbol{\Psi}\|_2\right)^{-1}\boldsymbol{\Psi} = \left(\sqrt{n}\right)^{-1}\mathbf{e}$. Then

[3] See footnote 4 in Chap. 2.

[4] For an exploration of the relationships between alternative measures of deviation, see Chap. 4.

$$d \equiv \|\mathbf{X}' - \boldsymbol{\Psi}'\|_2 = \sqrt{2(1 - \cos\theta)}$$

constitutes a measure of the deviation between $\boldsymbol{\chi}$ and $\boldsymbol{\psi}$, which is independent of both the choice of numeraire and physical measurement units. When all but one of the elements of $\mathbf{X}$ tend to zero, $\cos\theta$ tends to its *theoretically* minimum value of $(\sqrt{n})^{-1}$, and the d – distance tends to its maximum value of

$$D \equiv \sqrt{2\left[1 - (\sqrt{n})^{-1}\right]}$$

It then follows that, in our case, the cosine of the angle between $\overline{\mathbf{v}}\hat{\mathbf{e}}^{-1}$ and $\mathbf{e} = \mathbf{e}\hat{\mathbf{e}}^{-1}$ is approximately equal to 0.998 ($\theta \cong 3.21^0$), $d \cong 0.056$, $D \cong 0.919$ ($n = 3$) and the 'normalized d – distance' (Mariolis and Soklis 2010, p. 94), defined as dD^{-1}, is approximately equal to 0.061.

3.2.2 *Actual Prices and Profit Rates*

Production prices in the presence of depreciation and wages paid in advance can be written as (consider Eq. 2.1a)

$$\mathbf{p} = w\mathbf{l} + \mathbf{p}(\mathbf{A} + \mathbf{A}^{\mathrm{D}}) + r(w\mathbf{l} + \mathbf{pA}) \tag{3.2}$$

For the estimation of 'actual' production prices, we need the commodity vector, $\mathbf{b}^{\mathrm{T}}$, representing the real wage rate. This commodity vector has been estimated in the case of the US economy, for the year 1990, as follows:

$$\mathbf{b} \cong [0.508,\ \ 11.620,\ \ 23.960]$$

($\mathbf{vb}^{\mathrm{T}} \cong 0.704 < 1$; see Eq. 2.15). Substituting $w = \mathbf{pb}^{\mathrm{T}}$ in Eq. 3.2 yields

$$\mathbf{p} = \mathbf{pC} + \mathbf{pA}^{\mathrm{D}} + r\,\mathbf{pC},\ \ \mathbf{C} \equiv \mathbf{b}^{\mathrm{T}}\mathbf{l} + \mathbf{A}$$

or

$$\mathbf{p} = r\,\mathbf{pC}\left[\mathbf{I} - (\mathbf{C} + \mathbf{A}^{\mathrm{D}})\right]^{-1}$$

Consequently, r^{-1} is the P-F eigenvalue of $\mathbf{C}\left[\mathbf{I} - (\mathbf{C} + \mathbf{A}^{\mathrm{D}})\right]^{-1}$, and $\mathbf{p}$ is the corresponding left eigenvector. In terms of our numerical example, we get $r \cong 0.1717\ \left(< (\mathbf{vb}^{\mathrm{T}})^{-1} - 1\right)$; the maximum profit rate is approximately equal to 0.8428, i.e. $\rho \equiv rR^{-1} \cong 0.204$, and

$$\overline{\mathbf{p}} \equiv \left[(\mathbf{e}\overline{\mathbf{x}}^{\mathrm{T}})(\mathbf{p}\overline{\mathbf{x}}^{\mathrm{T}})^{-1}\right]\mathbf{p} \cong [0.952, \ \ 1.083, \ \ 0.924]$$

where $\overline{\mathbf{p}}\overline{\mathbf{x}}^{\mathrm{T}} = \mathbf{e}\overline{\mathbf{x}}^{\mathrm{T}}$. It then follows that:

(i) The deviation of $\overline{\mathbf{p}}$ from market prices is:

- 0.069 in terms of the MAD
- 0.078 in terms of the MAWD
- 0.070 in terms of the $d-$ distance

(ii) The deviation of $\overline{\mathbf{p}}$ from direct prices is:

- 0.058 in terms of the MAD
- 0.057 in terms of the MAWD
- 0.055 in terms of the $d-$ distance

(iii) The percentage deviation of the actual uniform profit rate, $r \cong 0.1717$, from the actual *average* profit rate in terms of market prices

$$r_{\mathrm{m}} \equiv \left(\mathbf{e}\left[\mathbf{I} - \mathbf{A}^{+} - \mathbf{b}^{\mathrm{T}}\mathbf{l}\right]\overline{\mathbf{x}}^{\mathrm{T}}\right)\left(\mathbf{e}\mathbf{C}\overline{\mathbf{x}}^{\mathrm{T}}\right)^{-1} \cong 0.1691$$

is almost 1.54 %, while its absolute percentage deviation from the actual average profit rate in terms of direct prices, $r_{\mathrm{d}} \cong 0.1711$, is almost 0.35 %.[5]

(iv) The $d-$ distance between the left P-F eigenvector of the matrix of vertically integrated technical coefficients, $\mathbf{H}^{+} = \mathbf{A}[\mathbf{I} - \mathbf{A}^{+}]^{-1}$, and $\overline{\mathbf{v}}$ is 0.298. Thus, it could be said that the system under consideration rather deviates from the equal value compositions of capital case (see Sects. 2.2.1.1 and 2.2.1.3).

3.2.3 Wage-Production Price-Profit Rate Curves

Figure 3.1 displays the production price-labour value ratios, in terms of Sraffa's Standard commodity (SCC), i.e.

$$\mathbf{p}\hat{\mathbf{v}}^{-1} = (1-\rho)\mathbf{v}[\mathbf{I} - \rho\mathbf{J}^{+}]^{-1}\hat{\mathbf{v}}^{-1}$$

as functions of the relative profit rate, $0 \leq \rho \leq 1$ (see Sect. 2.4.1), and their Taylor linear approximations about $\rho = 0$, i.e.

$$\mathbf{p}\hat{\mathbf{v}}^{-1} \approx \mathbf{e} + \rho\left(\mathbf{v}\mathbf{J}^{+}\hat{\mathbf{v}}^{-1} - \mathbf{e}\right)$$

[5] On the basis of an elegant proof, Shaikh (1984, pp. 55–59 and 80–82) argues that, in actual single-product economies, these deviations should be relatively low.

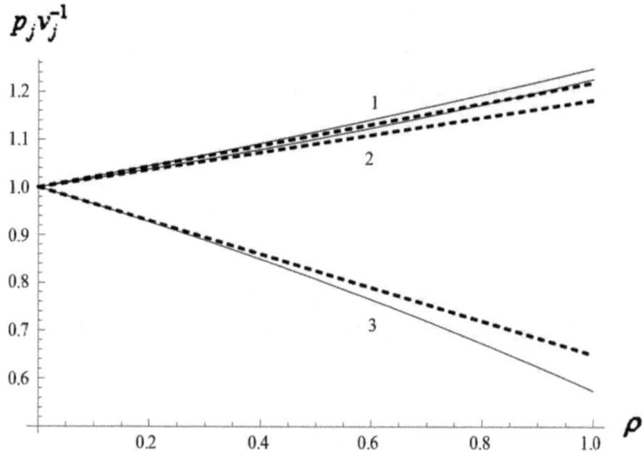

Fig. 3.1 The production price-relative profit rate curves in terms of SSC; USA, 1990, $n = 3$

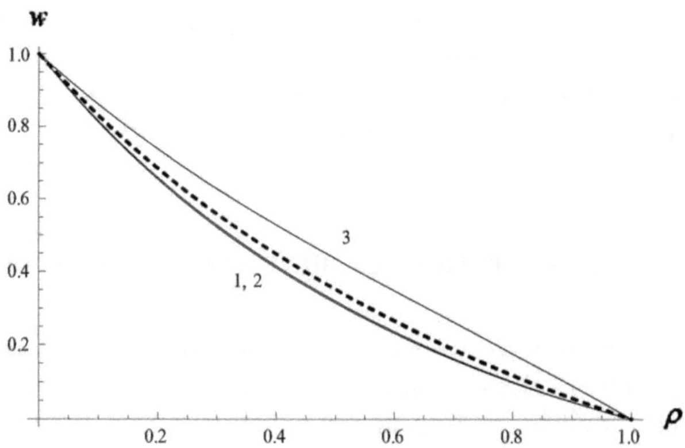

Fig. 3.2 Wage-relative profit rate curves; USA, 1990, $n = 3$

(depicted by dotted lines). Finally, Fig. 3.2 displays the wage-relative profit rate curves, in terms of the individuals commodities (the curves in terms of commodities 1 and 2 are almost indistinguishable from each other), i.e.

$$w = (1 + \rho R)^{-1}\left(1 - \rho\, \mathbf{p}\mathbf{J}_j^{+} v_j^{-1}\right)$$

and the Sraffian curve, i.e.

$$w^{\mathrm{S}} = (1 + \rho R)^{-1}(1 - \rho)$$

(depicted by a dotted line).[6] It then follows that (i) the price curves are almost linear, (ii) $\dot{k}_{\mathbf{z}} < 0$ (positive price Wicksell effects)[7] and (iii) the mean of the absolute percentage deviation of w from w^{S}, i.e.

$$\int_0^1 \left| w\left(w^{\mathrm{S}}\right)^{-1} - 1 \right| d\rho = \int_0^1 \left| \rho(1-\rho)^{-1}\left(1 - \mathbf{p}\mathbf{J}_j^{+} v_j^{-1}\right) \right| d\rho$$

is in the range of 9.2 % (commodity 2) to 28.0 % (commodity 3), which indicates that the price effect could be considered as weak and, therefore, for relatively low values of ρ, we can safely write

$$w \approx (1+\rho R)^{-1}\left(1 - \rho \mathbf{v}\mathbf{J}_j^{+} v_j^{-1}\right)$$

For instance, at the actual value of ρ ($\cong$0.204), the relative error in this approximation is in the range of 0.89 % (commodity 3) to 1.3 % (commodity 1), while at $\rho = 0.50$ or 0.80, this error is in the range of 9.1 % or 61.7 % (commodity 3) to 12.9 % or 85.7 % (commodity 1), respectively.

3.3 Price Estimates for Various Actual Economies

In what follows, we provide estimates of direct and actual production prices for a number of countries using, in most cases, a circulating capital model with wages paid in advance (the details of which have been developed in Chap. 2).[8] It should be noted that, throughout this chapter (unless stated otherwise), production prices are normalized with the use of SSC and the actual gross output vector as follows:

$$\mathbf{p}\bar{\mathbf{s}}^{\mathrm{T}} = \bar{\mathbf{v}}\bar{\mathbf{s}}^{\mathrm{T}}$$

where

$$\bar{\mathbf{s}} \equiv \left[\left(\bar{\mathbf{v}}\mathbf{x}^{\mathrm{T}}\right)\left(\bar{\mathbf{v}}\mathbf{x}_{\mathbf{A}1}^{\mathrm{T}}\right)^{-1}\right]\mathbf{x}_{\mathbf{A}1}^{\mathrm{T}}$$

These normalizations and Eq. 3.1 imply that

---

[6] See footnote 12 in Chap. 2.

[7] The wage curve in terms of commodity 3 switches from convex to concave at $\rho \cong 0.730$. If wages are paid *ex post*, then this curve is strictly concave to the origin (negative price Wicksell effect), while the other two curves are strictly convex.

[8] At the time of this research, the SIOTs of the Greek economy were available for the years 1988 through 1998. For the available data as well as the construction of relevant variables, see the Appendix 1 at the end of this chapter.

$$\mathbf{p}\bar{\mathbf{s}}^{\mathrm{T}} = \bar{\mathbf{v}}\bar{\mathbf{s}}^{\mathrm{T}} = \bar{\mathbf{v}}\bar{\mathbf{x}}^{\mathrm{T}} = \mathbf{e}\bar{\mathbf{x}}^{\mathrm{T}}$$

and, therefore, enable the expression of direct, production and market prices in common terms (Ochoa 1984, Chap. 4; Shaikh 1998, pp. 227–229).

3.3.1 Greece

The estimates that we got in the case of the Greek economy for the period 1988–1997 are displayed in Table 3.2 (DP, direct prices; PP, production prices; MP, market prices), which shows the MAD, MAWD, d – distance and the actual, maximum and relative profit rates ($n = 19$ and, therefore, $D \cong 1.241$). Thus, we conclude that:

(i) In terms of the d – distance, the deviation of actual production prices from market prices (from direct prices) does not vary widely over the years and is in the range of 0.21–0.29 (of 0.08–0.10), while the deviation of direct prices from market prices is in the range of 0.21–0.27.
(ii) The actual relative profit rate is in the range of 0.23–0.27.

3.3.2 Japan

Similar are the results with respect to Japan that we have data collected consistently over a fairly long period of time. In particular, the available data refer to the benchmark years 1970, 1975, 1980, 1985 and 1990, and the estimates are displayed in Table 3.3 ($n = 33$ and, therefore, $D \cong 1.285$).

3.3.3 Canada, China, Korea, UK and USA

Similar are, also, the results with respect to a number of quite diverse economies, that is, Canada (1997; $n = 34$ and $D \cong 1.287$), People's Republic of China (1997; $n = 38$ and $D \cong 1.294$), UK (1990; $n = 33$ for both circulating and fixed capital), Republic of Korea (for the years 1995 and 2000; $n = 27$ and $D \cong 1.271$ for both circulating and fixed capital) and, finally, USA (1990; $n = 32$ and $D \cong 1.283$ for both circulating and fixed capital). The estimates are displayed in Table 3.4,[9] while Fig. 3.3 is associated with the results of Tables 3.2, 3.3 and 3.4 and the circulating

[9] It is observed that, for the case of the US economy, the results differ significantly from those of the aggregated model (reported in Sect. 3.2).

Table 3.2 Measures of price deviations and profit rates; Greece, 1988–1997

Years	1988	1989	1990	1991	1992	1993	1994	1995	1996	1997	Measures
DP vs. MP	0.195	0.184	0.214	0.209	0.204	0.229	0.228	0.200	0.216	0.265	MAD
	0.221	0.215	0.212	0.196	0.200	0.210	0.206	0.168	0.189	0.191	MAWD
	0.227	0.219	0.229	0.226	0.216	0.212	0.216	0.236	0.217	0.273	*d*
PP vs. MP	0.178	0.174	0.205	0.200	0.196	0.220	0.231	0.208	0.204	0.250	MAD
	0.198	0.196	0.205	0.186	0.198	0.208	0.201	0.178	0.183	0.191	MAWD
	0.228	0.219	0.235	0.227	0.219	0.208	0.242	0.251	0.228	0.287	*d*
PP vs. DP	0.075	0.082	0.076	0.084	0.083	0.064	0.080	0.075	0.074	0.093	MAD
	0.081	0.081	0.060	0.078	0.087	0.079	0.077	0.077	0.089	0.085	MAWD
	0.093	0.098	0.090	0.100	0.097	0.079	0.089	0.090	0.089	0.094	*d*
r	0.211	0.220	0.218	0.243	0.275	0.236	0.254	0.230	0.247	0.238	
R	0.817	0.851	0.874	0.917	1.076	1.026	1.006	0.903	0.977	0.882	
$\rho \equiv rR^{-1}$	0.258	0.259	0.249	0.265	0.255	0.230	0.252	0.254	0.252	0.270	

Table 3.3 Measures of price deviations and profit rates; Japan, 1970–1990

Years	1970	1975	1980	1985	1990	Measures
DP vs. MP	0.271	0.171	0.172	0.147	0.127	MAD
	0.286	0.202	0.197	0.178	0.154	MAWD
	0.371	0.233	0.226	0.185	0.171	d
PP vs. MP	0.268	0.160	0.153	0.130	0.113	MAD
	0.266	0.173	0.155	0.141	0.122	MAWD
	0.323	0.216	0.212	0.181	0.161	d
PP vs. DP	0.112	0.089	0.107	0.117	0.115	MAD
	0.138	0.118	0.142	0.149	0.149	MAWD
	0.125	0.110	0.135	0.156	0.141	d
r	0.240	0.230	0.278	0.294	0.279	
R	0.788	0.770	0.788	0.795	0.842	
$\rho \equiv rR^{-1}$	0.305	0.298	0.344	0.371	0.331	

capital case and shows that there is a significant power function regression between ρ and the normalized distance, dD^{-1}, between production and direct prices.

3.4 Steedman's Polynomial Approximation

Tables 3.5 and 3.6 are associated with the Greek (for the year 1997) and Japanese (for the year 1980) economies, respectively, and present the results of Steedman's (1999) polynomial approximation, i.e.

$$\mathbf{p} = (1-\rho)\bar{\mathbf{v}}\sum_{h=0}^{+\infty}(\rho\mathbf{J})^h$$

(consider Eq. 2.51). The first two columns show the direct prices and the actual production prices,[10] whereas the remaining columns refer to the successive approximation of actual production prices. More specifically, column A gives the term $(1-\rho)\bar{\mathbf{v}}$, column B the term $(1-\rho)\bar{\mathbf{v}}[\mathbf{I}+\rho\mathbf{J}]$, column C the term $(1-\rho)\bar{\mathbf{v}}\left[\mathbf{I}+\rho\mathbf{J}+(\rho\mathbf{J})^2\right]$ and so forth for the column D. The deviations of these approximations from the estimated production prices, as measured by the MAD, are shown in the last row of the tables.

We thus observe that the approximation in column A displays a MAD equal to 23.4 % or 32.1 %, respectively, which drops sharply in column B to 5.9 % or 10.5 %. Clearly, the approximation with just a few terms is pretty accurate and depends crucially on the relatively low values of the relative profit rate,

[10] These estimates also measure interindustry 'pure forward linkages' (consider Eqs. 2.12 and 2.13).

Table 3.4 Measures of price deviations and profit rates; China, Canada, UK, Korea and USA

Countries and years	Canada 1997	China 1997	UK 1990	Korea 1995	Korea 2000	USA 1990	Measures
DP vs. MP	0.133	0.183	0.222	0.128	0.130	0.125	MAD
	0.149	0.160	0.186	0.131	0.143	0.094	MAWD
	0.180	0.196	0.285	0.182	0.167	0.163	*d*
PP vs. MP	0.126	0.170	0.199	0.151	0.152	0.126	MAD
	0.125	0.112	0.168	0.152	0.164	0.108	MAWD
	0.199	0.154	0.249	0.176	0.176	0.157	*d*
			Fixed capital	Fixed capital	Fixed capital	Fixed capital	Fixed capital
			0.169	0.156	0.174	0.139	MAD
			0.179	0.152	0.181	0.137	MAWD
			0.214	0.190	0.207	0.187	*d*
PP vs. DP	0.100	0.112	0.041	0.148	0.148	0.046	MAD
	0.098	0.109	0.045	0.161	0.173	0.061	MAWD
	0.140	0.114	0.055	0.179	0.177	0.059	*d*
			Fixed capital	Fixed capital	Fixed capital	Fixed capital	Fixed capital
			0.135	0.146	0.151	0.097	MAD
			0.176	0.151	0.154	0.129	MAWD
			0.210	0.174	0.174	0.127	*d*
r	0.250	0.220	0.168	0.268	0.253	0.167	
			Fixed capital	Fixed capital	Fixed capital	Fixed capital	
			0.092	0.123	0.133	0.085	
R	0.737	0.568	0.870	0.594	0.556	0.814	
			Fixed capital	Fixed capital	Fixed capital	Fixed capital	
			0.326	0.257	0.278	0.343	
$\rho \equiv rR^{-1}$	0.339	0.387	0.193	0.452	0.456	0.205	
			Fixed capital	Fixed capital	Fixed capital	Fixed capital	
			0.281	0.480	0.481	0.249	

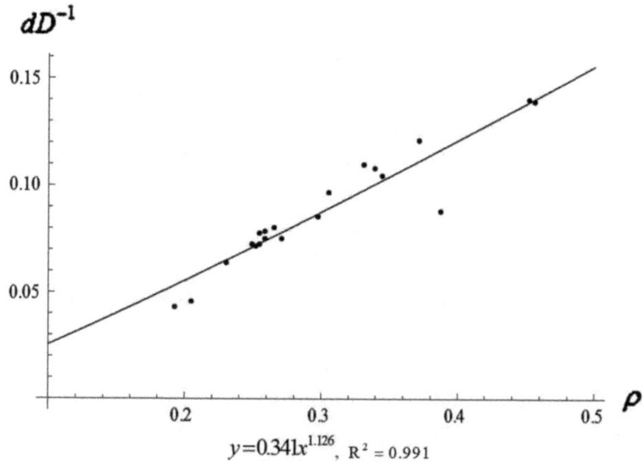

Fig. 3.3 Normalized d – distance, between production and direct prices, versus relative profit rate; circulating capital case

Table 3.5 Approximation of actual production prices; Greece, 1997

	Industries	DP	PP	A	B	C	D
1	Agriculture	1.034	0.909	0.755	0.872	0.876	0.876
2	Fish and fishing	1.580	1.302	1.152	1.266	1.268	1.268
3	Coal mining and oil	0.858	0.786	0.626	0.746	0.747	0.748
4	Other mining	1.215	1.039	0.886	1.000	1.001	1.001
5	Food, beverage and tobacco	1.073	1.121	0.783	1.046	1.072	1.077
6	Textiles	1.129	1.079	0.824	1.018	1.026	1.027
7	Wood and wood products	1.299	1.200	0.947	1.140	1.146	1.146
8	Pulp, paper and print	1.434	1.382	1.046	1.297	1.310	1.311
9	Petroleum refineries	0.845	0.924	0.617	0.853	0.878	0.882
10	Chemicals, rubber and plastic products	1.425	1.522	1.040	1.387	1.425	1.432
11	Other nonmetallic mineral products	1.023	0.985	0.746	0.929	0.932	0.933
12	Basic metals	1.185	1.369	0.864	1.222	1.247	1.250
13	Fabricated metals	1.338	1.385	0.976	1.263	1.280	1.282
14	Machin., radio, TV, etc.	2.134	2.086	1.557	1.944	1.968	1.970
15	Utilities	0.877	0.777	0.639	0.744	0.747	0.747
16	Construction	0.931	0.967	0.679	0.890	0.895	0.895
17	Wholesale and retail trade	0.784	0.687	0.572	0.660	0.662	0.662
18	Hotels and restaurants	0.721	0.687	0.526	0.649	0.652	0.652
19	Transportation and communications	1.195	0.998	0.871	0.969	0.970	0.970
MAD				0.234	0.059	0.050	0.049

Table 3.6 Approximation of actual production prices; Japan, 1980

	Industries	DP	PP	A	B	C	D
1	Agriculture, forestry and fishing	1.536	1.264	1.008	1.190	1.195	1.196
2	Mining and quarrying	0.610	0.514	0.400	0.482	0.482	0.482
3	Food, beverages and tobacco	1.100	1.123	0.722	1.017	1.039	1.041
4	Textiles, apparel and leather	1.381	1.361	0.906	1.221	1.240	1.242
5	Wood products and furniture	1.318	1.275	0.864	1.164	1.182	1.183
6	Paper and printing	1.130	1.167	0.741	1.028	1.056	1.061
7	Industrial chemicals	0.838	1.009	0.550	0.845	0.871	0.876
8	Drugs and medicines	0.812	0.798	0.533	0.715	0.718	0.718
9	Petroleum and coal products	0.560	0.599	0.367	0.540	0.559	0.563
10	Rubber and plastic products	1.011	1.057	0.663	0.919	0.934	0.936
11	Nonmetallic mineral products	0.976	0.927	0.640	0.844	0.850	0.851
12	Iron and steel	0.732	0.992	0.480	0.777	0.826	0.839
13	Nonferrous metals	0.721	0.822	0.473	0.709	0.727	0.729
14	Metal products	0.946	0.988	0.620	0.846	0.861	0.863
15	Non-electrical machinery	1.029	1.080	0.675	0.930	0.944	0.945
16	Office and computing machinery	0.940	0.969	0.616	0.848	0.854	0.855
17	Electrical apparatus, n.e.c.	0.934	0.989	0.612	0.856	0.863	0.863
18	Radio, TV, and commun. eqp.	0.891	0.939	0.585	0.819	0.827	0.828
19	Shipbuilding and repairing	1.041	1.055	0.683	0.919	0.928	0.929
20	Other transport	0.994	1.046	0.652	0.904	0.912	0.912
21	Motor vehicles	0.861	1.048	0.565	0.863	0.876	0.877
22	Aircraft	1.075	1.083	0.705	0.961	0.972	0.972
23	Professional goods	1.019	0.972	0.668	0.873	0.877	0.877
24	Other manufacturing	1.084	1.079	0.711	0.965	0.971	0.971
25	Electricity gas and water	0.608	0.597	0.399	0.542	0.548	0.548
26	Construction	1.105	1.038	0.725	0.938	0.942	0.942
27	Wholesale and retail trade	1.218	0.903	0.799	0.877	0.878	0.878
28	Restaurants and hotels	1.245	1.096	0.817	1.020	1.027	1.027
29	Transport and storage	1.268	1.087	0.832	1.012	1.016	1.016
30	Communication	0.964	0.711	0.632	0.689	0.689	0.689
31	Finance and insurance	0.926	0.695	0.608	0.673	0.673	0.673
32	Real estate and business services	0.585	0.493	0.384	0.461	0.461	0.461
33	Commun. soc. and pers. services	1.026	0.893	0.673	0.823	0.825	0.825
	MAD			0.321	0.105	0.094	0.092

i.e. $\rho \cong 0.270$ or 0.344 (see Tables 3.2 and 3.3), which are much *less* than 0.500 (see Sect. 2.3.2).[11]

[11] The results for the other years were similar, and we decided not to report them for reasons of economy in space.

It should be stressed that our findings are absolutely compatible with those of many other empirical studies.[12] Thus, it could be stated that, in actual single-product systems or, to be precise, in their SIOT simulacra:

(i) The actual production price (the market price)-labour value deviation is not less than 0.060 (than 0.070) and not considerably greater than 0.200 (than 0.370) in terms of the $d-$ distance. Remarkable exceptions can only be found in Steedman and Tomkins (1998, p. 383) and Soklis (2014, p. 49), where there are production price-labour value and market price-labour value deviations, respectively, even greater than 0.650 (also see Trigg 2002, which, however, uses an alternative analytic framework).
(ii) The actual relative profit rate is not less than 0.17 and not considerably greater than 0.4 (than 0.5), provided that wages are paid at the beginning (end) of the production period. Taking into account that ρ is no greater than the share of profits in the Sraffian Standard system (SSS; see Sect. 2.2.1.3), this seems to be in accordance with many well-known estimations of the share of profits (approximated by the net operating surplus) in actual economies. For instance, Ellis and Smith (2007) find that the share of profits in a sample of 20 OECD countries (for the period 1960–2005) only in a few years and a few countries has slightly exceeded the 40 % and, typically, fluctuates a few percentage points around an average of 30 %.[13]
(iii) The deviations of actual prices from labour values are not *too* sensitive to the type of measure used for their evaluation.

It is added that there are two empirical studies, based on SIOTs of the French and Swedish economies (for the years 1995 and 2005), which indicate that there exist vectors of commodity i values (see Eq. 2.9) that provide closer approximations to actual production and market prices than labour values (Soklis 2009a, 2014). The rather few empirical studies which are based on supply and use tables (SUTs) and, therefore, on models of *joint* production (see Eqs. 2.1b and 2.16b) indicate that[14]:

(i) The SUT simulacra of actual economies do not necessarily have the usual properties of single-product systems. For instance, the so-called vector of additive labour values, $\mathbf{v_B} \equiv \mathbf{l}[\mathbf{B} - \mathbf{A}]^{-1}$, and/or the matrices $[\mathbf{B} - \mathbf{A}]^{-1}$ contain

---

[12] See, e.g. Hejl et al. (1967), Fink (1981), Ochoa (1984, Chap. 7), Shaikh (1984, 1998, 2012, 2016), Petrović (1987, 1988), Valtukh (1987, Chap. 4), Bienenfeld (1988), Cockshott et al. (1995), Chilcote (1997, Chaps. 6 and 7), Cockshott and Cottrell (1997), Tsoulfidis and Maniatis (2002), Val'tukh (2005), Zachariah (2006), Sánchez and Ferràndez (2010), Mariolis and Soklis (2011), Flaschel et al. (2012), Mariolis et al. (2012, pp. 58–62), Flaschel et al. (2013), Fröhlich (2013), Nakajima (2013), Iliadi et al. (2014), Li (2014a) and Sánchez and Montibeler (2015).

[13] Also see, e.g. Harvie (2000), Izyumov and Alterman (2005), Yu and Feng (2007), Zachariah (2009), Karabarbounis and Neiman (2013) and Piketty (2013, Chap. 6).

[14] See Soklis (2006, 2011, 2012, Chap. 6, 2015), Mariolis and Soklis (2007, 2010, 2014), Wirkierman (2012) and Garbellini and Wirkierman (2014). For the SUTs, see the Appendix 2 at the end of this chapter, which is based on Mariolis and Soklis (2010).

negative elements, while positive 'surplus value' ($\mathbf{v_B b}^T < 1$) coexists with economically insignificant [r, $\mathbf{p}$].[15]

(ii) The deviations of market prices from additive labour values and actual production prices are considerably greater than those estimated on the basis of SIOTs. For instance, the normalized d – distance between market prices and additive labour values estimated from the 58×58 SUT of the Greek economy for the year 1995 is approximately equal to $0.870/1.318 \cong 0.660$ (Mariolis and Soklis 2010, pp. 93–94) and, therefore, considerably greater than the normalized d – distance between market prices and labour values estimated from the relevant 19×19 SIOT, which is approximately equal to $0.236/1.241 \cong 0.190$ (see Table 3.2). It goes without saying that such findings deserve further investigation.

(iii) There exist vectors of additive commodity values that provide closer approximations to actual production and market prices than additive labour values.

3.5 Intertemporal Price Comparisons

In the classical tradition, technological change takes place after the passage of sufficiently long time, and it diffuses across industries quite rapidly, although not necessarily uniformly. As a consequence, one does not expect sweeping changes in the structure of the economy from 1 year to the next.

The graphs in Fig. 3.4 depict the evolution of direct prices and actual production prices of the Greek economy, over the period 1988–1997, for each of the 19 industries.

The temporal paths of production prices to direct prices show that the ranking, in the majority of cases, remains the same over the years. However, for industries 6, 8, 14 and 18, the ranking changes. A more careful examination reveals that the two prices are very close to each other, and as technological change does not diffuse absolutely uniformly across industries, the (re-)switching of ranking of the two kinds of prices is entirely possible.

Similar are the results for the Japanese economy, which in the interest of brevity and clarity of presentation we display in a single Table 3.7 instead of a set of 33 graphs.[16] The interested reader may discern the rough concordance in the movement between direct and actual production prices, although there are deviations from this 'rule'.

It need hardly be emphasized that these findings are only tentative, and before we provide more definitive answers with respect to temporal price changes, more

[15] Soklis (2012) examines 79 SUTs of 11, quite diverse, economies and detects that the matrices $[\mathbf{B} - \mathbf{A}]^{-1}$ contain negative elements. Consequently, all those systems are not 'all-productive'.

[16] The industries are indicated in Table 3.6.

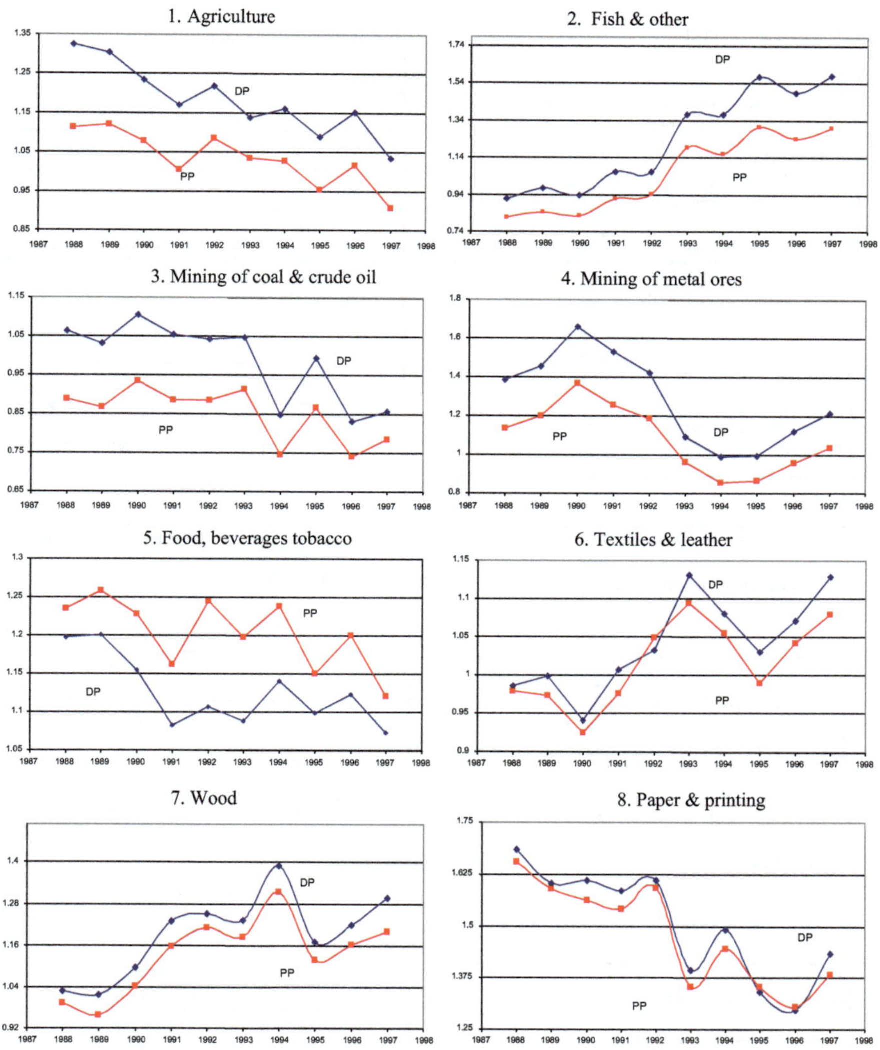

Fig. 3.4 (continued)

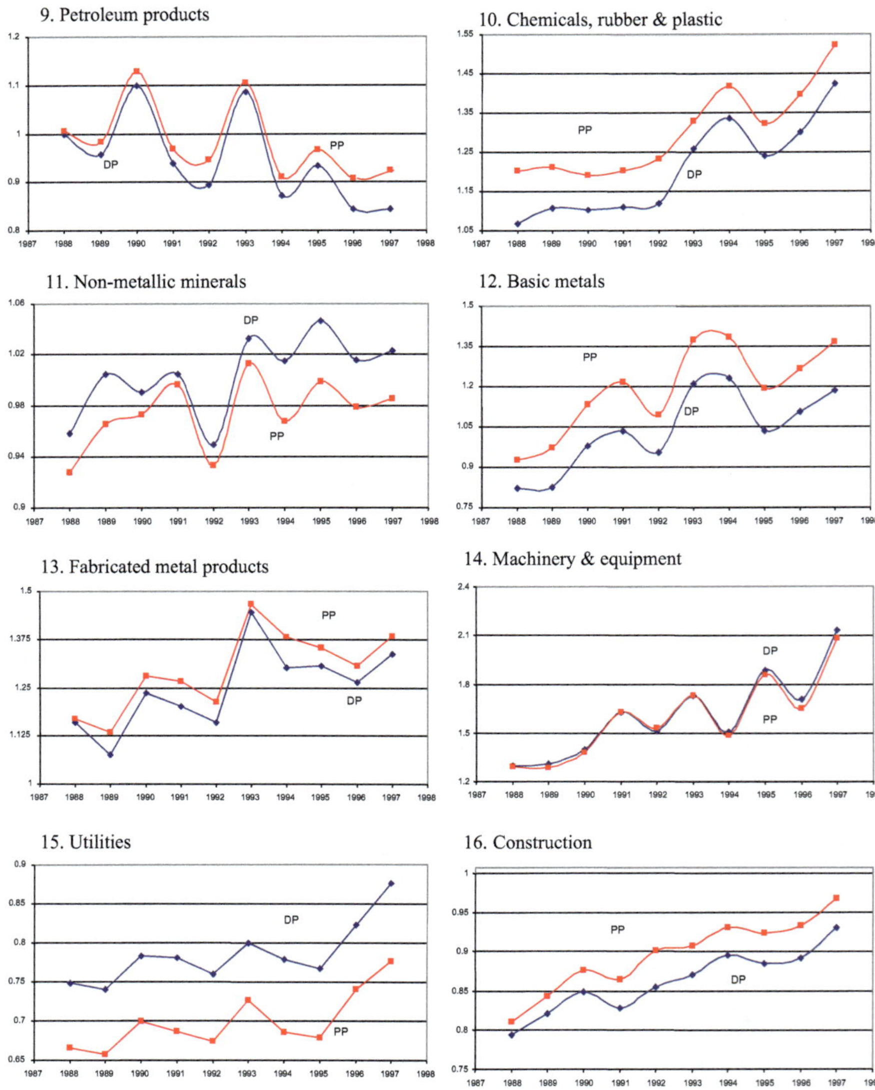

Fig. 3.4 (continued)

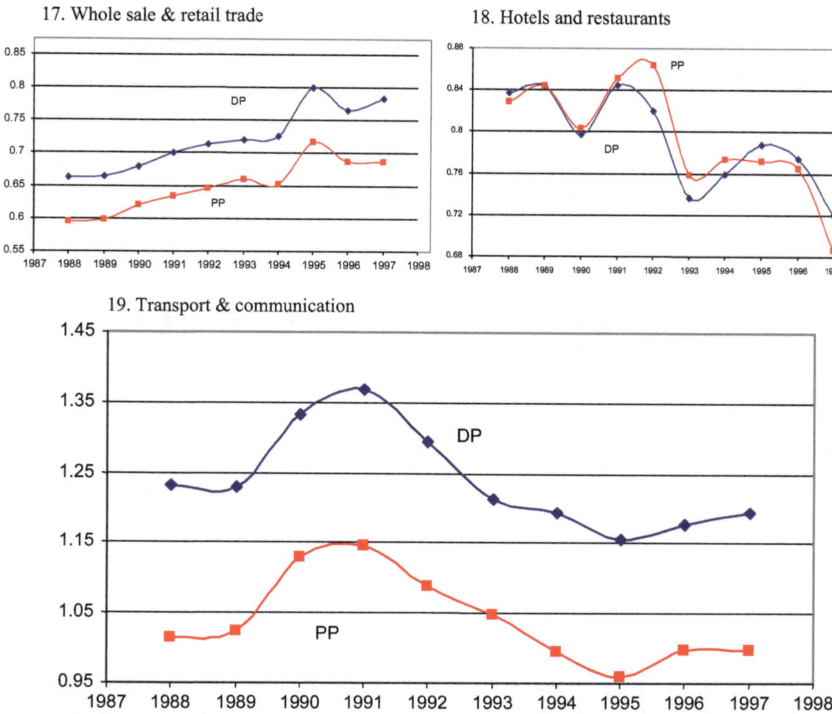

Fig. 3.4 Direct prices and actual production prices in 19 industries; Greek economy, 1988–1997

data are needed spanning a longer time period. Meanwhile, there are 'a few' issues which must be resolved. The available input-output tables for the Greek and Japanese economies are expressed in current prices, whereas the price indices for the individual commodities, which are needed for the derivation of physical input-output coefficients, are not currently available. Consequently, some caution must be exercised in the interpretation of the above results, especially in the face of significant changes in relative market prices. The reader interested in more relevant discussions may consult, among others, Han and Schefold (2006, pp. 750–752) and Miller and Blair (2009, pp. 307–308).

Table 3.7 Direct prices and production prices; Japan, 1970–1990

	DP	PP	DP	PP	DP	PP	DP	PP	DP	PP
Industry	1970	1970	1975	1975	1980	1980	1985	1985	1990	1990
1	2.399	1.790	1.715	1.392	1.536	1.264	1.314	1.073	1.381	1.159
2	0.882	0.698	0.702	0.581	0.610	0.514	0.868	0.687	0.971	0.866
3	1.490	1.410	1.244	1.247	1.100	1.123	1.023	1.039	1.015	1.052
4	1.333	1.292	1.343	1.314	1.381	1.361	1.320	1.301	1.228	1.220
5	1.632	1.507	1.305	1.246	1.318	1.275	1.190	1.124	1.218	1.186
6	0.975	0.956	1.063	1.064	1.130	1.167	1.104	1.074	1.038	1.020
7	0.692	0.713	0.832	0.921	0.838	1.009	0.806	0.955	0.802	0.931
8	0.566	0.537	0.707	0.667	0.812	0.798	0.802	0.760	0.800	0.807
9	0.515	0.501	0.631	0.645	0.560	0.599	0.698	0.720	0.653	0.724
10	0.873	0.845	0.975	0.959	1.011	1.057	0.968	1.001	0.911	0.985
11	0.887	0.790	0.942	0.877	0.976	0.927	0.934	0.862	0.943	0.916
12	0.635	0.832	0.751	0.982	0.732	0.992	0.800	1.122	0.806	1.070
13	0.773	0.798	0.833	0.849	0.721	0.822	0.873	1.004	0.900	1.066
14	0.822	0.824	0.912	0.909	0.946	0.988	0.984	1.026	0.969	1.015
15	0.840	0.865	0.981	0.989	1.029	1.080	0.953	0.971	0.944	0.992
16	0.771	0.797	1.004	0.983	0.940	0.969	0.900	0.920	0.874	0.988
17	0.795	0.815	0.941	0.940	0.934	0.989	0.930	0.970	0.925	0.995
18	0.791	0.813	0.943	0.932	0.891	0.939	0.876	0.928	0.900	0.992
19	0.942	0.936	0.979	0.982	1.041	1.055	1.083	1.100	1.020	1.093
20	0.863	0.886	0.963	0.973	0.994	1.046	0.968	1.088	0.964	1.179
21	0.746	0.837	0.851	0.936	0.861	1.048	0.886	1.122	0.952	1.264
22	0.706	0.679	1.059	1.032	1.075	1.083	0.840	0.925	0.950	1.010
23	0.926	0.877	0.996	0.920	1.019	0.972	1.000	0.952	0.996	0.979
24	1.072	1.022	1.068	1.039	1.084	1.079	0.988	0.996	1.003	1.033

25	0.516	0.443	0.634	0.599	0.608	0.597	0.616	0.585	0.633	0.619
26	1.005	0.959	0.992	0.938	1.105	1.038	1.155	1.042	1.092	1.022
27	1.075	0.812	1.171	0.902	1.218	0.903	1.322	0.952	1.310	1.003
28	1.337	1.211	1.231	1.092	1.245	1.096	1.229	1.042	1.211	1.079
29	1.062	0.853	1.242	1.046	1.268	1.087	1.286	1.014	1.124	0.991
30	0.893	0.639	1.042	0.783	0.964	0.711	0.920	0.658	0.969	0.732
31	0.714	0.528	0.818	0.635	0.926	0.695	0.928	0.682	1.029	0.806
32	0.489	0.431	0.532	0.472	0.585	0.493	0.643	0.518	0.679	0.564
33	0.862	0.726	0.926	0.818	1.026	0.893	0.998	0.834	1.048	0.863

3.6 Production-Direct Price Differences and Capital-Intensity Differences

The next logical step is to test whether the size differences in production-direct price deviations are proportional to the size differences between capital intensities from the economy-wide average (see Sect. 2.4). The first four columns of Table 3.8 refer to the 34 Canadian industries, where in the first column we display the number of each of the industries. The second column refers to the differences between actual production prices and direct prices, $p_j - \overline{v}_j$, where

$$\mathbf{p} = (1 + r)w\overline{\mathbf{v}}[\mathbf{I} - r\mathbf{H}]^{-1}$$

The signs of these differences are absolutely consistent with the difference in the industry's direct capital intensity (DCI), estimated as $\mathbf{pA}_j\overline{l}_j^{-1}$, where $\overline{\mathbf{l}} \equiv \left[\left(\mathbf{e}\overline{\mathbf{x}}^{\mathrm{T}}\right)\left(\mathbf{v}\overline{\mathbf{x}}^{\mathrm{T}}\right)^{-1}\right]\mathbf{l}$, from the average direct capital intensity (ADCI), estimated as $\mathbf{pA}\overline{\mathbf{x}}\left(\overline{\mathbf{l}}\overline{\mathbf{x}}\right)^{-1} \cong 20.28$ (third column). And the same holds true with regard to the differences of the vertically integrated capital intensities (VCI), estimated as $\mathbf{pH}_j\overline{v}_j^{-1}$, from the average vertically integrated capital intensity (AVCI), estimated as $\mathbf{pH}\overline{\mathbf{x}}(\overline{\mathbf{v}}\overline{\mathbf{x}})^{-1} \cong 10.40$ (fourth column). In the same Table 3.8, we display the relevant results for the Chinese economy (ADCI = 1.44 and AVCI = 1.57). With the exception of the industries 3, 5, 6 and 28 (of the industries 5 and 6), the differences $p_j - \overline{v}_j$ are directly related to those in direct (vertically integrated) capital intensities.

Figure 3.5 portrays the results from the two countries under examination. In all graphs, we plot on the vertical axis the differences of actual production prices-direct prices against the differences of the capital intensities from the average.

We finally apply the same exercise using data from the US economy for the year 1990. Hence, unlike the case of Canada and China, we test two cases: the first with circulating capital and the second with fixed capital. Such a comparison will be useful in the sense that it will allow us to evaluate the difference that capital stocks make in the various estimations. The results are displayed in Table 3.9 ($\mathrm{ADCI_C} \cong 83$, $\mathrm{AVCI_C} \cong 86$, $\mathrm{ADCI_F} \cong 178$ and $\mathrm{AVCI_F} \cong 195$).[17]

In Fig. 3.6, we plot the data of the Table 3.9 for the circulating capital case. The left-hand-side graph is associated with the direct capital intensities and displays a rather poor fit, which might be attributed to the presence of an obvious outlier of

[17] The subscript C (F) refers to the case of circulating (fixed) capital.

Table 3.8 Actual production price-direct price differences and differences of the actual capital intensities of industries from the economy's average; Canada, 1997, and China, 1997

Canada Industries	$p_j - \bar{v}_j$	DCI – ADCI	VCI – AVCI	China Industries	$p_j - \bar{v}_j$	DCI –ADCI	VCI –AVCI
1	0.08	11.45	7.01	1	−0.37	−1.04	−0.94
2	0.01	5.01	1.26	2	−0.09	−0.53	−0.27
3	0.18	57.61	18.82	3	−0.06	3.61	−0.06
4	0.04	9.28	4.47	4	0.03	1.18	0.33
5	0.14	31.63	13.12	5	−0.03	1.07	0.078
6	0.06	11.05	5.67	6	−0.004	0.53	0.17
7	0.16	188.02	22.22	7	0.06	5.54	0.53
8	0.11	38.90	15.53	8	0.08	1.99	0.61
9	0.06	10.49	6.73	9	0.02	1.52	0.30
10	0.03	8.52	3.10	10	0.10	2.16	0.69
11	0.12	34.13	14.07	11	0.02	0.62	0.27
12	0.06	6.74	5.50	12	0.10	1.96	0.68
13	0.08	14.46	8.77	13	0.12	3.24	0.82
14	0.61	123.33	54.60	14	0.10	1.49	0.71
15	0.09	16.43	9.27	15	0.08	0.88	0.60
16	0.13	31.82	14.17	16	0.20	3.08	1.27
17	0.36	94.98	38.90	17	0.15	2.44	0.99
18	−0.09	−10.25	−7.73	18	0.16	1.98	1.07
19	0.03	6.82	3.38	19	0.04	0.30	0.39
20	0.14	36.18	14.66	20	0.16	2.38	1.07
21	0.03	5.81	3.22	21	0.09	0.87	0.61
22	−0.03	−6.74	−5.82	22	−0.07	−0.38	−0.13
23	0.01	2.58	0.56	23	0.14	1.82	0.92
24	−0.13	−12.25	−11.79	24	0.03	0.99	0.36
25	−0.03	−4.81	−2.39	25	0.01	0.60	0.22
26	−0.03	−2.60	−3.02	26	0.01	0.25	0.23
27	−0.06	−6.92	−6.83	27	−0.10	−0.56	−0.30
28	−0.03	−1.34	−4.17	28	−0.08	0.26	−0.19
29	−0.11	−10.24	−10.20	29	−0.10	−0.65	−0.32
30	−0.11	−10.69	−10.51	30	0.02	0.31	0.36
31	−0.08	−4.69	−7.21	31	−0.08	−0.56	−0.32
32	−0.25	−17.53	−17.65	32	−0.05	−0.55	−0.30
33	−0.19	−16.01	−15.64	35	−0.12	−0.59	−0.39
34	−0.11	−10.10	−9.70	36	−0.06	−0.33	−0.10
				37	−0.19	−0.79	−0.51
				38	−0.30	−1.02	−0.78
				39	−0.09	−0.42	−0.17
				40	0.01	0.16	0.22

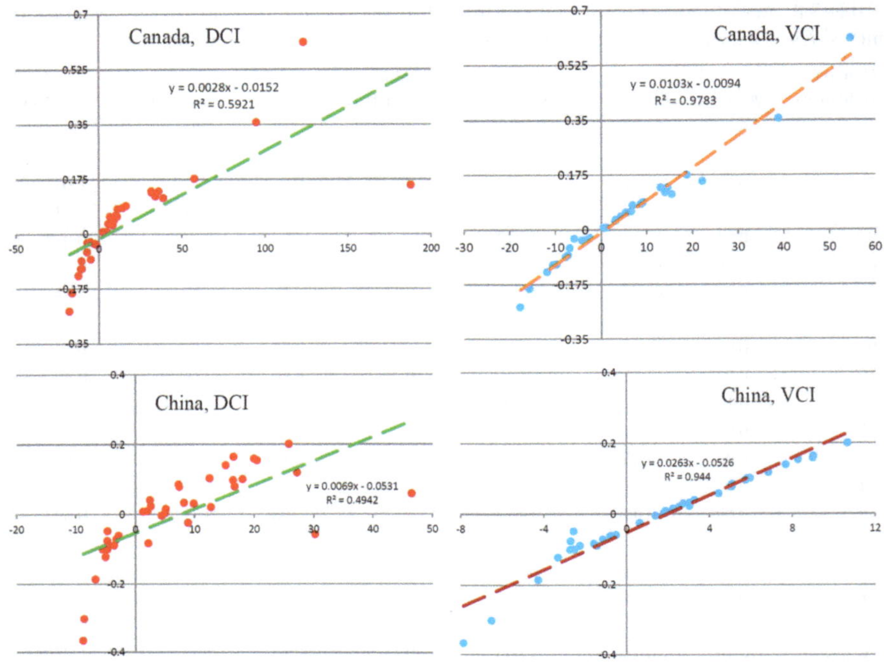

Fig. 3.5 Actual production price-direct price differences vs. actual capital-intensity differences; Canada, 1997, and China, 1997

industry 10 (rubber and plastic products), which when we removed it, the fit improved substantially, i.e. from an R-square of 46 %, we got an R-square of 78 %. The right-hand-side graph is associated with the vertically integrated capital intensities and displays much less variability. From the scatter plot, we observe one point that stands out away from all of the other points, an obvious outlier of industry 12 (Iron and steel), which when we removed it, the R-square improves from 90 % to 97 %.

The next pair of graphs in Fig. 3.7 refers to the fixed capital case. Thus, it can finally be concluded that, in all the tested cases, the results associated with the vertically integrated capital intensities are remarkably closer to Marx's position on production price-labour value deviations (see the Appendix to Chap. 2 and, especially, condition (2.99)).

Table 3.9 Actual production price-direct price differences and differences of the actual capital intensities of industries from the economy's average; USA, 1990

	Industries	DP	PP_C	PP_K	$PP_C - DP$	$DCI_C - ADCI_C$	$VCI_C - AVCI_C$	$PP_K - DP$	$DCI_F - ADCI_F$	$VCI_F - AVCI_F$
1	Agriculture, forest. and fishing	0.838	0.933	1.002	0.095	65.3	36	0.164	52	10.9
2	Mining and quarrying	0.690	0.666	1.091	−0.024	13.4	4.2	0.401	318	77.1
3	Food, beverages and tobacco	0.866	1.015	0.931	0.148	133.7	48.0	0.065	−74	−10.0
4	Textiles, apparel and leather	1.129	1.212	1.055	0.082	43.1	27.1	−0.074	−128	−34.1
5	Wood products and furniture	1.086	1.095	1.014	0.009	20.8	13.4	−0.072	−134	−34.3
6	Paper, and printing	1.152	1.149	1.104	−0.003	22.6	11.1	−0.048	−122	−30.0
7	Industrial chemicals	0.849	0.932	0.995	0.084	77.9	32.6	0.146	−12	6.8
8	Drugs and medicines	1.132	1.107	1.109	−0.025	22.1	6.9	−0.024	−178	−26.4
9	Petroleum and coal products	0.734	0.875	1.083	0.141	398.1	52.4	0.349	224	59.1
10	Rubber and plastic products	1.029	1.063	1.024	0.034	26.6	18.7	−0.005	−112	−23.7
11	Nonmetallic min. products	0.849	0.971	1.053	0.122	9.0	4.3	0.205	−76	−14.7
12	Iron and steel	0.939	1.001	0.956	0.061	53.4	25.5	0.017	−106	−19.8
13	Nonferrous metals	1.010	1.193	1.302	0.183	116.1	50.1	0.292	128	26.9
14	Metal products	1.315	1.283	1.236	−0.032	3.2	6.4	−0.079	−118	−33.2
15	Non-electrical machinery	1.096	1.082	1.033	−0.014	13.5	8.9	−0.064	−114	−32.8
16	Office and comput. machinery	0.945	0.961	1.350	0.016	30.2	15.3	0.405	295	51.1
17	Electrical apparatus, n.e.c.	1.085	1.104	0.973	0.018	25.9	15.2	−0.113	−170	−40.7
18	Radio, TV and commun. eqp.	1.140	1.130	0.990	−0.010	17.9	9.7	−0.150	−161	−45.6
19	Shipbuilding and repairing	1.208	1.146	1.067	−0.063	−1.2	0.6	−0.142	−144	−43.0
20	Other transport	0.927	1.068	1.089	0.141	139.1	44.0	0.163	218	7.4
21	Motor vehicles	1.177	1.340	1.093	0.164	80.9	41.2	−0.084	−118	−35.1
22	Aircraft	1.213	1.200	1.106	−0.013	17.3	9.3	−0.107	−130	−38.0
23	Professional goods	0.967	0.936	0.889	−0.031	9.9	4.9	−0.077	−147	−36.6
24	Other manufacturing	1.662	1.501	1.571	−0.160	−14.1	−8.9	−0.091	−102	−32.2
25	Electricity, gas and water	0.647	0.685	1.231	0.038	54.9	24.1	0.583	702	132.4
26	Construction	1.145	1.085	1.019	−0.061	3.4	0.3	−0.126	−164	−41.8

(continued)

Table 3.9 (continued)

	Industries	DP	PP_C	PP_K	$PP_C - DP$	$DCI_C - ADCI_C$	$VCI_C - AVCI_C$	$PP_K - DP$	$DCI_F - ADCI_F$	$VCI_F - AVCI_F$
27	Wholesale and retail trade	1.005	0.828	0.943	−0.176	−28.4	−25.8	−0.062	−129	−33.4
28	Restaurants and hotels	1.067	1.001	0.948	−0.066	−6.2	−1.6	−0.119	−178	−42.1
29	Transport and storage	0.984	0.878	1.103	−0.105	−13.1	−11.2	0.120	−2.9	−1.9
30	Communication	0.973	0.774	1.407	−0.199	−35.1	−31.9	0.434	172	54.0
31	Finance and insurance	1.144	0.996	1.169	−0.147	−12.4	−15.8	0.026	−82	−18.9
32	Real estate and bus. services	0.918	0.759	1.523	−0.159	−27.3	−25.3	0.605	296	90.6

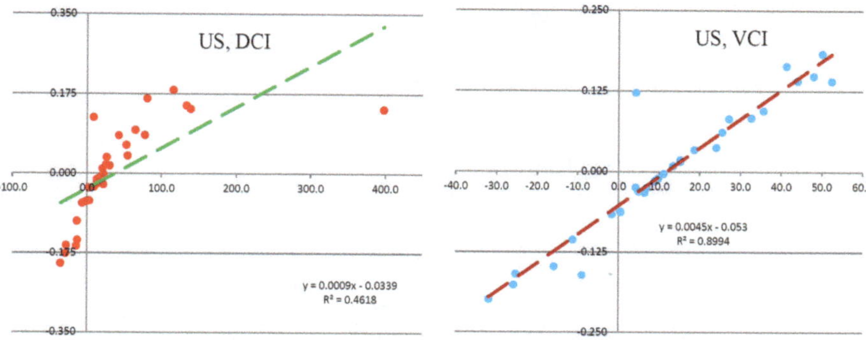

Fig. 3.6 Actual production price-direct price differences vs. actual capital-intensity differences in the circulating capital model; USA, 1990

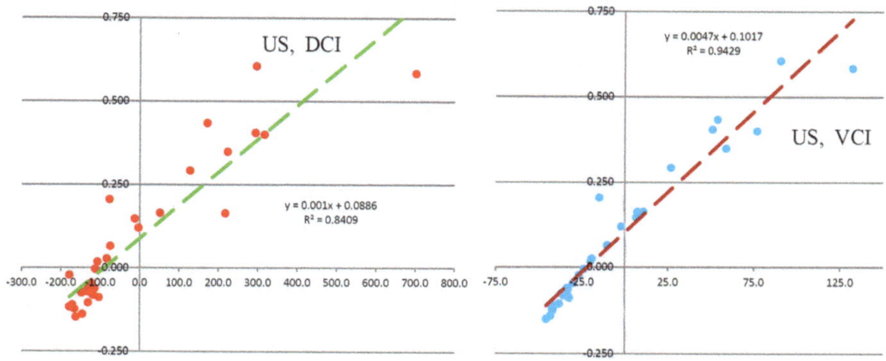

Fig. 3.7 Actual production price-direct price differences vs. actual capital-intensity differences in the fixed capital model; USA, 1990

3.7 Empirical Illustration of the Bounds for the Production Prices

The application of our analysis of the norm bounds for the price-relative profit rate curves (see Sect. 2.3.2) to the SIOTs of the Greek economy (for the period 1988–1997) gives the results summarized in Table 3.10, which displays:

(i) The values of m (see inequalities (2.58) and (2.59)) and the industries in which they occur (the industry numbers are indicated by [•]; see Table 3.5)

(ii) The values of the antilogarithm of the Hilbert distance $\Omega \equiv \|\boldsymbol{\omega}\|\|\hat{\boldsymbol{\omega}}^{-1}\|$ and the industries in which $\|\boldsymbol{\omega}\|$ and $\left(\|\hat{\boldsymbol{\omega}}^{-1}\|\right)^{-1}$ occur (the industry numbers are indicated by [•, •], where the first (second) number refers to $\|\boldsymbol{\omega}\|$ (to $\left(\|\hat{\boldsymbol{\omega}}^{-1}\|\right)^{-1}$)

Table 3.10 Norm bounds for the production prices; Greece, 1988–1997

		1988	1989	1990	1991	1992	1993	1994	1995	1996	1997
	$m \times 10^3$	0.534 [**18**]	0.590 [**18**]	0.585 [**18**]	0.593 [**18**]	0.680 [**18**]	0.755 [**18**]	0.773 [**18**]	0.788 [**18**]	0.813 [**18**]	0.678 [**18**]
	$\Omega \equiv \|\boldsymbol{\omega}\|\|\hat{\boldsymbol{\omega}}^{-1}\|$	7.342 [**1,10**]	7.591 [**19,12**]	7.612 [**4,12**]	6.814 [**4,12**]	5.069 [**19,10**]	5.895 [**2,12**]	6.562 [**19,12**]	8.049 [**2,12**]	6.833 [**2,12**]	6.728 [**2,12**]
$\rho = \rho^a$	$f(\rho)$	0.590	0.589	0.601	0.581	0.594	0.626	0.598	0.595	0.598	0.575
	$\|\boldsymbol{\pi}\|(\|\boldsymbol{\omega}\|)^{-1}$	0.840 [**1**]	0.832 [**19**]	0.824 [**4**]	0.820 [**4**]	0.840 [**19**]	0.869 [**2**]	0.834 [**19**]	0.830 [**2**]	0.838 [**2**]	0.824 [**2**]
	$\|\hat{\boldsymbol{\omega}}^{-1}\|(\|\hat{\boldsymbol{\pi}}^{-1}\|)^{-1}$	1.128 [**10**]	1.178 [**12**]	1.157 [**12**]	1.175 [**12**]	1.101 [**10**]	1.134 [**12**]	1.126 [**12**]	1.152 [**12**]	1.143 [**12**]	1.155 [**12**]
	$g(\rho)$	2.333	2.377	2.313	2.216	1.833	1.949	2.127	2.442	2.191	2.227
	$h(\rho)$	2.636	2.707	2.646	2.541	2.038	2.126	2.402	2.790	2.470	2.547
$\rho = 0.9$	$f(\rho)$	0.053	0.053	0.053	0.053	0.053	0.053	0.053	0.053	0.053	0.053
	$\|\boldsymbol{\pi}\|(\|\boldsymbol{\omega}\|)^{-1}$	0.336 [**1**]	0.360 [**19**]	0.337 [**4**]	0.366 [**1**]	0.395 [**19**]	0.404 [**2**]	0.355 [**2**]	0.323 [**2**]	0.350 [**2**]	0.354 [**2**]
	$\|\hat{\boldsymbol{\omega}}^{-1}\|(\|\hat{\boldsymbol{\pi}}^{-1}\|)^{-1}$	1.628 [**10**]	1.880 [**12**]	1.786 [**12**]	1.799 [**12**]	1.503 [**10**]	1.707 [**12**]	1.608 [**12**]	1.707 [**12**]	1.654 [**12**]	1.669 [**12**]
	$g(\rho)$	2.324	2.560	2.408	2.346	1.902	2.244	2.194	2.441	2.255	2.247
	$h(\rho)$	6.708	6.932	6.951	6.233	4.662	5.405	6.006	7.344	6.250	6.155

(iii) The values of $\|\boldsymbol{\pi}\|(\|\boldsymbol{\omega}\|)^{-1}$ and $\|\hat{\boldsymbol{\omega}}^{-1}\|\left(\|\hat{\boldsymbol{\pi}}^{-1}\|\right)^{-1}$, at the actual value of the profit rate (i.e. $\rho = \rho^{a}$ (see Table 3.2)) and at $\rho = 0.9$ (i.e. a 'high', somewhat unrealistic value), and the industries in which $\|\boldsymbol{\pi}\|$ and $\left(\|\hat{\boldsymbol{\pi}}^{-1}\|\right)^{-1}$ occur, respectively (the industry numbers are indicated by [•])
(iv) The relevant values of $f(\rho)$, $g(\rho)$ and $h(\rho)$ (see inequalities (2.59) and (2.60))

On the basis of these estimates, we may remark the following:

(i) m always occurs in the same industry, i.e. industry 18 (Hotel and restaurant services), and it is (much) less than 0.5, which implies that $f(\rho)$ is always strictly convex to the origin.[18]
(ii) $g(\rho)$ may be a non-monotonic function (consider the years 1988 and 1995).
(iii) Not quite unexpected, the relative errors in $f(\rho^{a})$ and $h(\rho^{a})$ (as bounds for $\|\boldsymbol{\pi}\|(\|\boldsymbol{\omega}\|)^{-1}$ and $\|\hat{\boldsymbol{\omega}}^{-1}\|\left(\|\hat{\boldsymbol{\pi}}^{-1}\|\right)^{-1}$, respectively) are less than the relative errors in $f(0.9)$ and $h(0.9)$, respectively. The relative error in $g(\rho^{a})$ (as a bound for $\|\hat{\boldsymbol{\omega}}^{-1}\|\left(\|\hat{\boldsymbol{\pi}}^{-1}\|\right)^{-1}$) is greater than the relative error in $g(0.9)$.
(iv) Within each year, $\left(\|\hat{\boldsymbol{\omega}}^{-1}\|\right)^{-1}$ and $\left(\|\hat{\boldsymbol{\pi}}^{-1}\|\right)^{-1}$ occur in the same industry. However, this does not hold true for $\|\boldsymbol{\omega}\|$ and $\|\boldsymbol{\pi}\|$. More precisely, they occur in different industries in the years 1991 and 1994 and at $\rho = 0.9$.

For reasons of clarity of presentation and economy of space, the following set of figures is associated with the year 1991. Figure 3.8 displays π_j as functions of ρ. Numerical calculations show that:

(i) Prices change more often than not in a strictly monotonic way.
(ii) π_1 and π_4, i.e. the largest elements of $\{\pi_j\}$, are strictly decreasing and equal to each other at $\rho \cong 0.846$, while π_{12}, i.e. $\left(\|\hat{\boldsymbol{\pi}}^{-1}\|\right)^{-1}$, is strictly increasing.
(iii) The case of a maximum point is observed in industries 5, 9 and 18, where $\omega_j > 1$, while the case of a minimum point is observed in industry 14, where $\omega_j < 1$ (see the dotted lines in Fig. 3.8).

Figure 3.9 displays $f(\rho)$, $\pi_1\omega_4^{-1}$ and $\pi_4\omega_4^{-1}$ as functions of ρ. Finally, Fig. 3.10 displays (i) $\pi_{12}\omega_{12}^{-1}$ as a function of ρ; (ii) the functions $g(\rho)$, associated with $\pi_1\omega_{12}^{-1}$ and $\pi_4\omega_{12}^{-1}$ and (iii) $h(\rho)$.

To the extent that, in the 'real' world, ρ is usually in the range of 0.17–0.40 (see, for instance, Tables 3.2, 3.3 and 3.4), the actual production prices obey the following inequalities (see inequalities (2.61) and (2.62)):

---

[18] It may be noted that also $\max_j\{m_{jj}\}$ always occurs in the same industry, i.e. industry 10 (Manufacture of chemicals and chemical products, manufacture of rubber and plastic products), and it is in the range of 0.619 (year 1989) to 0.740 (year 1988).

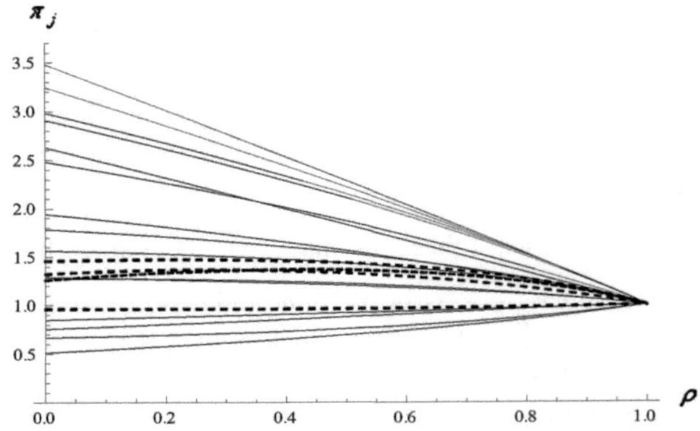

Fig. 3.8 The transformed production prices as functions of the relative profit rate; Greece, 1991

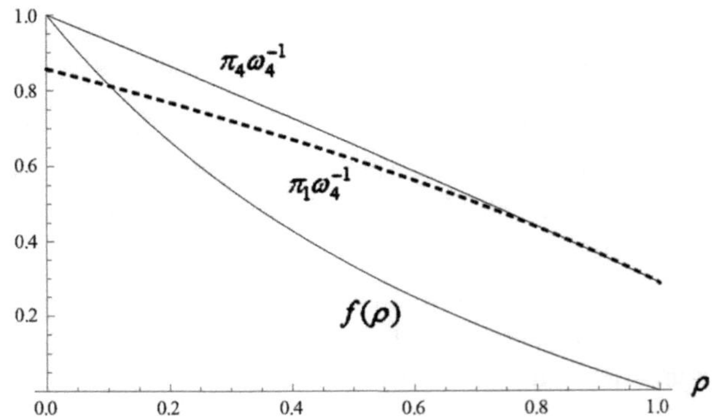

Fig. 3.9 $\|\boldsymbol{\pi}\|(\|\boldsymbol{\omega}\|)^{-1}$ and their lower bound; Greece, 1991

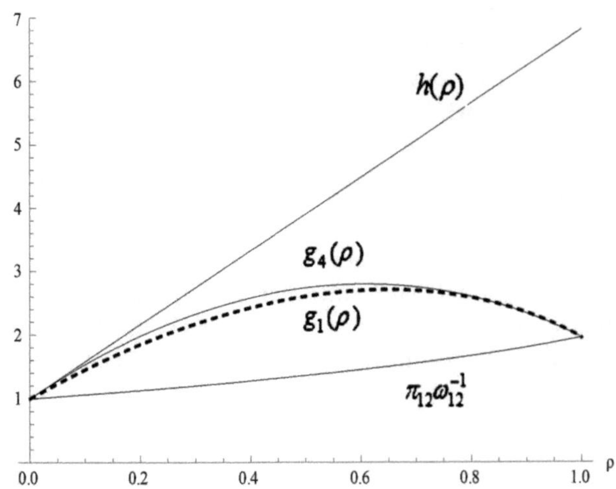

Fig. 3.10 $\|\hat{\boldsymbol{\omega}}^{-1}\|(\|\hat{\boldsymbol{\pi}}^{-1}\|)^{-1}$ and its upper bounds; Greece, 1991

$$\widetilde{f}(m) \leq \|\boldsymbol{\pi}\|(\|\boldsymbol{\omega}\|)^{-1} \leq 1$$

and

$$1 \leq \left\|\hat{\boldsymbol{\omega}}^{-1}\right\|\left(\left\|\hat{\boldsymbol{\pi}}^{-1}\right\|\right)^{-1} \leq \widetilde{h}(\boldsymbol{\omega})$$

where

$$3(7-4m)^{-1} \leq \widetilde{f}(m) \leq 83(117-34m)^{-1}$$

and

$$0.17\Omega + 0.83 \leq \widetilde{h}(\boldsymbol{\omega}) \leq 0.4\Omega + 0.6$$

It is concluded, therefore, that the detected bounds are not so loose.

3.8 The Monotonicity of the Production Price-Profit Rate Curves

The application of our analysis of the production price-profit rate curves, expressed in terms of SSC (see Sect. 2.4.1), to the SIOTs of the Chinese, Greek and Japanese economies (see Sect. 3.3) gives the following results:

3.8.1 China

Figure 3.11 displays the changes in the production price-labour value ratios, $p_j \overline{v}_j^{-1}$, induced by hypothetical changes in the relative profit rate. It is observed that, in most cases, prices move monotonically as ρ takes on values ranging from 0 to 1. However, there are price curves that have a maximum (industry 4, at $\rho \cong 0.5$; industry 6, at $\rho \cong 0.1$; industry 9, at $\rho \cong 0.4$; and industry 24, at $\rho \cong 0.8$) or minimum (industry 40, for $0 < \rho < 0.1$)[19] and cases of price-labour value reversals, which are observed in industries 4, 6, 9 and 40. In industries 4 and 9, the reversal occurs for $0.8 < \rho < 0.9$ and $0.7 < \rho < 0.8$, respectively, i.e. for values of ρ much higher than the actual one ($\rho^{a} \cong 0.387$; see Table 3.4), and in industries 6 and 40, the reversal occurs for $0.1 < \rho < 0.2$ and $0 < \rho < 0.1$, respectively.

[19] This minimum is not identified from a visual inspection of Fig. 3.11. It is discerned from more detailed data as well as from the movement of κ_{40} (see below).

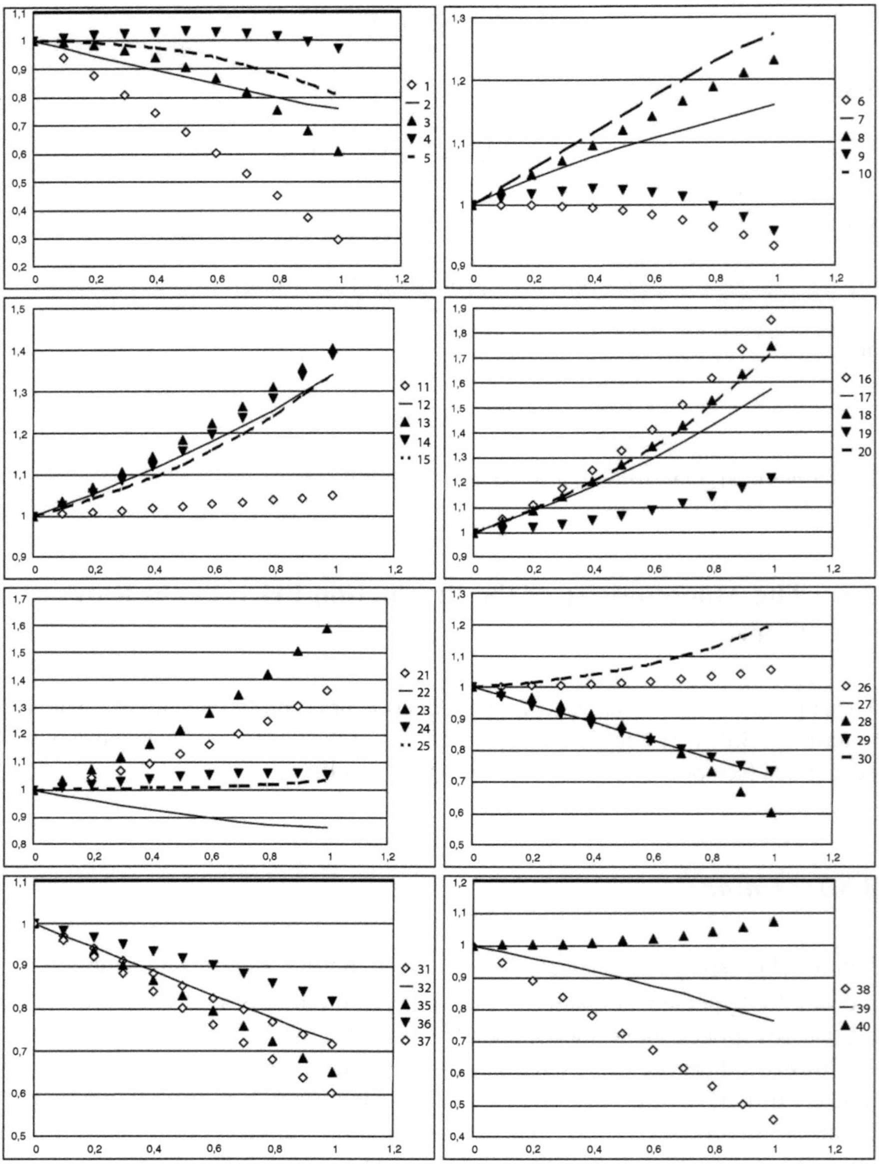

Fig. 3.11 The production price-relative profit rate curves; China, 1997

Figure 3.12 displays the changes in the vertically integrated capital intensities, κ_j, induced by changes in ρ. It is important to note that the movement of production price of an industry is almost in accordance to whether or not the associated capital intensity exceeds the capital intensity of the SSS, which in our case is $R^{-1} \cong 1.760$ (see Table 3.4).

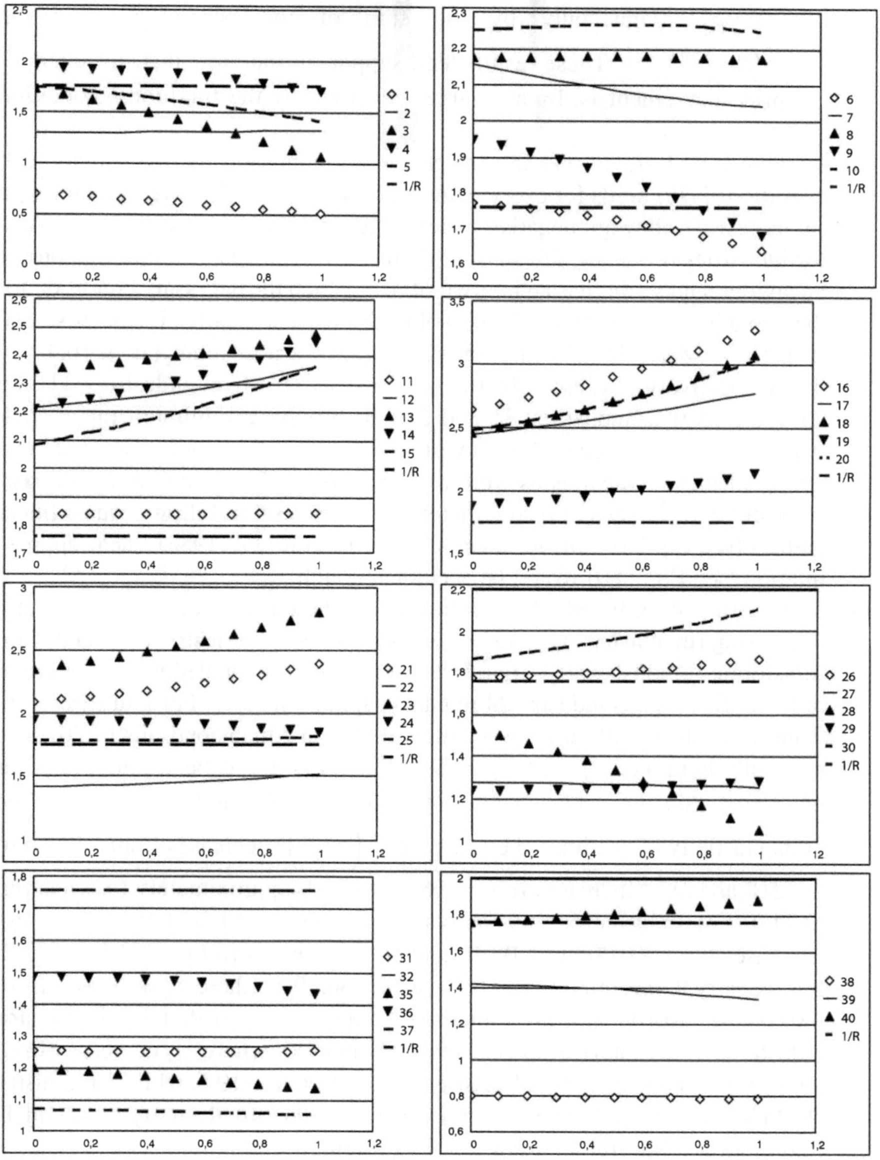

Fig. 3.12 The capital intensities of the vertically integrated industries as functions of the relative profit rate; China, 1997

From these figures and the associated numerical results, we arrive at the following conclusions:

(i) With the exception of industries 4, 6, 9, 24 and 40, the direction of the movement of $p_j\overline{v}_j^{-1}$ does not change, and it is not determined by the elasticity

$\eta_{\kappa j} \equiv \dot{\kappa}_j \rho \kappa_j^{-1}$ but only by the sign of the percentage deviation $D_j \equiv (R\kappa_j)^{-1} - 1$. These results lend support to the view that, for every ρ, the price movement is, by and large, governed by the traditional condition (2.70).

(ii) In industries 2, 7, 22 and 29, the *necessary* condition for the violation of condition (2.70) holds for every ρ, that is to say, $\eta_{\kappa j}$ and D_j have the same sign (in industry 7, they are negative, whereas for the rest, they are positive). Also for industries 8, 10, 11, 25, 31 and 32, the term κ_j displays a *non*-monotonic behaviour, and so there is an interval of ρ, in which the necessary condition for the violation of condition (2.70) holds. More specifically, in the first two industries (where $D_j < 0$), the term κ_j displays a maximum (at $\rho \cong 0.4$ and 0.6, respectively), whereas in the rest (where $D_j < 0$ in industries 11 and 25 and $D_j > 0$ in industries 31 and 32), it displays a minimum (at $\rho \cong 0.4$, 0.3, 0.6 and 0.5, respectively). Nevertheless, setting aside industries 7, 22 and 29, in all these industries as well as in industries 27, 37 and 38, κ_j is quasi-insensitive to changes in ρ and, therefore, prices tend to follow a quasi-linear pattern (see Eq. 2.67) or, in other words, Bienenfeld's (1988) linear approximation (see Eq. 2.80) would be accurate enough.

(iii) In industries 4, 6, 9 and 24 (in industry 40), the term κ_j constitutes a strictly decreasing (increasing) function of ρ. As ρ increases, industries 4, 6 and 9 are transformed (industry 40 is transformed) to labour (capital)-intensive relative to the SSS, whereas industry 24 remains capital intensive. For industries 4, 6, 9 and 24 (industry 40), there is an interval of ρ, in which condition (2.70) does not really hold, i.e. $\eta_{\kappa j} < D_j < 0$ $(0 < D_j < \eta_{\kappa j})$. It has been found that, for industry 4, this interval lies between the values $\rho = 0.5$ and $\rho = 0.9$, where the point elasticity $\eta_{\kappa j}$ (estimated by $(\Delta\kappa_j/\Delta\rho)\left(\rho\kappa_j^{-1}\right)$) decreases from -0.064 to -0.218 and D_j^{-1} increases from -16.3 to 175.4, approximately (see relation (2.71)). For industry 6, this interval lies between 0.1 and 0.2, where $\eta_{\kappa j}$ decreases from -0.005 to -0.010 and D_j^{-1} increases from -252.5 to 877.2. For industry 9, this interval lies between 0.4 and 0.8, where $\eta_{\kappa j}$ decreases from -0.051 to -0.168 and D_j^{-1} increases from -16.9 to 454.5. Finally, for industry 24, this interval lies between 0.8 and 1.0, where $\eta_{\kappa j}$ decreases from -0.071 to -0.086 and D_j^{-1} decreases from -14.6 to -19.5, while for industry 40, this interval lies between 0 and 0.1, where the arc elasticity of κ_j equals 0.002 and D_j^{-1} decreases from 397.4 to -430.5.

(iv) Although there are κ_j that display a non-monotonic behaviour, the approximation of the entire price vector through Bienenfeld's (1988) quadratic approximation (see Eq. 2.81) works pretty well. Table 3.11 reports a representative sample (compare with Fig. 3.11): The symbol ↑ (↓) indicates that the quadratic approximation of $p_j\overline{v}_j^{-1}$ is strictly increasing (decreasing) in the economically significant interval of ρ, ρ_j^* indicates the predictor of the value of ρ at which the function $p_j\overline{v}_j^{-1}$ has an extreme value and $\widetilde{\rho}_j = 2\rho_j^*$ indicates the predictor of a price-labour value reversal, i.e. $D_j(\widetilde{\rho}_j) = 0$ (see Eqs. 2.82 and 2.83).

Table 3.11 Bienenfeld's quadratic approximation of the production prices; China, 1997

Industry	$\kappa_j(0) - R^{-1}$	$\kappa_j(1) - \kappa_j(0)$	Monotonicity	ρ_j^*
1	−1.063	−0.188	↓	< 0
4	0.192	−0.244	↑, ↓	0.393 ($\tilde{\rho}_j \cong 0.786$)
6	0.015	−0.133	↑, ↓	0.056 ($\tilde{\rho}_j \cong 0.112$)
7	0.397	−0.114	↑	> 1
9	0.189	−0.267	↑, ↓	0.354 ($\tilde{\rho}_j \cong 0.708$)
11	0.082	0.005	↑	< 0
16	0.888	0.630	↑	< 0
22	−0.343	0.101	↓	> 1
24	0.194	−0.098	↑, ↓	0.989 ($\tilde{\rho}_j > 1$)
32	−0.488	0.003	↓	> 1
40	−0.004	0.129	↓, ↑	0.015 ($\tilde{\rho}_j \cong 0.030$)

3.8.2 *Greece*

Table 3.12 reports the characteristic features of the production price-relative profit rate curves, for $0 \leq \rho \leq 1$:

(i) The symbol ↑ (↓) indicates a strictly increasing (decreasing) function.
(ii) M [ρ^*] (m [ρ^*]) indicates that there is a maximum (minimum) at a value of the profit rate that is approximately equal to ρ^*.
(iii) r (α, β) indicates that a price-labour value reversal occurs in the interval $\alpha < \rho < \beta$.
(iv) The symbol → indicates that, at $\rho = 1$, the curve tends to intersect the line of price-labour value equality.

From these findings and the associated numerical results we arrive at the following conclusions:

(i) Non-monotonic production price-profit rate curves could not only be considered rare but also with no more than one extreme point. More specifically, there are 36 cases (or 36/190 ≅ 19 %) of non-monotonic movement and 29 cases (or 15 %) of price-labour value reversals. It then follows that the price movements are, by and large, governed by the traditional condition.
(ii) Having established the 'smooth' patterns of the production prices in terms of SSC, it is expected that the relative prices of any two commodities will also tend to move in a 'smooth' way (as well as the wage rate, expressed in terms of any numeraire; consider Eq. 2.78a). For instance, in terms of the corresponding actual net output vectors, there are 44 cases (or 23 %) of non-monotonic price curves. It is a remarkable empirical fact, however, that three of these curves display *two* extreme points (see Fig. 3.13; the second extreme point occurs at 'high' values of the relative rate of profit, i.e. for $\rho > 0.80$).
(iii) The price movement associated with each separate industry tends to be uniform over time. This fact may indicate that there exists a tendency towards the formation of a rather rigid ordering relation between $\kappa_j(0)$ and R^{-1} (also see Sect. 3.5).

Table 3.12 Characteristic features of the production price-relative profit rate curves; Greece, 1988–1997

j	1988	1989	1990	1991	1992	1993	1994	1995	1996	1997
1	↓	↓	↓	↓	↓	↓	↓	↓	↓	↓
2	↓	↓	↓	↓	↓	↓	↓	↓	↓	↓
3	↓	↓	↓	↓	↓	↓	↓	↓	↓	↓
4	↓	↓	↓	↓	↓	↓	↓	↓	↓	↓
5	M [0.3] r (0.4, 0.5)	M [0.3] r (0.6, 0.7)	M [0.4] r (0.7, 0.8)	M [0.4] r (0.7, 0.8)	M [0.7]	M [0.6] →	M [0.5] r (0.8, 0.9)	M [0.3] r (0.6, 0.7)	M [0.4] r (0.7, 0.8)	M [0.4] r (0.6, 0.7)
6	↓	↓	↓	↓	M [0.5] r (0.8, 0.9)	↓	↓	↓	↓	↓
7	↓	↓	↓	↓	↓	↓	↓	↓	↓	↓
8	↓	↓	↓	↓	↓	↓	↓	M [0.5] r (0.7, 0.8)	M [0.5] r (0.8, 0.9)	↓
9	M [0.2] r (0.3, 0.4)	M [0.2] r (0.4, 0.5)	M [0.2] r (0.4, 0.5)	M [0.3] r (0.5, 0.6)	M [0.3] r (0.6, 0.7)	M [0.2] r (0.4, 0.5)	M [0.4] r (0.6, 0.7)	M [0.3] r (0.5, 0.6)	M [0.5] r (0.9, 1.0)	M [0.6] →
10	↑	↑	↑	↑	↑	↑	↑	↑	↑	↑
11	↓	↓	↓	↓	↓	↓	↓	↓	↓	↓
12	↑	↑	↑	↑	↑	↑	↑	↑	↑	↑
13	M [0.9] →	↑	↑	↑	↑	↑	↑	↑	↑	↑
14	↓	m [0.8] →	m [0.6] r (0.9, 1.0)	m [0.2] r (0.4, 0.5)	↑	m [0.2] r (0.2, 0.3)	m [0.9] →	↓	↓	↓
15	↓	↓	↓	↓	↓	↓	↓	↓	↓	↓
16	M [0.6] →	↑	↑	↑	↑	↑	↑	↑	↑	↑
17	↓	↓	↓	↓	↓	↓	↓	↓	↓	↓
18	↓	M [0.1] r (0.2, 0.3)	M [0.2] r (0.3, 0.4)	M [0.2] r (0.4, 0.5)	M [0.6] r (0.9, 1.0)	M [0.5] r (0.7, 0.8)	M [0.3] r (0.5, 0.6)	↓	↓	↓
19	↓	↓	↓	↓	↓	↓	↓	↓	↓	↓

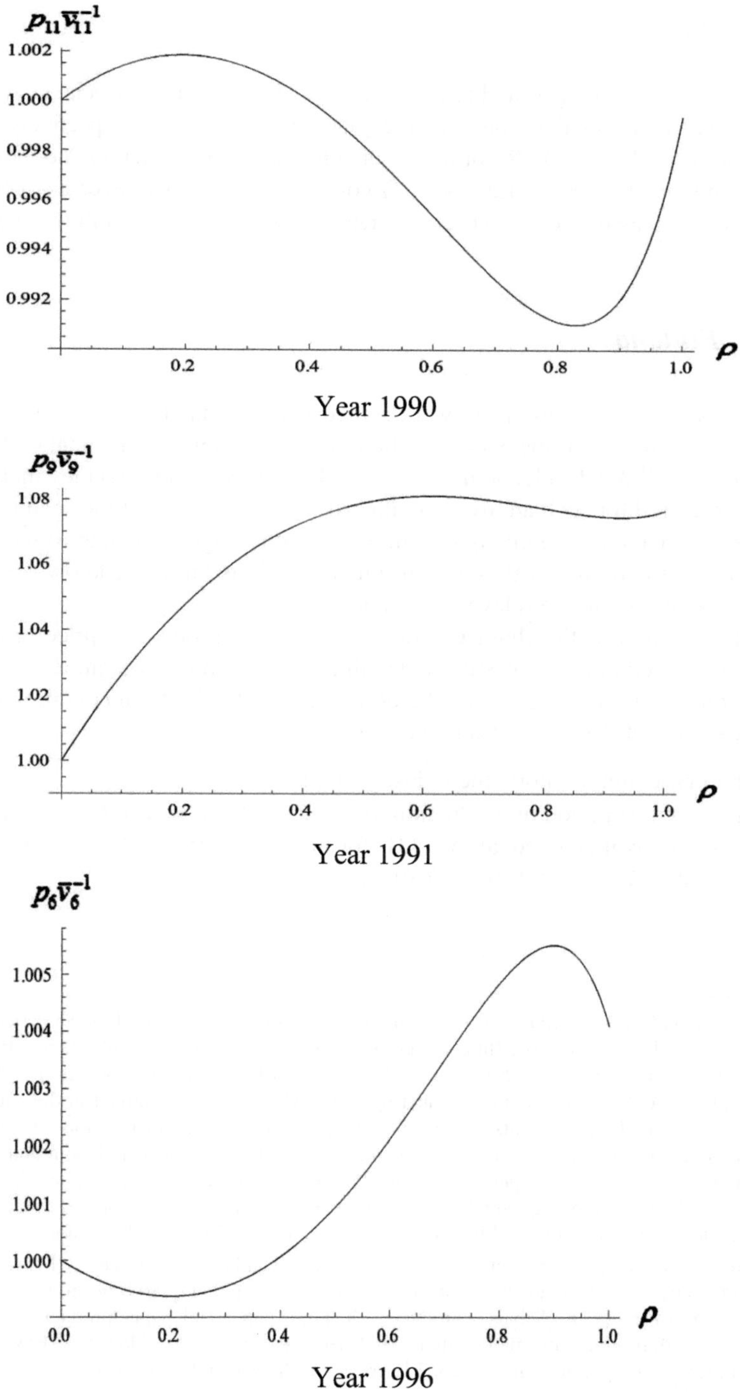

Fig. 3.13 Cases of production price curves with two extreme points; Greece

3.8.3 Japan

A similar picture emerges in Figs. 3.14 and 3.15, which are associated with the Japanese economy for the representative years 1980 and 1990, respectively. There are 23 cases (or 23/66 ≅ 35 %) of non-monotonic price curves (having no more than one extreme point) and 17 cases (or 26 %) of price-labour value reversals, while the price movement associated with each separate industry tends to be uniform over time.

3.8.4 Finland

Now we shall turn to Böhm-Bawerk's theory of capital (see the Appendix to Chap. 2) and apply it to the SIOTs of the Finnish economy for the years 1995 and 2004 ($n = 57$).[20] We decided to use these SIOTs mainly because (i) they include all the data required for such an investigation, (ii) the length of the time span between the selected years is long enough to allow for technological change to take place and give rise to possible differential results and (iii) as far as we know, such data have not been used in the relevant literature.

Table 3.13 reports the characteristic features of the production price-profit rate curves, expressed in terms of SSC, and within the economically significant interval of r, that are non-monotonic (and, therefore, violate the Austrian condition (2.98)) for at least one of the years of our analysis:

(i) The first column reports the industry number.[21]
(ii) The 'average period of production' of the SSS, $T_S(0) = 1 + R^{-1}$, is estimated to be approximately equal to 2.431, for the year 1995, and 2.550, for the year 2004 (and $\Delta T_j(0) \equiv T_j(0) - T_S(0)$).

[20] The SIOTs and the corresponding levels of sectoral employment of the Finnish economy are provided via the Eurostat website (http://ec.europa.eu/eurostat). At the time of this research, they were available for the years 1995 through 2004 and describe 59 products, which are classified according to CPA ('Classification of Product by Activity'; see the Appendix 1 at the end of this chapter). However, all the elements associated with the industry 'Uranium and thorium ores' equal zero and, therefore, we remove them from our analysis. Furthermore, since all labour and material inputs in the industry 'Crude petroleum and natural gas; services incidental to oil and gas extraction excluding surveying' equal zero, while the relevant product is imported to the system, we aggregate it with the industry 'Metal ores'. Thus, we derive SIOTs of dimensions 57×57.

[21] Industry classification: 1. Products of agriculture, hunting and related services; 3. Fish and other fishing products; services incidental of fishing; 6. Other mining and quarrying products; 7. Food products and beverages; 8. Tobacco products; 13. Pulp, paper and paper products; 15. Coke, refined petroleum products and nuclear fuels; 16. Chemicals, chemical products; 19. Basic metals; 21. Machinery and equipment n.e.c.; 23. Electrical machinery and apparatus n.e.c.; 24. Radio, television and communication equipment and apparatus; 26. Motor vehicles, trailers and semi-trailers; 27. Other transport equipment; 29. Recovered secondary raw materials; 45. Real estate services.

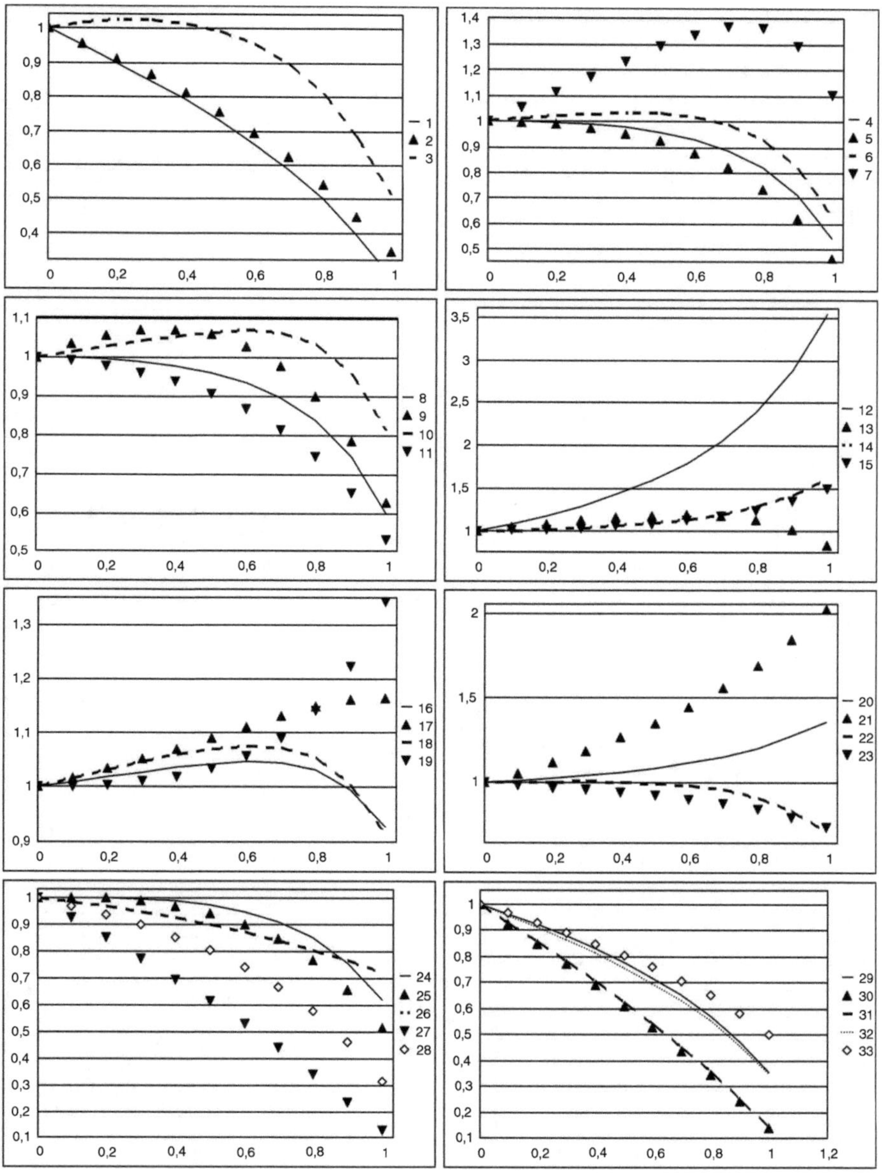

Fig. 3.14 The production price-relative profit rate curves; Japan, 1980

(iii) The actual profit rate is estimated as approximately equal to 0.323, for the year 1995, and 0.325, for the year 2004 (i.e. $\rho \cong 0.462$ or 0.504, respectively).

(iv) The symbol ↑ (↓) indicates that p_j is strictly increasing (decreasing).

(v) M[r*] (m[r*]) indicates that there is a maximum (minimum) at a value of the profit rate that is approximately equal to r^*.

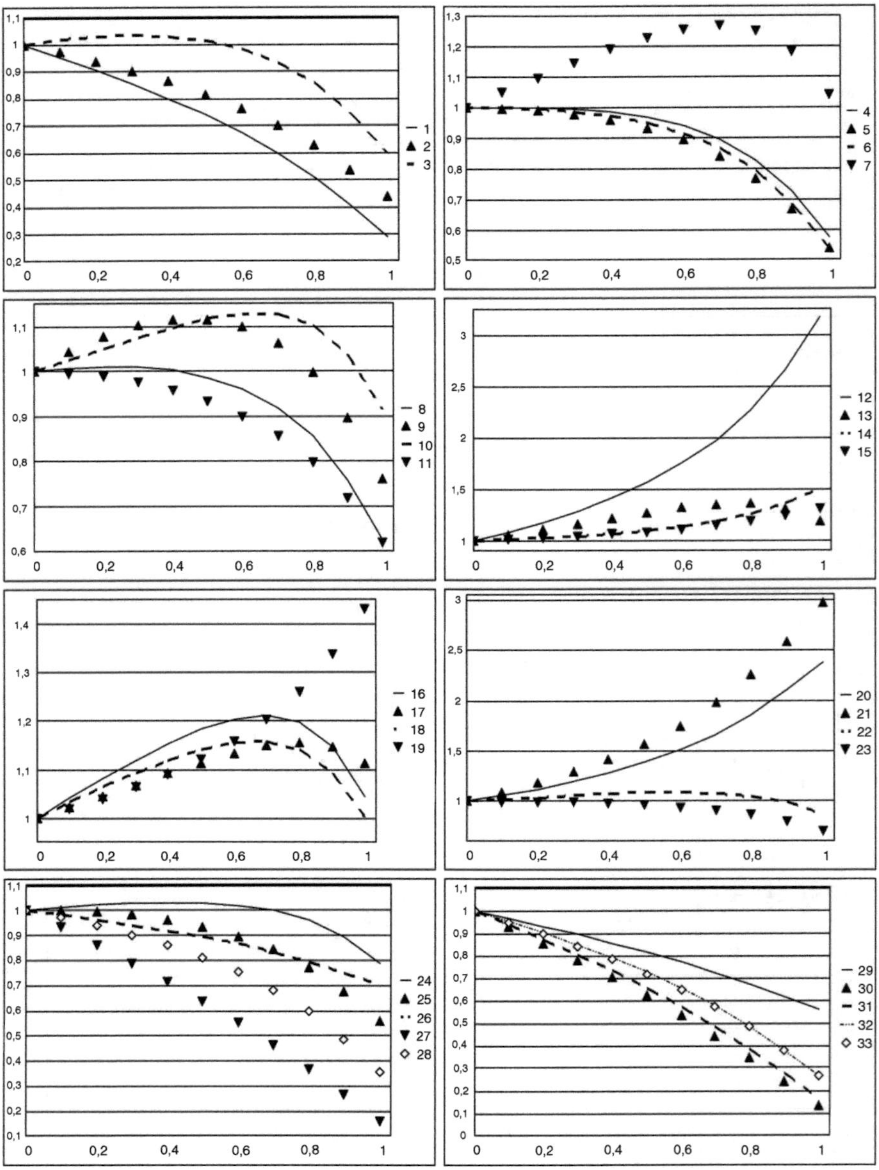

Fig. 3.15 The production price-relative profit rate curves; Japan, 1990

(vi) r[r^{**}] indicates that there is a price-labour value reversal at a positive value of the profit rate that is approximately equal to r^{**}.

In 76 cases (i.e. 32 cases for the year 1995 and 44 cases for the year 2004 or $76/114 \cong 67$ % of the tested cases), the ratios of means of production to labour, $\widetilde{\kappa}_j(r)$, in the jth golden sub-system (see condition (2.95)) are non-monotonic

Table 3.13 Characteristic features of the non-monotonic production price-profit rate curves; Finland, 1995 and 2004

j	1995	2004
1	$\Delta T_1(0) > 0$, M[0.54]	$\Delta T_1(0) > 0$, M[0.35], r[0.53]
3	$\Delta T_3(0) > 0$, M[0.22], r[0.39]	$\Delta T_3(0) < 0$, ↓
6	$\Delta T_6(0) < 0$, ↓	$\Delta T_6(0) > 0$, M[0.22], r[0.35]
7	$\Delta T_7(0) > 0$, M[0.61]	$\Delta T_7(0) > 0$, M[0.34], r[0.52]
8	$\Delta T_8(0) > 0$, M[0.03], r[0.08]	$\Delta T_8(0) < 0$, ↓
13	$\Delta T_{13}(0) > 0$, M[0.35], r[0.59]	$\Delta T_{13}(0) > 0$, M[0.08], r[0.015]
15	$\Delta T_{15}(0) > 0$, M[0.50]	$\Delta T_{15}(0) > 0$, M[0.39], r[0.58]
16	$\Delta T_{16}(0) > 0$, M[0.42], r[0.67]	$\Delta T_{16}(0) > 0$, M[0.23], r[0.40]
19	$\Delta T_{19}(0) > 0$, ↑	$\Delta T_{19}(0) > 0$, M[0.46], r[0.62]
21	$\Delta T_{21}(0) > 0$, ↑	$\Delta T_{21}(0) > 0$, M[0.11], r[0.21]
23	$\Delta T_{23}(0) > 0$, ↑	$\Delta T_{23}(0) > 0$, M[0.18], r[0.32]
24	$\Delta T_{24}(0) > 0$, ↑	$\Delta T_{24}(0) > 0$, M[0.02], r[0.04]
26	$\Delta T_{26}(0) < 0$, ↓	$\Delta T_{26}(0) > 0$, M[0.23], r[0.38]
27	$\Delta T_{27}(0) < 0$, m[0.34], r[0.56]	$\Delta T_{27}(0) < 0$, ↓
29	$\Delta T_{29}(0) > 0$, ↑	$\Delta T_{29}(0) > 0$, M[0.43], r[0.60]
45	$\Delta T_{45}(0) > 0$, M[0.16], r[0.31]	$\Delta T_{45}(0) > 0$, M[0.07], r[0.13]

functions (with no more than two extreme points). Nevertheless, there are 'only' 22 cases (or 19 %) of non-monotonic price movement (with no more than one extreme point), 11 cases (or 10 %) in which the extreme point occurs at a value of the profit rate which is less than the actual one, 19 cases (or 17 %) of price-labour value reversals and 7 cases (or 6 %) in which the price-labour value reversal occurs at a value of the profit rate which is less than the actual one. For instance, Fig. 3.16 is associated with industries 16, for the year 1995; 27, for the year 1995; and 20 (Fabricated metal products, except machinery and equipment), for the year 2004 and displays the differences in the 'r – average periods of production', $\Delta T_j(r)$; the Austrian production prices, $p_{j\mathrm{A}}(r)$ (depicted by dotted lines); and $p_j(r)$ (depicted by solid lines) (see conditions (2.96) and (2.98) and Eq. 2.97).[22] Finally, setting aside ten industries, i.e. nine industries that appear in Table 3.12 and industry 20, where $\Delta T_{20}(0) > (<)\ 0$ for the year 1995 (2004), the monotonicity of the production price-profit rate curves does not change over the years under consideration (as in the cases of the Greek and Japanese economies).

[22] The vector of relative labour values (of Austrian production prices) can be considered as a constant-term (a linear) approximation of the vector of relative production prices, which is exact when profits equal zero (which is derived from the 'rule of simple interest'). At the actual values of the profit rate, the d – distance between the vector of actual production prices and the vector of Austrian production prices (of labour values) is 0.070 (is 0.188). Moreover, labour values and actual Austrian production prices are 'equally' accurate approximations of the market prices: the deviation of the latter from labour values is in the range of 0.337–0.353, while their deviation from the actual Austrian production prices is in the range of 0.322–0.368.

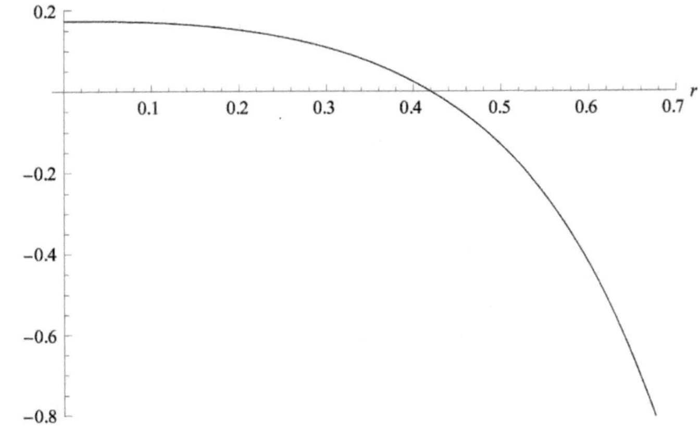

$\Delta T_{16}(r) > 0$ for $r < 0.419$

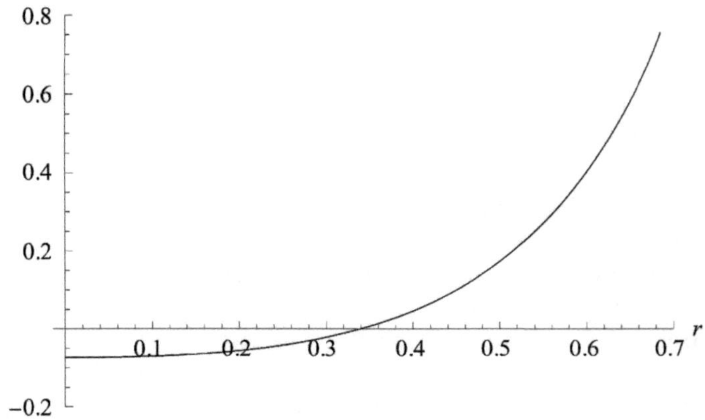

$\Delta T_{27}(r) > 0$ for $r > 0.340$

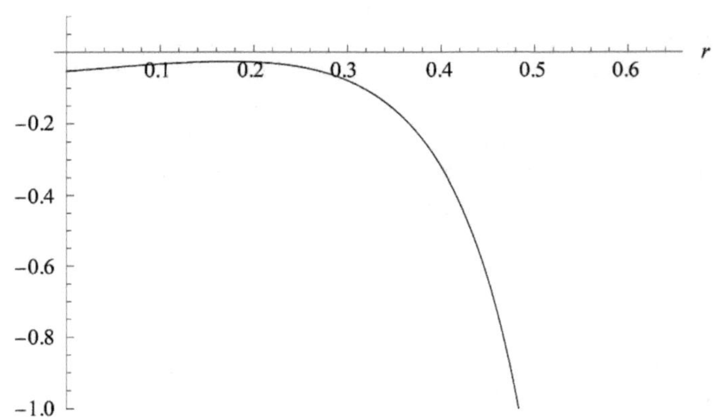

$\Delta T_{20}(r) < 0$

Fig. 3.16 (continued)

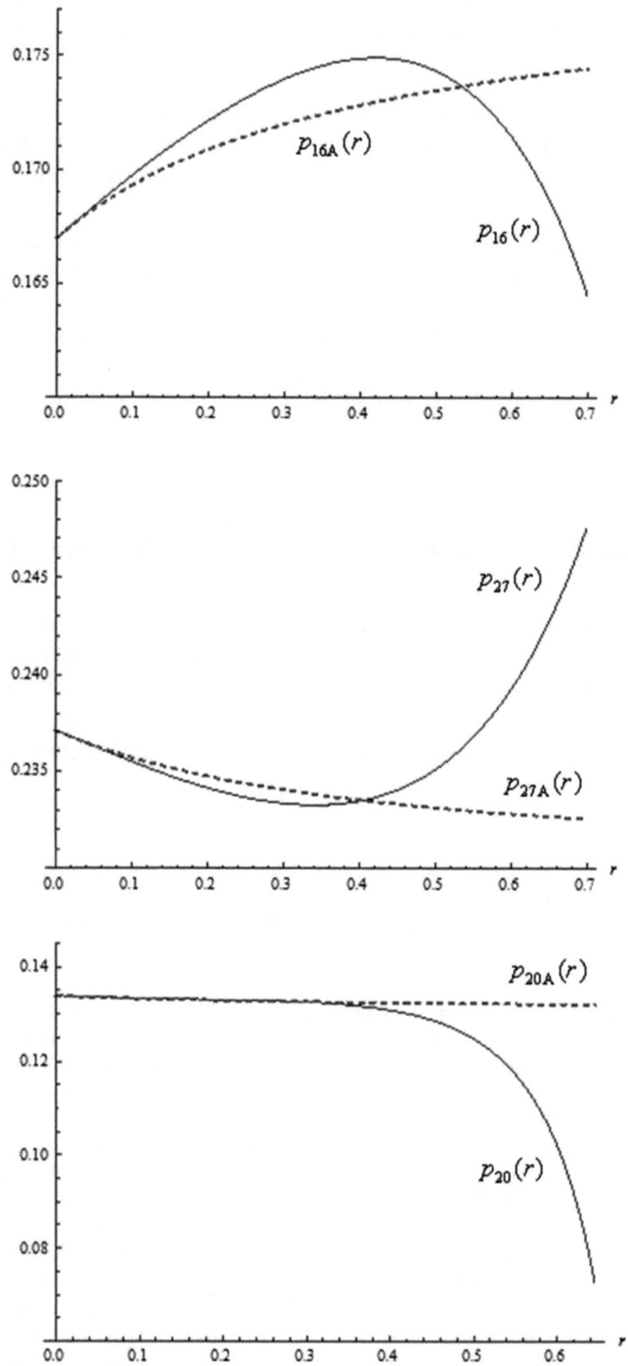

Fig. 3.16 Differences in the 'r – average periods of production' and Austrian production prices and production prices as functions of the profit rate; Finland, industries 16 (year 1995), 27 (year 1995) and 20 (year 2004)

The findings in this section are in absolute accordance with those of other empirical studies.[23] Thus, it could be stated that *within* the economically significant interval of the profit rate:

(i) The directions of relative price movements are, more often than not, governed by the traditional condition(s), that is to say, the 'capital-intensity effect' (direct or traditional effect) *dominates* the 'price effect' (indirect or Sraffian effect).
(ii) Non-monotonic production price-profit rate curves are relatively rare, i.e. not significantly more than 20 %, and have no more than one or, very rarely, two extreme points. Cases of price-labour value reversal are rarer. It then follows that actual single-product economies behave as *three*-industry systems with respect to the *shape* of these curves (see Sect. 2.2.1.3).
(iii) The price movement associated with each separate industry *tends* to be uniform over time.

3.9 Empirical Illustration of the Wage-Profit Rate Curve

The application of our analysis of the wage-relative profit rate curve (WPC; see Sects. 2.2.1.3 and 2.3.1), with *ex post* wages, to the flow SIOTs of the Greek (1988–1997), Danish (for the years 2000 and 2004), Finnish (for the years 1995 and 2004), French (for the years 1995 and 2005), German (for the years 2000 and 2002) and Swedish (for the years 1995 and 2005) economies gives the following results[24]:

---

[23] See, e.g. Kyn et al. (1967), Sekerka et al. (1970), Petrović (1987), Bienenfeld (1988), Da Silva and Rosinger (1992), del Valle Caballero (1993), Shaikh (1998, 2012, 2016) and Iliadi et al. (2014).

[24] The latter ten SIOTs have been used by Iliadi et al. (2014), who empirically examine the monotonicity of the production price-profit rate curves: non-monotonic curves, expressed in terms of SSC, are observed in about 19 % (105/559) of the tested cases. The data are provided via the Eurostat website and describe 59 products, which are classified according to CPA. However, there are cases in which all the elements or only the labour inputs or, finally, only the material inputs associated with certain industries are equal to zero. In order to derive 'Sraffa matrices' (Krause 1981, pp. 177–178), i.e. matrices with strictly positive left P-F eigenvectors, we remove them from our analysis or we make the appropriate aggregations. For example, in each SIOT, all the material inputs associated with the industry 'Private households with employed persons' are equal to zero and, therefore, we remove this industry. Or, in the SIOTs of the German economy, (i) all the elements associated with the product 'Uranium and thorium ores' are equal to zero, and, therefore, we remove them and (ii) all labour and material inputs in the industry 'Metal ores' are equal to zero, while the relevant product is imported to the system, and, therefore, we aggregate it with the industry 'Other mining and quarrying products'. Thus, $n = 55$ for Denmark, $n = 56$ for Finland, $n = 56$ for France, $n = 56$ for Germany, and $n = 52$ (year 1995) or $n = 50$ (year 2005) for Sweden.

(i) In terms of the corresponding actual net output vectors, and for $0 \leq \rho \leq 1$, nine WPCs for the Greek economy (i.e. those associated with the period 1988–1996) switch from convex to concave (it has not been found any case where the curvature switches more than one time), while all the other WPCs are strictly concave to the origin (negative price Wicksell effect). For clarity's and brevity's sake, we focus on the French, for the year 2005, and Greek, for the year 1994, economies. These results can be considered as sufficiently representative for the two samples: The Euclidean angle (measured in degrees), which depends on the choice of physical measurement units, between $\mathbf{p}(1)$ and $\mathbf{l}$ is in the range of 42.0° (Greece) to 47.4° (France). The relevant Hilbert distance is in the range of 1.23 (Greece) to 1.94 (France), and the $d-$ distance is in the range of 0.66 (Greece) to 0.79 (France). Thus, it could be said that these economies deviate considerably from the equal value compositions of capital case. Figure 3.17 displays the WPCs (depicted by a solid line), the bound curves (U, L), the Sraffian curve, $w^S \equiv 1 - \rho$ (depicted by a dotted line), and the values of ϕ, Ω and S (see inequalities (2.46) and Eqs. 2.47 and 2.48).[25] The WPC for the Greek economy crosses the w^S curve at $\rho \cong 0.194$ and switches from convex to concave at $\rho \cong 0.499$ ($k_{\mathbf{z}}$ increases for $\rho > 0.687$).

(ii) Finally, Table 3.14 displays results for four alternative numeraires that are of particular significance, i.e. the vectors of the actual gross outputs, $\overline{\mathbf{x}}^{\mathrm{T}}$; actual real wage rates, $\mathbf{b}^{\mathrm{T}}$; $\mathbf{e}_m^{\mathrm{T}}$ ($\omega_m = \min_j\{\omega_j\}$) and $\mathbf{e}_M^{\mathrm{T}}$ ($\omega_M = \max_j\{\omega_j\}$).[26] It then follows that the detected bounds are not so loose and the WPCs do not display many curvatures irrespective of the numeraire chosen (also see Figs. 3.18 and 3.19).

All these findings are in absolute accordance with those of other empirical studies.[27] Thus, it could be stated that within the economically significant interval of the profit rate, the WPCs are almost linear (experiments show that, more often than not, the correlation coefficients between the wage and profit rates tend to be above 99 %) and their second derivatives change sign no more than one or, very rarely, two times. It then follows that actual single-product economies behave or tend to behave as *corn-tractor* systems with respect to the *shape* of these curves.

---

[25] For the Greek economy, Ω is in the range of 5.069 (year 1992) to 8.049 (year 1995; see Table 3.10) and, therefore, the difference $S_{\max} - S_{\mathrm{sm}}$ is in the range of 0.016–0.031. For the other economies, Ω is in the range of 7.056 (Sweden, 1995) to 35.251 (Finland, 2004), and, therefore, $S_{\max} - S_{\mathrm{sm}}$ is in the range of 0.026–0.115.

[26] For the Greek economy, $m = 12$ (Basic metals and fabricated metal products) and $M = 19$ (Transports, water transport services, air transport services, post and telecommunications). For the French economy, $m = 28$ (Other transport equipment) and $M = 51$ (Education services).

[27] See studies mentioned in footnotes 12 and 23 in this chapter, and Krelle (1977), Leontief (1985), Hamilton (1986), Özol (1984, 1991), Cekota (1988, 1990), Michl (1991), Petrović (1991), Fujimori (1992), Da Silva (1993), Marzi (1994), Angeloussis (2006), Han and Schefold (2006), Degasperi and Fredholm (2010), García and Garzón (2011) and Li (2014b).

Fig. 3.17 The WPC, in terms of the actual net output vector, its bounds and the Sraffian curve; (a) France, 2005, and (b) Greece, 1994

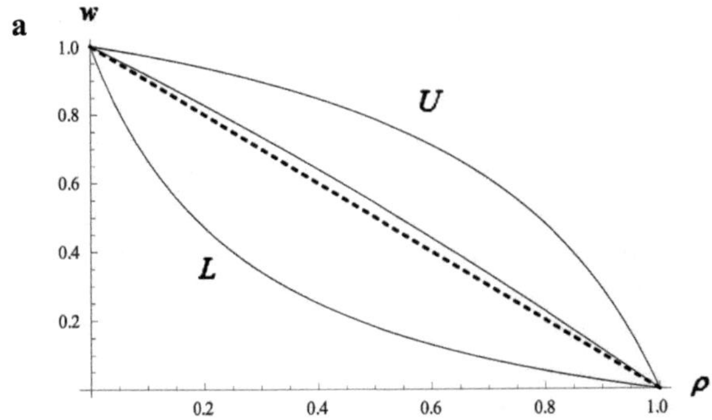

$\Omega \cong 16.513$, $\phi \cong 0.272$, $S(\phi) = 0.438$, $S_{sm} \cong 0.372$, $S_{max} \cong 0.439$ (at $\phi \cong 0.246$)

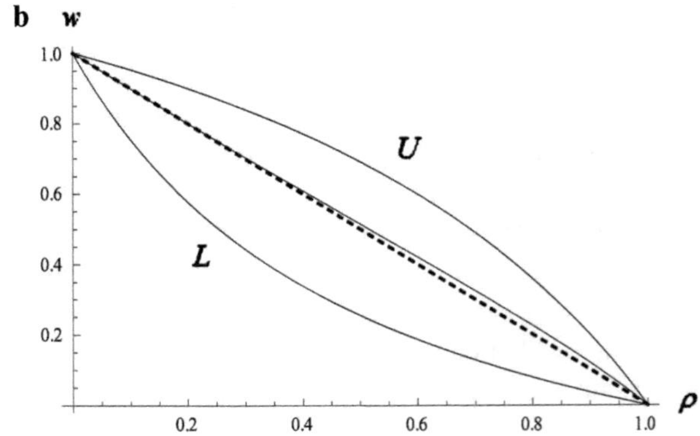

$\Omega \cong 6.563$, $\phi \cong 0.447$, $S(\phi) = 0.304$, $S_{sm} \cong 0.281$, $S_{max} \cong 0.305$ (at $\phi \cong 0.390$)

Table 3.14 Results for alternative numeraires; France, 2005, and Greece, 1994

	France, 2005			Greece, 1994		
$\mathbf{z}^{\mathrm{T}}$	ϕ	$S(\phi)$	$\ddot{w}$	ϕ	$S(\phi)$	$\ddot{w}$
$\overline{\mathbf{x}}^{\mathrm{T}}$	0.290	0.437	< 0	0.441	0.304	< 0
$\mathbf{b}^{\mathrm{T}}$	0.317	0.436	> 0	0.398	0.305	$> 0, \rho < 0.336$
						$< 0, \rho > 0.336$
$\mathbf{e}_m^{\mathrm{T}}$	1	0.372	> 0	1	0.281	> 0
$\mathbf{e}_M^{\mathrm{T}}$	0.061	0.372	< 0	0.152	0.281	< 0

The hitherto available evidence from the SUTs suggests that when the WPCs are strictly decreasing, they tend to be almost linear. Nevertheless, there are cases in which elements in the (positive) vector of labour-commanded prices decrease with the profit rate and, therefore, the monotonicity of the WPC depends on the numeraire chosen (see the empirical evidence provided by Soklis 2011).

Fig. 3.18 The WPC, in terms of $\mathbf{b}^{\mathrm{T}}$, its bounds and the Sraffian curve; (a) France, 2005, and (b) Greece, 1994

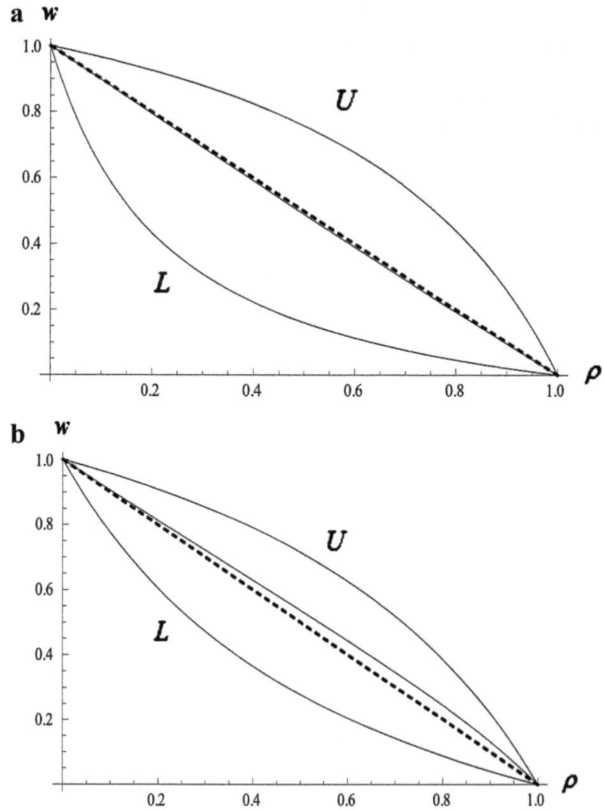

3.10 Concluding Remarks

The investigation of the relationships amongst prices, interindustry structure of production and income distribution in actual single-product economies gave the following results (which can be straightforwardly extended to the output-consumption-growth system; consider Sect. 2.2.1.4):

(i) The vectors of labour values, actual production prices and market prices are close to each other, as judged by alternative measures of deviation. More specifically, the deviations of actual production prices from labour values are, as a rule, much smaller than those of actual production prices from market prices. And there exist vectors of commodity values that are better approximations of the actual production and market prices than labour values.

(ii) The deviations of actual prices from labour values are not too sensitive to the type of measure used for their evaluation.

(iii) The actual uniform profit rate is usually no greater than 50 % of its maximum feasible value and, therefore, the polynomial approximation of the actual

Fig. 3.19 The WPC, in terms of $\mathbf{e}_M^{\mathrm{T}}$, its bounds and the Sraffian curve; (a) France, 2005, and (b) Greece, 1994

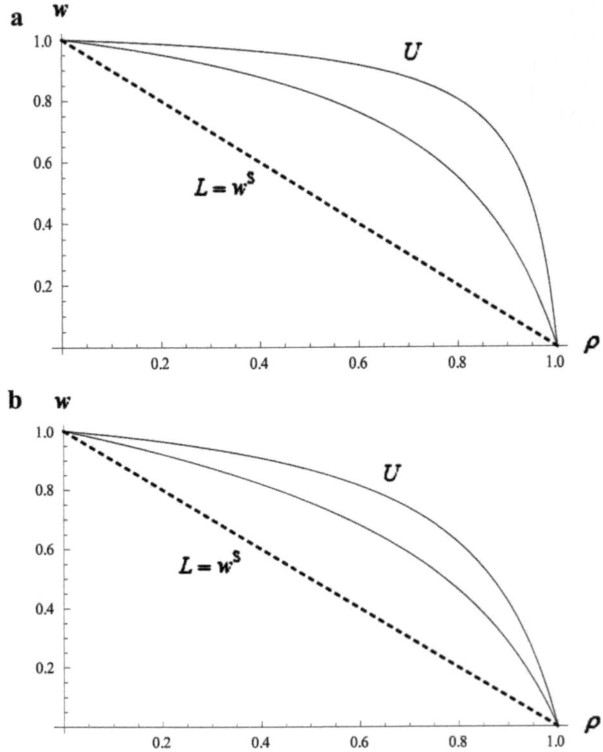

production prices, expressed in terms of Sraffa's Standard commodity, through dated quantities of embodied labour requires the inclusion of just a few terms. This also implies that the detected norm bounds for the actual production prices are not so loose. It is thus concluded that value-based approximations of actual economies could be considered as accurate enough.

(iv) Although the actual economies deviate considerably from the equal value compositions of capital case, they behave or tend to behave as corn-tractor systems with respect to the shape of the wage-profit rate curve and, at the same time, behave as three-industry systems with respect to the shape of the production price-profit rate curves. These findings indicate that the effective ranks of the matrices of vertically integrated technical coefficients or, equivalently, the effective dimensions of these economies appear to be relatively low, that is to say, between two and three. Hence, a *spectral* analysis of actual economies becomes absolutely necessary.

The detected insensitivity of actual price-labour value deviations and the spectral analysis of actual economies form the subjects of the following two chapters of this book. Future research should provide more empirical evidence from the fixed capital and joint production cases and, in parallel, concretize the analytic framework by incorporating turnover times, sectoral rates of capacity utilization, taxation (see Tsoulfidis 1990), labour of different kinds, noncompetitive imports and monetary factors. A crucial issue in these studies, which however has not attracted the attention that it may deserve, is that both direct and production prices are (weighted) average magnitudes and, therefore, they are not necessarily the best possible approximations to market prices (Tsoulfidis 2008, 2010, Chap. 5; Mariolis 2010b; Shaikh 2016; also see Schefold 1997, pp. 350–354 and 410–417). For instance, in agriculture and mining, the relevant direct and production prices are those that are formed on the 'marginal' lands and mines, and so the average direct price or the average production price is fraught with a certain degree of bias in approximating the respective market prices. This important aspect of the works of classical economists has received scant empirical attention over the years, possibly because the concept of marginal is chiefly associated with the neoclassical economics. Furthermore, the marginal conditions in actual economies are not easy to quantify (even in agriculture or mining, let alone the other industries). These difficulties, however, by no means should lead to the renouncement of efforts to make the marginal conditions amenable to further theorization with the aid of differential and integral calculus.

Appendix 1: Data Sources and Construction of Variables

A.1.1 Greece

The symmetric input-output tables of the Greek economy were available for the years 1988 through 1998 and at the 25 industries level of detail (Mylonas et al. 2000). However, the necessary data on employment and wage were not fully available for the year 1998, and so our analysis extends until the year 1997. From the 25 industries, only the first 19 are absolutely consistent with the requirements of our analysis: the concepts of labour values and production prices have no meaning in industries such as public administration and education, whereas the concept of output is problematic to industries such as finance and real estate. Thus, we decided to eliminate from our analysis the last 6 industries, making the necessary adjustments in the output vector.

These input-output tables are restricted to flow data so they do not include interindustry data on fixed capital stocks and also the noncompetitive imports. As a result, our investigation is restricted to a circulating capital model, where we cannot separate the foreign from the domestic sector of the economy. It is worth noting that the issue of noncompetitive imports leads to many complications (see Sect. 2.2.4).

The market prices of all products are taken to be equal to 1. Thus, the matrix of direct technical coefficients, $\mathbf{A}$, is obtained by dividing element-by-element the inputs of each industry by its gross output. In accordance with most of the relevant empirical studies, we use wage differentials to homogenize the sectoral employment, i.e. the vector of inputs in direct homogeneous labour, $\mathbf{l} \equiv [l_j]$, is estimated as

$$l_j = \left(\Lambda_j \overline{x}_j^{-1}\right)\left[w_{\mathrm{m}j}\left(\min_j\{w_{\mathrm{m}j}\}\right)^{-1}\right]$$

where Λ_j, $w_{\mathrm{m}j}$, $\overline{x}_j$ denote the total employment, money wage rate, in terms of market prices, and gross output of the industry j, respectively, and $\min_j \{w_{\mathrm{m}j}\}$ the minimum money wage rate in terms of market prices. Alternatively, the homogenization of employment could be achieved, for example, through the economy's average wage rate; in fact, the empirical results are robust to alternative normalizations with respect to homogenization of labour inputs.

Finally, by assuming that workers do not save and that their consumption has the same composition as the vector of the final consumption expenditures of the household sector, $\mathbf{f}^{\mathrm{T}}$, directly available in the input-output tables, the commodity vector defining the real wage rate is estimated as

$$\mathbf{b}^{\mathrm{T}} = \left[\min_j \{w_{\mathrm{m}j}\}\left(\mathbf{e}\,\mathbf{f}^{\mathrm{T}}\right)^{-1}\right]\mathbf{f}^{\mathrm{T}}$$

where $\mathbf{e}$ represents the vector of market prices (also see Okishio and Nakatani 1985, pp. 66–67; Ochoa 1989, p. 428). It goes without saying that the empirical results (on the deviations of production prices from labour values) are robust to the assumption that a certain relatively small fraction of wages, s_w, is saved; in that case, the vector of the real wage would be equal to $\left[(1 - s_w)\min_j\{w_{\mathrm{m}j}\}\left(\mathbf{e}\,\mathbf{f}^{\mathrm{T}}\right)^{-1}\right]\mathbf{f}^{\mathrm{T}}$.

A.1.2 Japan

The input-output tables of Japan are available from the OECD STAN database at the 35 industries level of detail. Industry 34 (Government and producer services) is eliminated from the analysis for it plays no role in the formation of the general profit rate and production prices. For the same reason, industry 35 (Other services) is also eliminated. In fact, the input-output tables for both industries report zero operating surplus.

The vector of direct labour coefficients is estimated using the wage bill of each industry (the product of annual wage times the number of employees) from the input-output table for each year of our analysis. The problem with this estimation is that the self-employed population is not accounted for. For this purpose, we created an index of self-employment calculated as the ratio of the total employed population (the number of employees plus the self-employed) to the number of employees. The estimation of the self-employed population is absolutely necessary for our analysis since in an economy such as the Japanese, self-employment is widespread.

For example, in agriculture in the year 1970, the number of self-employed was almost 12 times higher than that of the employees and dropped to approximately 6 times higher in the year 1990. The information on employment is available in the OECD STAN database. For a few industries, we could not collate data on the number of self-employed for the years 1970 and 1975, and so we used their percentage of the employed population in the year 1980. As the number of self-employed in these particular industries happened to be relatively small, it follows that our results are robust to this treatment. The industry names are given in Table 3.6.

A.1.3 China

The input-output tables of China for the year 1997 are available from the OECD STAN database at the 40 industries level of detail. Two industries 33 (Renting of machinery and equipment) and 34 (Computer and related activities) were eliminated from the analysis for they contain no data. The available input-output tables are restricted to flow data, and so our analysis will be carried out in terms of a circulating capital model. The flow vectors and matrices have been derived in a similar way with the above. The industries of the economy are the following:

1. Agriculture
2. Mining
3. Food
4. Textiles
5. Wood
6. Paper
7. Petroleum
8. Chemical
9. Pharmaceuticals
10. Rubber
11. Other nonmetallic mineral products
12. Iron and steel
13. Nonferrous metals
14. Fabricated metal products
15. Machinery and Equipment n.e.c.
16. Office accounting and computing machinery
17. Electrical machinery and apparatus n.e.c.
18. Radio and TV
19. Medical, precision and optical instruments
20. Motor vehicles
21. Building and repairing of ships and boats
22. Aircrafts and spacecraft
23. Railroad and transport equipment, n.e.c.

24. Manufacturing n.e.c.
25. Electricity, gas and water
26. Construction
27. Wholesale and retail trade
28. Hotels and restaurants
29. Transportation and storage
30. Communications
31. Finance insurance
32. Real estate
35. Research and development
36. Other business activities
37. Public administration
38. Education
39. Health and social work
40. Social services

A.1.4 Korea

Data limitations mainly on sectoral employment, wages, depreciation and capital stock restricted the analysis to 27 industries level of detail. In this classification, 'nonproductive' industries, such as, for example, the real estate and the public administration (whose output is really the wages of workers employed), are also included. The methodology applied for the construction of **A**, **l** and $\mathbf{b}^{\mathrm{T}}$ was similar to that applied to other countries. Since there is no matrix of capital stock coefficients, $\mathbf{A}^{\mathrm{C}}$, published for the Korean economy, we had to create one from the available data. To this end, we used the published fixed capital flow matrices companions of input-output tables of the years 1995 and 2000. This matrix allocates the gross fixed capital formation of each industry to itself and others. We use this matrix to form weights, assuming—in the absence of an actual capital stock matrix—that capital stock is allocated among producing industries in a way similar to that of gross investment. A gross capital stock vector corresponding to the 27 input-output industry detail is fortunately published by Shin (2005). This vector was allocated to each industry according to the weights that we formed with the fixed capital formation (for details, see Tsoulfidis and Rieu (2006)). Depreciation coefficients are directly provided by the Bank of Korea, and they are derived through the fixed capital flow matrices companions of the input-output data for the years 1995 and 2000. The depreciation coefficients matrix, $\mathbf{A}^{\mathrm{D}}$, is derived in a way similar to that of **A**. The industries of the economy that we used in our analysis are the following:

1. Agriculture, forestry, and fisheries
2. Mining and quarrying
3. Food, beverages and tobacco
4. Textile products and leather products

5. Wood and paper products
6. Printing, publishing and reproduction of recorded media
7. Petroleum and coal products
8. Chemicals and allied products
9. Nonmetallic mineral products
10. Primary metal products
11. Fabricated metal products
12. General machinery and equipment
13. Electronic and other electric equipment
14. Precision instruments
15. Transportation equipment
16. Furniture and other manufacturing products
17. Electric, gas, and water services
18. Construction
19. Wholesale and retail trade
20. Eating and drinking places, and hotels and other lodging places
21. Transportation and warehousing
22. Communications and broadcasting
23. Finance and insurance
24. Real estate and business service
25. Public administration and defence
26. Educational and health service
27. Social and other services

A.1.5 UK and USA

The input-output data for both countries are provided in the STAN basis of OECD. In the case of the UK, we managed to put together employment data (employed and self-employed). Provided that the wage data are available in the input-output tables, all we needed to carry out was an estimate of the wage equivalent of the self-employed population to obtain the total wage bill actually given and the imputed one for the self-employed population. The capital flow matrix for the case of the UK is provided in the OECD STAN database along with data on capital stock, which we corresponded to each of the 33 industries. The US input-output data were collated from the same source, and the industry names (the same with the UK) are given in Table 3.9.

A.1.6 Canada

The input-output tables of Canada are available from the OECD STAN database at the 34 industries level of detail. $\mathbf{A}$, $\mathbf{l}$ and $\mathbf{b}^{\mathrm{T}}$ are created following the standard procedure. The sectoral wages are given as a row of the input-output tables, whereas the sectoral average wage is derived by estimating the number of employees of each industry. The so-derived sectoral wage is multiplied by the index of self-employment calculated by the ratio of the total employed population (the number of employees plus the self-employed) to the number of employees. The information on employment in thousands is available in the OECD STAN database. The industries of the economy that we used in our analysis are the following:

1. Agriculture
2. Mining
3. Food
4. Textiles
5. Wood
6. Paper
7. Petroleum
8. Chemical
9. Rubber
10. Other nonmetallic mineral products
11. Machinery and equipment
12. Fabricated products
13. Machinery and equipment
14. Office machinery
15. Electrical machinery
16. Radio and TV
17. Motor vehicle
18. Aircrafts
19. Railroad equipment
20. Railroad equipment
21. Manufacturing n.e.c.
22. Utilities
23. Construction
24. Wholesale and retail trade
25. Hotels and restaurants
26. Transportation
27. Communications
28. Finance insurance and real estate
29. Computer equipment
30. Other business
31. Public administration
32. Education
33. Health
34. Social services

A.1.7 Denmark, Finland, France, Germany and Sweden

The described products (and their correspondence to CPA) are the following:

1. (CPA: 01). Products of agriculture, hunting and related services
2. (02). Products of forestry, logging and related services
3. (05). Fish and other fishing products; services incidental of fishing
4. (10). Coal and lignite; peat
5. (11). Crude petroleum and natural gas; services incidental to oil and gas extraction excluding surveying
6. (12). Uranium and thorium ores
7. (13). Metal ores
8. (14). Other mining and quarrying products
9. (15). Food products and beverages
10. (16). Tobacco products
11. (17). Textiles
12. (18). Wearing apparel; furs
13. (19). Leather and leather products
14. (20). Wood and products of wood and cork (except furniture); articles of straw and plaiting materials
15. (21). Pulp, paper and paper products
16. (22). Printed matter and recorded media
17. (23). Coke, refined petroleum products and nuclear fuels
18. (24). Chemicals, chemical products and man-made fibres
19. (25). Rubber and plastic products
20. (26). Other nonmetallic mineral products
21. (27). Basic metals
22. (28). Fabricated metal products, except machinery and equipment
23. (29). Machinery and equipment n.e.c.
24. (30). Office machinery and computers
25. (31). Electrical machinery and apparatus n.e.c.
26. (32). Radio, television and communication equipment and apparatus
27. (33). Medical, precision and optical instruments, watches and clocks
28. (34). Motor vehicles, trailers and semi-trailers
29. (35). Other transport equipment
30. (36). Furniture; other manufactured goods n.e.c.
31. (37). Secondary raw materials
32. (40). Electrical energy, gas, steam and hot water
33. (41). Collected and purified water, distribution services of water
34. (45). Construction work
35. (50). Trade, maintenance and repair services of motor vehicles and motorcycles; retail sale of automotive fuel
36. (51). Wholesale trade and commission trade services, except of motor vehicles and motorcycles

37. (52). Retail trade services, except of motor vehicles and motorcycles; repair services of personal and household goods
38. (55). Hotel and restaurant services
39. (60). Land transport; transport via pipeline services
40. (61). Water transport services
41. (62). Air transport services
42. (63). Supporting and auxiliary transport services; travel agency services
43. (64). Post and telecommunication services
44. (65). Financial intermediation services, except insurance and pension funding services
45. (66). Insurance and pension funding services, except compulsory social security services
46. (67). Services auxiliary to financial intermediation
47. (70). Real estate services
48. (71). Renting services of machinery and equipment without operator and of personal and household goods
49. (72). Computer and related services
50. (73). Research and development services
51. (74). Other business services
52. (75). Public administration and defence services; compulsory social security services
53. (80). Education services
54. (85). Health and social work services
55. (90). Sewage and refuse disposal services, sanitation and similar services
56. (91). Membership organisation services n.e.c.
57. (92). Recreational, cultural and sporting services
58. (93). Other services
59. (95). Private households with employed persons

Appendix 2: A Note on the Supply and Use Tables

The symmetric input-output tables can be derived from the 'System of National Accounts' framework of Supply and Use Tables (SUTs; see, e.g. United Nations 1999, Chaps. 2, 3, and 4; Eurostat 2008, Chap. 11), introduced in 1968 (see United Nations 1968, Chap. 3). Given that in the SUTs there are industries that produce more than one commodity, and commodities that are produced by more than one industry, it follows that the SUTs could be considered as the *counterpart* of joint production systems (see, e.g. Flaschel 1980, pp. 120–121; Bidard and Erreygers 1998, pp. 434–436). By contrast, in the SIOTs, there is no industry that produces more than one commodity nor commodity that is produced by more than one industry, and, therefore, the SIOTs could be considered as the counterpart of single production systems. Since joint production is the empirically relevant case (Steedman 1984; Faber et al. 1998; Kurz 2006), SUTs constitute a more realistic 'picture' (in the sense of multiproduct output resulting from a single plant or process) of the actual economic system than SIOTs. It has to be noted, however, that some of the 'joint' products that appear in the SUTs may result from statistical classification and, therefore, they do not correspond to the genuine notion of joint production (see, e.g. Semmler 1984, pp. 168–169; United Nations 1999, p. 77).

The SUTs are not necessarily 'square', i.e. the number of produced commodities does not necessarily equal the number of operated industries (see, e.g. United Nations 1999, p. 86; Eurostat (2008), p. 295). Square matrices are obtained by applying aggregation methods (then some important information may be lost). Moreover, in the Supply Tables, goods and services are measured at current 'basic prices', while in the Use Tables, all intermediate costs are measured in current 'purchasers' prices'. The derivation of the SUT at basic prices may be based on the method proposed by United Nations (1999, Chap. 3 and pp. 228–229).

For a review of the methods used to convert the SUT into SIOT, see, e.g. ten Raa and Rueda-Cantuche (2003, pp. 441–447). Amongst the various available methods, the so-called 'Commodity Technology Assumption' is the only one that fulfils a set of important properties of the input-output analysis (see Jansen and ten Raa 1990). However, the 'commodity technology assumption' is possible to generate economically insignificant results, i.e. negative elements in the input-output matrix. Ten Raa and Rueda-Cantuche (2013) offer a critical review of the various procedures proposed to overcome this inconsistency, while Lager (2007), Mariolis (2008) and Soklis (2009b) argue that the v. Neumann-Sraffa treatment of joint-product systems constitutes a preferable approach, not based on any of the restrictive (and debatable) assumptions of the conversion methods.

References

Angeloussis, A. (2006). *An empirical investigation of the reswitching of techniques phenomenon for the Greek economy, 1988–1992*. Master's Thesis, Athens: Department of Public Administration, Panteion University (in Greek).

Bidard, C., & Erreygers, G. (1998). Sraffa and Leontief on joint production. *Review of Political Economy, 10*(4), 427–446.

Bienenfeld, M. (1988). Regularity in price changes as an effect of changes in distribution. *Cambridge Journal of Economics, 12*(2), 247–255.

Cekota, J. (1988). Technological change in Canada (1961–80): An application of the surrogate wage function. *The Canadian Journal of Economics/Revue canadienne d'Economique, 21*(2), 348–358.

Cekota, J. (1990). The Soviet military sector and technological progress. *Defence Economics, 1*(4), 311–328.

Chilcote, E. B. (1997). *Interindustry structure, relative prices, and productivity: An input-output study of the U.S. and O.E.C.D. countries*. Ph.D. Dissertation, New York: New School for Social Research.

Cockshott, P., & Cottrell, A. (1997). Labour time versus alternative value bases: A research note. *Cambridge Journal of Economics, 21*(4), 545–549.

Cockshott, P., Cottrell, A., & Michaelson, G. (1995). Testing Marx: Some new results from UK data. *Capital and Class, 19*(1), 103–129.

Da Silva, E. A. (1993). The wage-profit curve in Brazil: An input-output model with fixed capital, 1975. *Review of Radical Political Economics, 23*(1–2), 104–110.
Da Silva, E. A., & Rosinger, J.-L. (1992). Prices, wages and profits in Brazil: An input-output analysis, 1975. In F. Moseley & E. N. Wolff (Eds.), *International perspectives on profitability and accumulation* (pp. 155–173). Aldershot: Edward Elgar.
Degasperi, M., & Fredholm, T. (2010). Productivity accounting based on production prices. *Metroeconomica, 61*(2), 267–281.
del Valle Caballero, J. (1993). *Structural change and factor prices* (Serie de Ensayos y Monografias, Vol. 66). Recinto de Río Piedras: Unidad de Investigaciones Económicas, Departamento de Economía, Universidad de Puerto Rico.
Ellis, L., & Smith, K. (2007). *The global upward trend in the profit share*. Bank for International Settlement, working paper no. 231. http://ssrn.com/abstract=1013997. Accessed 12 Dec 2014.
Eurostat. (2008). *Eurostat manual of supply, use and input-output tables*. Luxemburg: Office for the Official Publications of the European Communities.
Faber, M., Proops, J. L. R., & Baumgärtner, S. (1998). All production is joint production. A thermodynamic analysis. In S. Faucheux, J. Gowdy, & I. Nicolaï (Eds.), *Sustainability and firms: Technological change and the changing regulatory environment* (pp. 131–158). Cheltenham: Edward Elgar.
Fink, G. (1981). Price distortions in the Austrian and in the Hungarian economy. *Journal of Economics, 41*(1–2), 111–132.
Flaschel, P. (1980). The derivation and comparison of employment multipliers and labour productivity indexes using monetary and physical input-output tables. *Economics of Planning, 16* (3), 118–129.
Flaschel, P., Franke, R., & Veneziani, R. (2012). The measurement of prices of production: An alternative approach. *Review of Political Economy, 24*(3), 417–435.
Flaschel, P., Fröhlich, N., & Veneziani, R. (2013). The sources of aggregate profitability: Marx's theory of surplus value revisited. *European Journal of Economics and Economic Policies: Intervention, 10*(3), 299–312.
Fröhlich, N. (2013). Labour values, prices of production and the missing equalisation tendency of profit rates: Evidence from the German economy. *Cambridge Journal of Economics, 37*(5), 1107–1126.
Fujimori, Y. (1992). Wage-profit curves in a von Neumann-Leontief model: Theory and computation of Japan's economy 1970–1980. *Journal of Applied Input-Output Analysis, 1*(1), 43–54.
Garbellini, N., & Wirkierman, A. (2014). Productivity accounting in vertically (hyper-)integrated terms: Bridging the gap between theory and empirics. *Metroeconomica, 65*(1), 154–190.
García, M. M., & Garzón, C. A. R. (2011). La frontera de distribución en Colombia. *Revista de Economía Institucional, 13*(24), 357–372.
Hamilton, C. (1986). A general equilibrium model of structural change and economic growth, with application to South Korea. *Journal of Development Economics, 23*(1), 67–88.
Han, Z., & Schefold, B. (2006). An empirical investigation of paradoxes: Reswitching and reverse capital deepening in capital theory. *Cambridge Journal of Economics, 30*(5), 737–765.
Harvie, D. (2000). Testing Goodwin: Growth cycles in ten OECD countries. *Cambridge Journal of Economics, 24*(3), 349–376.
Hejl, L., Kyn, O., & Sekerka, B. (1967). Price calculations. *Czechoslovak Economic Papers, 8*, 61–81.
Iliadi, F., Mariolis, T., Soklis, G., & Tsoulfidis, L. (2014). Bienenfeld's approximation of production prices and eigenvalue distribution: Further evidence from five European economies. *Contributions to Political Economy, 33*(1), 35–54.
Izyumov, A., & Alterman, S. (2005). The general rate of profit in a new market economy: Conceptual issues and estimates. *Review of Radical Political Economics, 37*(4), 476–493.
Jansen, K. P., & ten Raa, T. (1990). The choice of model in the construction of input-output coefficients matrices. *International Economic Review, 31*(1), 213–227.

Karabarbounis, L., & Neiman, B. (2013). *Declining labor shares and the global rise of corporate saving*. National Bureau of Economic Research, working paper no. 18154. http://www.nber.org/papers/w18154. Accessed 12 Dec 2014.

Krause, U. (1981). Heterogeneous labour and the fundamental Marxian theorem. *The Review of Economic Studies, 48*(1), 173–178.

Krelle, W. (1977). Basic facts in capital theory. Some lessons from the controversy in capital theory. *Revue d'Economie Politique, 87*(2), 282–329.

Kurz, H. D. (2006). Goods and bads: Sundry observations on joint production waste disposal, and renewable and exhaustible resources. *Progress in Industrial Ecology—an International Journal, 3*(4), 280–301.

Kyn, O., Sekerka, B., & Hejl, L. (1967). A model for the planning of prices. In C. H. Feinstein (Ed.), *Socialism, capitalism and economic growth: Essays presented to Maurice Dobb* (pp. 101–124). London: Cambridge University Press.

Lager, C. (2007). *Why and when are there negative coefficients in joint production systems with 'commodity technology'?*. Paper presented at the 16th international input-output conference, Istanbul, Turkey, 2–6 July 2007.

Leontief, W. (1985). Technological change, prices, wages and rates of return on capital in the U.S. economy. In W. Leontief (Ed.) (1986), *Input-output economics* (pp. 392–417). Oxford: Oxford University Press.

Li, B. (2014a). Marx's labor theory of value and its implications for structural problems in China's economy. *Economic and Political Studies, 2*(2), 139–150.

Li, B. (2014b). Fixed capital and wage-profit curves *à la* von Neumann-Leontief: China's economy 1987–2000. *Research in Political Economy, 29*, 75–93.

Mariolis, T. (2008). *The conversion of the SUTs to SIOTs*. Internal report of the study group on Sraffian economics, 4 April 2008 (in Greek). Athens: Department of Public Administration, Panteion University.

Mariolis, T. (2010a). Norm bounds for a transformed price vector in Sraffian systems. *Applied Mathematical Sciences, 4*(9–12), 551–574.

Mariolis, T. (2010b). The system of David Ricardo: Falling profit rate and foreign trade. In T. Mariolis (Ed.), *Essays on the logical history of political economy* (in Greek) (pp. 107–141). Athens: Matura.

Mariolis, T. (2015). Norm bounds and a homographic approximation for the wage-profit curve. *Metroeconomica, 66*(2), 263–283.

Mariolis, T., & Soklis, G. (2007). On the empirical validity of the labour theory of value. In T. Mariolis (2010). *Essays on the logical history of political economy* (in Greek) (pp. 231–260). Athens: Matura.

Mariolis, T., & Soklis, G. (2010). Additive labour values and prices of production: Evidence from the supply and use tables of the French, German and Greek economies. *Economic Issues, 15*(2), 87–107.

Mariolis, T., & Soklis, G. (2011). On constructing numeraire-free measures of price-value deviation: A note on the Steedman-Tomkins distance. *Cambridge Journal of Economics, 35*(3), 613–618.

Mariolis, T., & Soklis, G. (2014). *The Sraffian multiplier for the Greek economy: Evidence from the supply and use table for the year 2010*. MPRA paper no 6253. http://mpra.ub.uni-muenchen.de/60253/. Accessed 12 Dec 2014.

Mariolis, T., & Tsoulfidis, L. (2009). Decomposing the changes in production prices into 'capital-intensity' and 'price' effects: Theory and evidence from the Chinese economy. *Contributions to Political Economy, 28*(1), 1–22.

Mariolis, T., Rodousakis, N., & Tsoulfidis, L. (2006). The rate of profit in the Greek economy, 1988–1997. An input-output analysis. *Archives of Economic History, 18*(2), 177–190.

Mariolis, T., Soklis, G., & Groza, E. (2012). Estimation of the maximum attainable economic dependency ratio: Evidence from the symmetric input-output tables of four European economies. *Journal of Economic Analysis, 3*(1), 52–71.

Mariolis, T., Soklis, G., & Zouvela, E. (2013). Testing Böhm-Bawerk's theory of capital: Some evidence from the Finnish economy. *The Review of Austrian Economics, 26*(2), 207–220.

Marzi, G. (1994). Vertically integrated sectors and the empirics of structural change. *Structural Change and Economic Dynamics, 5*(1), 155–175.

Michl, T. R. (1991). Wage-profit curves in US manufacturing. *Cambridge Journal of Economics, 15*(3), 271–286.

Miller, R. E., & Blair, P. D. (2009). *Input-output analysis: Foundations and extensions*. Cambridge: Cambridge University Press.

Mylonas, N. A., Economakou, M., Frankoulopoulos, N., Krasadakis, A., Molfetas, K., Stromplos, N., & Vlachos, P. (2000). *Natural resource accounts and environmental input-output tables for Greece 1988–1998*. Athens: Institute of Computer and Communications Systems (ICCS) of National Technical University of Athens (NTUA).

Nakajima, A. (2013). Determination of prices as comparison of market prices to natural prices: Input output analysis of Japan for 1951–2000. *Bulletin of Political Economy, 7*(2), 125–144.

Ochoa, E. (1984). *Labor values and prices of production: An interindustry study of the U.S. economy, 1947–1972*. Ph.D. Dissertation, New York: New School for Social Research.

Ochoa, E. (1989). Value, prices and wage-profit curves in the U.S. economy. *Cambridge Journal of Economics, 13*(3), 413–429.

Okishio, N., & Nakatani, T. (1985). A measurement of the rate of surplus value. In M. Krüger & P. Flaschel (Eds.) (1993), *Nobuo Okishio. Essays on political economy* (pp. 61–73). Frankfurt am Main: Peter Lang.

Özol, C. (1984). Parable and realism in production theory: The surrogate wage function. *The Canadian Journal of Economics/Revue canadienne d'Economique, 17*(2), 413–429.

Özol, C. (1991). The surrogate wage function and capital: Theory with measurement. *The Canadian Journal of Economics/Revue canadienne d'Economique, 24*(1), 175–191.

Petrović, P. (1987). The deviation of production prices from labour values: Some methodological and empirical evidence. *Cambridge Journal of Economics, 11*(3), 197–210.

Petrović, P. (1988). Price distortion and income dispersion in a labor-managed economy: Evidence from Yugoslavia. *Journal of Comparative Economics, 12*(4), 592–603.

Petrović, P. (1991). Shape of a wage-profit curve, some methodology and empirical evidence. *Metroeconomica, 42*(2), 93–112.

Piketty, T. (2013). *Le Capital au XXIe siècle*. Paris: Seuil.

Sánchez, C., & Ferràndez, M. N. (2010). Valores, precios de producción y precios de mercado a partir de los datos de la economía española. *Investigacion Economica, 69*(274), 87–118.

Sánchez, C., & Montibeler, E. E. (2015). The labour theory of value and the prices in China (in Spanish). *Economia e Sociedade, 24*(2), 329–354.

Schefold, B. (1997). *Normal prices, technical change and accumulation*. London: Macmillan.

Sekerka, B., Kyn, O., & Hejl, L. (1970). Price system computable from input-output coefficients. In A. P. Carter & A. Bródy (Eds.), *Contributions to input-output analysis* (pp. 183–203). Amsterdam: North-Holland.

Semmler, W. (1984). *Competition, monopoly, and differential profit rates. On the relevance of the classical and Marxian theories of production prices for modern industrial and corporate pricing*. New York: Columbia University Press.

Shaikh, A. M. (1984). The transformation from Marx to Sraffa: Prelude to a critique of the neo-Ricardians. In E. Mandel & A. Freeman (Eds.), *Ricardo, Marx, Sraffa: The Langston memorial volume* (pp. 43–84). London: Verso.

Shaikh, A. M. (1998). The empirical strength of the labour theory of value. In R. Bellofiore (Ed.), *Marxian economics: A reappraisal* (Vol. 2, pp. 225–251). New York: St. Martin's Press.

Shaikh, A. M. (2012). The empirical linearity of Sraffa's critical output-capital ratios. In C. Gehrke, N. Salvadori, I. Steedman, & R. Sturn (Eds.), *Classical political economy and modern theory. Essays in honour of Heinz Kurz* (pp. 89–101). London: Routledge.

Shaikh, A. M. (2016). *Capitalism: Competition, conflict, crises*. Oxford: Oxford University Press.

Shin, C.-S. (2005). Capital stock matrix for the Korean economy: 1995–2000. *Seoul Journal of Economics, 18*(1), 59–85.

Soklis, G. (2006). *Labour values and production prices: Exploration based on the joint production table of the Greek economy for the year 1999*. Master's Thesis, Athens: Department of Public Administration, Panteion University (in Greek).

Soklis, G. (2009a). Alternative value bases and prices: Evidence from the input-output tables of the Swedish economy. *Journal of Applied Input-Output Analysis, 15*(1), 21–39.

Soklis, G. (2009b). The conversion of the supply and use tables to symmetric input-output tables: A critical review. *Bulletin of Political Economy, 3*(1), 51–70.

Soklis, G. (2011). Shape of wage-profit curves in joint production systems: Evidence from the supply and use tables of the Finnish economy. *Metroeconomica, 62*(4), 548–560.

Soklis, G. (2012). *Labour values, commodity values, prices and income distribution: Exploration based on empirical input-output tables*. Ph.D. Dissertation, Athens: Department of Public Administration, Panteion University (in Greek).

Soklis, G. (2014). Contenido en mercancía de las mercancías y precios: Evidencia empírica a partir de los cuadros de insumo-producto de la economía francesa. *Investigacion Economica, 73* (288), 39–61.

Soklis, G. (2015). Labour versus alternative value bases in actual joint production systems. *Bulletin of Political Economy, 9*(1) 1–31.

Steedman, I. (1984). L'importance empirique de la production jointe. In C. Bidard (Ed.), *La Production jointe: Nouveaux débats* (pp. 5–20). Paris: Economica.

Steedman, I. (1999). Vertical integration and 'reduction to dated quantities of labour'. In G. Mongiovi & F. Petri (Eds.), *Value distribution and capital. Essays in honour of Pierangelo Garegnani* (pp. 314–318). London: Routledge.

Steedman, I., & Tomkins, J. (1998). On measuring the deviation of prices from values. *Cambridge Journal of Economics, 22*(3), 379–385.

ten Raa, T., & Rueda-Cantuche, J. M. (2003). The construction of input-output coefficients matrices in an axiomatic context: Some further considerations. *Economic Systems Research, 15*(4), 439–455.

ten Raa, T., & Rueda-Cantuche, J. M. (2013). The problem of negatives generated by the commodity technology model in input-output analysis: A review of the solutions. *Journal of Economic Structures*. doi:10.1186/2193-2409-2-5.

Trigg, A. (2002). Using micro data to test the divergence between prices and labour values. *International Review of Applied Economics, 16*(2), 169–186.

Tsoulfidis, L. (1990). Price effects of indirect and corporate income taxes: An input-output analysis. *Metroeconomica, 41*(2), 111–135.

Tsoulfidis, L. (2008). Price-value deviations: Further evidence from input-output data of Japan. *International Review of Applied Economics, 22*(6), 707–724.

Tsoulfidis, L. (2010). *Competing schools of economic thought*. Heidelberg: Springer-Verlag.

Tsoulfidis, L., & Maniatis, T. (2002). Values, prices of production and market prices: Some more evidence from the Greek economy. *Cambridge Journal of Economics, 26*(3), 359–369.

Tsoulfidis, L., & Mariolis, T. (2007). Labour values, prices of production and the effects of income distribution: Evidence from the Greek economy. *Economic Systems Research, 19*(4), 425–437.

Tsoulfidis, L., & Paitaridis, D. (2009). On the labor theory of value: Statistical artefacts or regularities? *Research in Political Economy, 25*, 209–232.

Tsoulfidis, L., & Rieu, D.-M. (2006). Labor values, prices of production, and wage-profit rate frontiers of the Korean economy. *Seoul Journal of Economics, 19*(3), 275–295.

United Nations. (1968). *A system of national accounts*. New York: United Nations.

United Nations. (1999). *Handbook of input – output table. Compilation and analysis. Studies in methods. Handbook of national accounting*. United Nations: New York.

Val'tukh, K. K. (2005). The theory of value: Statistical verification, generalization of information, and topical conclusions. *Herald of the Russian Academy of Sciences, 75*(5), 516–528.

Valtukh, K. K. (1987). *Marx's theory of commodity and surplus value. Formalised exposition.* Moscow: Progress Publishers.

Wirkierman, A. (2012). *Computable production prices with fixed capital as a joint product and technical progress. A simple case*. Paper presented at the 20th international input-output conference, Bratislava, Slovakia, 26–29 Jun 2012. http://www.iioa.org/conferences/20th/papers/files/815_20120520111_alw_pK_joint_products.pdf. Accessed 12 Dec 2014.

Yu, Z., & Feng, Z. (2007). The rate of surplus value, the composition of capital, and the rate of profit in the Chinese manufacturing industry: 1978–2004. *Bulletin of Political Economy, 1*(1), 17–42.

Zachariah, D. (2006). Labour value and equalisation of profit rates: A multi-country study. *Indian Development Review, 4*(1), 1–21. Reprinted in T. Mariolis, & L. Tsoulfidis (Eds.) (2006), *Distribution, development and prices. Critical perspectives* (pp. 1–21). New Delhi: Serials.

Zachariah, D. (2009). Determinants of the average profit rate and the trajectory of capitalist economies. *Bulletin of Political Economy, 3*(1), 13–36.

Chapter 4
Measures of Production Price-Labour Value Deviation and Production Conditions

Abstract Empirical studies indicate that the deviations of actual production prices from labour values are not too sensitive to the type of measure used for their evaluation. This chapter attempts to theorize this fact by focusing on the relationships between the 'traditional' and the numeraire-free measures of deviation. It also provides an illustration of these relationships using actual input-output data.

Keywords Measures of deviation • Production prices • Labour values • Sociotechnical conditions of production

4.1 Introduction

Empirical studies of single-product systems indicate that the deviations of actual production prices from labour values are not too sensitive to the type of measure used for their evaluation.[1] For instance, a study on the input-output table of the Chinese economy for the year 1997 (Mariolis and Tsoulfidis 2009, p. 12), in which the vector of production prices is normalized with the use of Sraffa's Standard commodity (SSC), indicates that the absolute error between the actual '$d-$distance' (Steedman and Tomkins 1998) and 'mean absolute deviation' (and 'mean absolute weighted deviation') is 0.2 % (is 0.5 %) and that the relevant relative error is 1.75 % (is 4.39 %).[2]

This chapter attempts to theorize this empirical fact by focusing on the relationships between the 'traditional' and the numeraire-free measures of deviation, where the former include the 'mean absolute deviation' (or MAD), the 'root-mean-square-percent-error' (or RMS%E) and the 'mean absolute weighted deviation'

[1] See Ochoa (1984, Chaps. 6–8; 1989, pp. 418–422), Petrović (1987, pp. 206–208), Chilcote (1997, Chaps. 6–7), Shaikh (1998, p. 233), Tsoulfidis and Maniatis (2002, pp. 365), Tsoulfidis and Rieu (2006, p. 289), Tsoulfidis and Mariolis (2007, p. 428), Tsoulfidis (2008, p. 715), Tsoulfidis and Paitaridis (2009, p. 221), Sánchez and Ferràndez (2010, p. 90), Mariolis and Soklis (2011, pp. 616–617), Sánchez and Montibeler (2015, pp. 336–339) and Chap. 3 in this book. What follows draws heavily on Mariolis and Tsoulfidis (2010, 2014) and Mariolis and Soklis (2011).

[2] Throughout the chapter, we use the term 'error' because we hypothesize that the $d-$distance represents the 'true or accepted' value of the deviation under study. However, see the Appendix at the end of this chapter.

© Springer Japan 2016

T. Mariolis, L. Tsoulfidis, *Modern Classical Economics and Reality*, Evolutionary Economics and Social Complexity Science 2, DOI 10.1007/978-4-431-55004-4_4

(or MAWD), while the latter include the d – distance and its variants.[3] More specifically, the main argument is that, for *realistic* values of the relative profit rate, a parameter reflecting the sociotechnical conditions of production, all these measures of deviation tend to be close to each other and, at the same time, follow certain rankings, which we can explore starting from a two-industry economy.

The remainder of the chapter is structured as follows. Section 4.2 deals with the measures of deviation in the case of a two-industry economy. Section 4.3 generalizes to the n – industry case. Section 4.4 provides an empirical illustration using input-output data from the Greek and Japanese economies. Finally, Sect. 4.5 concludes.

4.2 Theoretical Analysis of a Two-Industry Economy

Let us suppose a usual linear system of production with two industries, where prices are normalized by setting $\mathbf{pz}^{\mathrm{T}} = \mathbf{vz}^{\mathrm{T}}$ or

$$p_1 z_1 + p_2 z_2 = v_1 z_1 + v_2 z_2 \tag{4.1}$$

where $\mathbf{p}\equiv[p_j]$, $\mathbf{v}\equiv[v_j]$, are the vectors of production prices and labour values, respectively, and the semi-positive vector $\mathbf{z}^{\mathrm{T}}\equiv[z_i]$ represents the numeraire. Equation 4.1 can be rewritten as

$$p_2 - v_2 = (v_1 - p_1)z \tag{4.2}$$

where $z \equiv z_1 z_2^{-1}$.

Now, let d_{I} show the MAD. Substituting (4.2) in the definition of the MAD, i.e.

$$d_{\mathrm{I}} \equiv n^{-1} \sum_{j=1}^{n} \left| p_j v_j^{-1} - 1 \right| \tag{4.3}$$

where n is the number of commodities, yields

$$2d_{\mathrm{I}} = |p_1 - v_1| v_1^{-1} + \left(|v_1 - p_1| v_2^{-1}\right) z \tag{4.4}$$

In order to simplify our notation, we set

[3] For an alternative measure, i.e. the 'mean absolute eigen-deviation of labour-commanded prices from labour values', see Sect. 5.3.4.

$$f \equiv p_1 p_2^{-1} \tag{4.5}$$

where f is a monotonic function of the profit rat, and $f = v \equiv v_1 v_2^{-1}$ at $r = 0$.[4] From Eqs. 4.2 and 4.5, we obtain

$$p_1 = (v_1 z + v_2) f (1 + fz)^{-1} \tag{4.6}$$

For the sake of brevity and clarity of presentation, we focus on the case in which f is a strictly increasing function, i.e. $p_1 \geq v_1$. By combining Eqs. 4.4 and 4.6, we get

$$2d_{\mathrm{I}} = (\delta - 1) F_{\mathrm{I}}(z) \tag{4.7}$$

where $\delta \equiv f v^{-1} (>1 \text{ for } r > 0)$ represents the ratio of relative prices to relative labour values and $F_{\mathrm{I}}(z) \equiv (1 + vz)(1 + fz)^{-1}$ is a strictly decreasing function reflecting the dependence of d_{I} on z. For $z = 0$, we obtain $2d_{\mathrm{I}}(0) = \delta - 1$, whereas at the other extreme, i.e. as $z \to +\infty$, we obtain $2d_{\mathrm{I}}(+\infty) = 1 - \delta^{-1}$. Thus, we may write $d_{\mathrm{I}}(0)(d_{\mathrm{I}}(+\infty))^{-1} = \delta$,

$$\Delta_{\mathrm{I}} \equiv d_{\mathrm{I}}(0) - d_{\mathrm{I}}(+\infty) = \left[2^{-1}\left(\delta + \delta^{-1}\right)\right] - 1 = 2d_{\mathrm{I}}(0) d_{\mathrm{I}}(+\infty) \tag{4.8}$$

and using the Taylor expansion about $\delta = 1$,

$$\Delta_{\mathrm{I}} \approx 2^{-1}\left[(\delta - 1)^2 - (\delta - 1)^3\right] = 2(d_{\mathrm{I}}(0))^2 (2 - \delta) \tag{4.8a}$$

where this approximation is most reliable when $\delta < 1.18$.[5]

The next measure of deviation is the RMS%E, d_{II}, which is defined as

$$d_{\mathrm{II}} \equiv \sqrt{n^{-1} \sum_{j=1}^{n} \left(p_j v_j^{-1} - 1\right)^2} \tag{4.9}$$

or

$$d_{\mathrm{II}} = d_{\mathrm{I}} (\cos \phi)^{-1} \tag{4.9a}$$

where ϕ represents the angle between the vectors $\left|\mathbf{p}\hat{\mathbf{v}}^{-1} - \mathbf{e}\right|$ and the summation

[4] Iff the vector of direct labour coefficients is the left P-F eigenvector of the matrix of direct technical coefficients, then $f = v$ for each r (see Sect. 2.2.1.1).

[5] Throughout the chapter, 'most reliable' means that the relative error is less than 3 %. It may also be noted that $\Delta_{\mathrm{I}}(\delta) = \Delta_{\mathrm{I}}\left(\delta^{-1}\right)$. Moreover, when f decreases with r, (i) Eq. 4.7 holds with $(1 - \delta)$ and, therefore, (ii) $d_{\mathrm{I}}(+\infty) - d_{\mathrm{I}}(0)$ equals $2d_{\mathrm{I}}(0) d_{\mathrm{I}}(+\infty)$.

vector **e**. Thus, it holds true that $d_{\mathrm{I}} \leq d_{\mathrm{II}}$. Substituting Eqs. 4.2 and 4.6 in the definition of d_{II} yields

$$d_{\mathrm{II}} = 2^{-1}(\delta - 1)F_{\mathrm{II}}(z) = d_{\mathrm{I}}(0)F_{\mathrm{II}}(z) \tag{4.10}$$

where

$$F_{\mathrm{II}}(z) \equiv \sqrt{2\left[1 + (vz)^2\right]}(1 + fz)^{-1}$$

From Eqs. 4.7, 4.9a and 4.10, we obtain

$$\cos\phi = \left(\sqrt{2}\right)^{-1}(1 + vz)\left[1 + (vz)^2\right]^{-1/2}$$

which implies

$$\phi(Z) = \phi\left(Z^{-1}\right) \tag{4.11}$$

where $Z \equiv vz$. From the above, it follows that:

(i) At $z^* \equiv v^{-1}$ the absolute percentage deviations of prices from labour values are equal to each other and, therefore, it holds

$$\bar{d} \equiv d_{\mathrm{I}}\left(z^*\right) = d_{\mathrm{II}}\left(z^*\right) = (p_1 - v_1)v_1^{-1} = 2d_{\mathrm{I}}(0)(1 + \delta)^{-1}$$

i.e. $\cos\phi = 1$.

(ii) d_{II} (z) also equals $\bar{d}$ at $z = v^{-1}\left(\delta^2 + 2\delta - 1\right)\left(-\delta^2 + 2\delta + 1\right)^{-1}$.

(iii) F_{II} (z) is minimized at $z^{**} \equiv \delta v^{-1}$, where

$$\begin{aligned}(d_{\mathrm{II}})_{\min} \equiv d_{\mathrm{II}}\left(z^{**}\right) &= d_{\mathrm{I}}(0)\sqrt{2\left(1 + \delta^2\right)^{-1}} = \sqrt{1 - \cos^2\phi(z^{**})} \\ &= \sin\phi\left(z^{**}\right)\end{aligned}$$

or

$$(d_{\mathrm{II}})_{\min} = \sqrt{\bar{d}d_{\mathrm{I}}(z^{**})} \tag{4.12}$$

i.e. the minimum value of $d_{\mathrm{II}}(z)$ (a strictly increasing function of δ) equals $\sin\phi(z^{**})$ and constitutes the geometric mean of

$$\bar{d} = \sin\phi\left(z^{**}\right)\left(\cos\phi\left(z^{**}\right)\right)^{-1} = \tan\phi\left(z^{**}\right)$$

and

$$d_{\mathrm{I}}\left(z^{**}\right) = d_{\mathrm{I}}(0)(1+\delta)\left(1+\delta^2\right)^{-1}$$

Furthermore, using the Taylor expansion about $\delta = 1$, we get

$$\bar{d} \approx d_{\mathrm{I}}(0)(1 - d_{\mathrm{I}}(0))$$

and

$$(d_{\mathrm{II}})_{\min} \approx d_{\mathrm{I}}(0)(1 - d_{\mathrm{I}}(0))$$

where these approximations are most reliable when $\delta < 1.35$ and $\delta < 1.42$, respectively.

(iv) Since $d_{\mathrm{II}}(\bullet) = \sqrt{2}d_{\mathrm{I}}(\bullet)$, where $\bullet = 0, +\infty$ (see Eq. 4.8), then

$$\Delta_{\mathrm{II}} \equiv d_{\mathrm{II}}(0) - d_{\mathrm{II}}(+\infty) = \sqrt{2}\Delta_{\mathrm{I}} \tag{4.13}$$

Finally, substituting Eqs. 4.2 and 4.6 in the definition of the MAWD, d_{III}, i.e.

$$d_{\mathrm{III}} \equiv \sum_{j=1}^{n} \left| p_j v_j^{-1} - 1 \right| z_j \left(\mathbf{e}\mathbf{z}^{\mathrm{T}}\right)^{-1} \tag{4.14}$$

yields

$$d_{\mathrm{III}} = d_{\mathrm{I}}(0) F_{\mathrm{III}}(z) \tag{4.15}$$

where

$$F_{\mathrm{III}}(z) \equiv 2(1+v)z[(1+z)(1+fz)]^{-1}$$

From the above, it follows that:

(i) $F_{\mathrm{III}}(0) = F_{\mathrm{III}}(+\infty) = 0$ and $0 < F_{\mathrm{III}}(z) < 2$ for $0 < z < +\infty$.

(ii) F_{III} (z) is maximized at $z^{***} \equiv \left(\sqrt{\delta v}\right)^{-1}$, where

$$2(1+\delta)^{-1} \leq F_{\mathrm{III}}\left(z^{***}\right) = 2(1+v)\left(1+\sqrt{\delta v}\right)^{-2} < 2$$

and $F_{\mathrm{III}}(z^{***})$ tends to 2 (to $2\delta^{-1}$) as v tends to 0 (to $+\infty$). Moreover, $F_{\mathrm{III}}(z^{***})$ equals $2(1+\delta)^{-1}$ iff $v = \delta$. In that case, $d_{\mathrm{III}}\left(z^{***}\right) = \bar{d}$.

(iii) $d_{\mathrm{III}}(z^{***})$ is a strictly increasing function of δ that tends to $2d_{\mathrm{I}}$ (0) (to $2d_{\mathrm{I}}$ $(+\infty)$) as v tends to 0 (to $+\infty$).

(iv) $d_{\mathrm{I}}(z) < d_{\mathrm{III}}(z)$ when z lies between 1 and $z^{*}(\equiv v^{-1})$, while d_{III} also equals

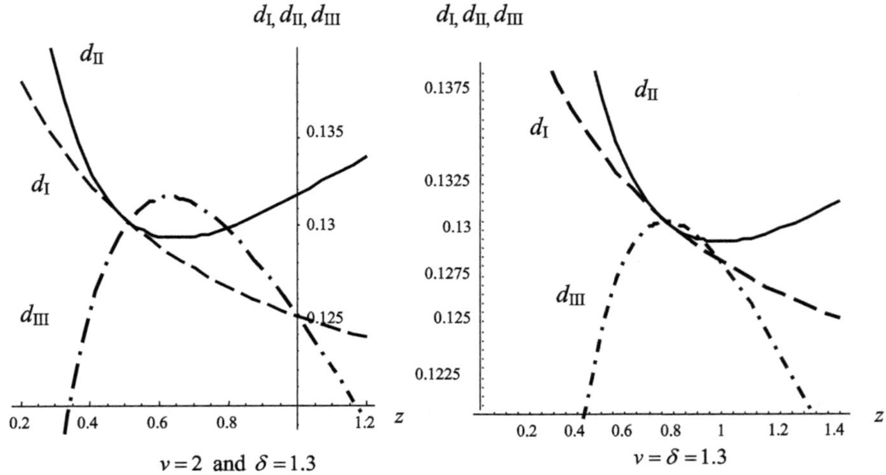

Fig. 4.1 The traditional measures of deviation as functions of the composition of the numeraire

$$d_{\mathrm{I}}(0)(1+v)(1+\delta v)^{-1}(=d_{\mathrm{III}}(1))$$

at $z=(\delta v)^{-1}=\left(z^{***}\right)^2$ (see the graphs in Fig. 4.1, where $v=2$ and $\delta=1.3$ or $v=\delta=1.3$, which represent the said measures of deviation as functions of z).

On the other hand, the numeraire-free measure d – distance is defined as

$$d\equiv\sqrt{2(1-\cos\theta)}$$

where θ is the angle between the vectors $\mathbf{p}\hat{\mathbf{v}}^{-1}$ and $\mathbf{e}$ and d is the Euclidean distance between the unit vectors $\left(\|\mathbf{p}\hat{\mathbf{v}}^{-1}\|_2\right)^{-1}\left(\mathbf{p}\hat{\mathbf{v}}^{-1}\right)$ and $\left(\|\mathbf{e}\|_2\right)^{-1}\mathbf{e}$ (Steedman and Tomkins 1998, pp. 381–382). Given that $\cos\theta$ can be expressed in terms of δ, i.e.

$$\cos\theta=\left(\sqrt{2}\right)^{-1}G(\delta)$$

where

$$G(\delta)\equiv(1+\delta)\left(\sqrt{(1+\delta^2)}\right)^{-1}$$

is maximized at $\delta=1(\cos\theta=1)$, and $G(\delta)=G\left(\delta^{-1}\right)$, it follows that

$$d^2=2-\sqrt{2}G(\delta) \tag{4.16}$$

or, recalling Eq. 4.12,

$$d^2 = 2D \tag{4.16a}$$

where $D \equiv 1 - (d_{II})_{min}\bar{d}^{-1}$ and, recalling Eqs. 4.9a and 4.11, $\theta = \phi(z^{**}) = \phi\left((\delta v)^{-1}\right)$. Thus, for $\delta > 1$, we may write $(d_{II})_{min} < d < \bar{d}$ or, approximately, $d \approx (d_{II})_{min}$ and $d \approx \bar{d}$, where these approximations are most reliable when $\delta < 3.3$ $(\theta^\circ < 28.1)$ and $\delta < 1.8$ $(\theta^\circ < 15.9)$, respectively. Finally, using the Taylor expansion of Eq. 4.16 about $\delta = 1$, we get

$$d^2 \approx (d_I(0))^2(2 - \delta)$$

or, recalling Eq. 4.8 and approximation (4.8a),

$$d^2 \approx 2^{-1}\Delta_I = d_I(0)d_I(+\infty) \tag{4.16b}$$

where these approximations are most reliable when $\delta < 1.22$ $(\theta^\circ < 5.7)$ and $\delta < 1.30$ $(\theta^\circ < 7.4)$, respectively.

From this analysis, it follows that:

(i) $d_I(+\infty) < d < d_I(0)$ for $\delta > 1$ (see Eqs. 4.7, 4.16 and Fig. 4.2).
(ii) $d < d_{II}(+\infty)$ for $1 < \delta < \delta' \cong 3.732$ and $d_I(0) < d_{II}(+\infty)$ for $1 < \delta < \sqrt{2}$.
(iii) The absolute errors between d and the *bounds* for the traditional measures, i.e. $\{d_I(\bullet), d_{II}(0), (d_{II})_{min}, (d_{III})_{max}\}$, increase with δ.
(iv) The relative errors between d and $\{d_I(\bullet), d_{II}(0), (d_{II})_{min}\}$ increase with δ (for instance, at $\delta = 1.1$, the relative error between d and $d_I(\bullet)$ lies between 4.5 % (i.e. $1 - d_I(+\infty)d^{-1} \approx 1 - \left(\sqrt{\delta}\right)^{-1}$; see approximation (4.16b)) and 5.1 % ($\approx \sqrt{\delta} - 1$), while at $\delta = 2$ it lies between 22.0 % and 56.1 %; see Table 4.1).[6]
(v) The monotonicity of the relative error between d and $(d_{III})_{max}$ depends on the value of v (for instance, see Fig. 4.3, where $v = 1$ (monotonic curve) or $v = 5$).

Now we shall approach δ as a function of the production technique and the profit rate, i.e. of the *sociotechnical* conditions of production. Let $\mathbf{A} \equiv [a_{ij}]$ be the irreducible matrix of direct technical coefficients, and let $\mathbf{l} \equiv [l_j]$ be the vector of direct labour coefficients. Then, in the case of our economy, we may write:

$$f = \{l[1 - (1 + r)a_{22}] + (1 + r)a_{21}\}[(1 + r)la_{12} + 1 - (1 + r)a_{11}]^{-1} \tag{4.17}$$

where $l \equiv l_1 l_2^{-1}$. From the definition of δ and Eq. 4.17, it follows that δ is a strictly decreasing function of l (for $r > 0$) and

[6] The relative error associated with $d_I(+\infty)$ and $(d_{II})_{min}$ tends to $1 - \left(2\sqrt{2 - \sqrt{2}}\right)^{-1} \cong 34.7\%$ and $1 - \left(\sqrt{4 - 2\sqrt{2}}\right)^{-1} \cong 7.6\%$, respectively.

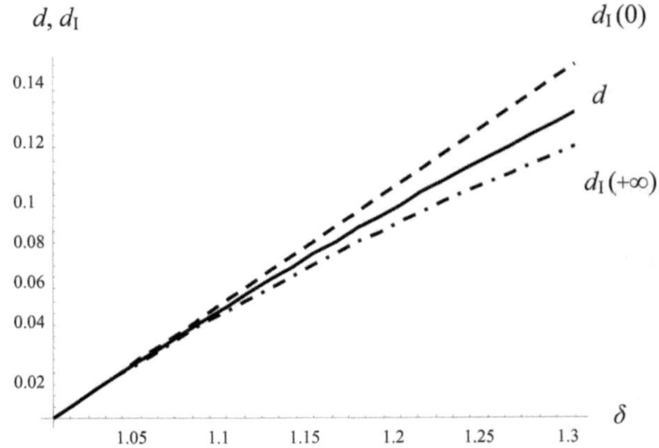

Fig. 4.2 The bounds for MAD and the d – distance as functions of the ratio of relative prices to relative labour values

$$\delta(0) \equiv \lim_{l \to 0} \delta = (1 + \rho R)\left(1 - \rho R R_1^{-1}\right)^{-1} (\geq 1) \tag{4.18}$$

$$\delta(l^*) \equiv \lim_{l \to l^*} \delta = 1 \tag{4.18a}$$

$$\delta(+\infty) \equiv \lim_{l \to +\infty} \delta = \left(1 - \rho R R_2^{-1}\right)(1 + \rho R)^{-1} (\leq 1) \tag{4.18b}$$

where l^* denotes the proportion given by the left P-F eigenvector of $\mathbf{A}$, $R_i \equiv a_{ii}{}^{-1} - 1$, $R \equiv \lambda_{\mathbf{A}1}^{-1} - 1$, the maximum profit rate, which increases with the elements a_{ij} (therefore $R < R_i$), and $\rho \equiv r R^{-1}$ the relative profit rate, which is less than or equal to the share of profits in the Sraffian Standard system (also see Fig. 4.4, where $0 < \rho_1 < \rho_2$). As $R R_1^{-1} \to 0$, we get $\delta(0) \to 1 + \rho R \left(= (\delta(+\infty))^{-1} \text{as } R R_2^{-1} \to 0 \right)$, while as $R R_1^{-1} \to 1$, we get $\delta(0) \to (1 + \rho R)(1 - \rho)^{-1}$ $(= (\delta(+\infty))^{-1}$ as $R R_2^{-1} \to 1$; see Eq. 4.18. Consequently, when f increases with r, the values

$$\delta^- \equiv 1 + \rho R \tag{4.19}$$

$$\delta^+ \equiv (1 + \rho R)(1 - \rho)^{-1} = \delta^-\left(1 + \rho + \rho^2 + \ldots\right) \tag{4.19a}$$

represent the *theoretically* possible lower and upper bounds for δ, respectively (while when f decreases with r, the values $(\delta^+)^{-1}$ and $(\delta^-)^{-1}$ represent the theoretically possible lower and upper bounds for δ, respectively). Thus, we may conclude that $|\delta - 1|$ (and, therefore, the errors between d and, for instance, $d_I(\bullet)$; also see Fig. 4.1) is directly related to the deviation of l from l^*, and ρ.

Table 4.1 Measures of deviation and the ratio of relative prices to relative labour values

δ	1.05	1.10	1.15	1.20	1.25	1.30	1.40	1.50	2.0	3.0
$d_{\mathrm{I}}(0)$	0.025	0.050	0.075	0.100	0.125	0.150	0.200	0.250	0.500	1.000
$d_{\mathrm{I}}(+\infty)$	0.024	0.045	0.065	0.084	0.100	0.115	0.143	0.167	0.250	0.333
Δ_{I}	0.001	0.005	0.010	0.016	0.025	0.035	0.057	0.083	0.250	0.667
$d_{\mathrm{II}}(0)$	0.035	0.071	0.106	0.141	0.177	0.212	0.283	0.354	0.707	1.414
$d_{\mathrm{II}}(+\infty)$	0.034	0.064	0.092	0.119	0.141	0.163	0.202	0.236	0.354	0.471
$\bar{d}$	0.0244	0.0476	0.0698	0.0909	0.1111	0.1304	0.1667	0.2000	0.3333	0.5000
$(d_{\mathrm{II}})_{\min}$	0.0244	0.0476	0.0696	0.0905	0.1104	0.1293	0.1644	0.1961	0.3162	0.4472
d	0.0244	0.0476	0.0696	0.0906	0.1106	0.1296	0.1650	0.1971	0.3204	0.4595
$d_{\mathrm{I}}(0)d^{-1}-1$ (%)	2.46	5.09	7.76	10.38	13.02	15.74	21.21	26.84	56.05	117.63
$1-d_{\mathrm{I}}(+\infty)d^{-1}$ (%)	1.64	4.46	6.61	7.28	9.58	11.27	13.33	15.27	21.97	27.53

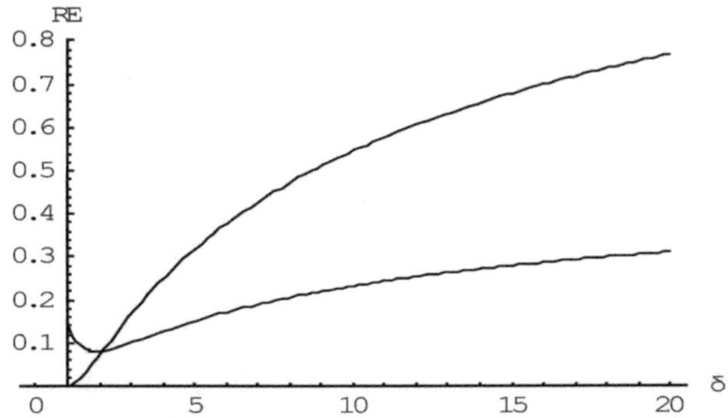

Fig. 4.3 The relative error between the d – distance and the upper bound for MAWD as a function of the ratio of relative prices to relative labour values

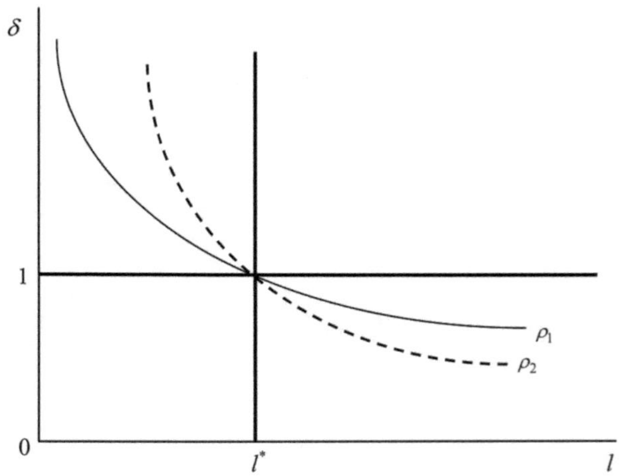

Fig. 4.4 The ratio of relative prices to relative labour values as a function of the relative direct labour inputs at different values of the relative profit rate

4.3 Generalization

In this section, we extend the argument to the n – industry case starting from the following definition of the ratios of relative prices to relative labour values

$$\boldsymbol{\delta} \equiv [\delta_j] \equiv \left[\left(p_j p_n^{-1}\right) \left(v_n v_j^{-1}\right) \right], \ j = 1, 2, .., n \tag{4.20}$$

where δ_j are *not* necessarily monotonic functions of the profit rate (see Sects. 2.4.1 and 3.8). Substituting Eq. 4.20 in the definition of d_{II} (see Eq. 4.9) yields

$$d_{\text{II}} \equiv \sqrt{n^{-1} \sum_{j=1}^{n} \left(\delta_j b - 1\right)^2} \tag{4.21}$$

where $b \equiv p_n v_n^{-1}$, and by invoking the normalization equation, we may write

$$b = \left(\boldsymbol{\delta}\hat{\mathbf{v}}\,\mathbf{z}^{\mathrm{T}}\right)^{-1}\mathbf{v}\mathbf{z}^{\mathrm{T}} \tag{4.21a}$$

Substituting Eq. 4.20 in the definition of $\cos\theta$ yields

$$\cos\theta = \left(1 + \tan^2\theta\right)^{-1/2} = \left(\sqrt{n}\right)^{-1}G(\boldsymbol{\delta}) \tag{4.22}$$

where

$$G(\boldsymbol{\delta}) \equiv \left(\sum_{j=1}^{n}\delta_j\right)\left(\sqrt{\sum_{j=1}^{n}(\delta_j)^2}\right)^{-1} \tag{4.22a}$$

From Eq. 4.22 it follows that $\cos\theta$ is maximized at $\boldsymbol{\delta} = \mathbf{e}(\cos\theta = 1)$ and, in contrast to the two-industry case, $G(\boldsymbol{\delta}) \neq G\left(\mathbf{e}\hat{\boldsymbol{\delta}}^{-1}\right)$. From Eqs. 4.20 to 4.22a, we obtain

$$(d_{\mathrm{II}})^2 = \left(1 + \tan^2\theta\right)\left(\mu\left(\mathbf{z}^{\mathrm{T}}\right)\right)^2 - 2\mu\left(\mathbf{z}^{\mathrm{T}}\right) + 1$$

where $\mu(\mathbf{z}^{\mathrm{T}}) \equiv n^{-1}\,\mathbf{p}\hat{\mathbf{v}}^{-1}\mathbf{e}^{\mathrm{T}}$ is the arithmetic mean of $p_j v_j^{-1}$ measured in terms of commodity $\mathbf{z}^{\mathrm{T}}$, a magnitude that equals $n^{-1}\left(\sum_{j=1}^{n}\delta_j\right)b$ and, therefore, varies from $n^{-1}\left(\sum_{j=1}^{n}\delta_j\right)\left(\min_j\left\{\delta_j^{-1}\right\}\right)$ to $n^{-1}\left(\sum_{j=1}^{n}\delta_j\right)\left(\max_j\left\{\delta_j^{-1}\right\}\right)$ (also see Steedman and Tomkins 1998, pp. 384–385).[7] By invoking Eqs. 4.3, 4.9a and 4.14, we derive the following:

(i) d_{I} is a piecewise, linear function of $\mu(\mathbf{z}^{\mathrm{T}})$.
(ii) $d_{\mathrm{I}}(\mathbf{z}^{\mathrm{T}}) = d_{\mathrm{II}}(\mathbf{z}^{\mathrm{T}})$, i.e. $\cos\phi = 1$, iff $\delta_k,\ k = 1, 2, \ldots, n-1$, are equal to each other and $b = 2(1+\delta_k)^{-1}$. In that case

$$\mu\left(\mathbf{z}^{\mathrm{T}}\right) = n^{-1}[1 + (n-1)\delta_k]b$$

and

$$d_{\mathrm{I}} = d_{\mathrm{III}} = |\delta_k - 1|(1+\delta_k)^{-1}$$

where $\mu(\mathbf{z}^{\mathrm{T}}) > 1$ and $d_{\mathrm{I}} > d$ iff $\delta_k > 1$.[8]

---

[7] It should be noted that to any given $z_n^{-1}\mathbf{z}^{\mathrm{T}}$ there corresponds a unique b, while the converse does not hold true.

[8] Given that the entire price vector cannot be proportional to that of labour values at a positive level of the profit rate (see Sect. 2.2.1.1), the case $\delta_k = 1,\ k = 1, 2, \ldots, n-1$, does not really exist.

(iii) At $\mathbf{z}^{\mathrm{T}^*} \equiv z_n v_n \hat{\mathbf{v}}^{-1}\mathbf{e}^{\mathrm{T}}$ it holds $\mu\left(\mathbf{z}^{\mathrm{T}^*}\right) = 1$ and, therefore,

$$d_{\mathrm{II}}\left(\mathbf{z}^{\mathrm{T}^*}\right) = \tan\theta = \sigma\left(\mathbf{z}^{\mathrm{T}^*}\right)(> d)$$

where $\sigma(\mathbf{z}^{\mathrm{T}}*)$ is the standard deviation of $p_j v_j^{-1}$ measured in terms of commodity $\mathbf{z}^{\mathrm{T}}*$, while

$$d_{\mathrm{I}}\left(\mathbf{z}^{\mathrm{T}^*}\right) = \cos\phi\left(\mathbf{z}^{\mathrm{T}^*}\right)\sigma\left(\mathbf{z}^{\mathrm{T}^*}\right)$$

(iv) $d_{\mathrm{II}}(\mathbf{z}^{\mathrm{T}})$ also equals $\tan\theta$ at $\mu(\mathbf{z}^{\mathrm{T}}) = \cos^2\theta - \sin^2\theta$.

(v) $d_{\mathrm{II}}(\mathbf{z}^{\mathrm{T}})$ is minimized at $\mathbf{z}^{\mathrm{T}^{**}} \equiv z_n v_n \hat{\boldsymbol{\delta}}\,\hat{\mathbf{v}}^{-1}\mathbf{e}^{\mathrm{T}}$, where

$$\mu\left(\mathbf{z}^{\mathrm{T}^{**}}\right) = n^{-1}(G(\boldsymbol{\delta}))^2 = \cos^2\theta$$

and

$$(d_{\mathrm{II}})_{\min} \equiv d_{\mathrm{II}}\left(\mathbf{z}^{\mathrm{T}^{**}}\right) = \sin\theta < d$$

(Fig. 4.5 corresponds to a four-industry case, where $\delta_1 = 1.1, \delta_2 = 0.9, \delta_3 = 1.3,$[9] and represents d_{I}, d_{II} and $\cos\phi$ as functions of $\mu(\mathbf{z}^{\mathrm{T}})$, respectively).

(vi) Equation 4.12 should be replaced by

$$(d_{\mathrm{II}})_{\min} = \sqrt{d_{\mathrm{II}}\left(\mathbf{z}^{\mathrm{T}^*}\right)\sigma\left(\mathbf{z}^{\mathrm{T}^{**}}\right)}$$

where $\sigma\left(\mathbf{z}^{\mathrm{T}^{**}}\right)\left(= \mu\left(\mathbf{z}^{\mathrm{T}^{**}}\right)\tan\theta\right)$ is the standard deviation of $p_j v_j^{-1}$ measured in terms of commodity $\mathbf{z}^{\mathrm{T}**}$.

(vii) At a given value of $\mu(\mathbf{z}^{\mathrm{T}})$, say $\bar{\mu}$, and for strictly positive $\mathbf{z}^{\mathrm{T}}$, d_{III} varies from the minimum to the maximum value of $\left|\left[n\bar{\mu}\delta_j\left(\sum_{j=1}^{n}\delta_j\right)^{-1}\right] - 1\right|$.

Leaving aside the fact that the relationships between the measures of deviation take more complicated forms, the main difference introduced here is that the ratios of relative prices to relative labour values are not necessarily monotonic functions of the profit rate. Consequently, the closeness of measures of deviation may occur not only at 'low' but also at 'high' values of ρ. This point can be illustrated with the aid of Sraffa's (1960, pp. 37–38) 'wine-oak' numerical example in which

---

[9] Consequently, $\cos\theta \cong 0.9906$, $\theta^\circ \cong 7.8$, $d \cong 0.137$, $d_{\mathrm{II}}\left(\mathbf{z}^{\mathrm{T}^*}\right) \cong 0.138$, $(d_{\mathrm{II}})_{\min} \cong 0.136$, $43/52 \leq \mu\left(\mathbf{z}^{\mathrm{T}}\right) \leq 43/36$ and $\mu\left(\mathbf{z}^{\mathrm{T}^*}\right) = \cos^2\theta \cong 0.981 > 43/44$.

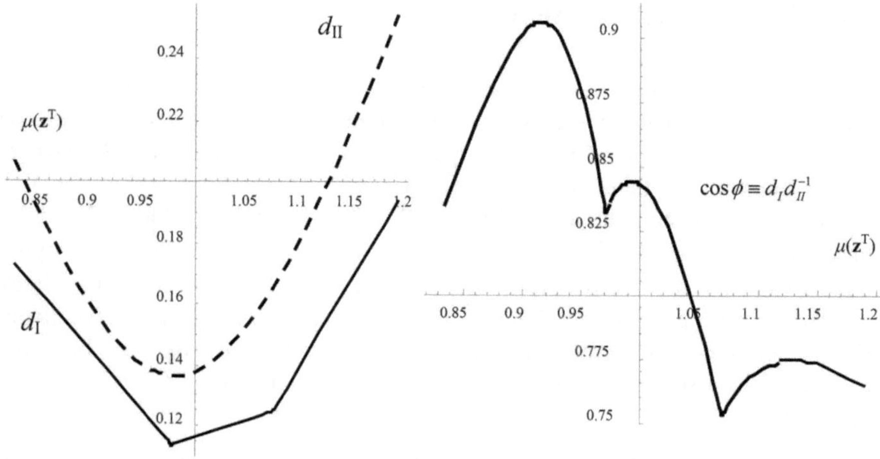

Fig. 4.5 The MAD, the RMS%E and their ratio as functions of the arithmetic mean of the production price-labour value ratios

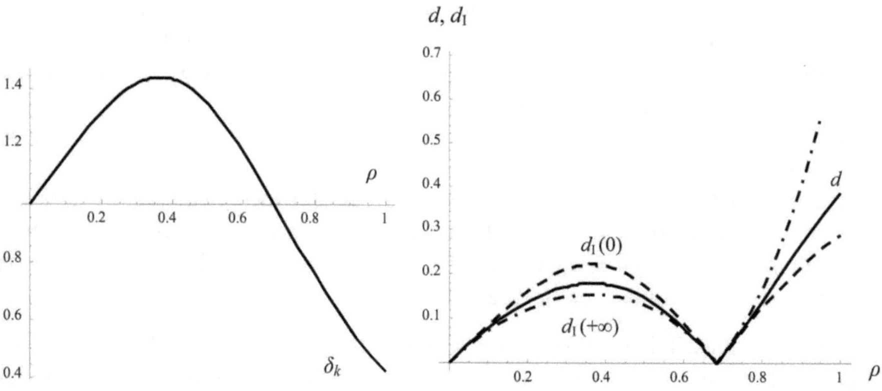

Fig. 4.6 The ratio of relative prices to relative labour values, the bounds for MAD and the d – distance as functions of the relative profit rate; Sraffa's 'wine-oak' numerical example

$$\delta = 20\left[19 + (1 + 0.25\rho)^{25}\right]^{-1}(1 + 0.25\rho)^{8}$$

and $R = 0.25$. As a consequence, δ equals 1 not only at $\rho = 0$ but also at $\rho \cong 0.684$, and, therefore, the ranking of the bounds for the MAD and the d – distance, associated with 'old wine' and 'oak chest', changes with ρ (see Fig. 4.6, which represents δ_k, and $d_{\mathrm{I}}(0)$, $d_{\mathrm{I}}(+\infty)$ and d as functions of ρ, respectively, and compare with Fig. 4.2).

4.4 Empirical Illustration

In order to get a realistic view of the trajectories of production price-labour value deviations for alternative measures and for different ρ in actual economies, we use input-output data from the Greek and Japanese economies for the year 1990 (where $n = 19$ and $n = 33$, respectively; see Sect. 3.3).

The results are summarized in Tables 4.2, 4.3, 4.4 and 4.5. Tables 4.2 and 4.3 present estimates of $\delta_k \equiv \left[\left(p_k p_n^{-1}\right)\left(v_n v_k^{-1}\right)\right]$, $k = 1, 2, .., n-1$, at different, hypothetical values of the relative profit rate, for each of the 19 industries of the Greek economy and for each of the 33 industries of the Japanese economy, respectively (the last columns in both tables give the arithmetic mean of $|\varepsilon_k| \equiv |\delta_k - 1|$). From the analysis of the associated numerical results and these estimates, we may derive the following:

(i) With one exception (i.e. the ratio δ_{32} of the Japanese economy), δ_k are monotonic functions of ρ (however, in terms of others commodities, there are production prices that are not monotonic functions of ρ).
(ii) The arithmetic means of $|\varepsilon_k|$ increase with ρ.
(iii) In the Greek (Japanese) economy, the Euclidean angle, measured in degrees, between the vector of direct labour coefficients and the left P-F eigenvector of the matrix of input-output coefficients is almost 47.18° (56.19°), and their d – distance is almost 0.71 (0.91).
(iv) In the Greek (Japanese) economy, the arithmetic mean of $|\varepsilon_k|$ is greater than 40 % for $\rho > 0.5$ ($\rho > 0.4$).
(v) Given that the *actual* value of ρ in the Greek (Japanese) economy is approximately equal to 0.249 (to 0.331), it follows that the actual arithmetic mean of $|\varepsilon_k|$ is less than 19.4 % (than 31.2 %). This is consistent with that expected on theoretical grounds (see Sect. 2.3.2).[10]

Finally, Tables 4.4 and 4.5 present estimates of (i) the measures of deviation (the production prices are normalized with the use of SSC and the actual gross output vector)[11] and (ii) the mean absolute error (MAE), the relative errors (e.g. $\mathrm{RE_I} \equiv |d_\mathrm{I} - d|d^{-1}$) and the mean relative error (MRE) associated with the traditional measures of deviation, at different, hypothetical values of ρ. Thus, it is observed that:

(i) Not quite unexpected, all the measures increase with ρ.
(ii) Setting aside d_I, the ranking of the measures changes with ρ (for instance, the Greek economy is characterized by $d_\mathrm{II} < d < d_\mathrm{III}$ for $0.1 \le \rho \le 0.4$, $d_\mathrm{II} < d_\mathrm{III} < d$ for $0.4 < \rho \le 0.5$ and $d_\mathrm{III} < d_\mathrm{II} < d$ for $0.5 < \rho \le 1$, while the Japanese

[10] In the Greek economy (1988–1997), the actual value of ρ lies between 0.230 (1993) and 0.270 (1997), and in the Japanese economy (1970, 1975, 1980, 1985, 1990), it lies between 0.298 (1975) and 0.371 (1985) (see Sect. 3.3).

[11] That is, $\mathbf{p}\,\bar{\mathbf{s}}^\mathrm{T} = \bar{\mathbf{v}}\,\bar{\mathbf{s}}^\mathrm{T} = \bar{\mathbf{v}}\bar{\mathbf{x}}^\mathrm{T} = \mathbf{e}\bar{\mathbf{x}}^\mathrm{T}$ (see Sect. 3.3).

Table 4.2 The ratios of relative prices to relative labour values and the relative profit rate; Greece 1990

Industries ρ	1	2	3	4	5	6	7	8	9	10	11	12	13	14	15	16	17	18	19	$(\Sigma\lvert\varepsilon_k\rvert)(n-1)^{-1}$ (%)
0.0	1.00	1.00	1.00	1.00	1.00	1.00	1.00	1.00	1.00	1.00	1.00	1.00	1.00	1.00	1.00	1.00	1.00	1.00	1.00	0.0
0.1	1.01	1.02	1.00	0.99	1.10	1.06	1.05	1.05	1.08	1.10	1.06	1.13	1.08	1.06	1.02	1.08	1.03	1.07	1.00	6.1
0.2	1.03	1.03	1.00	0.98	1.20	1.13	1.10	1.11	1.17	1.21	1.13	1.28	1.17	1.13	1.04	1.17	1.06	1.15	1.00	11.1
0.3	1.04	1.05	1.00	0.97	1.31	1.20	1.15	1.18	1.26	1.35	1.20	1.46	1.28	1.21	1.07	1.27	1.10	1.23	1.00	19.4
0.4	1.06	1.07	1.00	0.95	1.44	1.29	1.22	1.26	1.35	1.51	1.28	1.69	1.43	1.31	1.09	1.40	1.14	1.33	1.00	27.2
0.5	1.07	1.09	1.01	0.94	1.57	1.39	1.29	1.36	1.46	1.72	1.37	1.98	1.62	1.44	1.12	1.56	1.19	1.44	1.00	38.3
0.6	1.09	1.12	1.02	0.93	1.73	1.51	1.38	1.48	1.57	1.97	1.48	2.35	1.87	1.60	1.15	1.75	1.24	1.57	1.00	50.6
0.7	1.11	1.14	1.04	0.91	1.90	1.65	1.48	1.63	1.71	2.31	1.61	2.85	2.21	1.82	1.19	2.01	1.32	1.71	1.00	63.9
0.8	1.13	1.17	1.07	0.90	2.10	1.82	1.61	1.83	1.87	2.76	1.78	3.57	2.70	2.13	1.23	2.37	1.41	1.88	1.00	86.7
0.9	1.15	1.20	1.12	0.88	2.34	2.04	1.78	2.11	2.09	3.41	2.01	4.68	3.48	2.60	1.30	2.90	1.54	2.07	1.00	115.6
1.0	1.16	1.24	1.21	0.87	2.62	2.30	2.01	2.49	2.39	4.31	2.33	6.35	4.66	3.29	1.38	3.68	1.71	2.29	1.00	158.5

Table 4.3 The ratios of relative prices to relative labour values and the relative profit rate; Japan 1990

Industries ρ	1	2	3	4	5	6	7	8	9	10	11	12	13	14	15	16	17	18	19	20	21	22	23	24	25	26	27	28	29	30	31	32	33	$(\Sigma\|\varepsilon_k\|)$ $(n-1)^{-1}$ (%)
0.0	1.00	1.00	1.00	1.00	1.00	1.00	1.00	1.00	1.00	1.00	1.00	1.00	1.00	1.00	1.00	1.00	1.00	1.00	1.00	1.00	1.00	1.00	1.00	1.00	1.00	1.00	1.00	1.00	1.00	1.00	1.00	1.00	1.00	0.0
0.1	1.01	1.02	1.07	1.06	1.05	1.05	1.11	1.06	1.10	1.08	1.05	1.14	1.11	1.06	1.07	1.10	1.08	1.09	1.07	1.11	1.14	1.07	1.05	1.07	1.05	1.03	0.98	1.02	1.02	0.98	0.99	1.00	1.00	6.9
0.2	1.01	1.05	1.15	1.12	1.11	1.11	1.22	1.13	1.20	1.17	1.10	1.31	1.24	1.14	1.15	1.21	1.17	1.19	1.16	1.25	1.31	1.16	1.11	1.14	1.11	1.07	0.96	1.05	1.04	0.95	0.97	1.01	1.00	12.2
0.3	1.02	1.08	1.23	1.18	1.16	1.17	1.36	1.20	1.31	1.28	1.16	1.53	1.39	1.24	1.24	1.33	1.27	1.30	1.26	1.42	1.53	1.26	1.17	1.22	1.17	1.12	0.94	1.07	1.06	0.93	0.96	1.01	1.00	22.2
0.4	1.02	1.11	1.32	1.26	1.23	1.24	1.52	1.28	1.43	1.40	1.23	1.81	1.57	1.36	1.36	1.48	1.40	1.43	1.40	1.64	1.81	1.37	1.25	1.32	1.23	1.18	0.91	1.10	1.09	0.90	0.94	1.01	1.00	31.2
0.5	1.03	1.14	1.41	1.35	1.30	1.32	1.71	1.38	1.56	1.56	1.30	2.19	1.78	1.53	1.51	1.65	1.55	1.59	1.56	1.94	2.19	1.51	1.34	1.44	1.30	1.25	0.88	1.13	1.13	0.86	0.91	1.01	1.00	42.8
0.6	1.04	1.18	1.52	1.45	1.38	1.41	1.94	1.48	1.70	1.74	1.39	2.71	2.04	1.76	1.72	1.86	1.75	1.79	1.79	2.34	2.71	1.68	1.45	1.58	1.39	1.34	0.85	1.16	1.19	0.82	0.89	1.01	1.00	59.1
0.7	1.05	1.23	1.64	1.57	1.47	1.52	2.22	1.61	1.86	1.98	1.50	3.47	2.37	2.09	2.00	2.13	2.02	2.03	2.11	2.93	3.47	1.90	1.59	1.75	1.48	1.46	0.81	1.20	1.27	0.78	0.85	1.01	1.00	80.3
0.8	1.06	1.30	1.78	1.72	1.59	1.64	2.59	1.77	2.07	2.29	1.65	4.71	2.82	2.62	2.45	2.48	2.40	2.37	2.62	3.86	4.67	2.18	1.79	1.99	1.60	1.65	0.77	1.24	1.40	0.72	0.80	1.00	1.00	110.0
0.9	1.07	1.42	1.96	1.91	1.76	1.80	3.11	2.00	2.36	2.73	1.89	7.02	3.47	3.60	3.26	3.02	3.02	2.88	3.52	5.55	6.83	2.60	2.10	2.35	1.78	1.98	0.70	1.28	1.63	0.63	0.73	1.00	1.00	159.3
1.0	1.09	1.64	2.23	2.16	2.02	2.01	3.90	2.34	2.84	3.42	2.32	11.86	4.47	5.62	4.89	3.91	4.16	3.75	5.36	8.93	11.1	3.25	2.64	2.95	2.09	2.64	0.61	1.33	2.09	0.51	0.61	0.99	1.00	250.6

Table 4.4 The measures of deviation and the relative profit rate; Greece, 1990

ρ	d_{I} (%)	d_{II} (%)	d_{III}(%)	d (%)	MAE (%)	RE_{I} (%)	RE_{II} (%)	RE_{III} (%)	MRE (%)
0.0	0.00	0.00	0.00	0.00	0.00	–	–	–	–
0.1	3.00	3.56	3.71	3.64	0.26	17.58	2.20	1.92	7.23
0.2	6.08	7.28	7.52	7.42	0.53	18.06	1.90	1.35	7.10
0.3	9.22	11.18	11.45	11.36	0.80	18.84	1.58	0.79	7.07
0.4	12.49	15.30	15.56	15.55	1.11	19.68	1.61	0.06	7.12
0.5	16.05	19.72	19.92	20.04	1.48	19.91	1.60	0.60	7.37
0.6	20.11	24.62	24.60	24.94	1.83	19.37	1.28	1.36	7.34
0.7	24.58	29.96	29.72	30.40	2.31	19.14	1.45	2.24	7.61
0.8	29.85	35.86	35.43	36.62	2.91	18.49	2.08	3.25	7.94
0.9	36.25	42.48	41.98	43.88	3.64	17.39	3.19	4.33	8.30
1.0	43.01	49.19	48.90	51.66	4.63	16.74	4.78	5.34	8.95

Table 4.5 The measures of deviation and the relative profit rate; Japan, 1990

ρ	d_{I} (%)	d_{II} (%)	d_{III}(%)	d (%)	MAE (%)	RE_{I} (%)	RE_{II} (%)	RE_{III} (%)	MRE (%)
0.0	0.00	0.00	0.00	0.00	0.00	–	–	–	–
0.1	3.20	4.02	4.60	4.04	0.47	20.79	0.50	13.86	11.72
0.2	6.58	8.29	9.55	8.30	0.99	20.72	0.12	15.06	11.97
0.3	10.18	12.88	14.93	12.85	1.59	20.78	0.23	16.19	12.40
0.4	14.06	17.89	20.81	17.76	2.29	20.83	0.73	17.17	12.91
0.5	18.32	23.47	27.32	23.16	3.10	20.84	1.34	17.96	13.38
0.6	23.10	29.80	34.67	29.24	4.04	21.00	1.92	18.57	13.83
0.7	28.60	37.25	43.17	36.24	5.19	21.08	2.79	19.12	14.33
0.8	35.12	46.36	53.20	44.60	6.61	21.26	3.95	19.28	14.83
0.9	43.46	58.08	66.21	54.95	8.63	20.90	5.70	20.49	15.70
1.0	57.10	72.45	81.58	66.87	10.02	14.61	8.34	21.00	14.65

economy is characterized by $d_{\text{II}} < d < d_{\text{III}}$ for $0.1 \leq \rho \leq 0.2$ and $d < d_{\text{II}} < d_{\text{III}}$ for $0.3 \leq \rho \leq 1$).

(iii) Both the absolute and relative errors between d and the traditional measures may decrease with ρ.

(iv) In the Greek economy, the actual mean absolute (relative) error of the traditional measures of deviation is less than 0.80 % (lies between 7.07 % and 7.10 %), and in the Japanese economy, it is less than 2.29 % (12.91 %).

Since there is no relevant empirical study where ρ is considerably greater than 0.4 (than 0.5), provided that wages are paid at the beginning (end) of the production period (see Sect. 3.3), it is reasonable to *expect* that, in the 'real' world, all the considered measures of deviation are not far from each other.

4.5 Concluding Remarks

It has been argued that, for realistic values of the relative profit rate, which is no greater than the share of profits in the Sraffian Standard system, the traditional measures of production price-labour value deviations (i.e. the MAD, RMS%E and MAWD), which depend on the choice of numeraire, and the $d-$distance, which is a numeraire-free measure, tend to be close to each other. This does not imply, of course, that there is basis for not preferring the latter measure but rather that future research efforts should be focused on the sociotechnical conditions that determine the level of the relative profit rate in actual economies.

Appendix: Numeraire-Free Measures

Consider the price-wage-profit system described by

$$\mathbf{p} = w\mathbf{l} + (1 + r)\,\mathbf{pA}$$

or

$$\mathbf{p} = w\mathbf{v} + \rho\,\mathbf{pJ} \tag{4.23}$$

(see Eqs. 2.1 and 2.16). For $\rho = 0$, we get $\mathbf{p}(0) = w\mathbf{v}$, while for $\rho = 1$, we get $\mathbf{p}(1) = \mathbf{p}(1)\mathbf{J}$, i.e. $\mathbf{p}(1)$ is a left P-F eigenvector of $\mathbf{J}$. Postmultiplying Eq. 4.23 by $[\hat{\mathbf{p}}\,(\bar{\rho})]^{-1}$, where $\mathbf{p}(\bar{\rho})$ denotes the price vector associated with an *arbitrarily* chosen level, $\bar{\rho}$, of the relative profit rate, gives

$$\mathbf{p}^{*} = w\mathbf{v}^{*} + \rho\,\mathbf{p}^{*}\mathbf{J}^{*} \tag{4.24}$$

where $\mathbf{J}^{*} \equiv \hat{\mathbf{p}}\,(\bar{\rho})\mathbf{J}[\hat{\mathbf{p}}\,(\bar{\rho})]^{-1}$ denotes the transformed (via a diagonal similarity matrix formed from the elements of $\mathbf{p}(\bar{\rho})$) matrix of the system, the elements of which are independent of the normalization of $\mathbf{p}$, and $\mathbf{p}^{*} \equiv \mathbf{p}[\hat{\mathbf{p}}\,(\bar{\rho})]^{-1}, \mathbf{v}^{*} \equiv \mathbf{v}[\hat{\mathbf{p}}\,(\bar{\rho})]^{-1}$ the transformed vectors of prices and labour values, respectively.

Now suppose that one changes the units in which the various commodity quantities are measured. The shift of units converts $[\mathbf{A}, \mathbf{l}]$ to $\left[\widetilde{\mathbf{A}}, \widetilde{\mathbf{l}}\right]$, where $\widetilde{\mathbf{A}} \equiv \mathbf{DAD}^{-1}$, $\widetilde{\mathbf{l}} \equiv \mathbf{lD}^{-1}$ and $\mathbf{D}$ is a diagonal matrix with positive diagonal elements. However, no element in Eq. 4.24 changes, since the *original* (non-transformed) vectors of labour values and prices change to $\mathbf{vD}^{-1}$ and $\mathbf{pD}^{-1}$, respectively. Thus, the angle, θ, between $\mathbf{p}^{*}$ and $\mathbf{v}^{*}$, which is determined by

$$\cos\theta = \left(\|\mathbf{p}^*\|_2\|\mathbf{v}^*\|_2\right)^{-1}(\mathbf{p}^*\mathbf{v}^*)$$

is independent of the choice of physical measurement units. Let $d(\bar{\rho},\rho)$ be the Euclidean distance between the unit vectors $\mathbf{p}^{**}\equiv\left(\|\mathbf{p}^*\|_2\right)^{-1}\mathbf{p}^*$ and $\mathbf{v}^{**}\equiv\left(\|\mathbf{v}^*\|_2\right)^{-1}\mathbf{v}^*$ as a function of ρ.[12] Then

$$d(\bar{\rho},\rho)\equiv\|\mathbf{p}^{**}-\mathbf{v}^{**}\|_2=\sqrt{2(1-\cos\theta)}$$

constitutes a measure of price-value or, *equivalently*, value-price deviation, which is independent of any choice of numeraire and physical measurement units. If $\bar{\rho}=0$, then $\mathbf{p}^* = \mathbf{p}[w\hat{\mathbf{v}}]^{-1}$, $\mathbf{v}^* = w^{-1}\mathbf{e}$ and

$$d(0,\rho)=d_{\mathbf{p}}(\rho)\equiv\left\|\left(\|\mathbf{p}\hat{\mathbf{v}}^{-1}\|_2\right)^{-1}(\mathbf{p}\hat{\mathbf{v}}^{-1})-(\sqrt{n})^{-1}\mathbf{e}\right\|_2$$

i.e. $d(0,\rho)$ equals the d – distance, proposed by Steedman and Tomkins (1998, p. 382), and measures the deviation of the original prices from the original labour values, and not vice versa, in the sense that, in general,

$$d_{\mathbf{p}}(\rho)\neq d_{\mathbf{v}}(\rho)\equiv\left\|\left(\|\mathbf{v}\hat{\mathbf{p}}^{-1}\|_2\right)^{-1}(\mathbf{v}\hat{\mathbf{p}}^{-1})-(\sqrt{n})^{-1}\mathbf{e}\right\|_2$$

(except for the case where $n = 2$).[13] If $\bar{\rho}=1$, then $\mathbf{p}^* = \mathbf{p}[\hat{\mathbf{p}}(1)]^{-1}$, $\mathbf{v}^* = \mathbf{v}[\hat{\mathbf{p}}(1)]^{-1}$ and, in general, $d(1,\rho)\neq d_{\mathbf{p}}(\rho)$. Finally, at $\rho=\bar{\rho}$, we obtain $\mathbf{p}^* = \mathbf{e}$ and, therefore, $d(\bar{\rho},\bar{\rho}) = d_{\mathbf{v}}(\bar{\rho})$ measures the deviation of the original labour values from the original prices corresponding to $\bar{\rho}$ (and not vice versa).[14]

The empirical results provided by Mariolis and Soklis (2011, pp. 616–617) are associated with input-output data from the Swedish economy for the year 2005 ($n=50$), where the actual value of ρ is approximately equal to 0.520 or, if wages are

[12] The Euclidean distance between two normalized vectors is known as the 'Radner-McKenzie distance'. In this definition, the Euclidean norm of a vector $\boldsymbol{\chi}$ can be replaced by other norms such as $\sum_{j=1}^{n}|\chi_j|$ (Inada 1964).

[13] In accordance with most of the empirical studies on this topic, Steedman and Tomkins (1998) pay regard to measure 'the extent to which (with-profit) prices diverge from (zero-profit) values' (p. 379).

[14] It need hardly be said that, in terms (at least) of the Leontief-Bródy approach (see Eq. 2.16a), this construction remains valid for the (more realistic) case of fixed capital and/or differential profit rates (also see Steedman and Tomkins 1998, pp. 381–382).

paid ex ante, 0.368 ($R \cong 0.807$), and the distances (i) $d(0, \rho) = d_{\mathbf{p}}(\rho)$, (ii) $d(1, \rho)$, (iii) $d(\bar{\rho}, \rho)$, $\bar{\rho} = 0.8$ (for instance) and (iv) $d_{\mathbf{v}}(\rho)$. Those results suggest that:

(i) The distances increase with $\rho, 0 \leq \rho \leq 1$. Nevertheless, they tend to be close to each other for 'low' values of ρ. For instance, at the actual value of the relative profit rate, ρ^{a}, they are in the range of 0.184–0.216, i.e.

$$d_{\mathbf{p}}(\rho^{\mathrm{a}}) \cong 0.184 < d_{\mathbf{v}}(\rho^{\mathrm{a}}) \cong 0.202 < d(0.8, \rho^{\mathrm{a}}) \cong 0.215 < d(1, \rho^{\mathrm{a}}) \cong 0.216$$

or, if wages are paid ex ante, in the range of 0.127–0.144, i.e.

$$d_{\mathbf{p}}(\rho^{\mathrm{a}}) \cong 0.127 < d_{\mathbf{v}}(\rho^{\mathrm{a}}) \cong 0.134 < d(1, \rho^{\mathrm{a}}) \cong 0.141 < d(0.8, \rho^{\mathrm{a}}) \cong 0.144$$

(ii) As expected, the curve $d_{\mathbf{v}}(\rho)$ intersects the curves $d(1, \rho)$ and $d(0.8, \rho)$ at $\rho = 1$ and $\rho = 0.8$, respectively. The curve $d(1, \rho)$ also intersects the curves $d(0.8, \rho)$, $d_{\mathbf{v}}(\rho)$ and $d_{\mathbf{p}}(\rho)$ at $\rho \cong 0.470$, $\rho \cong 0.075$ and $\rho \cong 0.057$, respectively.

It emerges, therefore, that the ranking of these numeraire-free measures is a priori unknown (even when the measures are monotonic functions of the relative profit rate).

It has been shown that in order to construct a measure of price-value deviation, which does not depend on the choice of numeraire and physical measurement units, it suffices to transform the price-wage-profit system via a diagonal similarity matrix formed from the elements of the price vector corresponding to a value of the relative profit rate. This implies that there exists an *infinite* number of such measures, whose ranking is a priori unknown, and the choice between them depends either on the theoretical viewpoint or the aim of the observer. Schematically speaking, we could say that observers thinking in Marxian terms would prefer to use $d_{\mathbf{p}}(\rho)$, i.e. the d – distance, while those thinking in 'Marx after Sraffa' terms would prefer to use $d_{\mathbf{v}}(\rho)$, since the determination of prices is '*logically prior* to any determination of value magnitudes' (Steedman 1977, p. 65), or, more generally, $d(\bar{\rho}, \rho)$, with $\bar{\rho} > 0$.

References

Chilcote, E. B. (1997). *Interindustry structure, relative prices, and productivity: An input-output study of the U.S. and O.E.C.D. countries* (Ph.D. Dissertation, New School for Social Research, New York).

Inada, K.-I. (1964). Some structural characteristics of turnpike theorems. *The Review of Economic Studies, 31*(1), 43–58.

Mariolis, T., & Soklis, G. (2011). On constructing numeraire-free measures of price-value deviation: A note on the Steedman-Tomkins distance. *Cambridge Journal of Economics, 35* (3), 613–618.

Mariolis, T., & Tsoulfidis, L. (2009). Decomposing the changes in production prices into 'capital-intensity' and 'price' effects: Theory and evidence from the Chinese economy. *Contributions to Political Economy, 28*(1), 1–22.

Mariolis, T., & Tsoulfidis, L. (2010). Measures of production price-labour value deviation and income distribution in actual economies: A note. *Metroeconomica, 61*(4), 701–710.

Mariolis, T., & Tsoulfidis, L. (2014). Measures of production price-labour value deviation and income distribution in actual economies: Theory and empirical evidence. *Bulletin of Political Economy, 8*(1), 77–96.

Ochoa, E. (1984). *Labor values and prices of production: An interindustry study of the U.S. economy, 1947–1972* (Ph.D. Dissertation, New School for Social Research, New York).

Ochoa, E. (1989). Value, prices and wage-profit curves in the U.S. economy. *Cambridge Journal of Economics, 13*(3), 413–429.

Petrović, P. (1987). The deviation of production prices from labour values: Some methodological and empirical evidence. *Cambridge Journal of Economics, 11*(3), 197–210.

Sánchez, C., & Ferràndez, M. N. (2010). Valores, precios de producción y precios de mercado a partir de los datos de la economía española. *Investigacion Economica, 69*(274), 87–118.

Sánchez, C., & Montibeler, E. E. (2015). The labour theory of value and the prices in China (in Spanish). *Economia e Sociedade, 24*(2), 329–354.

Shaikh, A. M. (1998). The empirical strength of the labour theory of value. In R. Bellofiore (Ed.), *Marxian economics: A reappraisal* (Vol. 2, pp. 225–251). New York: St. Martin's Press.

Sraffa, P. (1960). *Production of commodities by means of commodities. Prelude to a critique of economic theory*. Cambridge: Cambridge University Press.

Steedman, I. (1977). *Marx after Sraffa*. London: New Left Books.

Steedman, I., & Tomkins, J. (1998). On measuring the deviation of prices from values. *Cambridge Journal of Economics, 22*(3), 379–385.

Tsoulfidis, L. (2008). Price-value deviations: Further evidence from input-output data of Japan. *International Review of Applied Economics, 22*(6), 707–724.

Tsoulfidis, L., & Maniatis, T. (2002). Values, prices of production and market prices: Some more evidence from the Greek economy. *Cambridge Journal of Economics, 26*(3), 359–369.

Tsoulfidis, L., & Mariolis, T. (2007). Labour values, prices of production and the effects of income distribution: Evidence from the Greek economy. *Economic Systems Research, 19*(4), 425–437.

Tsoulfidis, L., & Paitaridis, D. (2009). On the labor theory of value: Statistical artefacts or regularities? *Research in Political Economy, 25*, 209–232.

Tsoulfidis, L., & Rieu, D.-M. (2006). Labor values, prices of production, and wage-profit rate frontiers of the Korean economy. *Seoul Journal of Economics, 19*(3), 275–295.

Chapter 5
Spectral Decompositions of Single-Product Economies

Abstract This chapter follows a recently developed line of research, which focuses on the spectral analysis of the wage-price-profit rate relationships in actual single-product economies. It shows that main aspects of those relationships could be connected to the skew distribution of both the eigenvalues and the singular values of the system matrices. The results finally suggest that there is room for using low-dimensional models as surrogates for actual economies.

Keywords Eigenvalue and singular value distributions • Low-order approximations • Spectral decompositions

5.1 Introduction

Typical findings in many empirical studies (see Chap. 3) are that, within the economically relevant interval of the profit rate, actual single-product economies tend to behave as corn-tractor systems with respect to the shape of the wage-profit curve and, at the same time, behave as three-industry systems with respect to the shape of the production price-profit rate curves. This chapter shows that those findings could be connected to the *skew* distribution of the characteristic values of the system matrices, i.e. to the fact that, across countries *and* over time, the moduli of the first non-dominant eigenvalues and the singular values fall markedly, whereas the rest constellate in much lower values forming a 'long tail'.[1]

The remainder of the chapter is structured as follows. Section 5.2 presents spectral decompositions and reconstructions of the production price-wage-profit system. Section 5.3 brings in the empirical evidence by examining (i) the

[1] This chapter draws on Mariolis and Tsoulfidis (2011, 2014), Iliadi et al. (2014), Mariolis (2011, 2013, 2015) and Mariolis et al. (2015). In the present line of research, there have also been contributions by Schefold (2008, 2013) and Mariolis and Tsoulfidis (2009), while Bienenfeld (1988, p. 255) has already shown that, in the extreme case where the non-dominant eigenvalues of the matrix of vertically integrated technical coefficients equal zero, the production prices in terms of Sraffa's Standard commodity (SSC) are strictly linear functions of the profit rate, and Shaikh (1998) has noted that '[a] large disparity between first and second eigenvalues is another possible source of linearity.'. (p. 244; also see p. 250, note 9).

© Springer Japan 2016

T. Mariolis, L. Tsoulfidis, *Modern Classical Economics and Reality*, Evolutionary Economics and Social Complexity Science 2, DOI 10.1007/978-4-431-55004-4_5

distributions of the eigenvalues and singular values and (ii) various aspects of the wage-price-profit rate relationships. Finally, Sect. 5.4 concludes.

5.2 Spectral Decompositions

Consider a diagonalizable and regular (see Sect. 2.2.2) price-wage-profit system described by

$$w = (\mathbf{v}[\mathbf{I} - \rho\mathbf{J}]^{-1}\mathbf{z}^{\mathrm{T}})^{-1}, \quad \mathbf{v}\mathbf{z}^{\mathrm{T}} = 1 \tag{5.1}$$

$$\mathbf{p} = w\mathbf{v}[\mathbf{I} - \rho\mathbf{J}]^{-1} = \left(\mathbf{v}[\mathbf{I} - \rho\mathbf{J}]^{-1}\mathbf{z}^{\mathrm{T}}\right)^{-1}\mathbf{v}[\mathbf{I} - \rho\mathbf{J}]^{-1} \tag{5.2}$$

The vector of labour values, $\mathbf{v}$ ($=\mathbf{p}(0)$), can be expressed as a linear combination of the basis vectors $\mathbf{y}_{\mathbf{J}i}$, i.e.

$$\mathbf{v} = \sum_{i=1}^{n} c_i \mathbf{y}_{\mathbf{J}i} \tag{5.3}$$

while the numeraire commodity, $\mathbf{z}^{\mathrm{T}}$, can be expressed as a linear combination of the basis vectors $\mathbf{z}_{\mathbf{J}i}^{\mathrm{T}} \equiv [\mathbf{I} - \mathbf{A}]\mathbf{x}_{\mathbf{J}i}^{\mathrm{T}}$, i.e.

$$\mathbf{z}^{\mathrm{T}} = \sum_{i=1}^{n} d_i \mathbf{z}_{\mathbf{J}i}^{\mathrm{T}} \tag{5.4}$$

Postmultiplying Eq. 5.3 by $\mathbf{z}_{\mathbf{J}i}^{\mathrm{T}}$ gives

$$\mathbf{v}\mathbf{z}_{\mathbf{J}i}^{\mathrm{T}} = c_i \mathbf{y}_{\mathbf{J}i}\mathbf{z}_{\mathbf{J}i}^{\mathrm{T}} \tag{5.5}$$

since, for any two distinct eigenvalues of a matrix, the left eigenvector of one eigenvalue is orthogonal to the right eigenvector of the other. Premultiplying Eq. 5.4 by $\mathbf{v}$ gives

$$\mathbf{v}\mathbf{z}^{\mathrm{T}} = \sum_{i=1}^{n} d_i \mathbf{v}\mathbf{z}_{\mathbf{J}i}^{\mathrm{T}} \tag{5.6}$$

Hence, if $\mathbf{y}_{\mathbf{J}i}$, $\mathbf{z}_{\mathbf{J}i}^{\mathrm{T}}$ are normalized by setting

$\mathbf{y}_{\mathbf{J}i}\mathbf{z}_{\mathbf{J}i}^{\mathrm{T}} = 1$ and $\mathbf{v}\mathbf{z}_{\mathbf{J}i}^{\mathrm{T}} = 1$

then Eqs. 5.5, 5.6 and $\mathbf{v}\mathbf{z}^{\mathrm{T}} = 1$ imply that

$$c_i = 1 \text{ and } \sum_{i=1}^{n} d_i = 1 \tag{5.7}$$

Moreover, premultiplying Eq. 5.4 by $\mathbf{y}_{\mathbf{J}1}$ gives

$$\mathbf{y}_{\mathbf{J}1}\mathbf{z}^{\mathrm{T}} = d_1 \mathbf{y}_{\mathbf{J}1}\mathbf{z}_{\mathbf{J}1}^{\mathrm{T}} = d_1$$

and, given that $\mathbf{p}(1)\mathbf{z}^{\mathrm{T}} = 1$ and $\mathbf{p}(1)$ is the left P-F eigenvector of $\mathbf{J}$,

$$\mathbf{p}(1) = d_1^{-1}\mathbf{y}_{\mathbf{J}1} \tag{5.8}$$

Hence, Eqs. 5.7 and 5.8 imply that Eq. 5.3 can be written as

$$\mathbf{v} = \mathbf{p}(0) = d_1\,\mathbf{p}(1) + \sum_{k=2}^{n} \mathbf{y}_{\mathbf{J}k} \tag{5.3a}$$

5.2.1 Arbitrary Numeraire

The substitution of Eqs. 5.3a, 5.4 and 5.7 in Eqs. 5.1 and 5.2 yields

$$w = [(1-\rho)^{-1}d_1 + \Lambda_k^w]^{-1},\ \ \Lambda_k^w \equiv \sum_{k=2}^{n}(1-\rho\lambda_{\mathbf{J}k})^{-1}d_k \tag{5.9}$$

or

$$w = \Pi_0\left(\sum_{i=1}^{n}\Pi_i d_i\right)^{-1} \tag{5.9a}$$

and

$$\mathbf{p} = w[(1-\rho)^{-1}d_1\,\mathbf{p}(1) + \Lambda_k^{\mathbf{p}}],\ \ \Lambda_k^{\mathbf{p}} \equiv \sum_{k=2}^{n}(1-\rho\lambda_{\mathbf{J}k})^{-1}\mathbf{y}_{\mathbf{J}k} \tag{5.10}$$

or

$$\mathbf{p} = \left(\sum_{i=1}^{n}\Pi_i d_i\right)^{-1}\left(\sum_{i=1}^{n}\Pi_i \mathbf{y}_{Ji}\right) \tag{5.10a}$$

where

$$\Pi_0 \equiv (1-\rho)(1-\rho\lambda_{\mathbf{J}2})\ldots(1-\rho\lambda_{\mathbf{J}n}) = \det[\mathbf{I}-\rho\mathbf{J}]$$

and

$$\Pi_i \equiv \prod_{\substack{j=1 \\ j\neq i}}^{n} (1-\rho\lambda_{\mathbf{J}j})$$

Equations 5.9 and 5.10 represent *spectral forms* of the wage-relative profit rate curve (WPC) and production price-profit rate relationships, respectively, and the terms Λ_k^w, $\Lambda_k^{\mathbf{p}}$ represent the effects of non-dominant eigenvalues.[2]

From Eqs. 5.3a and 5.7 to 5.10, it follows that there are certain, particularly interesting, *polar* cases, which arise when the non-dominant eigenvalues are very close to each other, i.e. $\lambda_{\mathbf{J}k} \approx \lambda \equiv \alpha \pm i\beta$, where $i \equiv \sqrt{-1}$, for all k, or concentrate around two values:

Case 1 $\mathbf{J} \approx \mathbf{I}$, i.e. the system tends to be decomposed into n quasi-similar self-reproducing vertically integrated industries (also see Hartfiel and Meyer 1998). Thus, $\lambda_{\mathbf{J}k} = \lambda = \alpha \approx 1$ and, therefore,

$$w \approx \left[(1-\rho)^{-1}\sum_{i=1}^{n} d_i\right] = 1-\rho = w^{\mathrm{S}}$$

$$\mathbf{p} \approx w^{\mathrm{S}}\left[(1-\rho)^{-1}\left(d_1\,\mathbf{p}(1) + \sum_{k=2}^{n} \mathbf{y}_{\mathbf{J}k}\right)\right] = \mathbf{p}(0)$$

That is, the so-called pure labour theory of value tends to hold true or, in other words, the system tends to behave as a one-industry economy.

Case 2 *rank*[**J**] ≈ 1, i.e. there are strong quasi-linear dependencies amongst the technical conditions of production in all the vertically integrated industries. Thus,

---

[2] Steedman's (1999) numeraire entails that

$$\left(\sum_{i=1}^{n} \Pi_i d_i\right)^{-1} = 1$$

and, therefore, $w = \prod_0$ and

$$\mathbf{p} = \sum_{i=1}^{n} \Pi_i \mathbf{y}_{\mathbf{J}i}$$

(see Eqs. 5.9a and 5.10a). Thus, the w–ρ and $\mathbf{p}$–ρ relationships take on simpler forms in the sense that the former is expressed solely in terms of the eigenvalues of **J**, while the latter is expressed in terms of powers of ρ up to ρ^{n-1}.

$\lambda_{Jk} = |\lambda| \approx 0$ and, therefore, both the WPC and the relative production price-profit rate relationships tend to be rational functions of degree 1 (homographic functions):

$$w \approx \left[(1-\rho)^{-1}d_1 + \sum_{k=2}^{n} d_k\right] = w^{\mathrm{S}}[1+\rho(d_1-1)]^{-1} \tag{5.11}$$

$$\mathbf{p} \approx w^{\mathrm{S}}[1+\rho(d_1-1)]^{-1}\left[(1-\rho)^{-1}d_1\,\mathbf{p}(1) + \sum_{k=2}^{n} \mathbf{y}_{\mathrm{J}k}\right]$$

or

$$\mathbf{p} \approx [1+\rho(d_1-1)]^{-1}[\mathbf{p}(0) + \rho(d_1\,\mathbf{p}(1) - \mathbf{p}(0))] \tag{5.12}$$

That is, the system tends to behave as a reducible two-industry economy without self-reproducing non-basics. These approximations are exact when and only when $rank[\mathbf{J}] = 1$, i.e. $\mathbf{J} = \left(\mathbf{y}_{\mathrm{J1}}\mathbf{x}_{\mathrm{J1}}^{\mathrm{T}}\right)^{-1}\mathbf{x}_{\mathrm{J1}}^{\mathrm{T}}\mathbf{y}_{\mathrm{J1}}$. In that case, $\mathbf{J}$ can be transformed, via a semi-positive similarity matrix $\mathbf{T}$, into (Schur triangularization theorem; see, e.g. Meyer 2001, pp. 508–509)

$$\widetilde{\mathbf{J}} \equiv \mathbf{T}^{-1}\mathbf{J}\mathbf{T} = \begin{bmatrix} 1 & \widetilde{\mathbf{J}}_{12} \\ \mathbf{0}_{(n-1)\times 1} & \mathbf{0}_{(n-1)\times(n-1)} \end{bmatrix}$$

where the first column of $\mathbf{T}$ is $\mathbf{x}_{\mathrm{J1}}^{\mathrm{T}}$ (the remaining columns are arbitrary) and $\widetilde{\mathbf{J}}_{12}$ is a $1 \times (n-1)$ *positive* vector.[3] That is, the original system is economically equivalent to an $n \times n$ corn-tractor system, even if $\mathbf{J}$ is irreducible. Hence, the first row in the transformed matrix $\widetilde{\mathbf{J}}$ represents an industry which can be characterized as *hyper-basic*. This industry is no more than the Sraffian Standard system (SSS), while the remaining industries are not uniquely determined 'corn-like producing industries'.

It should, finally, be added that, when $\mathbf{J}$ is a *random* matrix, with identically and independently distributed entries, Bródy's (1997) conjecture implies that $|\lambda_{\mathrm{J2}}|$ tends to zero, with speed $n^{-0.5}$, when n tends to *infinity* (we shall return to this issue in Chap. 6).

Case 3 $\mathbf{J} \approx (1+\mathbf{y}\mathbf{x}^{\mathrm{T}})^{-1}(\mathbf{I}+\mathbf{x}^{\mathrm{T}}\mathbf{y})$ $(\geq \mathbf{0})$ and, therefore, $\lambda_{\mathrm{J}k} = \lambda = \alpha \approx (1+\mathbf{y}\mathbf{x}^{\mathrm{T}})^{-1}$.[4] Thus, it can be written that

---

[3] If, for instance, $\mathbf{T} = \left[\mathbf{x}_{\mathrm{J1}}^{\mathrm{T}}, \mathbf{e}_2^{\mathrm{T}}, \ldots, \mathbf{e}_n^{\mathrm{T}}\right]$, then $\widetilde{\mathbf{J}}_{12} = \left(\mathbf{y}_{\mathrm{J1}}\mathbf{x}_{\mathrm{J1}}^{\mathrm{T}}\right)^{-1}\left[y_{2\mathrm{J1}}, y_{3\mathrm{J1}}, \ldots, y_{n\mathrm{J1}}\right]$.

[4] Consider the theorem mentioned in footnote 31 of Chap. 2. It may be added that, if, for instance, $\mathbf{x} > \mathbf{0}$ and $y_{1i} = x_{i1}^{-1} + \delta_i$, where $\delta_i \geq 0$, then

$$w \approx w^{\mathrm{S}}(1-\rho\lambda)\{1+\rho[d_1(1-\lambda)-1]\}^{-1}$$
$$\mathbf{p} \approx \{1+\rho[d_1(1-\lambda)-1]\}^{-1}\{\mathbf{p}(0)+\rho[d_1(1-\lambda)\,\mathbf{p}(1)-\mathbf{p}(0)]\}$$

That is, for $-\infty << \mathbf{yx}^{\mathrm{T}} << 0$ or $0 << \mathbf{yx}^{\mathrm{T}} << +\infty$, the system tends to behave as a two-industry economy with only basic commodities. As $\mathbf{yx}^{\mathrm{T}} \rightarrow 0\ (\pm\infty)$, we obtain the *Case 1* (2).[5]

Case 4 $\mathbf{J} \approx (1+\lambda_{\Psi 1})^{-1}\left[\mathbf{I}+\sum_{i=1}^{2}\mathbf{x}_i^{\mathrm{T}}\mathbf{y}_i\right]$, where $\mathbf{x}_i^{\mathrm{T}}$, $\mathbf{y}_i$ are semi-positive vectors (or two pairs of complex conjugate vectors) and $\boldsymbol{\Psi} \equiv \left[\mathbf{y}_1^{\mathrm{T}}, \mathbf{y}_2^{\mathrm{T}}\right]^{\mathrm{T}}\left[\mathbf{x}_1^{\mathrm{T}}, \mathbf{x}_2^{\mathrm{T}}\right]$ (in either case, $\boldsymbol{\Psi}$ is a 2×2 matrix with only real eigenvalues). Thus, n–2 non-dominant eigenvalues of $\mathbf{J}$ tend to equal $(1+\lambda_{\Psi 1})^{-1}$, and the remaining tends to equal $(1+\lambda_{\Psi 2})(1+\lambda_{\Psi 1})^{-1}$ (consider the Corollary 3.4 in Ding and Zhou 2008, p. 635). The system tends to behave as a three-industry economy, and, therefore, the WPC may exhibit inflection points and the production price-profit rate relationships may be non-monotonic (the same holds true when $\lambda_{\mathbf{J}k} \approx \alpha \pm i\beta$, with $0 << |\beta|$, for all k).[6]

Case 5 The subdominant eigenvalue is complex, with $0 << |\beta|$ and $\lambda_{\mathbf{J}4} \approx \ldots \approx \lambda_{\mathbf{J}n} \approx 0$. The WPC tends to be a rational function of degree no greater than 3, and, therefore, the system tends to behave as a reducible four-industry economy without self-reproducing non-basics.

$$\lambda \approx \left(1+n+\sum_{i=1}^{n}x_{i1}\delta_i\right)^{-1} \leq (1+n)^{-1}$$

If $\mathbf{x} > \mathbf{0}$ and $y_{1i} = -x_{i1}^{-1}+\delta_i$, where $\delta_i \leq 0$, then

$$\lambda \approx \left(1-n+\sum_{i=1}^{n}x_{i1}\delta_i\right)^{-1} \geq (1-n)^{-1}$$

[5] It is noted that if we adopt Steedman's numeraire (see footnote 2 in this chapter) and $\lambda_{\mathbf{J}k} = \lambda = \alpha$, then

$$\mathbf{p} = (1-\rho\lambda)^{n-2}\left\{\mathbf{p}(0)+\rho\left[(1-\lambda)^{-n+2}\,\mathbf{p}(1)-\mathbf{p}(0)\right]\right\}$$

where $\mathbf{p}(1)$ is now equal to $(1–\lambda)^{n-1}\mathbf{y}_{\mathbf{J}1}$. Hence, the p_j–ρ curves are not necessarily monotonic.

[6] Any complex number is an eigenvalue of a positive 3×3 'circulant matrix' (Minc 1988, p. 167). To the best of our knowledge, however, the problem of determining necessary and sufficient conditions for a list of numbers to be the spectrum of a nonnegative matrix ('nonnegative inverse eigenvalue problem') remains unsolved (for a recent contribution, see Laffey and Šmigoc 2006).

Case 6 Consider the matrix

$$\mathbf{G} \equiv b\mathbf{S} + (1-b)\boldsymbol{\chi}^{\mathrm{T}}\mathbf{e}$$

where b is a real number such that $0 < b < 1$, known as a 'damping factor', $\mathbf{S}$ is a column stochastic matrix and $\boldsymbol{\chi}^{\mathrm{T}}$ is a semi-positive vector normalized by setting $\mathbf{e}\boldsymbol{\chi}^{\mathrm{T}} = 1$. It then follows that $\mathbf{G}$ is a column stochastic matrix ($\mathbf{eG} = b\mathbf{e} + (1-b)\mathbf{e} = \mathbf{e}$), known as a 'Google matrix', with eigenvalues $\{1, b\lambda_{\mathrm{S}2}, \ldots, b\lambda_{\mathrm{S}n}\}$ and, therefore, $|\lambda_{\mathrm{G}2}| \leq b$ (Haveliwala and Kamvar 2003; also see Ding and Zhou 2007, p. 1225). Thus, if for the column stochastic matrix $\mathbf{M} \equiv \hat{\mathbf{y}}_{\mathrm{J}1}\mathbf{J}\hat{\mathbf{y}}_{\mathrm{J}1}^{-1}$ (see Sect. 2.3.1) we can write $\mathbf{M} \approx \mathbf{G}$, then $|\lambda_{\mathrm{J}2}| \approx |\lambda_{\mathrm{G}2}| \leq b$.[7]

These six cases (and their possible combinations) indicate that the location of the non-dominant eigenvalues, $\lambda_{\mathrm{J}k}$, in the complex plane could be considered as an index for the degree of capital heterogeneity.

5.2.2 *Sraffa's Standard Commodity*

If SSC is chosen as the numeraire, i.e. $\mathbf{z}^{\mathrm{T}} = [\mathbf{I} - \mathbf{A}]\mathbf{x}_{\mathrm{J}1}^{\mathrm{T}}$, then $d_1 = 1$, $d_k = 0$ and Eqs. 5.9 and 5.10 become $w = w^{\mathrm{S}} \equiv 1 - \rho$ and

$$\mathbf{p} = \mathbf{p}(1) + (1-\rho)\boldsymbol{\Lambda}_k^{\mathbf{p}} \tag{5.13}$$

or

$$\mathbf{p} = \left[1, (1-\rho)(1-\rho\lambda_{\mathrm{J}2})^{-1}, \ldots, (1-\rho)(1-\rho\lambda_{\mathrm{J}n})^{-1}\right]\mathbf{Y}$$

where $\mathbf{Y} \equiv \left[\mathbf{p}(1)^{\mathrm{T}}, \mathbf{y}_{\mathrm{J}2}^{\mathrm{T}}, \ldots, \mathbf{y}_{\mathrm{J}n}^{\mathrm{T}}\right]^{\mathrm{T}}$ is a left eigenbasis and

$$\left[1, (1-\rho)(1-\rho\lambda_{\mathrm{J}2})^{-1}, \ldots, (1-\rho)(1-\rho\lambda_{\mathrm{J}n})^{-1}\right]$$

are the coordinates of the price vector in terms of $\mathbf{Y}$. Furthermore, it follows that:

(i) Differentiation of Eq. 5.13 with respect to ρ gives

$$\dot{\mathbf{p}} = -\boldsymbol{\Lambda}_k^{\mathbf{p}} + (1-\rho)\dot{\boldsymbol{\Lambda}}_k^{\mathbf{p}} = -\sum_{k=2}^{n}(1-\lambda_{\mathrm{J}k})(1-\rho\lambda_{\mathrm{J}k})^{-2}\mathbf{y}_{\mathrm{J}k}$$

which implies that the individual components of $\mathbf{p}$ can change in a complicated way as ρ changes. Nevertheless, it can be shown that there are

[7] Setting $b = (1 + \mathbf{y}\mathbf{x}^{\mathrm{T}})^{-1}, \mathbf{S} = \mathbf{I}, \boldsymbol{\chi}^{\mathrm{T}} = (\mathbf{y}\mathbf{x}^{\mathrm{T}})^{-1}\mathbf{x}^{\mathrm{T}}$ and replacing $\mathbf{e}$ by $\mathbf{y}$, we obtain *Case 3*.

commodity bundles whose prices decrease monotonically as ρ increases. Postmultiplying Eq. 5.13 by $\mathbf{z}_{\mathbf{J}\mu}^{\mathrm{T}}$, $\mu = 2, \ldots, n$ and $\mu \neq k$, gives

$$\mathbf{p}\mathbf{z}_{\mathbf{J}\mu}^{\mathrm{T}} = f_{\mu}(\rho) \equiv (1-\rho)\left(1-\rho\lambda_{\mathbf{J}\mu}\right)^{-1} \tag{5.14}$$

Now, it is necessary to distinguish between the following two cases:

Case 1: If $\mathbf{z}_{\mathbf{J}\mu}^{\mathrm{T}}$ is a real eigenvector, then $f_{\mu}(\rho) \geq 0$ is a strictly decreasing function of ρ, which is strictly concave (convex) to the origin for $\lambda_{\mathbf{J}\mu} > (<)$ 0,[8] while it coincides with 1–ρ for $\lambda_{\mathbf{J}\mu}=0$ and tends to 1 (to $(1-\rho)(1+\rho)^{-1}$) as $\lambda_{\mathbf{J}\mu} \rightarrow 1$ (as $\lambda_{\mathbf{J}\mu} \rightarrow -1$). Finally, multiplying both sides of Eq. 5.14 by $\lambda_{\mathbf{J}\mu}$ gives

$$\kappa_{\mu}\kappa_{\mathrm{S}}^{-1} = (1-\rho)(R_{\mu}R^{-1}-\rho)^{-1}$$

where $\kappa_{\mathrm{S}} \equiv R^{-1}$ equals the capital intensity of the SSS, $R_{\mu} \equiv \lambda_{\mathbf{A}\mu}^{-1} - 1$, $\kappa_{\mu} \equiv \mathbf{p}\mathbf{z}_{\mathbf{J}\mu}^{\mathrm{T}}R_{\mu}^{-1}$ equal the ratio of the net product to the means of production (or 'Standard ratio') and the capital intensity of the vertically integrated industry producing $\mathbf{z}_{\mathbf{J}\mu}^{\mathrm{T}}$ (or, alternatively, of an economically insignificant, non-Sraffian real (non-complex) Standard system),[9] respectively, and $|\kappa_{\mu}| < \kappa_{\mathrm{S}}$, since $R < |R_{\mu}|$.

Case 2: If $\mathbf{z}_{\mathbf{J}\mu}^{\mathrm{T}}$ and $\bar{\mathbf{z}}_{\mathbf{J}\mu}^{\mathrm{T}}$ are a pair of complex eigenvectors associated with $\lambda_{\mathbf{J}\mu} = \alpha + i\beta$, $|\lambda_{\mathbf{J}\mu}| \equiv \sqrt{\alpha^2+\beta^2} < 1$, $\beta \neq 0$, then from Eq. 5.13 we get

$$\mathbf{p}\left(\mathbf{z}_{\mathbf{J}\mu}^{\mathrm{T}} + \bar{\mathbf{z}}_{\mathbf{J}\mu}^{\mathrm{T}}\right) = F_{\mu}(\rho)$$

and

[8] It is easily checked that

$$\dot{f}_{\mu}(\rho) = -\left(1-\lambda_{\mathbf{J}\mu}\right)\left(1-\rho\lambda_{\mathbf{J}\mu}\right)^{-2} < 0$$

since $|\lambda_{\mathbf{J}\mu}| < 1$, and

$$\ddot{f}_{\mu}(\rho) = -2(1-\lambda_{\mathbf{J}\mu})\lambda_{\mathbf{J}\mu}(1-\rho\lambda_{\mathbf{J}\mu})^{-3}$$

[9] See Sraffa (1960, pp. 31, footnote 2, 48 and 53–54). For the non-Sraffian, real and/or complex, Standard commodities-systems, also see Goodwin (1976, 1977, 1984), Cozzi (1990), Pasinetti (1990), Punzo (1990), Aruka (1991), Steenge (1995) and Rodousakis (2012).

$$F_{\mu}(\rho) \equiv f_{\mu}(\rho) + \overline{f}_{\mu}(\rho) = 2(1-\rho)(1-\rho\alpha)\left[(1-\rho\alpha)^2 + (\rho\beta)^2\right]^{-1} \geq 0 \quad (5.15)$$

or

$$F_{\mu}(\rho) = 2(1-\rho)\left(1-\rho\left|\lambda_{\mathbf{J}\mu}\right|\cos\theta\right)\left[1-2\rho\left|\lambda_{\mathbf{J}\mu}\right|\cos\theta + \left(\rho\left|\lambda_{\mathbf{J}\mu}\right|\right)^2\right]^{-1} \quad (5.15a)$$

where $\theta \equiv \arccos\left(\alpha\left|\lambda_{\mathbf{J}\mu}\right|^{-1}\right)$. Given that Eq. 5.15 can be written as

$$2^{-1}F_{\mu}(\rho) = (g(\rho) + h(\rho))^{-1}$$

where $g(\rho) \equiv [(1-\rho)(1-\rho\alpha)]^{-1}(1-\rho\alpha)^2$ and $h(\rho) \equiv [(1-\rho)(1-\rho\alpha)]^{-1}(\rho\beta)^2$ are strictly increasing functions of ρ,[10] it follows that $F_{\mu}(\rho)$ is a strictly decreasing function of ρ. Moreover, Eq. 5.15a implies that $2^{-1}F_{\mu}(\rho)$ tends to $(1-\rho)$ as $\left|\lambda_{\mathbf{J}\mu}\right| \to 0$, to $(1-\rho)\left(1 \pm \rho\left|\lambda_{\mathbf{J}\mu}\right|\right)^{-1}$ (a function that is strictly concave (convex) to the origin) as $\cos\,\theta \to \pm 1$ and to $(1-\rho)\left[1+\left(\rho\left|\lambda_{\mathbf{J}\mu}\right|\right)^2\right]^{-1}$ (a function that has an inflection point in the interval $2-\sqrt{3}$ ($\cong 0.270$) $< \rho < 1/3$) as $\cos\theta \to 0$. Furthermore, the ratio of the capital intensity, $\kappa_{\mu} + \overline{\kappa}_{\mu}$, of the vertically integrated industry producing $\mathbf{z}^{\mathrm{T}}_{\mathbf{J}\mu} + \overline{\mathbf{z}}^{\mathrm{T}}_{\mathbf{J}\mu}$ to the capital intensity of the SSS is given by

$$\left(\kappa_{\mu} + \overline{\kappa}_{\mu}\right)\kappa_{\mathrm{S}}^{-1} = f_{\mu}(\rho)\lambda_{\mathbf{J}\mu} + \overline{f}_{\mu}(\rho)\overline{\lambda}_{\mathbf{J}\mu}$$

from which it follows that

$$\left|\kappa_{\mu} + \overline{\kappa}_{\mu}\right|\kappa_{\mathrm{S}}^{-1} < 2\left|f_{\mu}(\rho)\lambda_{\mathbf{J}\mu}\right| = 2(1-\rho)\left|\lambda_{\mathbf{J}\mu}\right|\left|1-\rho\lambda_{\mathbf{J}\mu}\right|^{-1}$$

or

$$\left|\kappa_{\mu} + \overline{\kappa}_{\mu}\right|\kappa_{\mathrm{S}}^{-1} < 2(1-\rho)\left|\lambda_{\mathbf{J}\mu}\right|\left(1-\rho\left|\lambda_{\mathbf{J}\mu}\right|\right)^{-1} < 2$$

Finally,

---

[10] It is easily checked that

$$\dot{g}(\rho) = (1-\rho)^{-2}(1-\alpha)$$

and

$$\dot{h}(\rho) = [(1-\rho)(1-\rho\alpha)]^{-2}\rho\beta^2[2-\rho(1+\alpha)]$$

Hence, $\dot{g}(\rho) > 0$ and $\dot{h}(\rho) > 0$, since $|\alpha| < 1$ and $\rho(1+\alpha) < 2$.

$$\left(\left|\kappa_{\mu}\right|^{-1}\kappa_{\mathrm{S}}\right)^{2}=\left|f_{\mu}(\rho)\lambda_{\mathbf{J}\mu}\right|^{-2}=\left[(1-\rho\alpha)^{2}+(\rho\beta)^{2}\right]\left[(1-\rho)\sqrt{\alpha^{2}+\beta^{2}}\right]^{-2}$$

is a strictly increasing function of ρ, since $\rho\alpha < 1$,[11] and, therefore, $|\kappa_{\mu}|$ is a strictly decreasing function of ρ (however, $\left|\kappa_{\mu}+\overline{\kappa}_{\mu}\right|$ does not necessarily decreases with ρ). Thus, we may conclude that when SSC is chosen as the numeraire, Ricardo's statement regarding the relationship between production prices and changes in income distribution (see Sect. 2.4.1) holds true with respect to the (real) commodity bundles $\mathbf{z}_{\mathbf{J}\mu}^{\mathrm{T}}$ and $\mathbf{z}_{\mathbf{J}\mu}^{\mathrm{T}}+\overline{\mathbf{z}}_{\mathbf{J}\mu}^{\mathrm{T}}$: they are labour-intensive relative to the numeraire, in the sense that $\left|\kappa_{\mu}\right|<\kappa_{\mathrm{S}}$ and $\left|\kappa_{\mu}+\overline{\kappa}_{\mu}\right|<2\kappa_{\mathrm{S}}$, respectively, and their prices decrease with increasing ρ.[12] However, this conclusion is not generally independent of the arbitrary choice of numeraire, since $\left|\kappa_{\mu}\right|\kappa_{S}^{-1}$ and, therefore, $\mathbf{p}\mathbf{z}_{\mathbf{J}\mu}^{\mathrm{T}}$ are not necessarily monotonic functions of ρ when $\mathbf{z}^{\mathrm{T}}\neq[\mathbf{I}-\mathbf{A}]\mathbf{x}_{\mathbf{J}1}^{\mathrm{T}}$.

(ii) If $\lambda_{\mathbf{J}k}=|\lambda|\approx 0$, then Eq. 5.13 reduces to

$$\mathbf{p}\approx\mathbf{p}(0)+\rho(\mathbf{p}(1)-\mathbf{p}(0))$$

(also see Eq. 5.12) which coincides with Bienenfeld's *linear* approximation formula for the price vector (see Eq. 2.80).

(iii) If $\rho|\lambda_{\mathbf{J}k}|<<1$, then

$$(1-\rho\lambda_{\mathbf{J}k})^{-1}=1+\rho\lambda_{\mathbf{J}k}+(\rho\lambda_{\mathbf{J}k})^{2}+\ldots\approx 1+\rho\lambda_{\mathbf{J}k}$$

and, therefore, Eq. 5.13 and $\mathbf{p}(0)=\mathbf{p}(1)+\sum_{k=2}^{n}\mathbf{y}_{\mathbf{J}k}$ imply that

---

[11] It is easily checked that the first derivative of $\left(\left|\kappa_{\mu}\right|^{-1}\kappa_{\mathrm{S}}\right)^{2}$ with respect to ρ equals

$$2[(1-\rho\alpha)(1-\alpha)+\rho\beta^{2}][(1-\rho)^{3}\sqrt{\alpha^{2}+\beta^{2}}]^{-1}$$

[12] It may be said that this is not unanticipated on the basis of Goodwin's (1976, 1977) contribution to the linear value and distribution theory. By following an approach which is closer to our, Bidard and Ehrbar (2007, pp. 203–204) show that $|\kappa_{\mu}|$ decrease with ρ, and if κ_{μ} is complex, then the derivative of its argument does not change sign, i.e. κ_{μ} moves monotonically, either clockwise or counterclockwise, across the complex plane. Since there are statements in the foreign trade theory (e.g. Stolper-Samuelson effect, 'factor price' equalization theorem) that depend crucially on the existence of monotonic price-profit rate relationships, our conclusion would seem to be of some importance for that theory (also see Mariolis 2004).

$$\mathbf{p} \approx \mathbf{p}(0) + \rho(\mathbf{p}(1) - \mathbf{p}(0)) + \rho\sum_{k=2}^{n} \lambda_{\mathbf{J}k}\mathbf{y}_{\mathbf{J}k} - \rho^2\sum_{k=2}^{n} \lambda_{\mathbf{J}k}\mathbf{y}_{\mathbf{J}k} \tag{5.16}$$

Postmultiplying $\mathbf{p}(0) = \mathbf{p}(1) + \sum_{k=2}^{n} \mathbf{y}_{\mathbf{J}k}$ by $\mathbf{J}$ gives

$$\mathbf{p}(0)\mathbf{J} = \mathbf{p}(1) + \sum_{k=2}^{n} \lambda_{\mathbf{J}k}\mathbf{y}_{\mathbf{J}k} \tag{5.17}$$

Substituting Eq. 5.17 in approximation (5.16) yields

$$\mathbf{p} \approx \mathbf{p}(0) + \rho(\mathbf{p}(0)\mathbf{J} - \mathbf{p}(0)) + \rho^2(\mathbf{p}(1) - \mathbf{p}(0)\mathbf{J})$$

which coincides with Bienenfeld's *quadratic* formula (see Eq. 2.81).

(iv) Writing $(1-\rho\lambda_{\mathbf{J}k})^{-1}$ as $1 + \rho\lambda_{\mathbf{J}k}(1 - \rho\lambda_{\mathbf{J}k})^{-1}$ and substituting in Eq. 5.13 yields

$$\mathbf{p} = \mathbf{p}(1) + (1-\rho)\sum_{k=2}^{n} \mathbf{y}_{\mathbf{J}k} + (1-\rho)\sum_{k=2}^{n} \rho\lambda_{\mathbf{J}k}(1-\rho\lambda_{\mathbf{J}k})^{-1}\mathbf{y}_{\mathbf{J}k}$$

or

$$\mathbf{p} = \mathbf{p}(0) + \rho(\mathbf{p}(1) - \mathbf{p}(0)) + (1-\rho)\sum_{k=2}^{n} \rho\lambda_{\mathbf{J}k}(1-\rho\lambda_{\mathbf{J}k})^{-1}\mathbf{y}_{\mathbf{J}k} \tag{5.18}$$

Thus, if the moduli of the last $n-\nu$, $2 \leq \nu \leq n-1$, eigenvalues are sufficiently small that can be considered as negligible, then Eq. 5.18 reduces to

$$\mathbf{p} \approx \mathbf{p}(0) + \rho(\mathbf{p}(1) - \mathbf{p}(0)) + \sum_{k=2}^{\nu} f_{sk}(\rho)\mathbf{y}_{\mathbf{J}k} \tag{5.19}$$

where

$$f_{sk}(\rho) \equiv (1-\rho)\rho\lambda_{\mathbf{J}k}(1-\rho\lambda_{\mathbf{J}k})^{-1}$$

The sum of the first two terms in Eq. 5.19 coincides with Bienenfeld's linear approximation, and if $\lambda_{\mathbf{J}k}$ is positive (negative), then the nonlinear term $f_{sk}(\rho)$ is a semi-positive (semi-negative) and strictly concave (convex) function of ρ, which is maximized (minimized) at $\rho^* \equiv (1 - \sqrt{1-\lambda_{\mathbf{J}k}})\lambda_{\mathbf{J}k}{}^{-1}$, where $-1 + \sqrt{2} \cong 0.414 < \rho^* < 1$ and $-3 + 2\sqrt{2} \cong -0.172 < f_{sk}(\rho^*) < 1$, since $|\lambda_{\mathbf{J}k}| < 1$.

Relation (5.19) could be called a 'ν-th order eigenvalue decomposition (EVD) approximation' and is exact at the extreme values of ρ. If $\mathbf{X}_\mathbf{J}$ and the diagonal matrix $\hat{\boldsymbol{\lambda}}_\mathbf{J}$ are matrices formed from the right eigenvectors and the eigenvalues of $\mathbf{J}$, respectively, then $\hat{\boldsymbol{\lambda}}_\mathbf{J} = \mathbf{X}_\mathbf{J}^{-1}\mathbf{J}\mathbf{X}_\mathbf{J}$. Let $\hat{\boldsymbol{\lambda}}_\mathbf{J}^{[\nu]}$ be the matrix derived from $\hat{\boldsymbol{\lambda}}_\mathbf{J}$ by replacing the last $n-\nu$ eigenvalues by zeroes and

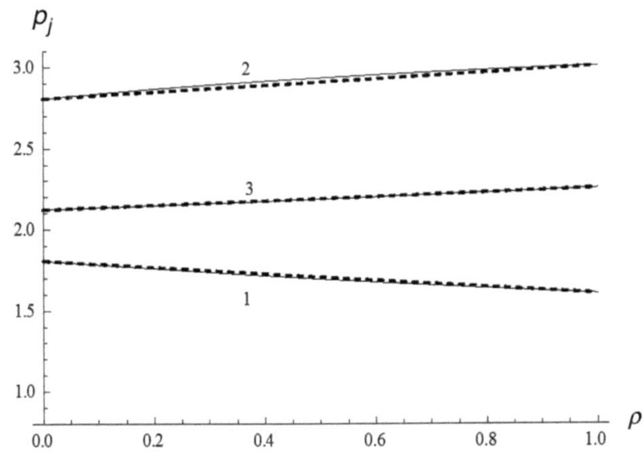

Fig. 5.3 The production price-relative profit rate curves and their first-order EVD approximations

$$\mathbf{J}^{[1]} \cong \begin{pmatrix} 0.333 & 0.625 & 0.468 \\ 0.178 & 0.333 & 0.250 \\ 0.237 & 0.444 & 0.333 \end{pmatrix}, \quad \left\|\mathbf{J} - \mathbf{J}^{[1]}\right\|_{SP} \cong 0.487, \quad \left\|\mathbf{J} - \mathbf{J}^{[1]}\right\|_{F} \cong 0.561$$

and

$$\tilde{\mathbf{J}}^{[1]} \cong \begin{pmatrix} 1 & 0.836 & 0.627 \\ 0 & 0 & 0 \\ 0 & 0 & 0 \end{pmatrix}$$

Figure 5.3 displays the production prices as functions of the relative profit rate and their first-order EVD approximations (depicted by dotted lines). It is noted that the actual $p_2 p_3^{-1} - \rho$ curve has a *maximum* at $\rho \cong 0.546$, although (i) the actual p_j–ρ curves are almost linear and (ii) there is no capital intensity reversal.

Now we turn to the SVD low-rank approximations of **J**:

$$\sigma_{J1} \cong 1.270, \quad \sigma_{J1}\sigma_{J2}^{-1} \cong 3.661, \quad \sigma_{J1}\sigma_{J3}^{-1} \cong 4.676,$$
$$\left\|\mathbf{J} - \overline{\mathbf{J}}^{[1]}\right\|_{SP} \cong 0.347, \quad \left\|\mathbf{J} - \overline{\mathbf{J}}^{[1]}\right\|_{F} \cong 0.440$$

the P-F eigenvalue of $\overline{\mathbf{J}}^{[1]}$ is approximately equal to 0.814, and $\varepsilon_{J1} \cong 0.107$, which indicates a rather high degree of inseparability. Indeed, the graphs in Fig. 5.4 show that the first-order approximations do not work well, while the second-order approximations are accurate enough: $\varepsilon_{J2} \cong 0.041$, the P-F eigenvalue of $\overline{\mathbf{J}}^{[2]}$ ($> \mathbf{0}$) is approximately equal to 1.005, its subdominant eigenvalue is approximately equal to -0.030 and the approximate $p_2 p_3^{-1} - \rho$ curve has a maximum at $\rho \cong 1.038$.[15]

[15] It is noted that, in this example, **M** is 'circulant' (since **A** is cyclic) and, therefore, 'normal' ($\mathbf{M}\mathbf{M}^{T} = \mathbf{M}^{T}\mathbf{M}$) and doubly stochastic: $\sigma_{M1} = |\lambda_{J1}| = 1$, $\sigma_{M2} = \sigma_{M3} = |\lambda_{J2,3}|$ and $\varepsilon_{M1} \cong 0.193$, $\varepsilon_{M2} \cong 0.097$ (see, e.g. Meyer 2001, pp. 379 and 555).

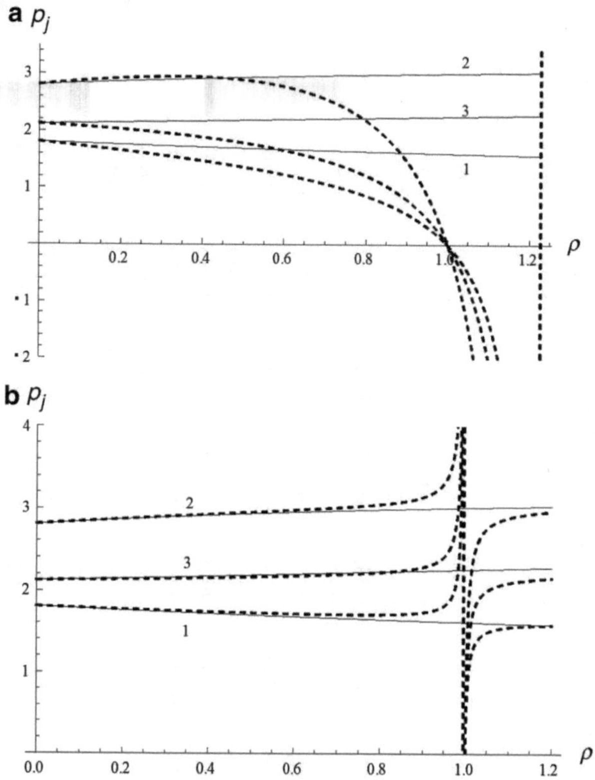

Fig. 5.4 The production price-relative profit rate curves and their SVD approximations; **(a)** first-order approximations and **(b)** second-order approximations

5.3 Empirical Evidence

Using input-output data from a number of quite diverse economies or from the same economy over the years, this section provides empirical results on:

(i) Eigenvalue and singular value distributions
(ii) Wage-price-profit rate approximations
(iii) Price effects of total productivity shift
(iv) Eigen-deviation of labour-commanded prices from labour values

5.3.1 Eigenvalue and Singular Value Distributions

Tables 5.1 and 5.2 are associated with the flow SIOTs of China, Greece, Japan, Korea and USA. Table 5.1 reports the moduli of the eigenvalues of **J** (in descending

Table 5.1 The distribution of the moduli of the non-dominant eigenvalues for the circulating capital case: China, Greece, Japan, Korea and USA

	CHN 1997	GRC 1970	GRC 1988	GRC 1989	GRC 1990	GRC 1991	GRC 1992	GRC 1993	GRC 1994	GRC 1995	GRC 1996	GRC 1997	
Rank													
1	1.000	1.000	1.000	1.000	1.000	1.000	1.000	1.000	1.000	1.000	1.000	1.000	
2	0.376	0.726	0.643	0.683	0.675	0.657	0.624	0.667	0.678	0.655	0.664	0.641	
3	0.304	0.539	0.416	0.436	0.418	0.397	0.443	0.433	0.420	0.382	0.382	0.350	
4	0.282	0.470	0.409	0.377	0.376	0.382	0.443	0.353	0.357	0.382	0.382	0.307	
5	0.231	0.453	0.362	0.377	0.376	0.382	0.406	0.320	0.327	0.281	0.313	0.279	
6	0.224	0.319	0.259	0.308	0.311	0.326	0.308	0.268	0.261	0.246	0.233	0.249	
7	0.224	0.319	0.187	0.207	0.218	0.226	0.242	0.234	0.207	0.202	0.214	0.249	
8	0.167	0.243	0.187	0.207	0.218	0.226	0.242	0.234	0.207	0.202	0.214	0.210	
9	0.167	0.243	0.083	0.104	0.110	0.101	0.108	0.110	0.109	0.098	0.098	0.103	
10	0.165	0.218	0.083	0.082	0.089	0.094	0.105	0.105	0.097	0.092	0.088	0.098	
11	0.142	0.201	0.079	0.082	0.089	0.094	0.105	0.105	0.097	0.092	0.088	0.098	
12	0.126	0.201	0.079	0.080	0.080	0.078	0.081	0.083	0.082	0.085	0.086	0.087	
13	0.122	0.166	0.071	0.080	0.080	0.078	0.081	0.068	0.082	0.085	0.086	0.042	
14	0.114	0.106	0.071	0.031	0.039	0.034	0.053	0.068	0.059	0.023	0.072	0.035	
15	0.114	0.106	0.027	0.031	0.028	0.034	0.029	0.026	0.026	0.023	0.029	0.035	
16	0.102	0.103	0.027	0.024	0.022	0.023	0.027	0.026	0.026	0.015	0.029	0.017	
17	0.102	0.100	0.020	0.024	0.022	0.023	0.027	0.017	0.023	0.015	0.019	0.017	
18	0.062	0.092	0.009	0.007	0.009	0.008	0.005	0.006	0.007	0.005	0.002	0.013	
19	0.058	0.088	0.006	0.006	0.006	0.005	0.003	0.002	0.006	0.004	0.001	0.001	
20	0.058	0.074	....	....	....	....	....	....	....	....	....	....	
21	0.052	0.060	....	....	....	....	....	....	....	....	....	....	
22	0.044	0.060	....	....	....	....	....	....	....	....	....	....	
23	0.041	0.043	....	....	....	....	....	....	....	....	....	....	
24	0.041	0.043	....	....	....	....	....	....	....	....	....	....	

25	0.034	0.037	….	….	….	….	….	….	….	….	….	….	
26	0.034	0.037	….	….	….	….	….	….	….	….	….	….	
27	0.033	0.030	….	….	….	….	….	….	….	….	….	….	
28	0.025	0.029	….	….	….	….	….	….	….	….	….	….	
29	0.025	0.023	….	….	….	….	….	….	….	….	….	….	
30	0.021	0.015	….	….	….	….	….	….	….	….	….	….	
31	0.021	0.008	….	….	….	….	….	….	….	….	….	….	
32	0.018	0.008	….	….	….	….	….	….	….	….	….	….	
33	0.006	0.003	….	….	….	….	….	….	….	….	….	….	
34	0.006	….	….	….	….	….	….	….	….	….	….	….	
35	0.005	….	….	….	….	….	….	….	….	….	….	….	
36	0.005	….	….	….	….	….	….	….	….	….	….	….	
37	0.002	….	….	….	….	….	….	….	….	….	….	….	
38	0.001	….	….	….	….	….	….	….	….	….	….	….	
AM	0.096	0.161	0.168	0.175	0.176	0.176	0.185	0.174	0.171	0.161	0.167	0.157	
GM	0.048	0.083	0.086	0.086	0.088	0.087	0.089	0.081	0.088	0.074	0.074	0.073	
SF	0.499	0.517	0.511	0.490	0.500	0.495	0.483	0.469	0.513	0.459	0.446	0.462	
π_2	11 %	14 %	21 %	22 %	21 %	21 %	19 %	21 %	22 %	23 %	22 %	23 %	
RE	0.873	0.856	0.829	0.824	0.829	0.831	0.837	0.835	0.836	0.822	0.834	0.832	
REN	62 %	59 %	61 %	61 %	61 %	61 %	61 %	61 %	61 %	61 %	61 %	61 %	
	JPN 1970	JPN 1975	JPN 1980	JPN 1985	JPN 1990	KOR 1995	KOR 2000	USA 1947	USA 1958	USA 1963	USA 1967	USA 1972	USA 1977
Rank													
1	1.000	1.000	1.000	1.000	1.000	1.000	1.000	1.000	1.000	1.000	1.000	1.000	1.000
2	0.652	0.711	0.762	0.735	0.737	0.638	0.683	0.620	0.571	0.638	0.639	0.648	0.527
3	0.434	0.445	0.474	0.653	0.604	0.421	0.517	0.462	0.571	0.582	0.552	0.512	0.386
4	0.388	0.381	0.474	0.572	0.604	0.373	0.422	0.436	0.451	0.479	0.421	0.400	0.378
5	0.346	0.381	0.362	0.538	0.424	0.314	0.321	0.390	0.451	0.461	0.421	0.400	0.378

(continued)

Table 5.1 (continued)

	JPN 1970	JPN 1975	JPN 1980	JPN 1985	JPN 1990	KOR 1995	KOR 2000	USA 1947	USA 1958	USA 1963	USA 1967	USA 1972	USA 1977
6	0.303	0.332	0.321	0.396	0.351	0.271	0.303	0.334	0.376	0.461	0.399	0.306	0.330
7	0.303	0.340	0.318	0.396	0.351	0.266	0.303	0.325	0.358	0.323	0.277	0.306	0.330
8	0.263	0.261	0.318	0.336	0.320	0.266	0.286	0.282	0.327	0.264	0.268	0.286	0.263
9	0.244	0.261	0.292	0.328	0.320	0.185	0.198	0.257	0.261	0.264	0.265	0.242	0.226
10	0.244	0.258	0.270	0.219	0.303	0.111	0.141	0.205	0.255	0.257	0.265	0.236	0.226
11	0.218	0.200	0.260	0.219	0.236	0.111	0.128	0.205	0.236	0.237	0.255	0.236	0.220
12	0.177	0.169	0.165	0.157	0.191	0.107	0.128	0.197	0.230	0.237	0.243	0.212	0.220
13	0.152	0.169	0.153	0.152	0.178	0.079	0.127	0.197	0.230	0.216	0.228	0.212	0.198
14	0.152	0.067	0.153	0.137	0.166	0.068	0.127	0.185	0.212	0.203	0.228	0.196	0.180
15	0.116	0.067	0.144	0.132	0.152	0.062	0.093	0.161	0.212	0.203	0.182	0.182	0.147
16	0.107	0.149	0.120	0.132	0.146	0.048	0.076	0.139	0.174	0.181	0.182	0.150	0.147
17	0.094	0.109	0.120	0.132	0.143	0.048	0.076	0.131	0.174	0.171	0.160	0.150	0.137
18	0.094	0.109	0.088	0.132	0.143	0.047	0.073	0.131	0.163	0.171	0.150	0.142	0.137
19	0.082	0.116	0.085	0.123	0.124	0.033	0.036	0.102	0.161	0.138	0.150	0.126	0.116
20	0.056	0.058	0.082	0.099	0.105	0.033	0.036	0.102	0.120	0.138	0.138	0.126	0.102
21	0.046	0.058	0.067	0.070	0.100	0.027	0.028	0.096	0.120	0.133	0.129	0.107	0.102
22	0.046	0.098	0.055	0.070	0.085	0.015	0.024	0.091	0.116	0.133	0.129	0.107	0.086
23	0.037	0.041	0.048	0.058	0.051	0.015	0.022	0.083	0.101	0.090	0.088	0.096	0.086
24	0.036	0.090	0.048	0.051	0.051	0.004	0.018	0.080	0.101	0.090	0.088	0.078	0.082
25	0.036	0.051	0.040	0.051	0.039	0.001	0.005	0.080	0.097	0.089	0.085	0.078	0.082
26	0.034	0.051	0.037	0.050	0.039	....	....	0.071	0.060	0.089	0.085	0.066	0.059
27	0.034	0.036	0.037	0.036	0.027	....	....	0.066	0.060	0.076	0.075	0.051	0.059
28	0.028	0.020	0.030	0.026	0.027	....	....	0.066	0.057	0.053	0.075	0.047	0.046
29	0.011	0.020	0.019	0.020	0.026	....	....	0.051	0.057	0.041	0.046	0.036	0.035
30	0.011	0.004	0.019	0.020	0.026	....	....	0.031	0.030	0.041	0.046	0.036	0.031

31	0.008	0.004	0.014	0.014	0.024	....	....	0.029	0.030	0.036	0.037	0.031	0.031
32	0.008	0.003	0.009	0.012	0.024	....	....	0.029	0.026	0.036	0.037	0.031	0.030
33	0.001	0.005	0.000	0.008	0.003	....	....	0.025	0.024	0.027	0.033	0.026	0.030
34	....	....	....	....	....	....	....	0.008	0.024	0.027	0.033	0.026	0.024
35	....	....	....	....	....	....	....	0.008	0.019	0.024	0.020	0.019	0.019
36	....	....	....	....	....	....	....	0.006	0.014	0.018	0.015	0.016	0.014
37	....	....	....	....	....	....	....	0.006	0.012	0.012	0.015	0.009	0.008
38	....	....	....	....	....	....	....	0.004	0.002	0.012	0.015	0.009	0.008
39	....	....	....	....	....	....	....	0.004	0.002	0.009	0.002	0.007	0.007
AM	0.149	0.158	0.168	0.190	0.191	0.148	0.174	0.150	0.171	0.175	0.171	0.156	0.144
GM	0.074	0.079	0.074	0.103	0.108	0.068	0.098	0.078	0.090	0.104	0.101	0.091	0.086
SF	0.495	0.497	0.440	0.544	0.562	0.459	0.563	0.523	0.527	0.593	0.591	0.583	0.597
π_2	14 %	14 %	14 %	12 %	12 %	18 %	16 %	11 %	9 %	10 %	10 %	11 %	10 %
RE	0.863	0.866	0.866	0.863	0.875	0.837	0.862	0.880	0.888	0.891	0.897	0.888	0.894
REN	61 %	63 %	63 %	59 %	63 %	58 %	63 %	63 %	66 %	66 %	68 %	66 %	66 %

Table 5.2 The distribution of the moduli of the non-dominant eigenvalues and the level of aggregation for the circulating capital case; Japan, 1980–2005

	1980	1980	1985	1985	1990	1990	1995	1995	2000	2000	2005	2005
n	21	100	21	100	21	100	21	100	21	100	21	100
Rank												
1	1.000	1.000	1.000	1.000	1.000	1.000	1.000	1.000	1.000	1.000	1.000	1.000
2	0.529	0.522	0.546	0.527	0.520	0.550	0.496	0.541	0.465	0.499	0.517	0.519
3	0.342	0.379	0.391	0.390	0.415	0.448	0.496	0.497	0.436	0.499	0.443	0.512
4	0.342	0.379	0.383	0.386	0.413	0.410	0.383	0.393	0.436	0.410	0.443	0.421
5	0.330	0.351	0.383	0.386	0.413	0.410	0.383	0.393	0.355	0.410	0.342	0.421
6	0.301	0.351	0.295	0.342	0.316	0.352	0.359	0.363	0.355	0.370	0.310	0.394
7	0.200	0.296	0.276	0.342	0.229	0.352	0.249	0.363	0.264	0.352	0.236	0.355
8	0.159	0.296	0.145	0.309	0.229	0.345	0.249	0.346	0.219	0.352	0.179	0.331
9	0.140	0.270	0.145	0.309	0.145	0.337	0.182	0.339	0.219	0.333	0.144	0.308
10	0.140	0.270	0.140	0.271	0.133	0.337	0.145	0.339	0.133	0.323	0.144	0.282
11	0.097	0.251	0.115	0.254	0.133	0.334	0.122	0.257	0.133	0.238	0.082	0.258
12	0.097	0.251	0.096	0.213	0.079	0.232	0.079	0.257	0.068	0.238	0.062	0.258
13	0.075	0.192	0.066	0.205	0.079	0.232	0.079	0.247	0.068	0.230	0.062	0.232
14	0.075	0.191	0.066	0.201	0.079	0.230	0.067	0.247	0.060	0.225	0.058	0.191
15	0.054	0.191	0.051	0.188	0.071	0.230	0.067	0.234	0.060	0.225	0.044	0.182
16	0.022	0.166	0.044	0.184	0.071	0.226	0.061	0.219	0.048	0.202	0.044	0.182
17	0.012	0.166	0.019	0.184	0.016	0.218	0.013	0.196	0.021	0.190	0.023	0.177
18	0.012	0.144	0.011	0.156	0.015	0.205	0.012	0.196	0.018	0.190	0.018	0.177
19	0.010	0.144	0.011	0.147	0.010	0.197	0.005	0.172	0.018	0.188	0.018	0.175
20	0.005	0.136	0.007	0.133	0.007	0.191	0.005	0.172	0.006	0.182	0.013	0.175
21	0.002	0.128	0.005	0.133	0.005	0.174	0.004	0.164	0.003	0.162	0.003	0.166
22	....	0.124	....	0.125	....	0.163	....	0.164	....	0.152	....	0.149
23	....	0.124	....	0.125	....	0.163	....	0.162	....	0.152	....	0.146
24	....	0.123	....	0.123	....	0.156	....	0.162	....	0.150	....	0.146

25	…	0.123	…	0.123	…	0.147	…	0.162	…	0.150	…	0.138
26	…	0.122	…	0.121	…	0.147	…	0.156	…	0.149	…	0.138
27	…	0.120	…	0.117	…	0.142	…	0.156	…	0.149	…	0.119
28	…	0.110	…	0.117	…	0.142	…	0.143	…	0.139	…	0.119
29	…	0.107	…	0.106	…	0.137	…	0.140	…	0.137	…	0.115
30	…	0.107	…	0.100	…	0.132	…	0.140	…	0.128	…	0.115
AM	0.147	0.090	0.160	0.091	0.169	0.106	0.173	0.110	0.169	0.105	0.159	0.099
GM	0.067	0.035	0.078	0.040	0.085	0.051	0.077	0.056	0.083	0.052	0.079	0.048
SF	0.452	0.389	0.487	0.440	0.501	0.482	0.448	0.511	0.491	0.498	0.499	0.487
π_2	18 %	6 %	17 %	6 %	15 %	5 %	14 %	5 %	14 %	5 %	16 %	5 %
RE	0.840	0.879	0.841	0.878	0.852	0.887	0.844	0.894	0.850	0.888	0.837	0.878
REN	62 %	57 %	62 %	57 %	64 %	59 %	62 %	61 %	63 %	60 %	61 %	57 %

order)[16] and six measures of the distribution of the moduli of the non-dominant eigenvalues, namely:

(i) The arithmetic mean, *AM*, that gives equal weight to all moduli.
(ii) The geometric mean, *GM*, which assigns more weight to lower moduli and, therefore, is more appropriate for detecting the central tendency of an exponential set of numbers. In our case, it can be written as

$$GM = |\det\mathbf{J}|^{(n-1)^{-1}} = \left(\prod_{i=1}^{n}\sigma_{\mathbf{J}i}\right)^{(n-1)^{-1}} = (\sigma_{\mathbf{J}1})^{n(n-1)^{-1}}\left(\prod_{i=1}^{n}\sigma_{\mathbf{J}i}\sigma_{\mathbf{J}1}^{-1}\right)^{(n-1)^{-1}}$$

where $\sigma_{\mathbf{J}i}\sigma_{\mathbf{J}1}^{-1}$ are the normalized singular values of **J**.
(iii) The so-called spectral flatness, $SF \equiv GM(AM)^{-1}$.
(iv) $\pi_2 \equiv \max_k\left\{\pi_k \equiv |\lambda_{\mathbf{J}k}|\left(\sum_{k=2}^{n}|\lambda_{\mathbf{J}k}|\right)^{-1}\right\}$, where π_k represents a set of relative frequencies.
(v) The relative (or normalized) entropy, *RE*, defined as the ratio of the 'information content or Shannon entropy', *E*, to its maximum possible value, i.e. $RE \equiv EE_{\max}^{-1}$, where

$$E \equiv -\sum_{k=2}^{n}\pi_k\log\pi_k$$

and $E_{\max} \equiv \log(n-1)$ is the maximum value of *E* corresponding to $\pi_k = (n-1)^{-1}$ for all *k*.
(vi) The relative 'equivalent number', $REN \equiv EN(n-1)^{-1}$, where *EN* denotes the so-called equivalent number, which is determined by the equation $\log EN = E$ and represents the number of eigenvalues with equal moduli that would result in the same amount of entropy.

The spectral flatness and the relative entropy are known to be alternative, but different, measures of similarity (or closeness) of the moduli and take on values from near zero to one. When all $|\lambda_{\mathbf{J}k}|$ are equal to each other, then $AM = GM$, $\pi_k = (n-1)^{-1}$ and, therefore, $SF = RE = REN = 1$. However, a low *SF* rather reflects

[16] The dimensions of those SIOTs vary from 19 industries (Greece, 1988–1997) to 39 industries (USA). The tables of China and Japan are available from the OECD STAN database. Those of Greece and Korea are provided by the National Statistical Service of Greece and the Bank of Korea, respectively (also see Chap. 3). Finally, those of USA are from the Bureau of Economic Analysis (BEA) and have been compiled by Juillard (1986) (the data used in the studies by Ochoa 1984; Bienenfeld 1988 and Shaikh 1998 are from the same source although at 71 × 71 industry detail).

the presence of a much lower than the average $\min_k \{\pi_k\}$, whereas a low *RE* rather reflects the presence of a much higher than the average π_2.[17]

From the numerical results of Table 5.1, it becomes apparent that the moduli fall quite rapidly in the 'beginning' and then constellate in much lower values. In plotting these data for each of the countries and years, and after experimentation with various possible functional forms, we found that a single exponential functional form fits all the data pretty well, as this can be judged by the high R-square, R^2, and the fact that all the estimated coefficients are statistically significant, with zero probability values. This form is

$$y = \alpha_0 + \alpha_1 \exp(x^{\alpha_2}), \quad \alpha_0 < 0, \quad \alpha_1 > 0, \quad \alpha_2 < 0 \tag{5.21}$$

where $\alpha_2 = -0.2$, 0.721 (China) $\leq \alpha_1 \leq$ 1.040 (Greece, 1989), -1.827 (Greece, 1989) $\leq \alpha_0 \leq -1.174$ (China) and 90.5 % (China) $\leq R^2 \leq$ 99.4 % (Greece, 1970) (also see Fig. 5.5).[18] It is expected, therefore, that the *SF* would be relatively low and that the opposite would hold true regarding *RE*. Indeed, it is found that the former is in the range of 0.440 (Japan, 1980) to 0.597 (USA, 1977), while the latter is in the range of 0.822 (Greece, 1995) to 0.897 (USA, 1967), and the relevant maxima relative frequencies, π_2, are 23 % and 10 %, respectively. Moreover, the *REN* is in the range of 58 % (Korea, 1995) to 68 % (USA, 1967).[19] Thus, it could be concluded that these measures in combination give a quite good description of the central tendency and also the skewness of the distribution of the moduli.

---

[17] Finkelstein and Friedberg (1967) discuss *E* and *EN* and apply them to studies of industrial competition and concentration, while Jasso (1982) and Bailey (1985) discuss *SF* and *RE*, respectively, and apply them to studies of income distribution. It may also be noted that there is a connection between *SF* and entropy: using π_k, the former can be expressed as

$$SF = (n-1) \prod_{k=2}^{n} \pi_k^{(n-1)^{-1}}$$

or, taking the logarithm of both sides,

$$\log SF = E_{\max} - \left[-(n-1)^{-1} \sum_{k=2}^{n} \log \pi_k \right]$$

where log *SF* is known as the Wiener entropy and the term in brackets can be conceived as a 'cross-entropy' expression.

[18] In fact, we tried an optimization procedure to find the best possible form, and from the many possibilities, we opted for a simple but, at the same time, general enough to fit the moduli of the eigenvalues of all countries and years.

[19] It should be noted that we have also experimented with the flow SIOTs of Canada (1997, 34 × 34; source: OECD STAN database), Japan (1995–1997, 41 × 41; source: OECD STAN database), UK (1998, 40 × 40; source: OECD STAN database) and USA (1997, 40 × 40; source: BEA, compilation through the OECD STAN database), and the results were quite similar, i.e. *SF*, 0.359 (USA)–0.500 (UK); π_2, 8 % (UK)–18 % (Canada); *RE*, 0.811 (Canada)–0.888 (UK); and *REN*, 52 % (Canada)–67 % (UK).

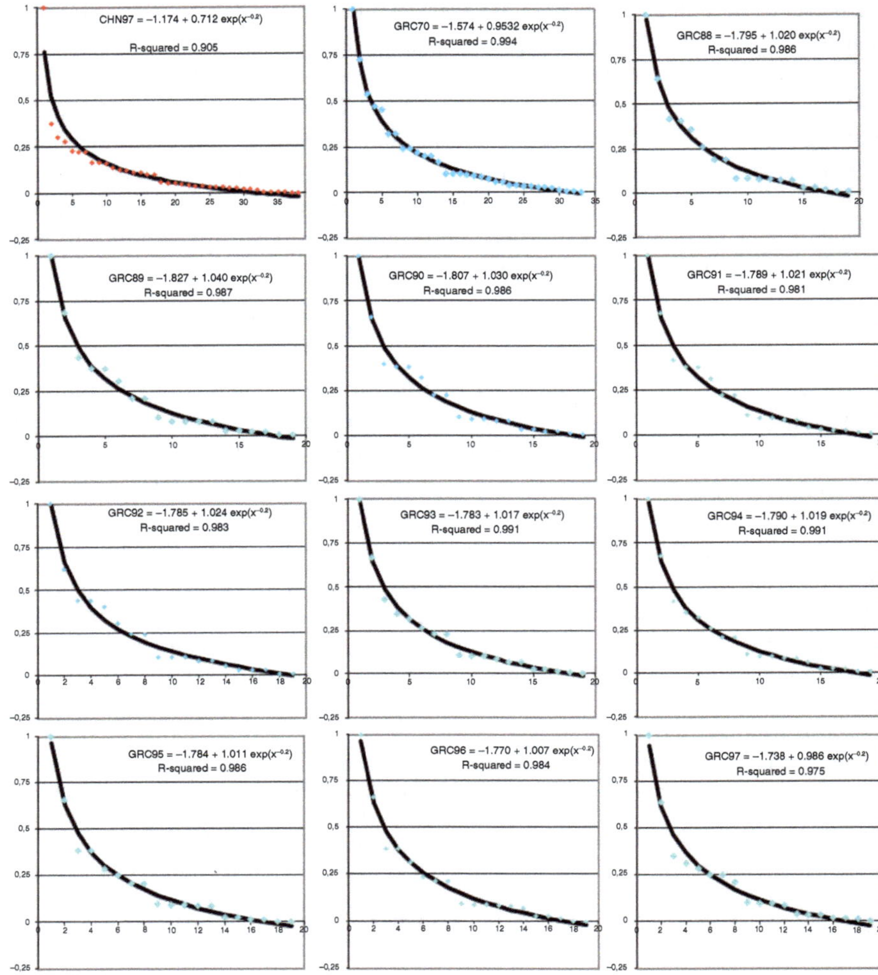

Fig. 5.5 (continued)

For reasons of clarity of presentation and economy of space, the numerical results displayed in Table 5.2 are only associated with the flow SIOTs of Japan and seek to detect the dependence of the distribution of the moduli on the level of *aggregation*, that is to say, n (also consider Bródy's (1997) conjecture). More specifically, we experimented with SIOTs for every 5 years starting from 1980 until 2005 for the 100×100 industry structure, and we also repeated the experiment

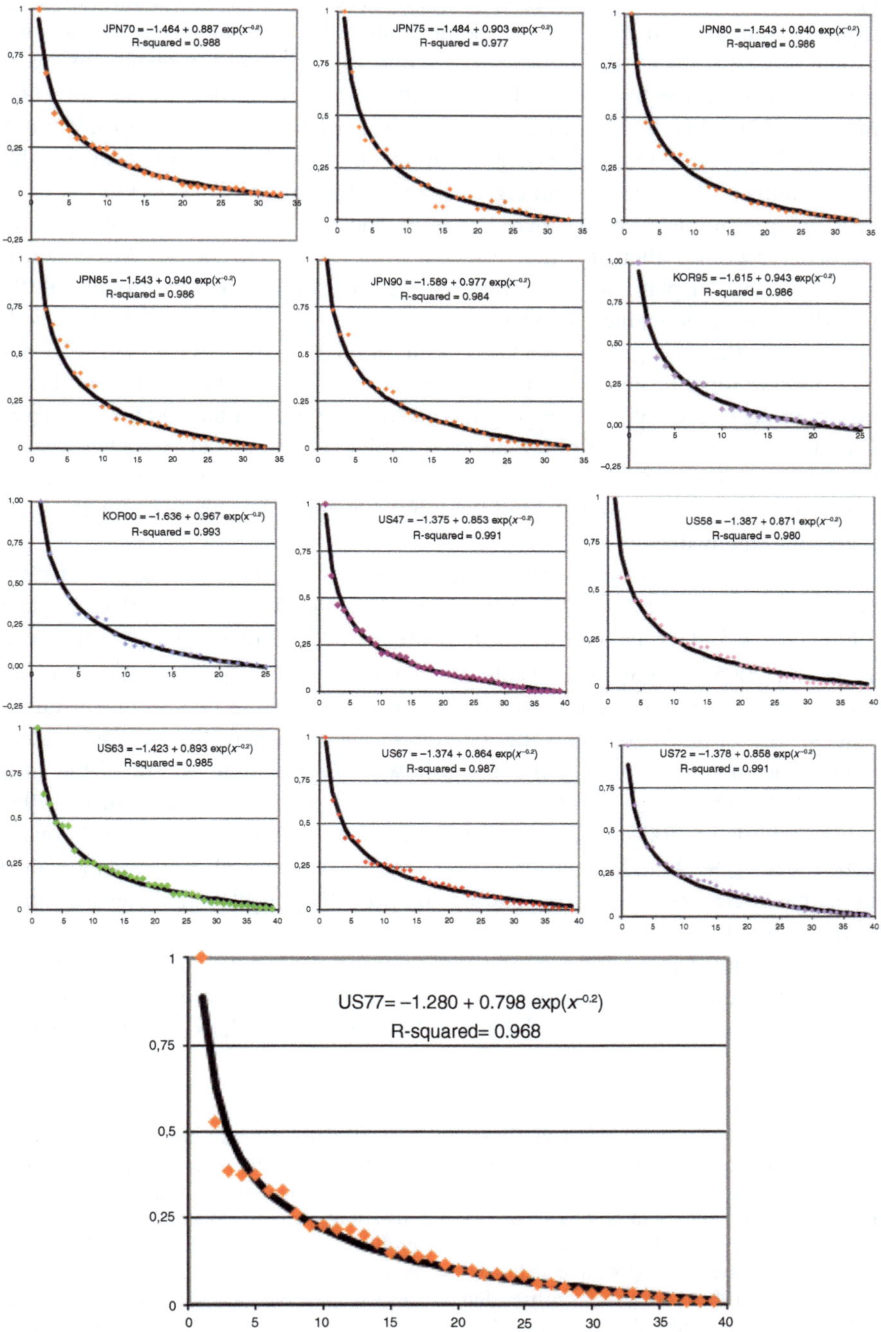

Fig. 5.5 Exponential fit of the distribution of the moduli of the eigenvalues for the circulating capital case; China, Greece, Japan, Korea and USA

aggregating each of these SIOTs into 21 industries.[20] In our aggregation, we put together similar industries, and we kept mainly the manufacturing as the most disaggregated from all the industries. Finally, for reasons of economy in space, we present only the first 30 moduli, and the last six rows display the statistical measures of the distribution. Clearly, the results suggest that *RE* decreases, while π_2 and *REN* increases, with decreasing *n*. On the other hand, they do *not* suggest that the modulus of the subdominant eigenvalues (as well as *SF*) tends to increase with decreasing *n*: it could be considered as rigid, and the 'small' relative changes that we observe go to either direction (varying from −8.3 % to 3.6 %). Moreover, in Fig. 5.6a, we display the histogram of the distribution of the moduli of the non-dominant eigenvalues associated with the 21×21 SIOTs, and in Fig. 5.6b, we display the histogram associated with the 100×100 SIOTs, i.e. 120 and 594 observations, respectively. On the top of each bar, we report the number of observations in each of our five bins, the mean value of each bin and the bin edges. Clearly, the majority of the observations (i.e. 62 (51.6 %) or 411 (69.2 %), respectively) constellate in the lowest bin, whereas 9 (7.5 %) or 10 (1.7 %) observations constellate in the highest bin (and are on an average less than one-half of the dominant eigenvalue).

A rather similar 'picture' emerges from the flow SIOTs of the Danish (for the years 2000 and 2004), Finnish (for the years 1995 and 2004), French (for the years 1995 and 2005), German (for the years 2000 and 2002) and Swedish (for the years 1995 and 2005) economies.[21] Table 5.3 reports $|\lambda_{J2}|^{-1}$, $|\lambda_{J3}|^{-1}$, $|\lambda_{Jn}|^{-1}$ and the statistical measures of the distribution of the moduli of the non-dominant eigenvalues, while Fig. 5.7 displays the location of all the eigenvalues in the complex plane. The moduli of the eigenvalues follow an exponential pattern of the form of Eq. 5.21, where $\alpha_2 = -3$, 0.630 (Sweden, 2005) $\leq \alpha_1 \leq$ 0.754 (France, 1995), −1.012 (Finland, 2004) $\leq \alpha_0 \leq$ −0.857 (Sweden, 2005) and 95.9 % (Germany, 2000) $\leq R^2 \leq$ 99.4 % (Finland, 1995): see Table 5.4, which also reports the values of the parameter α_2 that approximately maximize R^2, as well as the relevant values of α_1, α_2 and R^2.

Furthermore, Table 5.5 reports the moduli of the eigenvalues for the case of fixed capital and a uniform profit rate (see Chap. 3), as well as the statistical measures of the distribution of the moduli of the non-dominant eigenvalues. It is important to

[20] The original input-output data comprised 108 industries and are published by the Statistical Service of Japan. The problem with this data set is that eight of the industries have zero rows (i.e. they do not deliver any output to the other sectors and to themselves), which give rise to an input-output structure with non-basic sectors and, therefore, zero eigenvalues corresponding to each of these eight industries. To sidestep this problem, we aggregated each of these eight industries to corresponding similar industries so as the resulting input-output structure consists of dimensions 100×100 basic industries. Finally, it should be noted that the results displayed in Table 5.2 are not comparable with those displayed in Table 5.1, since the 33 industries SIOTs of Japan are constructed using different sources and also methodology.

[21] See Sect. 3.9. For completeness reasons, here, as well as in Sect. 5.3.2.1, we do not remove the elements associated with the industry 'private households with employed persons'.

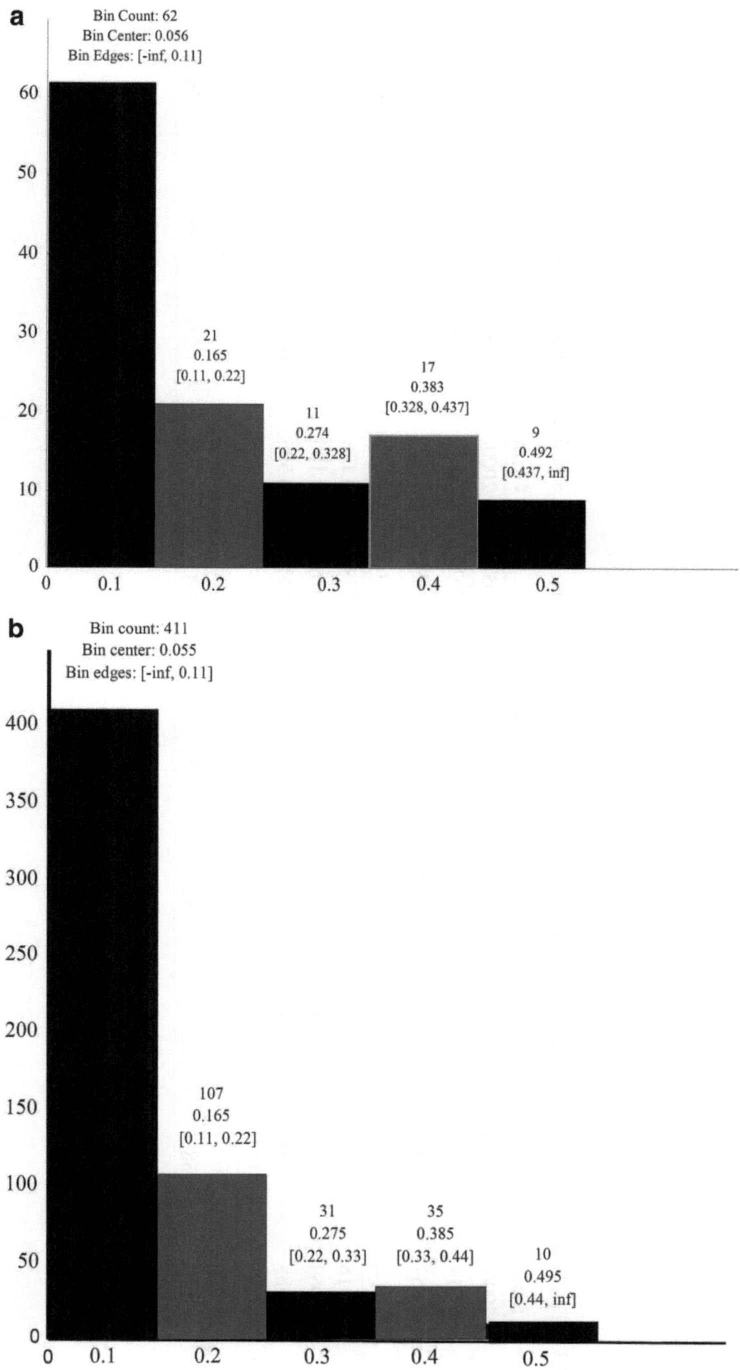

Fig. 5.6 Histogram of the distribution of the moduli of the non-dominant eigenvalues; Japan 1985–2000: (**a**) 21×21 flow SIOTs, (**b**) 100×100 flow SIOTs

Table 5.3 The distribution of the moduli of the non-dominant eigenvalues for the circulating capital case; five European economies: ten SIOTs

	Denmark		Finland		France		Germany		Sweden	
	2000	2004	1995	2004	1995	2005	2000	2002	1995	2005
$\lvert\lambda_{J2}\rvert^{-1}$	1.914	1.568	1.676	1.177	1.636	1.702	1.753	1.641	1.881	2.369
$\lvert\lambda_{J3}\rvert^{-1}$	2.057	1.990	2.308	1.990	1.889	2.208	2.013	1.939	2.302	2.563
$\lvert\lambda_{Jn}\rvert^{-1}$	1541.750	815.370	735.900	2517.050	29324.400	817.635	729.625	158.114	299.881	1092.060
AM	0.118	0.108	0.100	0.103	0.131	0.128	0.178	0.178	0.098	0.099
GM	0.069	0.065	0.047	0.047	0.059	0.076	0.106	0.111	0.050	0.052
SF	0.585	0.602	0.470	0.456	0.450	0.594	0.596	0.624	0.510	0.525
π_2	8 %	11 %	11 %	15 %	8 %	8 %	6 %	6 %	10 %	9 %
RE	0.870	0.863	0.825	0.821	0.856	0.880	0.900	0.900	0.828	0.849
REN	60 %	58 %	50 %	48 %	57 %	63 %	66 %	66 %	50 %	56 %

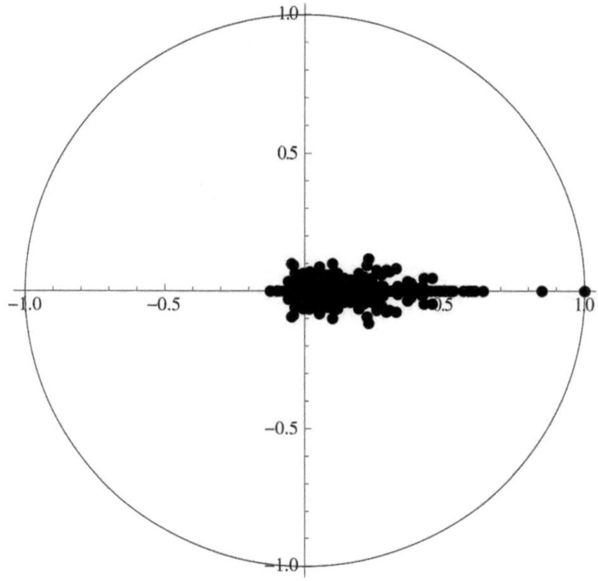

Fig. 5.7 The location of all the eigenvalues in the complex plane for the circulating capital case; five European economies: ten SIOTs

stress at this point that, in the capital stock matrix, the consumer commodities producing industries as they do not normally sell investment commodities their respective rows will contain many zeros or near-zero (higher than the fifth decimal) elements, and, therefore, we end up with many zero or near-zero eigenvalues. In other words, all the zero eigenvalues come from the fact that the capital stock matrix is reducible without self-reproducing non-basics. We could have sidestepped the problem of zero eigenvalues by accounting as part of the matrix of capital stocks the inventories as well as the matrix of workers' necessary consumption ('wage fund'). However, these data are hard to come by with the possible exception of the US economy. Thus, in the interest of brevity and clarity of presentation, we opted not to use inventories, and in the same spirit, we did *not* use matrices of depreciation coefficients. As a consequence, we present estimates of the moduli of eigenvalues only for the economies that we had access to data on their capital stocks, i.e. for Greece (1970), Korea (1995 and 2000) and USA (1947, 1958, 1963, 1967, 1972 and 1977). It might be remarked in passing that in the case of the US economy, we employ data on industry turnover times and in so doing we included the matrix of inventories of intermediate commodities along with the matrix of fixed capital stock coefficients. Thus, we avoided the zero eigenvalues that appear in the results of Greece and Korea without, at the same time, affecting in any quantitatively significant way the estimated eigenvalues.

An inspection of the results reveals that the presence of fixed capital stocks leads to considerably lower moduli and to higher π_2 than the corresponding flow data.

Table 5.4 Estimates of the exponential fit of the moduli of the eigenvalues for the circulating capital case; five European economies: ten SIOTs

	Denmark		Finland		France		Germany		Sweden	
	2000	2004	1995	2004	1995	2005	2000	2002	1995	2005
α_2	−0.3	−0.3	−0.3	−0.3	−0.3	−0.3	−0.3	−0.3	−0.3	−0.3
α_1	0.679	0.675	0.702	0.742	0.754	0.680	0.730	0.737	0.682	0.630
α_0	−0.902	−0.906	−0.956	−1.012	−1.000	−0.892	−0.918	−0.930	−0.934	−0.857
R^2	0.991	0.987	0.994	0.977	0.987	0.987	0.959	0.964	0.992	0.975
α_2^*	−0.3	−0.4	−0.3	−0.4	−0.2	−0.3	−0.1	−0.1	−0.4	−0.5
α_1^*	–	0.653	–	0.717	0.845	–	1.168	1.177	0.656	0.601
α_0^*	–	−0.781	–	−0.873	−1.323	–	−2.254	−2.273	−0.801	−0.668
$(R^2)^*$	–	0.993	–	0.979	0.994	–	0.982	0.985	0.995	0.983

Table 5.5 The distribution of the moduli of the nonzero non-dominant eigenvalues for the fixed capital case; Greece, Korea and USA

	GRC	KR	KR	USA	USA	USA	USA	USA	USA
	1970	1995	2000	1947	1958	1963	1967	1972	1977
Rank									
1	1.000	1.000	1.000	1.000	1.000	1.000	1.000	1.000	1.000
2	0.037	0.084	0.063	0.408	0.309	0.309	0.473	0.549	0.461
3	0.035	0.059	0.063	0.117	0.090	0.105	0.116	0.069	0.069
4	0.035	0.057	0.057	0.069	0.057	0.057	0.065	0.069	0.058
5	0.015	0.057	0.057	0.069	0.045	0.057	0.065	0.062	0.058
6	0.012	0.026	0.025	0.050	0.045	0.053	0.051	0.062	0.054
7	0.004	0.007	0.009	0.048	0.043	0.049	0.051	0.062	0.054
8	0.004	0.004	0.009	0.048	0.043	0.049	0.047	0.054	0.041
9	0.002	0.004	0.008	0.044	0.037	0.043	0.034	0.049	0.036
10	0.002	0.003	0.003	0.044	0.035	0.043	0.034	0.049	0.036
11	3.8E-4	0.000	0.003	0.040	0.035	0.042	0.034	0.034	0.036
12	3.7E-4	0.000	0.000	0.040	0.033	0.038	0.032	0.034	0.036
13	3.7E-4	0.000	0.000	0.040	0.031	0.038	0.032	0.034	0.031
14	9.8E-5	0.000	0.000	0.029	0.031	0.030	0.029	0.034	0.031
15	2.1E-19	0.000	0.000	0.029	0.029	0.027	0.029	0.030	0.029
16	4.3E-20	0.000	0.000	0.027	0.018	0.022	0.028	0.030	0.029
17	1.1E-20	0.000	0.000	0.024	0.017	0.021	0.028	0.029	0.023
18	0.000	0.000	0.000	0.021	0.017	0.021	0.027	0.027	0.022
19	0.000	0.000	0.000	0.017	0.017	0.021	0.021	0.021	0.022
20	0.000	0.000	0.000	0.017	0.017	0.021	0.021	0.020	0.017
21	0.000	0.000	0.000	0.016	0.014	0.018	0.017	0.020	0.016
22	0.000	0.000	0.000	0.016	0.013	0.016	0.016	0.019	0.015
23	0.000	0.000	0.000	0.016	0.013	0.016	0.016	0.015	0.014

(continued)

Table 5.5 (continued)

	GRC	KR	KR	USA	USA	USA	USA	USA	USA
	1970	1995	2000	1947	1958	1963	1967	1972	1977
24	0.000	0.000	0.000	0.012	0.012	0.010	0.015	0.012	0.014
25	0.000	0.000	0.000	0.012	0.012	0.008	0.015	0.011	0.012
26	0.000	....	....	0.012	0.007	0.007	0.010	0.011	0.012
27	0.000	....	....	0.010	0.006	0.007	0.009	0.010	0.009
28	0.000	....	....	0.008	0.006	0.007	0.009	0.010	0.008
29	0.000	....	....	0.007	0.005	0.006	0.009	0.010	0.008
30	0.000	....	....	0.007	0.005	0.006	0.007	0.006	0.006
31	0.000	....	....	0.006	0.005	0.006	0.007	0.006	0.006
32	0.000	....	....	0.003	0.002	0.004	0.007	0.005	0.005
33	0.000	....	....	0.003	0.002	0.004	0.006	0.003	0.003
34	....	....	....	0.002	0.002	0.003	0.002	0.003	0.003
35	....	....	....	0.001	0.002	0.002	0.001	0.002	0.002
36	....	....	....	0.001	0.002	0.002	0.001	0.002	0.001
37	....	....	....	0.001	0.0003	0.001	0.001	0.001	0.001
38	....	....	....	0.00003	0.0003	0.0003	0.001	0.0002	0.001
39	....	....	....	0.00002	0.000002	0.00005	0.0002	0.0002	0.0004
AM	0.009	0.027	0.027	0.035	0.028	0.031	0.036	0.039	0.034
GM	2.2E-06	0.006	0.010	0.012	0.009	0.012	0.014	0.015	0.013
SF	2.4E-04	0.223	0.387	0.352	0.338	0.406	0.394	0.377	0.394
π_2	25 %	28 %	21 %	31 %	29 %	26 %	35 %	38 %	36 %
RE	0.668	0.734	0.791	0.767	0.782	0.800	0.753	0.736	0.748
REN	39 %	53 %	61 %	43 %	45 %	48 %	41 %	38 %	40 %

Fig. 5.8 The normalized singular values and the moduli of the eigenvalues

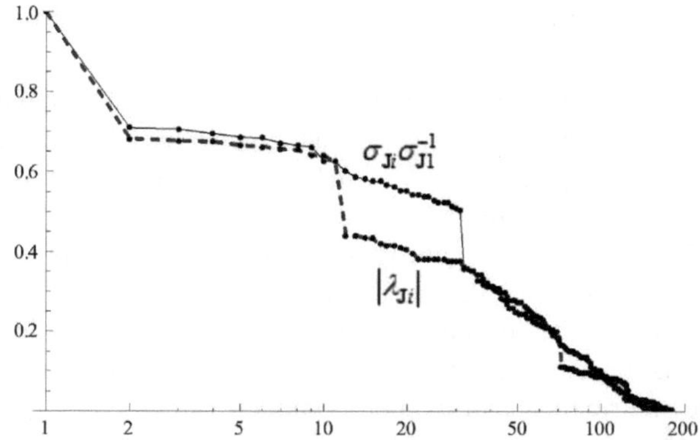

$AM(\sigma_{Jk}\sigma_{J1}^{-1}) \cong 0.190$, $GM(\sigma_{Jk}\sigma_{J1}^{-1}) \cong 0.066$

$AM(|\lambda_{Jk}|) \cong 0.171$, $GM(|\lambda_{Jk}|) \cong 0.082$

Greek economy; circulating capital case: ten SIOTs

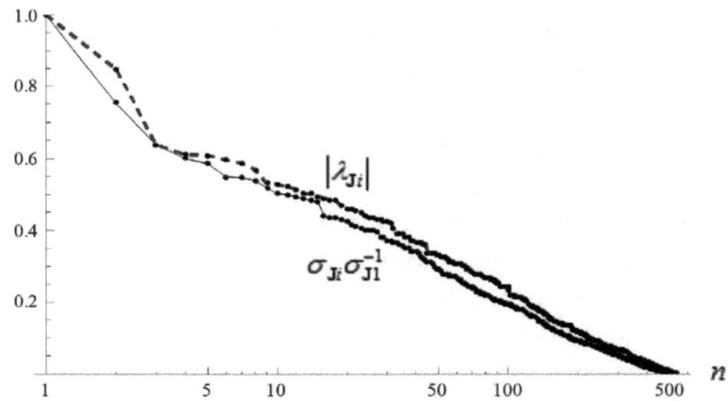

$AM(\sigma_{Jk}\sigma_{J1}^{-1}) \cong 0.106$, $GM(\sigma_{Jk}\sigma_{J1}^{-1}) \cong 0.041$

$AM(|\lambda_{Jk}|) \cong 0.127$, $GM(|\lambda_{Jk}|) \cong 0.065$

Five European economies; circulating capital case: ten SIOTs

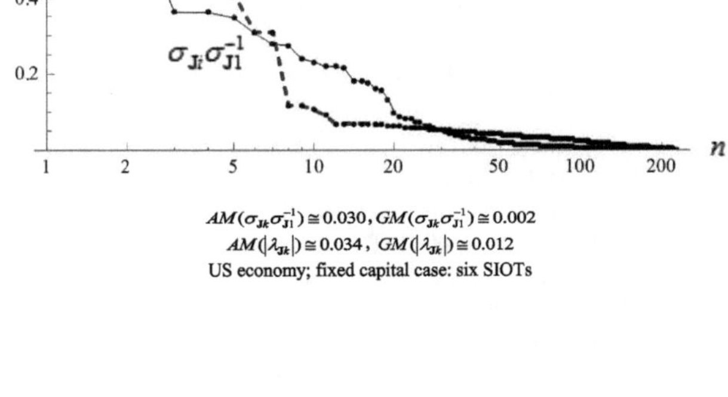

$AM(\sigma_{Jk}\sigma_{J1}^{-1}) \cong 0.030$, $GM(\sigma_{Jk}\sigma_{J1}^{-1}) \cong 0.002$

$AM(|\lambda_{Jk}|) \cong 0.034$, $GM(|\lambda_{Jk}|) \cong 0.012$

US economy; fixed capital case: six SIOTs

Thus, we observe that our statistics *SF*, *RE* and *REN*, displayed in Table 5.5, are by far lower than those of Tables 5.1, 5.2 and 5.3.[22]

Finally, the configuration of the normalized singular values, $\sigma_{\mathbf{J}i}\sigma_{\mathbf{J}1}^{-1}$, is not so different from that of the relevant eigenvalues. For instance, consider the representative graphs in Fig. 5.8, which are associated with the (i) ten flow SIOTs of the Greek economy for the period 1988–1997 (see Table 5.1), (ii) ten flow SIOTs of the aforementioned five European economies (see Table 5.3) and (iii) six SIOTs of the US economy for the fixed capital case (see Table 5.5), respectively. The graphs display all the normalized singular values and the moduli of all the eigenvalues (the horizontal axes are plotted in *logarithmic* scale), and the relevant arithmetic and geometric means of the non-dominant values.

From all these findings, the associated numerical results and the hitherto analysis, we arrive at the following conclusions:

(i) The moduli of the non-dominant eigenvalues fall quite rapidly in the 'beginning', and figuratively speaking their falling pattern can be described by an exponential curve that approaches asymptotically much lower values, where it is observed a concentration of moduli. Further analysis reveals that the distribution of the moduli tends to be remarkably uniform across countries and over time.

(ii) The complex (as well as the negative) eigenvalues tend to appear in the lower ranks, i.e. their modulus is relatively small. However, even in the cases that they appear in the higher ranks, i.e. second or third rank, the real part has been found to be much larger than the imaginary part ($\cos\theta \cong 1$; see Sect. 5.2), which is equivalent to saying that the imaginary part may even be ignored. Moreover, in the fewer cases that the imaginary part of an eigenvalue exceeds the real one, not only their ratio is relatively small but also the modulus of the eigenvalue can be considered as a negligible quantity. Finally, by inspecting all of our eigenvalues, we observe that, in *general*, the imaginary part gets progressively smaller. Consequently, first, the already detected distribution of the moduli can be viewed as a fair representation of the distribution of the eigenvalues, and, second, the majority of the prices of the non-SSCs in terms of SSC are almost linear functions of the relative profit rate and close to the

[22] It may be recalled that

$$rank\left[\mathbf{A}^{\mathrm{C}}\right] + rank[\mathbf{I}-\mathbf{A}] - n \leq rank\left[\mathbf{A}^{\mathrm{C}}[\mathbf{I}-\mathbf{A}]^{-1}\right] \leq \min\left\{rank\left[\mathbf{A}^{\mathrm{C}}\right],\ rank[\mathbf{I}-\mathbf{A}]\right\}$$

(see, e.g. Meyer 2001, p. 211). We also experimented with an aggregation in a 3×3 SIOT for the USA (1977): in the flow version, the modulus of the subdominant (complex) eigenvalue equals 0.146; in the stock version, the subdominant eigenvalue equals 0.031, while the third eigenvalue equals –0.0001. The aggregation in a 3×3 SIOT for Greece (1970) did not give any different results: in the flow version, the modulus of the subdominant (complex) eigenvalue equals 0.087; in the stock version, the subdominant eigenvalue equals –0.027, while the third eigenvalue equals zero (see Tsoulfidis 2010, pp. 150–155). Also consider the evidence provided by Steenge and Thissen (2005).

Table 5.6 Non-dominant eigenvalues and mean of the relative error between the prices of the non-SSCs and the WPC in terms of SSC; Greece, 1994

λ_{Jk}	*MRE*
0.678	67.1 %
0.420	29.1 %
0.357	23.7 %
0.327	21.1 %
0.261	15.9 %
$0.199 \pm i0.057$	11.3 %
0.109	5.9 %
$-0.071 \pm i0.066$	3.5 %
$0.071 \pm i0.041$	3.7 %
0.059	3.1 %
$-0.013 \pm i0.023$	0.7 %
0.023	1.2 %
−0.007	0.3 %
0.006	0.3 %
	AM = 13.4 %

curve $w^{\mathrm{S}} \equiv 1 - \rho$. For instance, we may consider the representative case of the Greek economy for the year 1994: Table 5.6 reports the non-dominant eigenvalues and the mean of the relative error, *MRE*, between w^{S} and $f_\mu(\rho)$ or $2^{-1}F_\mu(\rho)$ (see Eqs. 5.14 and 5.15), i.e.

$$MRE \equiv \int_0^1 \left|1 - f(\rho)(1-\rho)^{-1}\right| d\rho$$

where $f(\rho)$ denotes $f_\mu(\rho)$ or $2^{-1}F_\mu(\rho)$.

(iii) Setting aside the polar *Case 1* presented in Sect. 5.2.1, all the other cases therein, and especially those including reducible systems with hyper-basic commodities, constitute useful *ideal types* that model the essential properties of the actual economies. Flaschel (2010) has remarked that:

> [T]he concept of 'basic commodities' needs reformulation from the empirical point of view, since it may (on the physical level) include basics of very minor importance ('pencils'). These types of commodities must in some way or another be classified as non-basics. (p. 247). [...] To give the notion of a basic commodity operational significance as well as economic content, it may be useful to look for criteria which help to eliminate 'minor basics' form the list of basics, i.e. which serve to eliminate corresponding weak price dependencies as far as possible. (p. 254)

(iv) Although the level of aggregation affects both the central tendency and skewness of the eigenvalue distribution, it is expected that it does not drastically affect the monotonicity of the production price-profit rate relationship, since the higher non-dominant eigenvalues exhibit small relative changes that go to either direction.

(v) Moving from the flow to the more realistic stock input-output data, the above conclusions are further supported by the fact that the moduli of the non-dominant eigenvalues fall even more abruptly, whereas the third or fourth eigenvalues tend to become 'indistinguishable' from the rest, which are crowded near zero.

(vi) An analogous pattern holds for the singular value distribution. Both these spectral patterns suggest that the effective ranks of the matrices of vertically integrated technical coefficients are relatively low and, therefore, actual single-product economies can be adequately described by only a few eigensectors, which regulate their production wage-price-profit rate relationships.

5.3.2 *Wage-Price-Profit Rate Approximations*

5.3.2.1 Bienenfeld's Approximation

The results summarized in Tables 5.7 and 5.8 are associated with the aforementioned ten SIOTs of the Danish, Finnish, French, German and Swedish economies, and Bienenfeld's approximation (with wages paid *ex ante*).

Table 5.7 reports (i) the maximum and the 'actual', absolute and relative, profit rates (i.e. the profit rates that correspond to the 'actual' real wage rate, which is estimated on the basis of the available input-output data) and (ii) the deviation between the vector of the actual production prices and the vector of the approximate production prices, which is estimated using Bienenfeld's quadratic approximation, and the actual value of the relative profit rate. This deviation is measured by the *d*–distance, *d*, and the normalized *d*– distance, dD^{-1}.

Table 5.8 reports the Euclidean angles (measured in degrees) and the *d*–distances between $\mathbf{p}(1)$ and $\mathbf{l}$, and between $\mathbf{p}(1)$ and $\mathbf{p}(0)\mathbf{J}^m$, $m = 0, 1, 2, \ldots, 5$ (see relations (2.77)): the angles (distances) are denoted by ϕ_{L} (d_{L}) and $\phi_m(d_m)$, respectively.

From all the results associated with these European economies, we arrive at the following conclusions:

(i) Although the actual relative profit rate is relatively low, i.e. in the range of 0.342–0.504, there are cases (Denmark and Sweden) where the deviation

Table 5.7 The actual profit rates and the deviation between the actual production prices and their Bienenfeld's quadratic approximation; five European economies: ten SIOTs

	Denmark		Finland		France		Germany		Sweden	
	2000	2004	1995	2004	1995	2005	2000	2002	1995	2005
R	0.920	0.867	0.699	0.645	0.899	0.855	1.000	1.052	0.859	0.807
r	0.344	0.326	0.323	0.325	0.322	0.308	0.342	0.362	0.336	0.297
ρ	0.374	0.376	0.462	0.504	0.358	0.360	0.342	0.344	0.392	0.368
d	0.325	0.372	0.012	0.057	0.007	0.028	0.034	0.033	0.247	0.436
dD^{-1}	0.247	0.283	0.009	0.043	0.005	0.021	0.026	0.025	0.188	0.333

between the actual production prices and their quadratic approximation is considerably high (see Table 5.7). The reader need hardly be reminded of the fact that Bienenfeld's approximation is certainly exact only at the extreme values of ρ.

(ii) In all cases, $\mathbf{p}(1)$ deviates considerably from $\mathbf{l}$ (see Table 5.8). However, setting aside the Finnish economy for the year 2004, $\mathbf{p}(0)\mathbf{J}^m$ tends rather quickly to $\mathbf{p}(1)$: ϕ_5 is in the range of 0.17° (Sweden, 2005) to 1.68° (Denmark, 2004), d_5 is in the range of 0.002 (Sweden, 2005) to 0.023 (Denmark, 2004) and, as it is easily checked, the average percentage decrease of d_m, i.e.

$$\overline{\hat{d}} \equiv 5^{-1}\sum_{m=0}^{4} 1 - d_{m+1}d_m^{-1}$$

is in the range of 45.8 % (Denmark, 2004) to 64.9 % (Sweden, 2005), while for the Finnish economy, 2004, d_5 is 0.166 and $\overline{\hat{d}}$ is 25.1 %. Thus, it is expected that low-order Bienenfeld's approximations would be adequate. Finally, it should be noted that there is a direct relationship between $|\lambda_{J2}|^{-1}$ and $\overline{\hat{d}}$: Spearman's coefficient is 0.721, and the regression $y = bx^a$ gives an R^2 value of 0.989 and statistically significant coefficients ($a \cong 0.990$ and $b \cong 0.296$).

(iii) Non-monotonic price-profit rate curves could not only be considered as rare but also have no more than one extreme point, and, therefore, Bienenfeld's quadratic approximation tracks down accurately enough the trajectories of the actual prices of production. More specifically, there are 105 cases of non-monotonic price movement (i.e. 105/559 ≅ 18.8 % of the tested cases)

Table 5.8 Indicators of the accuracy of Bienenfeld's approximation; five European economies; ten SIOTs

	Denmark		Finland		France		Germany		Sweden	
	2000	2004	1995	2004	1995	2005	2000	2002	1995	2005
ϕ_L	47.96°	51.73°	54.83°	61.23°	46.99°	51.72°	49.67°	49.59°	46.03°	48.07°
ϕ_0	28.50°	33.06°	36.34°	47.96°	28.82°	31.22°	30.87°	31.14°	27.11°	27.01°
ϕ_1	8.33°	13.67°	13.81°	35.77°	9.27°	11.51°	9.65°	9.99°	6.71°	5.35°
ϕ_2	3.75°	7.64°	7.04°	31.12°	3.90°	6.46°	4.80°	5.31°	3.01°	2.13°
ϕ_3	1.86°	4.48°	3.84°	27.32°	1.64°	3.83°	2.51°	3.03°	1.46°	0.91°
ϕ_4	0.98°	2.72°	2.18°	23.89°	0.72°	2.33°	1.34°	1.76°	0.72°	0.39°
ϕ_5	0.52°	1.68°	1.26°	20.79°	0.35°	1.41°	0.72°	1.03°	0.36°	0.17°
d_L	0.686	0.792	0.838	0.915	0.782	0.801	0.731	0.729	0.765	0.923
d_0	0.419	0.502	0.557	0.729	0.478	0.483	0.472	0.485	0.408	0.404
d_1	0.151	0.230	0.218	0.438	0.177	0.186	0.186	0.201	0.120	0.101
d_2	0.066	0.122	0.099	0.307	0.072	0.087	0.084	0.093	0.049	0.034
d_3	0.030	0.067	0.052	0.241	0.027	0.042	0.044	0.051	0.022	0.013
d_4	0.014	0.038	0.029	0.198	0.010	0.023	0.024	0.030	0.011	0.005
d_5	0.007	0.023	0.017	0.166	0.004	0.013	0.013	0.018	0.005	0.002

and the arithmetic mean of the mean of the relative errors, $\overline{MRE}$, between the actual, $p_j(\rho)$, and the approximate, $p_{Bj}(\rho)$, curves, i.e.

$$\overline{MRE} \equiv n^{-1}\sum_{j=1}^{n} MRE_j$$

where

$$MRE_j \equiv \int_0^1 \left| \left(p_j(\rho) - p_{Bj}(\rho)\right)\left(p_j(\rho)\right)^{-1} \right| d\rho$$

is in the range of 0.267 % (Sweden, 2005) to 7.069 % (Finland, 2004) (see Table 5.9, which reports the percentage of non-monotonic curves, indicated by n.-m., $\min_j\{MRE_j\}$, $\max_j\{MRE_j\}$ and $\overline{MRE}$). For reasons of clarity of presentation and economy of space, in Fig. 5.9 we display only a set of three graphs associated with the Danish (2004), Finnish (2004) and Swedish (2005) economies, respectively, and some of the actual (depicted by solid lines) and the approximate (depicted by dotted lines) curves. Finally, it should be noted that there is an inverse relationship between $|\lambda_{J2}|^{-1}$ (or $\bar{\hat{d}}$) and $\overline{MRE}$: Spearman's coefficient is -0.770 (or -0.976) and the regression $y = bx^a$ gives an R^2 value of 0.993 (or 0.995) and statistically significant coefficients ($a \cong -5.870$ (or -2.985) and $b \cong 18.370$ (or 0.114); see Fig. 5.10).

(iv) Since Bienenfeld's quadratic approximation works extremely well, the capital intensities, κ_j, of the vertically integrated industries producing commodities $j = 1, 2, \ldots, n$ are almost linear functions of the relative profit rate (see relation (2.83)). Figure 5.11 is representative and displays the capital intensities of the French economy, $\kappa_{\mathbf{y}} \equiv \mathbf{pH}\overline{\mathbf{y}}^{\mathrm{T}}\left(\mathbf{v}\overline{\mathbf{y}}^{\mathrm{T}}\right)^{-1}$, where $\overline{\mathbf{y}}^{\mathrm{T}}$ denotes the net output vector of the economy, as functions of ρ. They are strictly increasing functions,[23] and the mean of the relative errors between the actual and the linear curves are in the range of 0.129 % (1995) to 0.548 % (2005). As is well known, an almost linear $\kappa_{\mathbf{y}}$–ρ curve implies that the WPC, measured in terms of $\overline{\mathbf{y}}^{\mathrm{T}}$, *tends* to be either strictly convex or strictly concave to the origin. And it has usually been argued that such shapes reduce the probability of reswitching of techniques. Nevertheless, Mainwaring and Steedman (2000) find, by means of a two-sector model, that the highest reswitching probabilities are observed in the cases where the WPCs exhibit low curvature and, thus, conclude:

> That this is so in a two-sector model should make us particularly wary of claiming a *simple* relationship between probability and curvature in theoretical or actual multi-sector economies. (p. 346; emphasis added)

[23] The same holds true for the German economy, while the functions associated with all the other economies of this sample are strictly decreasing.

Table 5.9 The percentage of non-monotonic price-profit rate curves and the accuracy of Bienenfeld's quadratic approximation; five European economies: ten SIOTs

	Denmark		Finland		France		Germany		Sweden	
	2000	2004	1995	2004	1995	2005	2000	2002	1995	2005
n.-m. (%)	23.2	32.1	15.8	22.8	18.9	14.0	15.8	12.3	20.8	11.8
$\min_j \{MRE_j\}$ (%)	0.042	0.042	0.023	2.152	0.015	0.012	0.042	0.003	0.020	0.000
$\max_j \{MRE_j\}$ (%)	2.243	4.431	2.667	17.199	3.096	6.947	3.926	5.264	1.897	1.498
$\overline{MRE}$ (%)	0.651	1.394	1.208	7.069	0.614	0.712	0.757	0.818	0.517	0.267

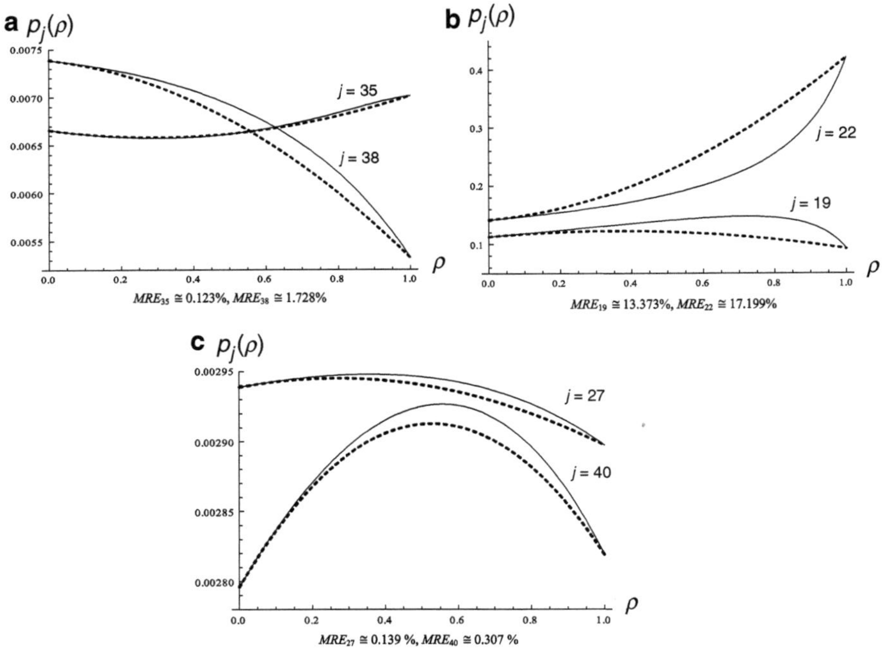

Fig. 5.9 Actual and approximate production price-relative profit rate curves: (**a**) Denmark, 2004; (**b**) Finland, 2004; and (**c**) Sweden, 2005

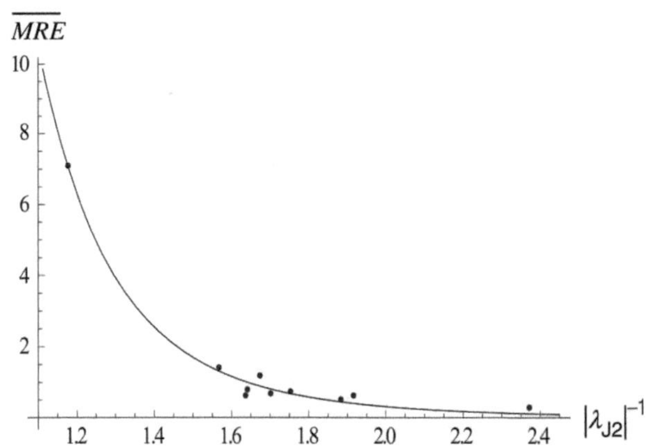

Fig. 5.10 Mean error of Bienenfeld's quadratic approximation vs. damping ratio; five European economies: ten SIOTs

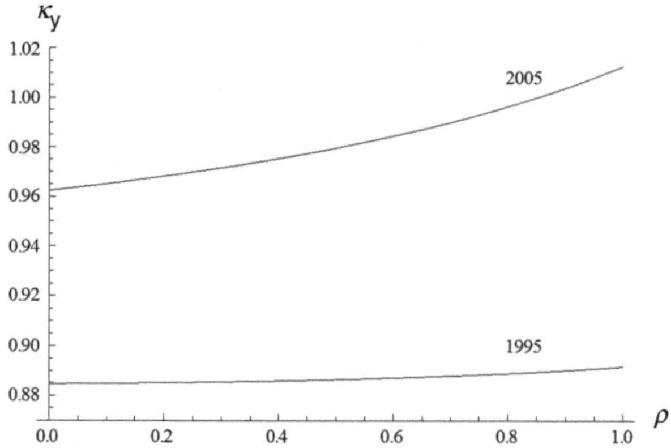

Fig. 5.11 The capital intensities of the French economy as functions of the relative profit rate

5.3.2.2 Eigenvalue Decomposition, Singular Value Decomposition and Steedman's Approximations

For clarity's and brevity's sake, we only report figures for the French economy and the year 2005. These figures can be considered as sufficiently representative. In all figures, the actual price curves are depicted by solid lines. The graphs in Fig. 5.12 display their fifth-order EVD approximations (depicted by dotted lines; see relation (5.19)). The graphs in Fig. 5.13 display their fifth-order SVD approximations (depicted by dotted lines; see relation (5.20)). Finally, the graphs in Fig. 5.14 display their fifth-order Steedman's approximations (depicted by dotted lines that cross the ρ–axis at $\rho = 1$), i.e.

$$\mathbf{p} \approx (1-\rho)\,\mathbf{p}(0)\sum_{h=0}^{5}(\rho\mathbf{J})^{5}$$

or

$$\mathbf{p} \approx (1-\rho)\,\mathbf{p}(0)\mathbf{X_J}\left[\sum_{h=0}^{5}(\rho\hat{\lambda}_{\mathbf{J}})^{h}\right]\mathbf{X_J^{-1}}$$

(see Eq. 2.51 and Sects. 3.4 and 5.2.2). It is added that $\lambda_{\mathbf{J}4,5} \cong 0.332 \pm i0.015$, $\sigma_{\mathbf{J}5}\sigma_{\mathbf{J}1}^{-1} \cong 0.299$, the dominant eigenvalue of $\bar{\mathbf{J}}^{[5]}$ is approximately equal to 1.088, $\left\|\mathbf{J}-\bar{\mathbf{J}}^{[5]}\right\|_{\mathrm{SP}} \cong 0.426$, $\left\|\mathbf{J}-\bar{\mathbf{J}}^{[5]}\right\|_{\mathrm{F}} \cong 1.237$ and the inseparability index $\varepsilon_{\mathbf{J}5}$ is approximately equal to 0.200.

These figures suggest that even the SVD and Steedman's approximations work pretty well, *although* for low or, more precisely, 'realistic' values of the relative profit rate (its actual value is approximately equal to 0.360; see Table 5.7). Finally, it may be noted that the price curves corresponding to these two approximations are somewhat 'symmetric' with respect to the actual price curves.

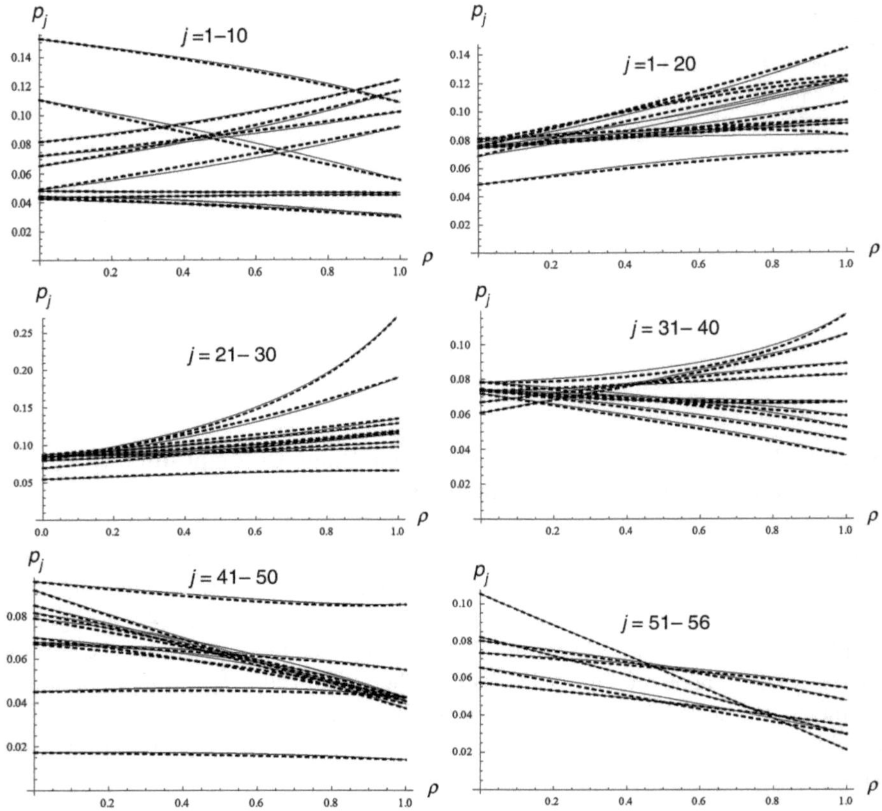

Fig. 5.12 The production price-relative profit rate curves and their fifth-order EVD approximations; France, 2005

5.3.2.3 Homographic Approximation of the Wage-Profit Rate Curve

We have already seen (Sect. 5.2.1, *Case 2*) that if $rank[\mathbf{J}] \approx 1$, i.e. $\mathbf{J} \approx \left(\mathbf{y}_{\mathbf{J}1}\mathbf{x}_{\mathbf{J}1}^{\mathrm{T}}\right)^{-1}\mathbf{x}_{\mathbf{J}1}^{\mathrm{T}}\mathbf{y}_{\mathbf{J}1}$, then the WPC tends to be a homographic function:

$$w \approx w^{\mathrm{S}}[1 + \rho(d_1 - 1)]^{-1}$$

An alternative derivation of this approximation can be based on the bound curves for the WPC (Sect. 2.3.1). If $rank[\mathbf{J}] \approx 1$, then

$$\mathbf{M} \approx \left(\mathbf{y}_{\mathbf{M}1}\mathbf{x}_{\mathbf{M}1}^{\mathrm{T}}\right)^{-1}\mathbf{x}_{\mathbf{M}1}^{\mathrm{T}}\mathbf{y}_{\mathbf{M}1} \tag{5.22}$$

Equation 2.41, i.e. $\boldsymbol{\Xi} \equiv \mathbf{M}\left[\mathbf{I} + (1-w)^{-1}w\boldsymbol{\zeta}^{\mathrm{T}}\boldsymbol{\omega}\right]$, and relation (5.22) imply that

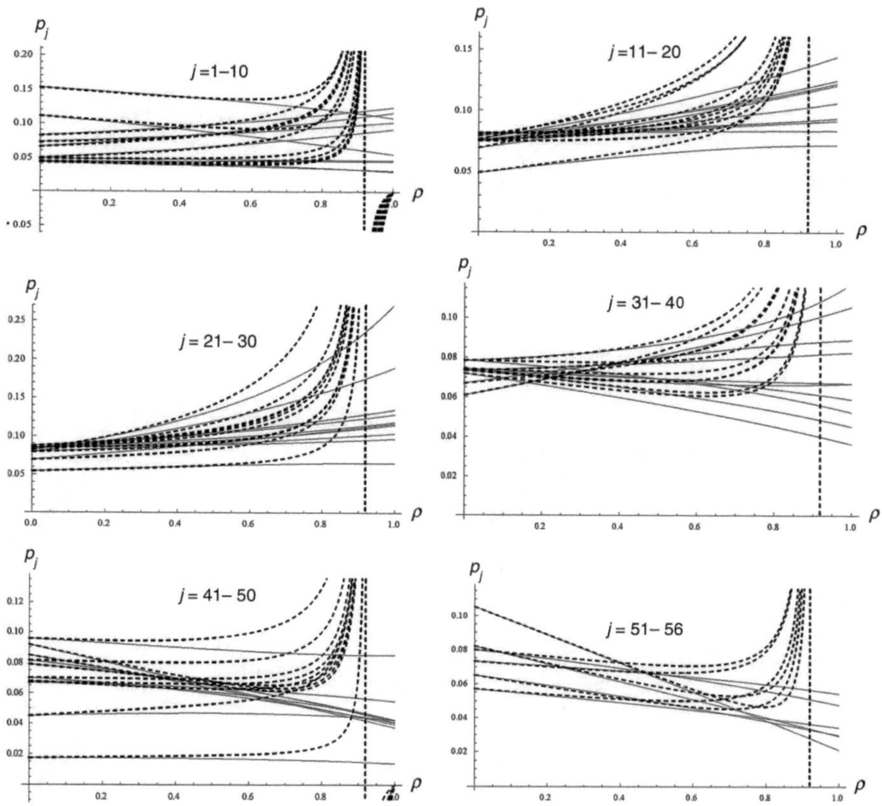

Fig. 5.13 The production price-relative profit rate curves and their fifth-order SVD approximations; France, 2005

$$\boldsymbol{\Xi} \approx \left[\left(\mathbf{y}_{\mathbf{M}1}\mathbf{x}_{\mathbf{M}1}^{\mathrm{T}}\right)^{-1}\mathbf{x}_{\mathbf{M}1}^{\mathrm{T}}\right]\left[\mathbf{y}_{\mathbf{M}1}\left[\mathbf{I}+(1-w)^{-1}w\boldsymbol{\zeta}^{\mathrm{T}}\boldsymbol{\omega}\right]\right]$$

or $rank[\boldsymbol{\Xi}] \approx 1$, from which it directly follows that

$$\lambda_{\boldsymbol{\Xi}1} \approx 1+(1-w)^{-1}w\left(\mathbf{y}_{\mathbf{M}1}\mathbf{x}_{\mathbf{M}1}^{\mathrm{T}}\right)^{-1}\mathbf{y}_{\mathbf{M}1}\boldsymbol{\zeta}^{\mathrm{T}}\boldsymbol{\omega}\mathbf{x}_{\mathbf{M}1}^{\mathrm{T}}$$

or, because of $\mathbf{y}_{\mathbf{M}1}\boldsymbol{\zeta}^{\mathrm{T}}\boldsymbol{\omega}\mathbf{x}_{\mathbf{M}1}^{\mathrm{T}} = \boldsymbol{\omega}\mathbf{x}_{\mathbf{M}1}^{\mathrm{T}}\mathbf{y}_{\mathbf{M}1}\boldsymbol{\zeta}^{\mathrm{T}}$ and relation (5.22),

$$\lambda_{\boldsymbol{\Xi}1} \approx \lambda_{\boldsymbol{\Xi}1}^{\mathrm{A}} \equiv 1+(1-w)^{-1}w\boldsymbol{\omega}\mathbf{M}\boldsymbol{\zeta}^{\mathrm{T}} \tag{5.23}$$

In that case, Eq. (2.42), i.e. $\rho^{-1} = \lambda_{\boldsymbol{\Xi}1}$, and relation (5.23) imply that

$$w \approx w^{\mathrm{A}} \equiv w^{\mathrm{S}}\left[1+\rho\left(\phi^{*}-1\right)\right]^{-1} \tag{5.24}$$

where

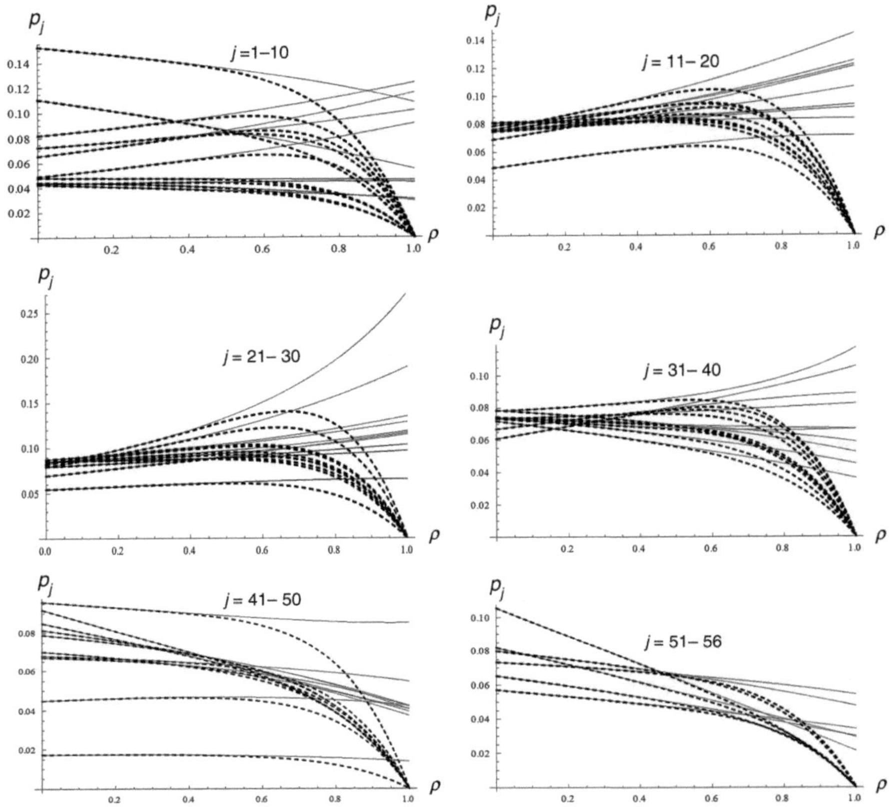

Fig. 5.14 The production price-relative profit rate curves and their fifth-order Steedman's approximations; France, 2005

$$\phi^* \equiv \boldsymbol{\omega}\mathbf{M}\boldsymbol{\zeta}^{\mathrm{T}} = \mathbf{v}\mathbf{J}\mathbf{z}^{\mathrm{T}} \approx \left(\mathbf{y}_{\mathbf{J}1}\mathbf{x}_{\mathbf{J}1}^{\mathrm{T}}\right)^{-1}\mathbf{v}\left(\mathbf{x}_{\mathbf{J}1}^{\mathrm{T}}\mathbf{y}_{\mathbf{J}1}\right)\mathbf{z}^{\mathrm{T}} = \mathbf{y}_{\mathbf{J}1}\mathbf{z}^{\mathrm{T}}$$

or

$$\phi^* \approx d_1$$

$$\phi \equiv \left(\left\|\hat{\boldsymbol{\omega}}^{-1}\right\|\right)^{-1}\left\|\boldsymbol{\zeta}^{\mathrm{T}}\right\| \leq \phi^* \leq \Phi \equiv \|\boldsymbol{\omega}\|\left\|\boldsymbol{\zeta}^{\mathrm{T}}\right\|$$

and $\phi^* > 1$ iff $\mathbf{vHz}^{\mathrm{T}} > R^{-1}$, i.e. the capital-net output ratio (measured in terms of labour values) in the vertically integrated industry producing the numeraire commodity is greater than the capital-net output ratio in the SSS. From Eq. 5.9 it follows that the relative error in the homographic approximation of the WPC can be written as

$$|w - w^{\mathrm{A}}|w^{-1} = |(1 - d_1 - \Lambda_k^w) - \rho(1 - \phi^* - \Lambda_k^w)|[1 + \rho(\phi^* - 1)]^{-1} \quad (5.25)$$

Finally, it should be noted that if $rank[\mathbf{J}] = 1$, then the Hilbert distance between $\mathbf{y}_{\mathbf{J}1}$ and $\mathbf{vJ}$ equals zero and $\phi^*\Phi^{-1} = \phi^*(\Omega\phi)^{-1}$ is numeraire-free.

For instance, the application of this analysis to the flow SIOTs of the French (for the year 2005) and the Greek (for the year 1994) economies gives the following results (also consider Sect. 3.9):

(i) The Hilbert distance between $\mathbf{y}_{\mathbf{J}1}$ and $\mathbf{l}$ is in the range of 1.23 (Greece) to 1.94 (France). By contrast, the distance between $\mathbf{y}_{\mathbf{J}1}$ and $\mathbf{vJ}$ is in the range of 0.32 (Greece) to 0.42 (France).

(ii) If wages are measured in terms of the corresponding actual net output vectors, then ϕ^* is in the range of 0.830 (France) to 1.025 (Greece), and $\phi^*\phi^{-1}$ is in the range of 2.293 (Greece) to 3.051 (France; also see Fig. 3.17). Given that the WPC for the French economy is strictly concave to the origin, while the WPC for the Greek economy crosses the w^{S} curve at $\rho \cong 0.194$, and switches from convex to concave at $\rho \cong 0.499$, it follows that the value of ϕ^* predicts the curvature of the WPC in the case of the French economy but not in that of the Greek economy for $\rho > 0.499$. Furthermore, the approximations (5.23)–(5.24) work well: the relative error in the approximation (5.23), i.e.

$$RE \equiv |\lambda_{\Xi 1}^{\mathrm{A}} - \lambda_{\Xi 1}|\lambda_{\Xi 1}^{-1} = |\lambda_{\Xi 1}^{\mathrm{A}} - \rho^{-1}|\rho$$

takes its *maximum* value of 0.920 % (France) or 4.597 % (Greece) at $w \cong 0.450$ or 0.390, respectively, and the mean of the relative error in the homographic approximation (5.24), i.e.

$$MRE \equiv \int_0^1 |w - w^{\mathrm{A}}|w^{-1}d\rho$$

is approximately equal to 1.650 % (France) or 0.630 % (Greece). This *MRE* can be conceived of as an aggregate measure of the effect of non-dominant eigenvalues on WPC (see Eq. 5.25). Figures 5.15 and 5.16 display the *RE* and the absolute error $|w - w^{\mathrm{A}}|$ as functions of the distributive variables.

(iii) Table 5.10 and Fig. 5.17 display the results for four alternative numeraires that are of particular significance, i.e. the vectors of the actual gross outputs, $\bar{\mathbf{x}}^{\mathrm{T}}$, actual real wage rates, $\mathbf{b}^{\mathrm{T}}$, $\mathbf{e}_m^{\mathrm{T}}$ ($\omega_m = \min_j\{\omega_j\}$) and $\mathbf{e}_M^{\mathrm{T}}$ ($\omega_M = \max_j\{\omega_j\}$; also see Table 3.14 and Figs. 3.18 and 3.19). It follows that with the exception of the Greek economy for $\mathbf{z}^{\mathrm{T}} = \mathbf{b}^{\mathrm{T}}$, the values of ϕ^* predict the curvatures of the WPCs. Moreover, although $\phi^*\phi^{-1}$ vary considerably with the numeraire, the homographic approximation of the WPC works well.

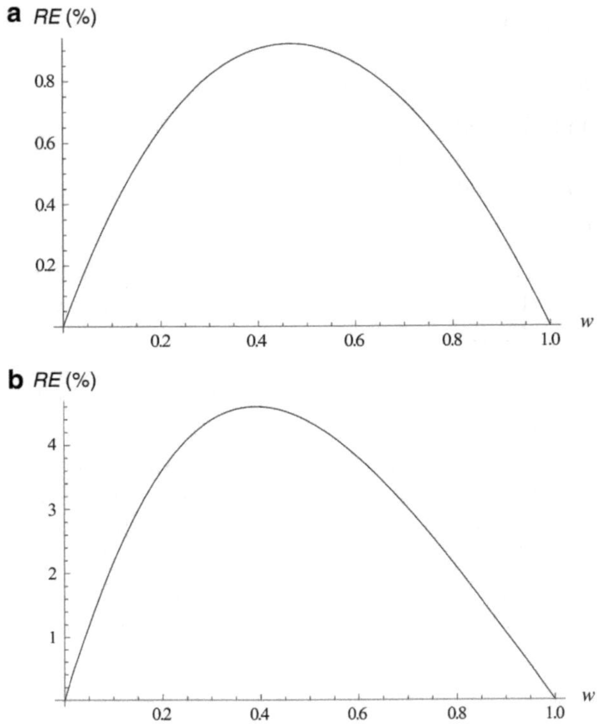

Fig. 5.15 The relative error in the approximation of the relative profit rate; (**a**) France, 2005, and (**b**) Greece, 1994

5.3.3 *Relative Price Effects of Total Productivity Shift*

Now consider our theoretical analysis of the relative price effects of total productivity shift (Sect. 2.4.2), and assume the case of (i) differential profit rates, $\bar{\mathbf{r}} \equiv [\bar{r}_j] \neq \mathbf{0}$, $\bar{r}_j > -1$ and (ii) a uniform rate of productivity change, i.e. $\widehat{\boldsymbol{\tau}} = \tau \mathbf{e}$. If $rank[\boldsymbol{\Theta}] \approx 1$, where now $\theta_{ij} \equiv p_i a_{ij}(1+\bar{r}_j)p_j^{-1}$ $(\mathbf{p} > \mathbf{0})$ and $\boldsymbol{\Theta} = \hat{\mathbf{p}}\left[\mathbf{A}\left[\mathbf{I}+\hat{\bar{\mathbf{r}}}\right]\right]\hat{\mathbf{p}}^{-1}$, then

$$\boldsymbol{\Theta} \approx \lambda_{\Theta 1}\left(\mathbf{y}_{\Theta 1}\mathbf{x}_{\Theta 1}^{\mathrm{T}}\right)^{-1}\mathbf{x}_{\Theta 1}^{\mathrm{T}}\mathbf{y}_{\Theta 1}$$

and, therefore,

$$[\mathbf{I}-\boldsymbol{\Theta}]^{-1} \approx \mathbf{I}+D^{-1}\boldsymbol{\Theta}, \ \ 0 < D \equiv \det[\mathbf{I}-\boldsymbol{\Theta}] \approx 1-\lambda_{\Theta 1} \tag{5.26}$$

(by applying the Sherman-Morrison formula). Substituting relations (5.26) in Eq. 2.89 yields

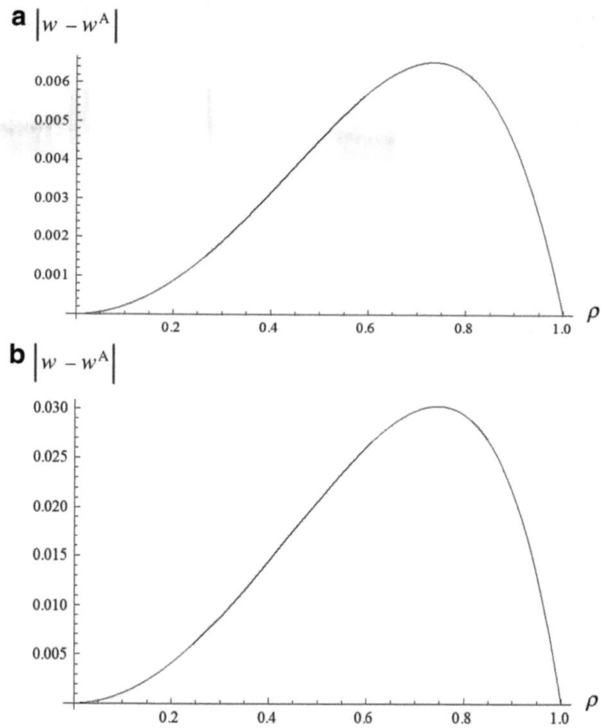

Fig. 5.16 The absolute error in the approximation of the WPC; (**a**) France, 2005, and (**b**) Greece, 1994

Table 5.10 Results for alternative numeraires; France, 2005, and Greece, 1994

	France, 2005				Greece, 1994			
$\mathbf{z}^T$	ϕ^*	$\phi^*\phi^{-1}$	$\ddot{w}$	*MRE %*	ϕ^*	$\phi^*\phi^{-1}$	$\ddot{w}$	*MRE %*
$\overline{\mathbf{x}}^T$	0.927	3.194	<0	1.098	0.957	2.170	<0	5.075
$\mathbf{b}^T$	1.025	3.234	>0	0.777	0.944	2.371	$>0, \rho<0.336$	6.603
							$<0, \rho>0.336$	
$\mathbf{e}_m^T$	1.862	1.862	>0	19.677	1.465	1.465	>0	4.791
$\mathbf{e}_M^T$	0.212	3.493	<0	4.778	0.356	2.337	<0	6.387

$$\widehat{p}_i - \widehat{p}_j \approx -\tau\mathbf{e}\left[\mathbf{I} + (1-\lambda_{\Theta 1})^{-1}\mathbf{\Theta}\right]\left(\mathbf{e}_i^T - \mathbf{e}_j^T\right)$$

or

$$\widehat{p}_i - \widehat{p}_j \approx \tau(1-\lambda_{\Theta 1})^{-1}E_{i-j}^I = \tau E_{i-j}^I + \tau\left[\lambda_{\Theta 1}E_{i-j}^I + (\lambda_{\Theta 1})^2 E_{i-j}^I + \ldots\right] \quad (5.27)$$

where $E_{i-j}^I \equiv \theta_{Li} - \theta_{Lj}$ represents the 'direct' effect. Thus, it may be concluded that the accuracy of approximation (5.27) and, therefore, the validity of the traditional labour cost condition

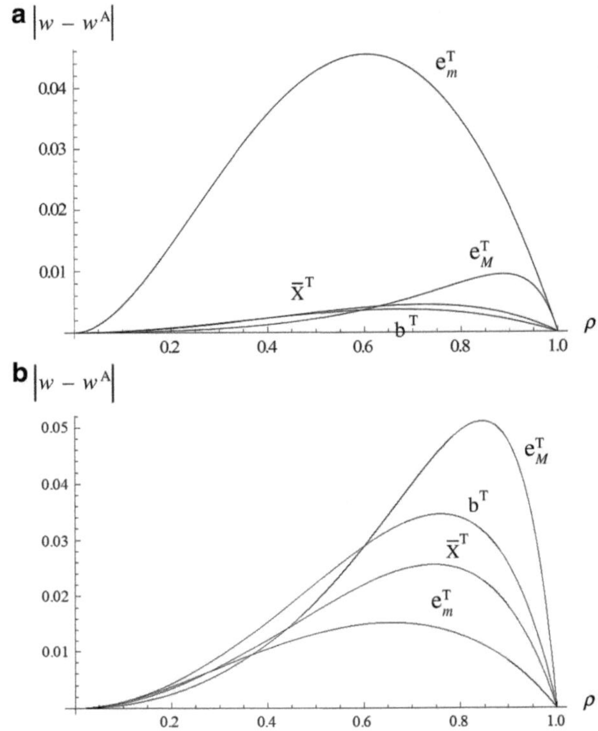

Fig. 5.17 The absolute error in the approximation of the WPC; alternative numeraires: (**a**) France, 2005, and (**b**) Greece, 1994

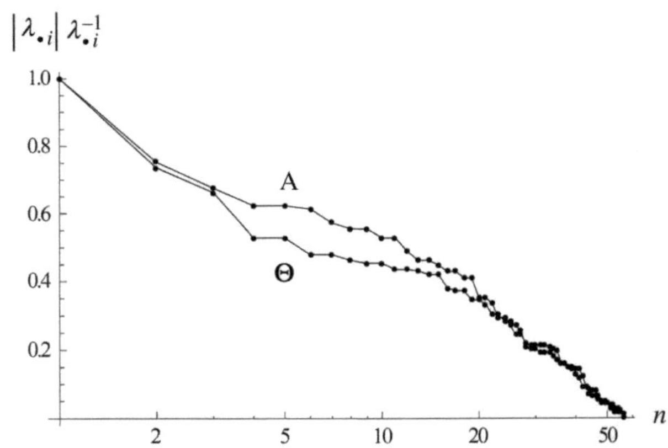

Fig. 5.18 The moduli of the normalized eigenvalues of **Θ** and **A**; Germany, 2002

$$E^{\mathrm{I}}_{i-j} > (<)\, 0 \Leftrightarrow \widehat{p}_i > (<)\, \widehat{p}_j$$

are inversely related to the magnitudes of $|\lambda_{\Theta k}|\lambda_{\Theta 1}^{-1}$.

For instance, the application of our analysis to the flow SIOT of the German economy, for the year 2002, gives the results summarized in Tables 5.11, 5.12

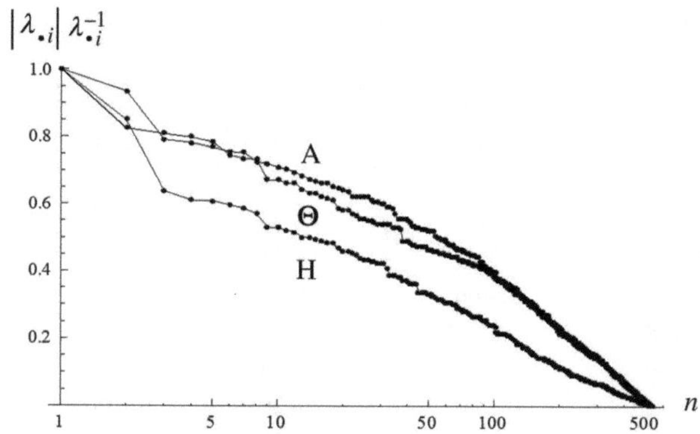

Fig. 5.19 The moduli of the normalized eigenvalues of all the matrices **H**, **Θ** and **A**; five European economies: ten SIOTs

Table 5.11 The relative shares of labour; Germany, 2002

j	θ_{Lj}	j	θ_{Lj}	j	θ_{Lj}	j	θ_{Lj}
1	0.173	15	0.056	29	0.173	43	0.239
2	0.230	16	0.205	30	0.210	44	0.162
3	0.119	17	0.283	31	0.218	45	0.036
4	0.954	18	0.288	32	0.290	46	0.056
5	0.141	19	0.194	33	0.457	47	0.464
6	0.255	20	0.333	34	0.397	48	0.366
7	0.177	21	0.323	35	0.451	49	0.308
8	0.137	22	0.159	36	0.346	50	0.585
9	0.266	23	0.357	37	0.431	51	0.729
10	0.187	24	0.265	38	0.060	52	0.466
11	0.197	25	0.339	39	0.153	53	0.185
12	0.234	26	0.196	40	0.217	54	0.697
13	0.205	27	0.266	41	0.187	55	0.282
14	0.245	28	0.294	42	0.342	56	0.159

and 5.13.[24] Table 5.11 reports the relative shares of labour. Relative price movements (estimated from Eq. 2.89, with $\tau = 1$) are displayed in Table 5.12:

(i) The symbol 'I' indicates that the two effects work in the same direction and, at the same time, the direct one is stronger in absolute value.
(ii) '*' indicates that the two effects work in opposite directions and, at the same time, the direct effect is stronger.

[24] It is noted that (i) **p** is identified with **e**; (ii) for the construction of [**A**,**l**] and the estimation of w, we follow the usual procedure; and (iii) the sectoral 'profit factors' are estimated from

$$1 + \bar{r}_j = \left(1 - wl_j\right)\left(a_{1j} + \ldots + a_{nj}\right)^{-1}$$

Table 5.12 Relative price movements; Germany, 2002

i–j	$\widehat{p}_i - \widehat{p}_j$	*i–j*	$\widehat{p}_i - \widehat{p}_j$	*i–j*	$\widehat{p}_i - \widehat{p}_j$
1–2	−0.322	20–21	−0.047 [**]	39–40	−0.609
2–3	0.531	21–22	0.895	40–41	0.410
3–4	−3.418	22–23	−1.061	41–42	−0.746
4–5	3.117	23–24	0.473	42–43	0.459
5–6	−0.396	24–25	−0.322	43–44	0.477
6–7	0. 466	25–26	0.682	44–45	0.159 [I]
7–8	0.035 [*]	26–27	−0.427	45–46	0.975 [**]
8–9	−0.539	27–28	−0.079	46–47	−2.857
9–10	0.254	28–29	0.758	47–48	0.161 [I]
10–11	0.049 [**]	29–30	−0.632	48–49	0.642
11–12	−0.131	30–31	0.198 [**]	49–50	−1.073
12–13	0.151	31–32	−0.224	50–51	−0.697
13–14	−0.208	32–33	−0.603	51–52	1.192
14–15	1.026	33–34	0.201	52–53	1.074
15–16	−0.862	34–35	−0.136	53–54	−2.081
16–17	−0.311	35–36	0.499	54–55	1.750
17–18	−0.148	36–37	−0.535	55–56	0.813
18–19	0.520	37–38	1.824		
19–20	−0.672	38–39	−0.447		

Table 5.13 Relative contributions (%) of the direct effect and relative errors (%) in the approximation of relative price movements; Germany, 2002

i–j	RC^{I}_{i-j}	$RE_{i\text{–}j}$	*i–j*	RC^{I}_{i-j}	$RE_{i\text{–}j}$	*i–j*	RC^{I}_{i-j}	$RE_{i\text{–}j}$
1–2	17.6	29.9	22–23	18.6	25.6	41–42	20.8	17.1
2–3	20.1	17.1	23–24	19.4	22.6	42–43	22.4	10.1
3–4	24.4	2.4	24–25	22.8	9.1	43–44	16.1	35.9
4–5	26.1	4.2	25–26	20.9	16.5	44–45	79.0	215.6
5–6	28.8	15.0	26–27	16.4	34.6	46–47	14.3	42.9
6–7	16.8	33.0	27–28	34.7	38.6	47–48	60.8	142.9
8–9	24.3	2.7	28–29	16.0	36.0	48–49	9.1	63.8
9–10	31.1	24.4	29–30	5.8	76.8	49–50	25.8	3.2
11–12	28.7	14.5	31–32	32.3	29.2	50–51	20.5	17.9
12–13	19.2	23.2	32–33	27.7	10.7	51–52	22.0	12.1
13–14	19.6	23.8	33–34	30.2	20.6	52–53	56.2	4.6
14–15	18.4	26.5	34–35	39.7	58.6	53–54	24.6	1.7
15–16	17.2	31.1	35–36	21.0	16.3	54–55	23.7	5.3
16–17	25.1	0.30	36–37	15.8	36.8	55–56	15.1	39.6
17–18	3.6	85.5	37–38	20.3	18.9	$MRC^{\mathrm{I}}_{i-j} = 22.3$		
18–19	17.2	31.1	38–39	20.8	17.1			
19–20	20.1	19.8	39–40	10.6	57.7	$MRE_{i-j} = 32.4$		
21–22	18.3	26.7	40–41	7.4	70.5			

(iii) '**' indicates that the traditional condition is violated.

Setting aside the 'perverse' cases (ii)–(iii), in Table 5.13, we report:

(i) The relative contributions of the direct effect, i.e.

$$RC^{\mathrm{I}}_{i-j} \equiv E^{\mathrm{I}}_{i-j}(E^{\mathrm{t}}_{i-j})^{-1}, \; E^{\mathrm{t}}_{i-j} \equiv E^{\mathrm{I}}_{i-j} - E^{\mathrm{II}}_{i-j}$$

and their arithmetic mean, MRC^{I}_{i-j}.

(ii) The relative errors in the approximation (5.27), i.e.

$$RE_{i-j} \equiv \left| 1 - (1 - \lambda_{\Theta 1})^{-1} E^{\mathrm{I}}_{i-j}\left(E^{\mathrm{t}}_{i-j}\right)^{-1} \right|$$

where $\lambda_{\Theta 1} \cong 0.750$, and their arithmetic mean, MRE_{i-j}.

From these tables and the associated numerical results, we arrive at the following two conclusions:

(i) Although the mean relative contribution of the direct effect is rather small, the direction of the relative price movements is, more often than not, governed by this effect. There are five cases (5/55 ≅ 9 % of the tested cases) where the two effects work in opposite directions and four cases (≅7 %) where the traditional condition is violated. It may be added that, in terms of commodity $i = 1$ or 56, i.e. $\widehat{p}_i = 0$, there are three or four cases, respectively, of violation: $j = 5$, 22, 29 or 3, 5, 8, 39 (consider Tables 5.11 and 5.12). In terms of commodity 45, $\theta_{\mathrm{L}45} = \min_j\{\theta_{\mathrm{L}j}\}$, there are three cases of violation, $j = 15$, 38, 46, while in terms of commodity 4, $\theta_{\mathrm{L}4} = \max_j\{\theta_{\mathrm{L}j}\}$, there is no such case. Finally, in terms of the '$\bar{\mathbf{r}}$−SSC', i.e.

$$\mathbf{s}^{*\mathrm{T}} \equiv (\mathbf{l}\mathbf{x}^{\mathrm{T}}_{\mathbf{A}^*1})^{-1}\mathbf{x}^{\mathrm{T}}_{\mathbf{A}^*1}, \; \mathbf{A}^* \equiv \mathbf{A}[\mathbf{I} + \hat{\bar{\mathbf{r}}}], \; \theta_{\mathrm{Ls}^*} \cong 0.250$$

(the arithmetic mean of $\theta_{\mathrm{L}j}$ is approximately equal to 0.281), there are four cases of violation: $j = 14$, 30, 31, 40. It could, therefore, be stated that the violation of the traditional condition is 'more unlikely' the greater is the difference between $\theta_{\mathrm{L}i}$ and $\theta_{\mathrm{L}j}$.

(ii) The 'crude' approximation (5.27) is not without some validity. This is due rather to the distribution of the moduli of the normalized eigenvalues of $\mathbf{\Theta}$, $|\lambda_{\Theta i}|\lambda_{\Theta 1}^{-1}$. As Fig. 5.18 shows, the horizontal axis of which is plotted in logarithmic scale, the moduli of the first non-dominant eigenvalues of both $\mathbf{\Theta}$ and $\mathbf{A}$ fall quite markedly, whereas the rest constellate in much lower values.

Experiments with the other nine flow SIOTs of the aforementioned five European economies (i.e. Danish, Finnish, French, German and Swedish) give rise to similar results with respect to their eigen-configuration and, therefore, to the conjecture that, in actual economies, the relative price effects of total productivity shift are, by and large, governed by the direct effect. As it has already been stated, the issue at hand is formally equivalent to that of price movements arising from changes in the uniform profit rate. And there is no

Table 5.14 The distribution of the moduli of the normalized non-dominant eigenvalues of $\mathbf{\Theta}$ and $\mathbf{A}$; five European economies: ten SIOTs

	Denmark		Finland		France		Germany		Sweden	
	2000	2004	1995	2004	1995	2005	2000	2002	1995	2005
$\lvert\lambda_{\Theta 2}\rvert\lambda_{\Theta 1}^{-1}$	0.584	0.672	0.732	0.825	0.799	0.611	0.809	0.736	0.634	0.541
$\lvert\lambda_{\Theta 3}\rvert\lambda_{\Theta 1}^{-1}$	0.584	0.630	0.617	0.785	0.672	0.588	0.645	0.662	0.574	0.491
$AM(\mathbf{\Theta})$	0.207	0.199	0.198	0.212	0.221	0.227	0.255	0.253	0.171	0.179
$GM(\mathbf{\Theta})$	0.135	0.133	0.115	0.123	0.120	0.149	0.165	0.169	0.100	0.108
$AM(\mathbf{A})$	0.206	0.194	0.189	0.197	0.222	0.228	0.283	0.278	0.175	0.186
$GM(\mathbf{A})$	0.130	0.128	0.102	0.111	0.115	0.145	0.184	0.188	0.099	0.107

little empirical evidence that, due to the eigenvalue distribution of the matrices of vertically integrated technical coefficients, $\mathbf{H}$, which tends to be remarkably uniform across countries over time, the directions of the latter movements are mainly governed by the differences in the relevant vertically integrated capital intensities. The results in Table 5.14 and Fig. 5.19 (also see Table 5.3), which displays the moduli of all the normalized eigenvalues of that sample (the horizontal axis is once again plotted in logarithmic scale), suggest that the eigenvalues of $\mathbf{H}$ and $\mathbf{\Theta}$ follow similar patterns and, at the same time, the spread between them is not so wide. They therefore provide support to our conjecture.

5.3.4 *Eigen-Deviation of Labour-Commanded Prices from Labour Values*

Sraffa (1960) remarks that:

> [T]he quantity of *labour* that can be purchased by the *Standard* net product [is] a variable quantity of labour, which, however, varies according to a *simple* rule which is *independent of prices*. (p. 32; emphasis added – also see p. 94)

This remark provides the basis for the proposal of an alternative measure of price-labour value deviation for diagonalizable and regular single-product systems, which may be called the 'mean absolute eigen-deviation' (MAED) of labour-commanded prices from labour values. We do not by any means advocate the superiority of the proposed measure over the existing ones (see Chap. 4), but rather its simplicity and usefulness.

Using $\mathbf{p}_w \equiv w^{-1}\mathbf{p}$ and $\hat{\boldsymbol{\lambda}}_{\mathbf{J}} = \mathbf{X}_{\mathbf{J}}^{-1}\mathbf{J}\mathbf{X}_{\mathbf{J}}$, Eq. 5.2 can be written as

$$\mathbf{p}_w = \mathbf{v}\mathbf{X}_{\mathbf{J}}\left[\mathbf{I} - \rho\hat{\boldsymbol{\lambda}}_{\mathbf{J}}\right]^{-1}\mathbf{X}_{\mathbf{J}}^{-1}$$

or, postmultiplying by $\mathbf{X}_{\mathbf{J}}\hat{\tilde{\mathbf{v}}}^{-1}$,

$$\tilde{\mathbf{p}}_w\hat{\tilde{\mathbf{v}}}^{-1} = \mathbf{e}\left[\mathbf{I} - \rho\hat{\boldsymbol{\lambda}}_{\mathbf{J}}\right]^{-1}$$

or, in terms of the *j*th commodity,

$$\widetilde{p}_{wj}\widetilde{v}_j^{-1} = \left(1 - \rho\lambda_{\mathbf{J}j}\right)^{-1} \tag{5.28}$$

where $\widetilde{\mathbf{p}}_w \equiv \mathbf{p}_w\mathbf{X}_\mathbf{J}$, $\widetilde{\mathbf{v}} \equiv \mathbf{v}\mathbf{X}_\mathbf{J}$ represent the transformed vectors of prices and labour values, respectively, $\left[\mathbf{I} - \rho\hat{\boldsymbol{\lambda}}_\mathbf{J}\right]^{-1}$ the linear diagonal operator that 'transforms' $\tilde{\mathbf{v}}$ into $\widetilde{\mathbf{p}}_w$, $\widetilde{p}_{w1}$ the quantity of labour that can be purchased by the Sraffian Standard net product and $\widetilde{p}_{w1}\widetilde{v}_1^{-1} = (1-\rho)^{-1}$, $\widetilde{p}_{wk}\widetilde{v}_k^{-1} = (1 - \rho\lambda_{\mathbf{J}k})^{-1}$ the price-labour value ratios of the Sraffian and non-Sraffian Standard commodities, respectively (also see Sect. 2.2.1.3).

The MAED of labour-commanded prices from labour values, i.e. the mean absolute deviation of $\widetilde{\mathbf{p}}_w$ from $\tilde{\mathbf{v}}$, is defined as

$$\text{MAED} \equiv n^{-1}\sum_{j=1}^{n}\left|\left(\widetilde{p}_{wj} - \widetilde{v}_j\right)\widetilde{v}_j^{-1}\right| \tag{5.29}$$

Substituting Eq. 5.28 in Eq. 5.29 yields

$$\text{MAED} = n^{-1}\left(d_1 + \sum_{k=2}^{n} d_k\right) \tag{5.30}$$

where $d_1 \equiv \rho(1-\rho)^{-1}$ equals the profit-wage ratio in the SSS (and, at the same time, the elasticity of $\widetilde{p}_{w1}$ with respect to ρ), a strictly increasing and convex function of ρ, tending to infinity as ρ approaches 1 from below, and

$$d_k \equiv \left|\rho\lambda_{\mathbf{J}k}(1 - \rho\lambda_{\mathbf{J}k})^{-1}\right| = \rho|\lambda_{\mathbf{J}k}||1 - \rho\lambda_{\mathbf{J}k}|^{-1} \tag{5.31}$$

equals the moduli of the profit-wage ratios in the non-SSSs.[25]

Now consider the following four cases:

(i) If $\rho|\lambda_{\mathbf{J}k}| > 0$, then

$$d_k \leq \rho|\lambda_{\mathbf{J}k}|(1 - \rho|\lambda_{\mathbf{J}k}|)^{-1} = \rho\left(|\lambda_{\mathbf{J}k}|^{-1} - \rho\right)^{-1} < d_1 \tag{5.32}$$

which implies that

$$\text{MAED} < n^{-1}[d_1 + (n-1)d_1] = d_1 \tag{5.33}$$

(ii) If the moduli of the last *n*–*v*, $1 \leq v \leq n-1$, eigenvalues are sufficiently small that can be considered as negligible, then Eq. 5.30 reduces to

---

[25] For instance, the 'root-mean-square-percent-error' or the distances *à la* Steedman-Tomkins (consider Chap. 4) lead to more complicated expressions. Thus, it is much more convenient to focus on the MAED.

$$\mathrm{MAED} \approx \mathrm{MAED}_1 \equiv n^{-1} d_1, \ \text{ if } \ v = 1 \tag{5.34}$$

and

$$\mathrm{MAED} \approx \mathrm{MAED}_\nu \equiv n^{-1}(d_1 + \sum_{k=2}^{\nu} d_k), \ \text{ if } \ v \geq 2 \tag{5.34a}$$

(iii) If $\rho|\lambda_{\mathbf{J}k}| << 1$, which implies that

$$\widetilde{p}_{wj}\widetilde{v}_j^{-1} = \left(1 - \rho\lambda_{\mathbf{J}j}\right)^{-1} \approx 1 + \rho\lambda_{\mathbf{J}j}$$

then

$$\mathrm{MAED} \approx \mathrm{MAED}_\mathrm{L} \equiv n^{-1}\rho\left(1 + \sum_{k=2}^{n} |\lambda_{\mathbf{J}k}|\right) \tag{5.35}$$

which is a linear approximation of the MAED.

(iv) If $rank[\mathbf{J}] = 1$, then

$$\mathrm{MAED} = \mathrm{MAED}_1 \tag{5.36}$$

i.e. the MAED equals the profit-wage ratio in the SSS divided by the number of produced commodities.

Hence, for the general case, we can write

$$\mathrm{MAED}_\nu \leq \mathrm{MAED} \leq d_1 \tag{5.37}$$

Furthermore, since $\lambda_{\mathbf{J}k} = \alpha \pm i\beta$, Eq. 5.31 can be rewritten as

$$d_k = \rho|\lambda_{\mathbf{J}k}|D_k$$

where $D_k \equiv \left[1 - 2\rho\alpha + (\rho|\lambda_{\mathbf{J}k}|)^2\right]^{-0.5}$. Taking the first partial derivatives of d_k^2 with respect to ρ, α and β, i.e.

$2|\lambda_{\mathbf{J}k}|^2\rho(1-\rho\alpha)D_k^4, 2\rho^2\left[\alpha + \rho\left(\beta^2 - \alpha^2\right)\right]D_k^4$ and $2\beta\rho^2(1-2\rho\alpha)D_k^4$ respectively, it follows that d_k:

(i) Increases with increasing ρ, since $\rho\alpha < 1$
(ii) Increases with $\alpha > 0$
(iii) Decreases with $\alpha < 0$, when $\beta \leq \alpha$
(iv) Decreases with $\alpha < 0$ for $\rho < -\alpha(\beta^2 - \alpha^2)^{-1}(< 1)$, when $\alpha(\alpha-1) < \beta^2$
(v) Increases with $|\beta|$, when $\alpha \leq 0$
(vi) Increases with $|\beta|$ for $\rho < (2\alpha)^{-1}(> 2^{-1})$, when $\alpha > 0$ (see, for instance, Fig. 5.20a, where $\alpha = -0.4$ or -0.1 and $\beta = 0.8$, and Fig. 5.20b, where

Fig. 5.20 Components of the MAED as functions of the relative profit rate

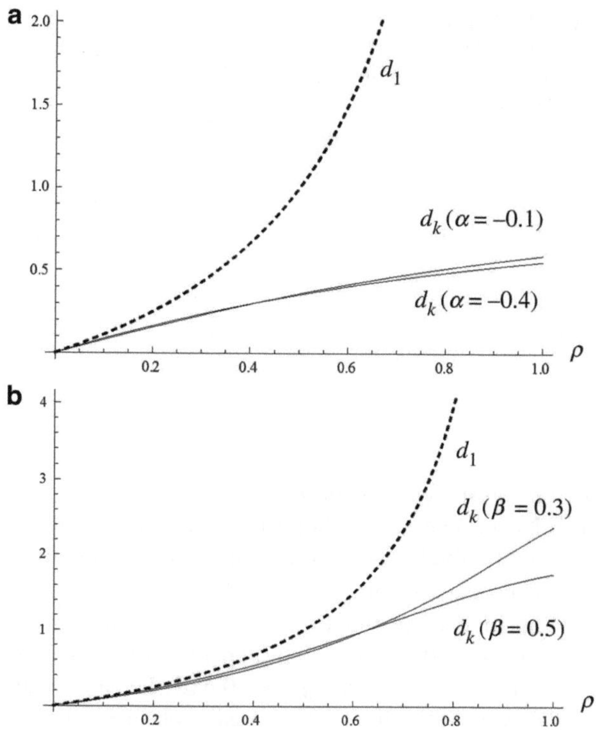

$\alpha = 0.8$ and $\beta = 0.3$ or $\beta = 0.5$; the dotted line represents d_1, and the solid lines represent d_k)

Finally, consider the first derivative, with respect to ρ, of $\left(d_k d_1^{-1}\right)^2$, i.e.

$$2\left(d_k d_1^{-3}\right)\left(\dot{d}_k d_1 - d_k \dot{d}_1\right) = -2|\lambda_{Jk}|^2(1-\rho)\left[(1-\alpha)(1-\rho\alpha)+\rho\beta^2\right]D_k^4$$

Its negativity implies $d_k \dot{d}_1 - \dot{d}_k d_1 > 0$, which in its turn implies $\dot{d}_1 - \dot{d}_k > 0$, since $0 < d_k < d_1$ for $\rho > 0$ (see relation (5.32)). It then follows that:

(i) The relative error between the MAED and the MAED_1, i.e.

$$\text{RE}_1 \equiv 1 - \text{MAED}_1(\text{MAED})^{-1} = 1 - \left(1 + \sum_{k=2}^{n} d_k {d_1}^{-1}\right)^{-1} \tag{5.38}$$

or, alternatively, the accuracy of the approximation (5.34), is a strictly decreasing function of ρ, tending to $\left(\sum_{k=2}^{n}|\lambda_{Jk}|\right)\left(1+\sum_{k=2}^{n}\lambda_{Jk}\right)^{-1}$ (tending to 0) as ρ tends to 0 (tends to 1).

Fig. 5.21 Relative errors between the MAED and the MAED$_2$ as functions of the relative profit rate

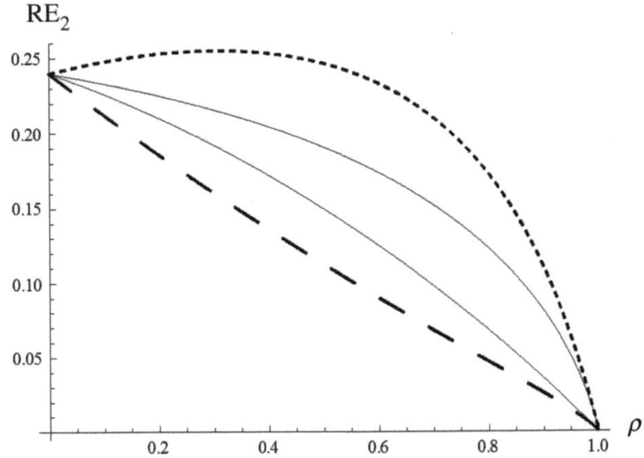

(ii) d_1–d_k increases with ρ.

(iii) Nevertheless, the relative error between the MAED and the MAED$_\nu$, $\nu \geq 2$, or, alternatively, the accuracy of the approximation (5.34a), does not necessarily decrease monotonically with ρ, since $d_{k-1}d_k^{-1}$, $k \geq 3$, is not necessarily an increasing function of ρ. See, for instance, Fig. 5.21, where $n = 3$ and (a) $\lambda_{J2} = 0.9$, $\lambda_{J3} = 0.6$ (upper solid line); (b) $\lambda_{J2} = -0.9$, $\lambda_{J3} = 0.6$ (dotted line); (c) $\lambda_{J2} = 0.9$, $\lambda_{J3} = -0.6$ (dashed line); and (d) $\lambda_{J2} = -0.9$, $\lambda_{J3} = -0.6$ (lower solid line). It is easily checked that a necessary condition for a non-monotonic RE$_2$ is $\{\lambda_{J2} < 0,\ \lambda_{J3} > 0\}$.

Thus, we conclude that the MAED constitutes a simple measure of price-labour value deviation. In effect, this measure:

(i) Leads to an algebraically simple, monotonic and economically interpretable expression
(ii) Does not require the prior computation of the values and prices
(iii) Provides a transparent separation between the effects of income distribution, as represented by ρ, and of the technical conditions of production, as represented by $|\lambda_{\mathbf{J}k}|$.[26]

It goes without saying that, depending on her/his theoretical viewpoint or his aim, the observer may use one of the numeraire-free measures: the said properties (ii) and (iii) continue to hold, while it is expected that, for realistic values of the

[26] The effects of technical changes on the eigenvalues of $\mathbf{A}$ (and, therefore, on $\lambda_{\mathbf{J}k}$) are unknown a priori. It could be noted that the first partial derivatives of $\lambda_{\mathbf{A}j}$ with respect to the elements of $\mathbf{A}$ are given by

$$\partial\lambda_{\mathbf{A}j}/\partial\mathbf{A} \equiv \left[\partial\lambda_{\mathbf{A}j}/\partial a_{ij}\right] = \left(\mathbf{y}_{\mathbf{A}j}\mathbf{x}_{\mathbf{A}j}^{\mathrm{T}}\right)^{-1}\left(\mathbf{y}_{\mathbf{A}j}^{\mathrm{T}}\mathbf{x}_{\mathbf{A}j}\right)$$

(see, e.g. Phillips 1982 and Ipsen 1998).

Table 5.15 Non-dominant eigenvalues and actual relative profit rate for the circulating capital case; Greece, 1988–1997

λ_{Jk}	λ_{Jk}	λ_{Jk}	λ_{Jk}	λ_{Jk}
1988	**1989**	**1990**	**1991**	**1992**
0.643	0.683	0.675	0.657	0.624
0.416	0.436	0.418	0.397	$0.442 \pm i0.023$
0.409	$0.376 \pm i0.025$	$0.376 \pm i0.011$	$0.382 \pm i0.016$	0.406
0.361	0.308	0.311	0.326	0.308
0.259	$0.199 \pm i0.060$	$0.207 \pm i0.069$	$0.217 \pm i0.065$	$0.230 \pm i0.075$
$0.178 \pm i0.0588$	0.104	0.110	0.101	0.108
$0.065 \pm i0.052$	$0.067 \pm i0.047$	$-0.058 \pm i0.068$	$-0.066 \pm i0.068$	$-0.075 \pm i0.073$
$-0.054 \pm i0.057$	$-0.052 \pm i0.062$	$0.066 \pm i0.046$	$0.063 \pm i0.046$	$0.068 \pm i0.044$
$0.070 \pm i0.013$	$0.028 \pm i0.013$	0.039	$0.030 \pm i0.015$	0.053
$-0.017 \pm i0.022$	$-0.015 \pm i0.018$	0.028	$-0.013 \pm i0.018$	0.029
0.020	−0.007	$-0.013 \pm i0.018$	0.008	$-0.017 \pm i0.021$
−0.009	0.006	0.009	−0.005	−0.005
0.006	–	−0.006	–	0.003
ρ^a	ρ^a	ρ^a	ρ^a	ρ^a
0.411	0.414	0.399	0.409	0.420
1993	**1994**	**1995**	**1996**	**1997**
0.667	0.678	0.655	0.664	0.641
0.433	0.420	$0.382 \pm i0.008$	$0.382 \pm i0.008$	0.350
0.353	0.357	0.281	0.313	0.307
0.320	0.327	0.246	0.233	0.279
0.268	0.261	$0.196 \pm i0.050$	$0.204 \pm i0.062$	$0.238 \pm i0.072$
$0.224 \pm i0.069$	$0.199 \pm i0.057$	0.098	0.098	0.210
0.110	0.109	$-0.066 \pm i0.064$	$0.083 \pm i0.029$	0.103
$-0.075 \pm i0.073$	$-0.071 \pm i0.066$	$0.077 \pm i0.036$	$-0.058 \pm i0.064$	$-0.066 \pm i0.072$
0.083	$0.071 \pm i0.041$	$0.019 \pm i0.013$	0.072	0.087
$0.058 \pm i0.037$	0.059	$-0.010 \pm i0.011$	$-0.016 \pm i0.024$	0.042
$-0.015 \pm i0.021$	$-0.013 \pm i0.023$	0.005	0.019	$0.027 \pm i0.022$
0.017	0.023	−0.004	0.002	$-0.009 \pm i0.015$
−0.006	−0.007	–	−0.001	0.013
0.002	0.006	–	–	0.001
ρ^a	ρ^a	ρ^a	ρ^a	ρ^a
0.388	0.421	0.419	0.423	0.438

relative profit rate, all these measures (as well as the traditional ones) will tend to be close to each other.

The application of this analysis to the SIOTs of the Greek economy gives the results summarized in Tables 5.15, 5.16 and 5.17 (we assume that wages are paid at the *end* of the production period).

Table 5.16 The MAED (%) and its approximations for the circulating capital case; Greece, 1988–1997

		1988	1989	1990	1991	1992	1993	1994	1995	1996	1997
$\rho=\rho^{a}$	MAED	11.3	11.8	11.3	11.6	12.5	10.7	11.8	11.3	11.7	11.7
	$MAED_1$	3.7	3.7	3.5	3.6	3.8	3.3	3.8	3.8	3.9	4.1
	$MAED_5$	8.6	8.9	8.3	8.5	9.2	7.8	8.8	8.5	8.7	8.7
	RE_1	67.3	68.6	69.1	69.0	69.6	69.2	67.8	66.4	66.7	65.0
	RE_5	23.9	24.6	26.5	26.7	26.4	27.1	25.4	24.8	25.6	25.6
$\rho=0.9$	MAED	69.8	71.6	71.4	71.0	72.0	70.6	70.4	68.7	69.5	67.6
	$MAED_1$	47.4	47.4	47.4	47.4	47.4	47.4	47.4	47.4	47.4	47.4
	$MAED_5$	63.3	64.6	64.1	63.4	64.1	63.2	63.5	62.2	62.8	60.7
	RE_1	32.1	33.8	33.6	33.2	34.2	32.9	32.7	31.0	31.8	29.9
	RE_5	9.3	9.8	10.2	10.7	11.0	10.5	9.8	9.5	9.6	10.2

Table 5.17 The nonzero non-dominant eigenvalues, the MAED (%) and its approximations for the fixed capital case; Greece, 1970

λ_{Jk}	ρ	MAED	$MAED_1$	$MAED_5$	$MAED_L$	RE_1	RE_5	RE_L
−0.035	0.328	1.62	1.48	1.59	1.13	8.64	1.85	30.25
$-0.002 \pm i0.033$	0.900	27.65	27.27	27.59	3.11	1.37	0.22	88.75
−0.015								
0.011								
$0.002 \pm i0.004$								
0.002								
−0.002								
0.0004								
$-0.0002 \pm i0.0003$								
0.0001								
$(-2.62 \pm i3.56)$E-19								
−2.03E-21								

Tables 5.15 and 5.16 are associated with the flow SIOTs, spanning the period 1988–1997. Table 5.15 reports (i) λ_{Jk} and (ii) the actual relative profit rate, ρ^{a} (also consider Tables 3.2 and 5.1).

Table 5.16 reports, in percentage terms, the MAED, $MAED_1$ and $MAED_5$ of $\widetilde{\mathbf{p}}_{w}$ from $\tilde{\mathbf{v}}$, and the relevant relative errors (see Eqs. 5.30 and 5.38 and approximations (5.34) and (5.34a)) at $\rho=\rho^{a}$ and $\rho=0.9$ (i.e. a 'high', somewhat unrealistic value), while Fig. 5.22 displays these errors as functions of ρ, for the representative years 1988 (dotted lines) and 1997 (solid lines; compare with Fig. 5.21). Thus, it is observed that approximations of the MAED on the basis of only a few of the largest modulus eigenvalues are not so bad and the errors RE_5 decrease monotonically with ρ. Clearly, these findings are due, respectively, to the following 'stylized facts' (see Sect. 5.3.1): (i) the first non-dominant eigenvalues fall quite rapidly and (ii) the negative eigenvalues, as well as the complex eigenvalues with negative real part, tend to appear in the lower ranks, while the (positive) real part of complex eigenvalues that appear in the higher ranks is much larger than the imaginary part.

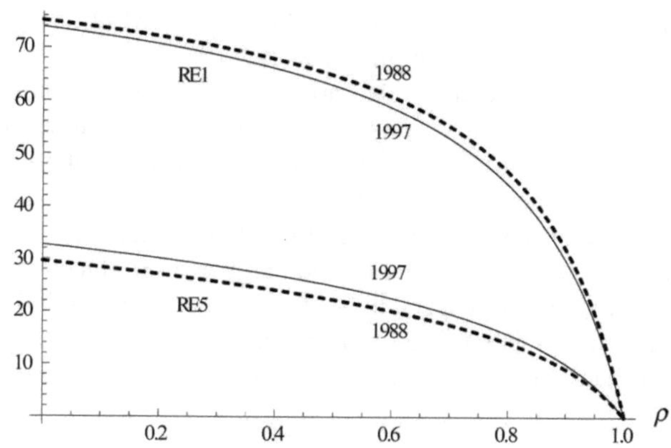

Fig. 5.22 Relative errors (%) between the MAED and its approximations as functions of the relative profit rate for the circulating capital case; Greece, 1988 and 1997

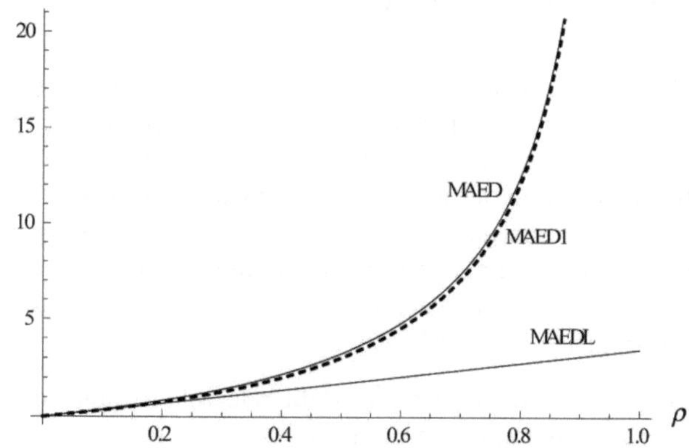

Fig. 5.23 The MAED (%), MAED_1 (%) and MAED_L (%) as functions of the relative profit rate for the fixed capital case; Greece, 1970

Table 5.17 is associated with the SIOT of the Greek economy for the year 1970 and the fixed capital case with a uniform profit rate.[27] It reports (i) the nonzero non-dominant eigenvalues of $\mathbf{J}$ (all the zero eigenvalues come from the fact that $\mathbf{A}^C$ is reducible without self-reproducing non-basics) and (ii) the MAED, MAED_ν, where $\nu = 1$ or 5, $\mathrm{MAD}_L \cong 33^{-1}(\rho 1.141)$ (see relation (5.35)), RE_ν and RE_L, at $\rho = \rho^a \cong 0.328$ (actual value) and $\rho = 0.9$. Thus, it is observed that the moduli of the non-dominant eigenvalues fall even more abruptly and, therefore, the approximation of the MAED through the MAED_1 works pretty well (also see Fig. 5.23, which displays the MAED, MAED_1 and MAED_L as functions of ρ; it is easily checked that $\mathrm{MAED}_1 > \mathrm{MAED}_L$ for $\rho > 0.124$). Taking also into account the results reported in Table 5.5, where $|\lambda_{J2}|^{-1}$ is in the range of 1.8 (USA, 1972) to 15.9 (Korea, 2000) and $|\lambda_{J3}|^{-1}$ is in the range of 8.5 (USA, 1947) to 16.9 (Korea,

[27] We postulate that $\mathbf{H} \equiv \mathbf{A}^C\left[\mathbf{I} - \left(\mathbf{A} + \mathbf{A}^D\right)\right]^{-1}$ (see Eq. 2.16a). It is also noted that the flow SIOT for the year 1970 (see Table 5.1) gives results similar to those reported in Tables 5.15 and 5.16.

1995), it is reasonable to expect that the MAED_1 is a good (and easily computed) approximation for empirical work.

The labour-commanded prices of the Standard commodities depend in a simple way on the relative profit rate and the eigenvalues of the vertically integrated technical coefficients matrix. This implies that there is a basis for constructing workable measures of price-labour value deviation. In actual economies, the MAED of labour-commanded prices from labour values tends to the profit-wage ratio in the SSS divided by the number of produced commodities. Thus, it can be concluded that, especially in the case of fixed capital (*à la* Leontief-Bródy), the quantity of labour that can be purchased by the *Sraffian* Standard net product provides a tangible and useful measure of price-labour value deviation.

5.4 Concluding Remarks

On the basis of spectral decompositions of linear single-product systems, it has been shown that main aspects of the wage-price-profit rate relationships (and, implicitly, of the consumption-output-growth rate relationships) depend to a great extent on the distribution of the characteristic values of the system matrices. The examination of input-output data of many diverse economies suggested that the majority of the non-dominant eigenvalues and singular values concentrate at very low values, and this means that the actual systems can be adequately described by only a few non-Sraffian Standard systems. It then follows that:

(i) The production price-profit rate relationship tends to be monotonic and its approximation through low-order spectral formulae works extremely well.
(ii) A homographic approximation to the wage-profit curve is empirically powerful.
(iii) The relative price effects of total productivity shift are, more often than not, governed by the traditional labour cost condition.
(iv) The mean absolute eigen-deviation of labour-commanded prices from labour values tends to the profit-wage ratio in the Sraffian Standard system divided by the number of produced commodities.

The results of this exploration indicate not the irrelevance of Sraffian analysis but rather that, within the economically significant interval of the profit rate, there is room for using corn-tractor or three-industry models as surrogates for actual single-product systems (or, to be precise, for their SIOT simulacra). More specifically, it appears that little is gained by considering higher dimensions and a lot is lost by postulating a one-commodity world. If this is indeed the case, our findings may be of some importance for both the theory and the empirics of capital.

Future research should primarily focus on the joint production case and then provide relevant evidence from the Supply and Use Tables of actual economies.

References

Aruka, Y. (1991). Generalized Goodwin's theorems on general coordinates. *Structural Change and Economic Dynamics, 2*(1), 69–91. Reprinted in Y. Aruka (Ed.) (2011), Complexities of production and interacting human behaviour (pp. 39–66). Heidelberg: Physica-Verlag.

Bailey, K. D. (1985). Entropy measures of inequality. *Sociological Inquiry, 55*(2), 200–211.

Bidard, C., & Ehrbar, H. G. (2007). Relative prices in the classical theory: Facts and figures. *Bulletin of Political Economy, 1*(2), 161–211.

Bienenfeld, M. (1988). Regularity in price changes as an effect of changes in distribution. *Cambridge Journal of Economics, 12*(2), 247–255.

Bródy, A. (1997). The second eigenvalue of the Leontief matrix. *Economic Systems Research, 9* (3), 253–258.

Cozzi, T. (1990). A comparison between Goodwin's normalized general coordinates and Pasinetti's vertical integration methods. In K. Velupillai (Ed.), *Nonlinear and multisectoral macrodynamics* (pp. 165–172). New York: New York University Press.

Ding, J., & Zhou, A. (2007). Eigenvalues of rank-one updated matrices with some applications. *Applied Mathematics Letters, 20*(12), 1223–1226.

Ding, J., & Zhou, A. (2008). Characteristic polynomials of some perturbed matrices. *Applied Mathematics and Computation, 199*(2), 631–636.

Finkelstein, M. O., & Friedberg, R. M. (1967). The application of an entropy theory of concentration to the Clayton act. *The Yale Law Journal, 76*(4), 677–717.

Flaschel, P. (2010). *Topics in classical micro- and macroeconomics. Elements of a critique of neoricardian theory*. Heidelberg: Springer.

Goodwin, R. M. (1976). Use of normalized general co-ordinates in linear value and distribution theory. In K. R. Polenske & J. V. Skolka (Eds.), *Advances in input-output analysis* (pp. 581–602). Cambridge, MA: Ballinger.

Goodwin, R. M. (1977). Capital theory in orthogonalised general co-ordinates. In R. M. Goodwin (Eds.), (1983), *Essays in linear economic structures* (pp. 153–172). London: Macmillan.

Goodwin, R. M. (1984). Disaggregating models of fluctuating growth. In R. M. Goodwin, M. Krüger, & A. Vercelli (Eds.), *Nonlinear models of fluctuating growth* (pp. 67–72). Berlin: Springer.

Hartfiel, D. J., & Meyer, C. D. (1998). On the structure of stochastic matrices with a subdominant eigenvalue near 1. *Linear Algebra and its Applications, 272*(1–3), 193–203.

Haveliwala, T. H., & Kamvar, S. D. (2003). *The second eigenvalue of the Google matrix* (Technical Report 2003-20). Stanford: Computer Science Department, Stanford University.

Horn, R. A., & Johnson, C. R. (1991). *Topics in matrix analysis*. Cambridge: Cambridge University Press.

Iliadi, F., Mariolis, T., Soklis, G., & Tsoulfidis, L. (2014). Bienenfeld's approximation of production prices and eigenvalue distribution: Further evidence from five European economies. *Contributions to Political Economy, 33*(1), 35–54.

Ipsen, I. C. F. (1998). Relative perturbation results for matrix eigenvalues and singular values. *Acta Numerica, 7*, 151–201.

Jasso, G. (1982). Measuring inequality: Using the geometric mean/arithmetic mean ratio. *Sociological Methods and Research, 10*(3), 303–326.

Juillard, M. (1986). *The input-output database for a departmental study of the US economy*. New York: New School for Social Research. Mimeo.

Laffey, T. J., & Šmigoc, E. (2006). Nonnegative realization of spectra having negative real parts. *Linear Algebra and its Applications, 416*(1), 148–159.

Mainwaring, L. (1978). The interest rate equalisation theorem with non-traded goods. *Journal of International Economics, 8*(1), 11–19. Reprinted in I. Steedman (Ed.) (1979), *Fundamental Issues in Trade Theory* (pp. 90–98). London: Macmillan.

Mainwaring, L., & Steedman, I. (2000). On the probability of re-switching and capital reversing in a two-sector Sraffian model. In H. D. Kurz (Ed.), *Critical essays on Piero Sraffa's legacy in economics* (pp. 323–354). Cambridge: Cambridge University Press.

Mariolis, T. (2004). A Sraffian approach to the Stolper-Samuelson theorem. *Asian-African Journal of Economics and Econometrics, 4*(1), 1–11.

Mariolis, T. (2011). A simple measure of price-labour value deviation. *Metroeconomica, 62*(4), 605–611.

Mariolis, T. (2013). Applying the mean absolute eigen-deviation of labour commanded prices from labour values to actual economies. *Applied Mathematical Sciences, 7*(104), 5193–5204.

Mariolis, T. (2015). Norm bounds and a homographic approximation for the wage-profit curve. *Metroeconomica, 66*(2), 263–283.

Mariolis, T., & Tsoulfidis, L. (2009). Decomposing the changes in production prices into 'capital-intensity' and 'price' effects: Theory and evidence from the Chinese economy. *Contributions to Political Economy, 28*(1), 1–22.

Mariolis, T., & Tsoulfidis, L. (2011). Eigenvalue distribution and the production price-profit rate relationship: Theory and empirical evidence. *Evolutionary and Institutional Economics Review, 8*(1), 87–122.

Mariolis, T., & Tsoulfidis, L. (2014). On Bródy's conjecture: Theory, facts and figures about instability of the US economy. *Economic Systems Research, 26*(2), 209–223.

Mariolis, T., Rodousakis, N., & Christodoulaki, A. (2015). Input-output evidence on the relative price effects of total productivity shift. *International Review of Applied Economics, 29*(2), 150–163.

Meyer, C. D. (2001). *Matrix analysis and applied linear algebra*. New York: Society for Industrial and Applied Mathematics.

Minc, H. (1988). *Nonnegative matrices*. New York: Wiley.

Ochoa, E. (1984). *Labor values and prices of production: An interindustry study of the U.S. economy, 1947–1972* (Ph.D. Dissertation, New School for Social Research, New York, USA).

Pasinetti, L. L. (1990). Normalised general coordinates and vertically integrated sectors in a simple case. In K. Velupillai (Ed.), *Nonlinear and multisectoral macrodynamics* (pp. 151–164). New York: New York University Press.

Phillips, P. C. B. (1982). A simple proof of the latent root sensitivity formula. *Economics Letters, 9*(1), 57–59.

Punzo, L. F. (1990). Generalised diagonal coordinates in dynamical analysis, and capital and distribution theory. In K. Velupillai (Ed.), *Nonlinear and multisectoral macrodynamics* (pp. 173–197). New York: New York University Press.

Rodousakis, N. (2012). Goodwin's Lotka-Volterra model in disaggregative form: A correction note. *Metroeconomica, 63*(4), 599–613.

Schefold, B. (2008). Families of strongly curved and of nearly linear wage curves: A contribution to the debate about the surrogate production function. *Bulletin of Political Economy, 2*(1), 1–24.

Schefold, B. (2013). Approximate surrogate production functions. *Cambridge Journal of Economics, 37*(5), 1161–1184.

Shaikh, A. M. (1998). The empirical strength of the labour theory of value. In R. Bellofiore (Ed.), *Marxian economics: A reappraisal* (Vol. 2, pp. 225–251). New York: St. Martin's Press.

Sraffa, P. (1960). *Production of commodities by means of commodities. Prelude to a critique of economic theory*. Cambridge: Cambridge University Press.

Steedman, I. (1999). Values do follow a simple rule! *Economic Systems Research, 11*(1), 5–11.

Steenge, A. E. (1995). Sraffa and Goodwin: A unifying framework for standards of value in the income distribution problem. *Journal of Economics, 62*(1), 55–75.

Steenge, A. E., & Thissen, M. J. P. M. (2005). A new matrix theorem: Interpretation in terms of internal trade structure and implications for dynamic systems. *Journal of Economics, 84*(1), 71–94.

Treitel, S., & Shanks, J. L. (1971). The design of multistage separable planar filters. *Institute of Electrical and Electronics Engineers Transactions on Geoscience Electronics, 9*(1), 10–27.

Tsoulfidis, L. (2010). *Competing schools of economic thought*. Heidelberg: Springer.

Chapter 6
Bródy's Stability and Disturbances

Abstract Bródy's conjecture regarding the instability of economies is submitted to an empirical test using input-output flow tables of varying size for the US economy, for the benchmark years 1997 and 2002, as well as for the period 1998–2011. The results obtained lend support to the view of increasing instability of the US economy over the period considered. Furthermore, our analysis shows that only a few vertically integrated industries are enough to shape the behaviour of the entire economy in the case of a disturbance. These results may, on the one hand, provide empirical evidence on the speed of convergence of Marxian iterative procedures 'transforming' labour values into production prices; on the other hand, they may usefully be contrasted with those derived in a parallel literature on aggregate fluctuations from microeconomic 'idiosyncratic' shocks.

Keywords Bródy's conjecture • Eigenvalue distribution • Idiosyncratic shocks • Marxian iterative procedures • Speed of convergence

6.1 Introduction

The Perron-Frobenius (P-F) theorems for semi-positive matrices imply that the maximum uniform profit-interest (and, at the same time, growth) factor is identified with the reciprocal of the dominant eigenvalue of the system input-output matrix, whereas the long-run relative price and output vectors are equal to the relevant eigenvectors (von Charasoff-von Neumann growth path; see Sect. 2.2.1.1).[1] However, as Goodwin (1970) notes:

> [I]n a system subject to continual and sometimes violent outside disturbances, the short-run outputs and prices will certainly diverge from these eigenvector values. (p.194)[2]

On the basis of the so-called power method or iteration,[3] Bródy (1997) noticed that, under certain conditions, if an arbitrary vector is repeatedly multiplied by the diagonalizable matrix of input-output coefficients, then the result converges to the

[1] This chapter draws on Mariolis and Tsoulfidis (2014).

[2] Also consider Samuelson (1970) and Hua (1984).

[3] See footnote 30 in Chap. 2.

© Springer Japan 2016
T. Mariolis, L. Tsoulfidis, *Modern Classical Economics and Reality*, Evolutionary Economics and Social Complexity Science 2, DOI 10.1007/978-4-431-55004-4_6

P-F (or equilibrium) eigenvector of that matrix.[4] This iterative process can be conceived of as

> [A]n exact analogue of certain dynamic market processes, and that likewise dynamic stability and convergence to a solution are analogues and are both assured by viability. (Goodwin 1970, p. 194)

In more general terms, it might be considered that

> [a]n electronic analogue (servo-mechanism) simulates the working of the market. This statement, however, may be reversed: the market simulates the electronic analogue computer. In other words, the market may be considered as a computer *sui generis* which serves to solve a system of simultaneous equations. [. . .] There may be (and there are) economic processes so complex in terms of the number of commodities and the type of equations involved that no computer can tackle them. Or it may be too costly to construct computers of such large capacity. In such cases nothing remains but to use the old-fashioned market servo-mechanism which has a much broader working capacity. (Lange 1967, pp. 159–160)

Bródy (1997) also argued that the speed of convergence depends on the ratio of the modulus of the subdominant eigenvalue to the dominant one. More precisely, the closer to zero that eigenvalue ratio is, the faster is the convergence to the equilibrium eigenvector. Then he experimented with large-sized randomly generated $n \times n$ Leontief-type matrices, in particular with identically and independently distributed (i.i.d.) entries, until he derived that, for n tending to infinity, that eigenvalue ratio in fact tends to zero, with speed $n^{-0.5}$: the estimated eigenvalues fluctuate around their theoretical distribution, but the amplitude of these deviations progressively dwindles. Hence, the larger the system is, the faster is the convergence, which is equivalent to saying that in a 'very large' system convergence to equilibrium may be attained in just a few iterations (for an extension of this approach to a monetary multiplier, where the flow of money is described as a Markov chain, see Leontief and Bródy 1993, Bródy 2000b).

Bródy's conjecture is not necessarily an investigation in pure mathematics, and right from the introduction of his paper, it becomes evident that the focus is not on mathematics per se but rather on the behaviour of actual single-product economies, as these are described by their flow and stock input-output structures. More specifically, he seems to assume that input-output data of dimensions of about 100 industries would be adequate enough for what is true for the large random matrices, and therefore the same theorem might be applicable to actual economies. Bidard and Schatteman (2001) argue that Bródy's conjecture is of statistical nature based on the 'law of large numbers', while Sun (2008) shows that it can be proved

[4] For an application of that method to the classical competitive process, which includes simultaneous adjustments in prices and outputs ('cross-dual dynamics'), see Egidi (1975). For more recent and general formulations of the cross-dual dynamics, see Steedman (1984), Duménil and Lévy (1989), Halpern and Molnár (1997), Bródy (2000a) and Flaschel (2010, Part 3) and the references therein.

using theorems provided by Goldberg et al. (2000) (also see Goldberg and Neumann 2003),[5] and remarks:

> One important insight implied by Bródy's hypothesis is that a market economy of a large size, once and if off its golden equilibrium, converges to equilibrium more quickly *than* one of a smaller size. In other words, if the economy is of a very large size, the market mechanism, allowing for many erroneous decisions independently made in different sectors, may work fairly efficiently in re-establishing its equilibrium in only a few steps. This can be seen as one more tribute to the superiority of the market mechanism over alternatives. (p. 430; emphasis added)

Meanwhile, surprisingly enough, there has been a parallel literature with essentially the same object of analysis, which is whether 'idiosyncratic' shocks buffeting particular industries may generate non-trifling aggregate fluctuations in the entire economy. In particular, the degree of volatility, measured by the standard deviation of the logarithm of aggregate output, is related to the degree of connectedness of particular industries with the rest of the economy. A low degree of connectedness implies that there are asymmetries across sectors and these might become the source of instability, which quickly propagates throughout the economy. This literature also encompasses the kind of ('downstream or upstream') networks that industries may develop with each other, using the supplier-buyer relations reflected in input-output tables, while the analytical techniques are mainly based on graph theory (Lucas 1977; Long and Plosser 1983; Acemoglu et al. 2012, amongst others).

In what follows, we present results for the US economy using the flow SIOTs of the years 1997 and 2002 (as well as for the period 1998–2011). For these two benchmark years, we have input-output data for industry classifications with dimensions varying from 12 up to 488 industries. More specifically, the tables for 1997 contain 12, 129 and 488 industries, whereas for the year 2002, the industry detail varies from 15 to 133 and 426 industries.[6] These input-output tables provide an ideal terrain to test Bródy's conjecture in the context of actual data and not just on randomly generated matrices of various dimensions. The reason is that Bródy's conjecture holds for randomly computer-generated matrices with sizes tending to infinity; however, to the best of our knowledge, there are no published SIOTs larger than 488 industries, for the US economy at least. Certainly given these dimensions, especially the extra-large one, we can submit the conjecture to what we think a fair empirical test. It should be stressed at the outset, however, that our investigation is carried out on the basis of circulating capital (intermediate inputs), as there are no suitable data on capital flow matrices which are necessary for the construction of the corresponding matrices of fixed capital stocks.

[5] It has also been repeatedly conjectured in the literature that, for n tending to infinity, the moduli of the non-dominant eigenvalues (as well as the normalized non-dominant singular values) of random stochastic matrices are uniformly distributed in the interval $[0, n^{-0.5}]$.

[6] The SIOTs are provided via the Bureau of Economic Analysis (BEA) website (http://www.bea.gov/iTable/iTable.cfm?ReqID=5&step=1).

The remainder of the chapter is structured as follows. Section 6.2 presents facts and figures from the US economy. Section 6.3 brings some empirical evidence on Marxian iterative procedures 'transforming' labour values into production prices. Section 6.4 offers a connection with the current research on microeconomic 'idiosyncratic' shocks. Finally, Sect. 6.5 concludes.[7]

6.2 Bródy's Conjecture: Facts and Figures from the US Economy

We shall focus on matrix **J** (instead of **A**), which is similar to a stochastic matrix, since its eigenvalue distribution regulates not only the behaviour of the dynamic price system (2.34)–(2.35) but also the shapes of the production price (output)-wage (consumption)-profit (growth) rate relationships (see Chaps. 2 and 5). It should also be recalled that:

(i) $|\lambda_{\mathbf{J}k}|\lambda_{\mathbf{J}1}^{-1} = |\lambda_{\mathbf{J}k}| < |\lambda_{\mathbf{A}k}|\lambda_{\mathbf{A}1}^{-1}$ holds for all k. Thus, by focusing on the eigenvalues of **J** rather than on those of **A**, we give more credence to Brody's conjecture.
(ii) $R_k \equiv \lambda_{\mathbf{A}k}^{-1} - 1 = \lambda_{\mathbf{H}k}^{-1}$ represents the maximum uniform profit (growth) rate of the kth eigensector (or non-Sraffian Standard system).
(iii) The location of the non-dominant eigenvalues, $\lambda_{\mathbf{J}k} = \alpha_k \pm i\beta_k$, in the complex plane could be considered as an index for the degree of capital heterogeneity.

The location of the eigenvalues in the complex plane for the year 1997 is displayed in the left-hand-side graphs of Fig. 6.1, while the right-hand-side graphs display the location of all the eigenvalues for the year 2002 (in the vertical dimension, the panels are ordered from high levels of aggregation at the top to low levels in the bottom part: $n = 12$, 129 and 488, for 1997, and $n = 15$, 133 and 426, for 2002). Moreover, Table 6.1 reports:

(i) The eigenvalues $\lambda_{\mathbf{H}1}$ and $|\lambda_{\mathbf{J}2}|$ to $|\lambda_{\mathbf{J}4}|$.
(ii) The top value of k for which $|\lambda_{\mathbf{J}k}| \geq 0.1$.
(iii) The arithmetic mean, AM, of all the $|\lambda_{\mathbf{J}k}|$. The symbol '*' indicates a complex eigenvalue, $\theta_k \equiv \arctan(\beta_k \alpha_k^{-1})$ denotes its argument, and the period of the produced oscillation equals $2\pi\theta_k^{-1}$.

From these results, which are absolutely consistent, both qualitatively and quantitatively, with those exposed in Chap. 5, we arrive at the following conclusions:

[7] The two Appendices, at the end of this chapter, briefly extend the analysis to consider the Sraffian multiplier (Appendix 1) and the price effects of currency devaluation (Appendix 2).

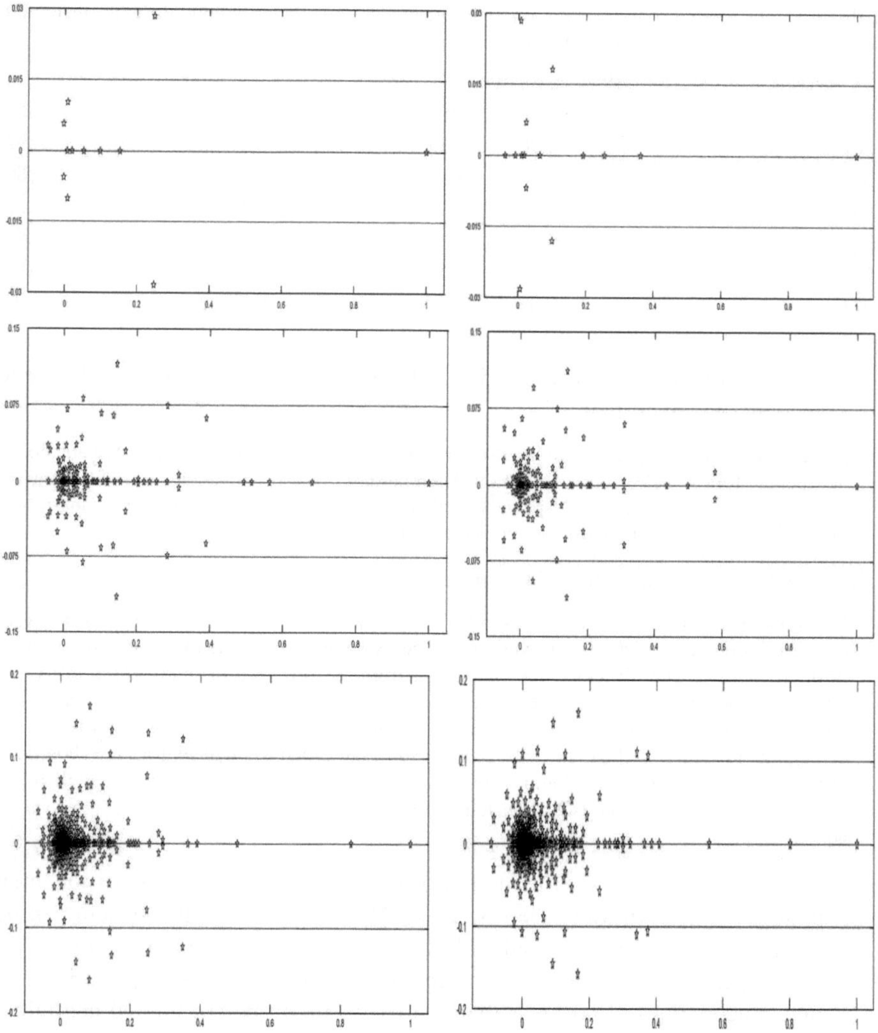

Fig. 6.1 The location of the eigenvalues in the complex plane; USA, 1997 ($n = 12, 129, 488$) and 2002 ($n = 15, 133, 426$)

(i) Although $\lambda_{\mathbf{H}1}$ for all aggregations are near to each other (in fact, for the year 2002, they differ in the third decimal), $|\lambda_{\mathbf{J}2}|$ increases with the size of the matrices casting doubt on Bródy's conjecture.[8] Both $|\lambda_{\mathbf{J}3}|$ and $|\lambda_{\mathbf{J}4}|$ increase from the small size matrices to the large ones and decreases for the extra-large

[8] Also consider the empirical evidence on $|\lambda_{\mathbf{A}2}|\lambda_{\mathbf{A}1}^{-1}$, from 22 European Union countries, and for the year 2005, where $n = 16, 30, 59$, provided by Gurgul and Wójtowicz (2015).

Table 6.1 The moduli of the second to fourth eigenvalues and the arithmetic mean of the moduli of the non-dominant eigenvalues; USA, 1997 and 2002

	1997			2002		
n	12	129	488	15	133	426
$\lambda_{\mathbf{H}1}$	0.97	0.96	1.06	0.92	0.92	0.92
$\lvert\lambda_{\mathbf{J}2}\rvert$	$0.25^{*}(\theta_2 \cong 6.55°)$	0.68	0.83	0.36	$0.58^{*}(\theta_2 \cong 1.35°)$	0.80
$\lvert\lambda_{\mathbf{J}3}\rvert$	0.25	0.56	0.51	0.25	0.58	0.56
$\lvert\lambda_{\mathbf{J}4}\rvert$	0.15	0.52	0.39	0.19	0.50	0.41
k	5	31	65	5	28	70
AM	0.08	0.08	0.05	0.08	0.08	0.05

matrices (also consider Table 5.2 and Fig. 5.6a, b). It should be taken into account, however, that

> [T]he coefficients computed from input-output tabulations are not evenly distributed and do not seem to follow a clear-cut distribution. Their pattern is skew, with a few large and many small and zero elements. [...] A special distribution and/or a special structure of the matrix may still permit exceptions [to the conjecture].[9] (Bródy's 1997, p. 255)

(ii) Bidard and Schatteman (2001) note:

> For economists, the crucial hypothesis in Bródy's conjecture is that the entries of I-O tables can be considered as i.i.d. random variables. The hypothesis is but the expression of our a priori ignorance. The difficulty does not come from the presence of many zeros in I-O tables but from specific linkages between some industries. It would be interesting to check whether the existence of patches of intense relationships between some sectors resists disaggregation and is sufficient to reverse the result established when the entries are chosen at random. [...] Since the randomness hypothesis is economically unrealistic, an application of the theorem to actual I-O tables remains subject to *practical tests*. (p. 297; emphasis added)

As Fig. 6.2 indicates, the moduli of the eigenvalues follow an exponential pattern of the form described by Eq. 5.21 and, therefore, the system can be adequately represented by only a few eigensectors or, alternatively, by only a few hyper-basic industries, which regulate its adjustment to equilibrium. In fact, since values of $\lvert\lambda_{\mathbf{J}k}\rvert$ less than 0.40–0.30 might be considered negligible from a 'practical' point of view (see Chap. 5), the extra-large matrices tend to correspond to reducible economies with low dimensions (say 12 or 13 industries at most).

(iii) The negative eigenvalues, as well as the complex eigenvalues with negative real part, tend to appear in the lower ranks, while the (positive) real part of complex eigenvalues that appear in the higher ranks is much larger than the imaginary part.

[9] Also see Molnár and Simonovits (1998), who examine deterministic matrices, and Białas and Gurgul (1998), whose focus is on column stochastic matrices.

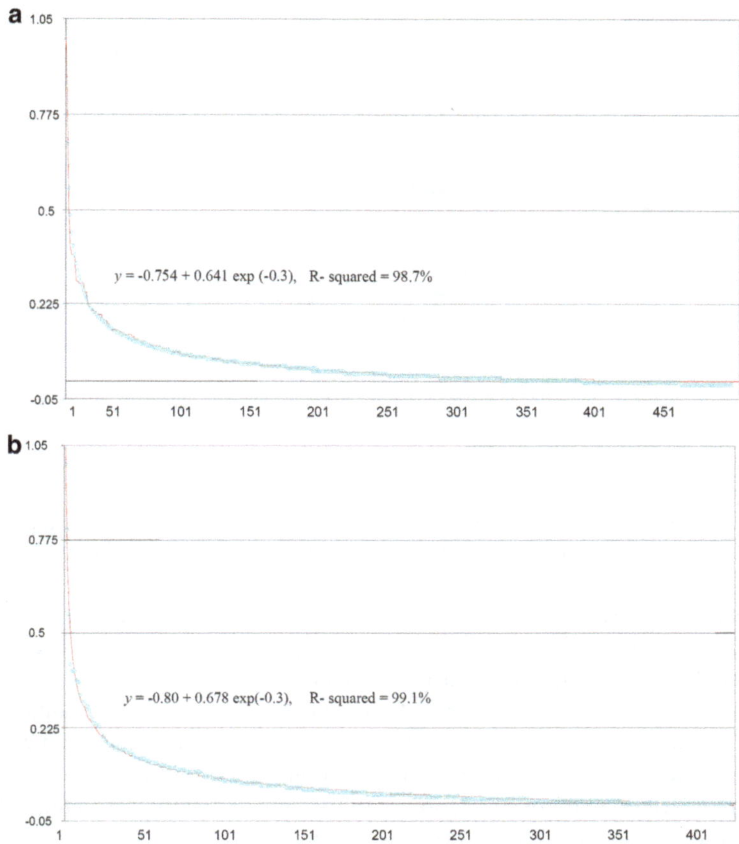

Fig. 6.2 Exponential fit of the moduli of the eigenvalues; USA, (**a**) 1997, $n = 488$; and (**b**) 2002, $n = 426$

Apart from the benchmark years 1997 and 2002, the BEA provides input-output data spanning the period 1998–2011, and the dimensions of these tables are of 15 and 65 industries. The industry structure and the methods of assembling the data are the same, and so we put together, in Fig. 6.3, $|\lambda_{J2}|$, $|\lambda_{J3}|$ and the *AM* of $|\lambda_{Jk}|$, in order to observe their evolution during a period of 14 years (we also display the linear regression trend lines). The time series results spanning the period 1998–2011 are consistent with the findings for the years 1997 and 2002. More specifically, for both the 65 and the 15 industry detail, $|\lambda_{J2}|$ follow upward trends and $(|\lambda_{J2}|)_{15} < (|\lambda_{J2}|)_{65}$. Moreover, $(|\lambda_{J3}|)_{15} < (|\lambda_{J3}|)_{65}$, where the former (the latter) follows a downward (upward) trend. Finally, for both 65 and 15 industry detail, the arithmetic means move pretty much parallel to the horizontal axis and, as expected, the $(AM)_{65}$ ($\cong$0.099 over the whole period) is somewhat higher than the $(AM)_{15}$ ($\cong$0.085 over the whole period) because the second and the third eigenvalues in the 15 industry structure are lower than those in the 65 industry structure.

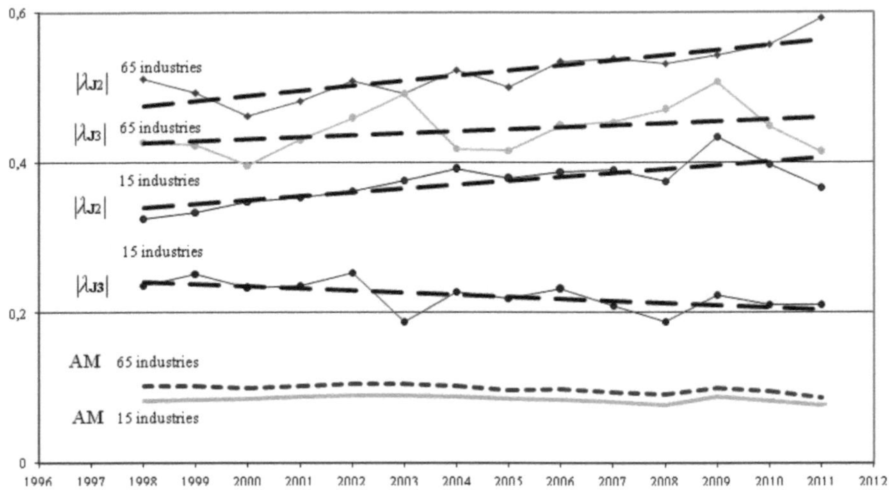

Fig. 6.3 The evolution of the moduli of the second and third eigenvalues and of the arithmetic mean of the moduli of the non-dominant eigenvalues; USA, period 1998–2011, $n = 15, 65$

To sum up, these findings do not support Bródy's conjecture. Since, however, hitherto produced empirical evidence suggests that, in the case of fixed capital (*à la* Leontief-Bródy), the eigenvalue decay is remarkably faster than that in the circulating capital case (see Tables 5.5, 5.17 and Fig. 5.8), it follows that Bródy's conjecture deserves further investigation. On the other hand, these same findings reveal that, regardless of the level of aggregation, actual single-product economies can be represented in terms of a 'core' of only a few vertically integrated industries that conditions the motion of the entire economic system.

6.3 Marxian Iterative Procedures

Now consider the Marxian iterative procedure (2.84) 'transforming' labour values into production prices, i.e.

$$\mathbf{p}^{(m)} = (1 + r^{(m-1)})\,\mathbf{p}^{(m-1)}\mathbf{C},\ \ 1 + r^{(m-1)} = (\mathbf{p}^{(m-1)}\mathbf{x}^{\mathrm{T}})(\mathbf{p}^{(m-1)}\mathbf{C}\mathbf{x}^{\mathrm{T}})^{-1},\ \ \mathbf{p}^{(0)} = \mathbf{v}$$

where $\mathbf{C} \equiv \mathbf{b}^{\mathrm{T}}\mathbf{l} + \mathbf{A}$ and $\mathbf{x}^{\mathrm{T}}$ is an arbitrary gross output vector.

The representative graphs in Fig. 6.4 correspond to (a) the 65×65 SIOTs of the US economy for the years 1998 and 2011 and (b) the ten SIOTs of the five European economies that we have already used in Chap. 5 (see Table 5.3). These graphs, the horizontal axes of which are plotted in logarithmic scale, display the moduli of the eigenvalues of $\mathbf{J}$ and of the normalized eigenvalues of $\mathbf{C}$. Moreover, Table 6.2 reports the dominant eigenvalue ratios, $|\lambda_{\bullet 2}|\lambda_{\bullet 1}^{-1}$, associated with the following matrices:

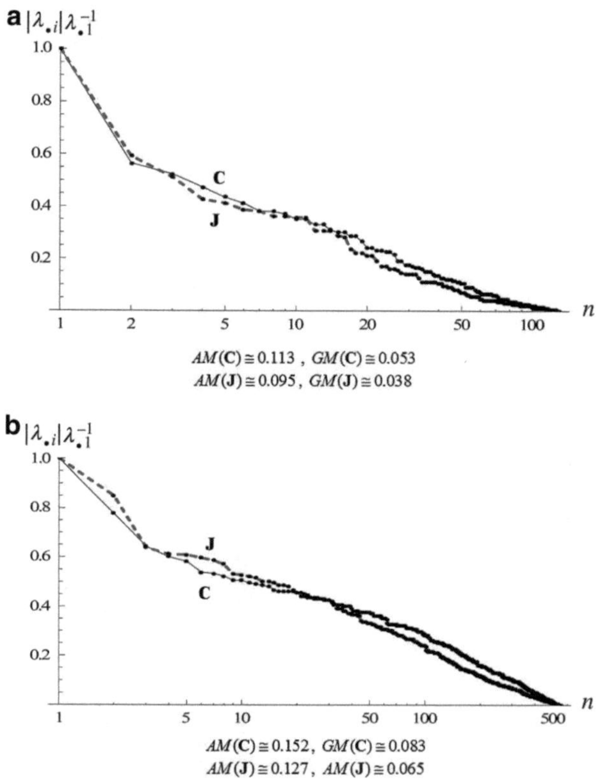

Fig. 6.4 The moduli of the normalized eigenvalues of matrices **C** and **J**; (**a**) US economy: two SIOTs, (**b**) five European economies: ten SIOTs

(i) **C**.

(ii) $\mathbf{\Gamma} \equiv \mathbf{A}\left[\mathbf{I} - \mathbf{b}^{\mathrm{T}}\mathbf{l}\right]^{-1} = \mathbf{A}\left[\mathbf{I} + \left(1 - \mathbf{l}\mathbf{b}^{\mathrm{T}}\right)^{-1}\mathbf{b}^{\mathrm{T}}\mathbf{l}\right]$.

(iii) $\mathbf{K} \equiv \mathbf{J}\left[\mathbf{I} - \mathbf{b}^{\mathrm{T}}\mathbf{v}\right]^{-1} = \mathbf{J}\left[\mathbf{I} + \left(1 - \mathbf{v}\mathbf{b}^{\mathrm{T}}\right)^{-1}\mathbf{b}^{\mathrm{T}}\mathbf{v}\right]$ (see Eqs. 2.4 and 2.19, respectively; also consider Tables 5.7 and 5.8).

From these results, we observe that the eigenvalues of **C** and **J** follow similar patterns and, at the same time, the spread between them is relatively narrow. It is expected, therefore, that, setting aside the Finnish economy for the year 2004, the procedure with iteration matrix **C** would converge quickly to the long-run equilibrium price vector and profit rate. Figure 6.5 is representative and shows the rapid convergence of $r^{(m-1)}\left(\lambda_{\mathbf{C}1}^{-1} - 1\right)^{-1}$ to 1:

(i) $\mathbf{x}^{\mathrm{T}}$ are identified with the corresponding actual gross output vectors, $\overline{\mathbf{x}}^{\mathrm{T}}$, while the normalized $d-$ distances between the vectors $\mathbf{x}_{\mathbf{C}1}^{\mathrm{T}}$ and $\overline{\mathbf{x}}^{\mathrm{T}}$ are almost 0.91 (Finland, 2004), 0.80 (Germany, 2002) and 0.61 (Sweden, 2005).

(ii) The normalized $d-$ distances between $\mathbf{p}^{(0)}$ and $\mathbf{y}_{\mathbf{C}1}$ are 0.15 (Finland, 2004), 0.13 (Germany, 2002) and 0.11 (Sweden, 2005), while those between $\mathbf{p}^{(1)}$ and $\mathbf{y}_{\mathbf{C}1}$ are 0.05, 0.03 and 0.03, respectively.

Table 6.2 The dominant eigenvalue ratios for alternative system matrices; USA and five European economies

	USA		Denmark		Finland		France		Germany		Sweden	
	1998	2011	2000	2004	1995	2004	1995	2005	2000	2002	1995	2005
$\lvert\lambda_{C2}\rvert\lambda_{\mathbf{C}1}^{-1}$	0.435	0.565	0.507	0.583	0.643	0.778	0.535	0.539	0.486	0.496	0.524	0.439
$\lvert\lambda_{\Gamma 2}\rvert\lambda_{\mathbf{\Gamma}1}^{-1}$	0.494	0.626	0.558	0.641	0.684	0.836	0.592	0.590	0.547	0.564	0.572	0.486
$\lvert\lambda_{K2}\rvert\lambda_{\mathbf{K}1}^{-1}$	0.244	0.367	0.297	0.364	0.397	0.605	0.315	0303	0.290	0.313	0.301	0.218

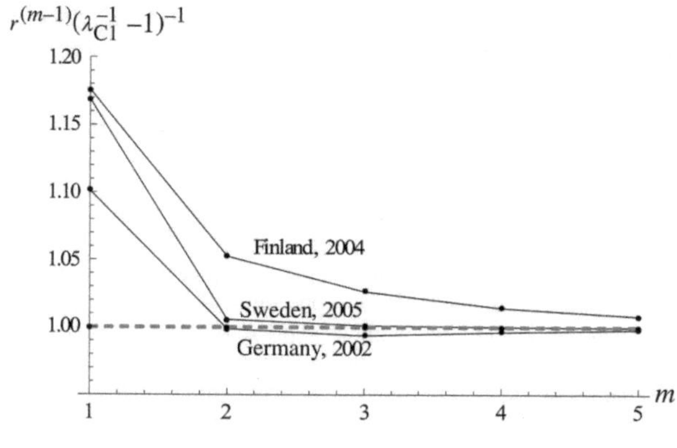

Fig. 6.5 The convergence of the Marxian procedure; three European economies

Finally, the same holds true, analogously, for the procedures with iteration matrices $\mathbf{\Gamma}$ and, in particular, $\mathbf{K}$ (setting aside the Finnish economy for the year 2004, $|\lambda_{\Gamma 2}|\lambda_{\Gamma 1}^{-1} < 0.690$ and $|\lambda_{\mathbf{K}2}|\lambda_{\mathbf{K}1}^{-1} < 0.400$; see Table 6.2).

6.4 Aggregate Fluctuations from Sectoral Shocks

According to Lucas' (1977) 'standard diversification argument', microeconomic 'idiosyncratic' shocks to firms (or disaggregated sectors) cannot generate sizable aggregate fluctuations. More precisely, as the number of sectors tends to infinity, aggregate volatility (defined as the standard deviation of the logarithm of aggregate output) tends to zero, at the rate implied by the 'law of large numbers', i.e. $n^{0.5}$. Nevertheless, in a recent paper, Acemoglu et al. (2012) contend that, in the general case, that rate is determined by the linkage structure of the networks naturally captured in input-output description of economic activities and, therefore, aggregate volatility depends directly on the asymmetry (or relative importance) in the roles that industries play as (direct and/or indirect) input suppliers to others. Asymmetric sectoral interconnections may imply that aggregate volatility decays at a rate slower than $n^{1-\gamma^{-1}}$, where $1 < \gamma < 2$, and that latter rates

> may have two related but distinct causes. First, they may be due to *first-order interconnections*: shocks to a sector that is a supplier to a disproportionally large number of other sectors propagate directly to those sectors. Second, they may be due to *higher-order interconnections*: low productivity in one sector leads to a reduction in production of not only its immediate downstream sectors but also a sequence of sectors interconnected to one another, creating cascade effects. (Acemoglu et al. 2012, p. 1981)

This approach is in sharp contrast to Lucas' (1977) averaging out process amounting to negligible aggregate effects and also ends the debate between Dupor (1999), who argued that, for a wide class of input-output structures, interdependence is a poor mechanism for turning independent sectoral shocks into aggregate fluctuations, and Horvath (1998, 2000), who argued against such a view and supported that the sparseness of the input-output matrix (which increases with disaggregation) contributes to increased volatility.

All the aforementioned papers build on Long and Plosser's (1983) multisectoral model of 'real business cycles', in which the total 'factor' productivity shocks are assumed to be i.i.d. over time and across sectors. It then follows that the matrix of the relative shares of the capital commodities in the cost of outputs, $\mathbf{\Theta}$ (see Sects. 2.4.2 and 5.3.3)

> provides the *only* intertemporal link between deviations of outputs [and prices] from their normal (expected) values. [. . .] Stability of the system is ensured if the eigenvalues of $\mathbf{\Theta}$ have modulus less than one. In our example, stability is guaranteed since $\mathbf{\Theta}$ is nonnegative, and the row sums, which are one minus labor's cost share in production, are strictly less than one. [. . .] [T]he output [and price] of good i depends on its own contemporaneous and lagged shocks as well as the past history of shocks to all of the other sectors. Given the nature of the assumptions above about [the productivity shocks], this propagation mechanism is completely summarized by $\mathbf{\Theta}$. (Long and Plosser 1983, pp. 53 and 55; using our symbol)

By applying their framework to the input-output data of the US economy, spanning the period 1972–2002, Acemoglu et al. (2012) find that (i) there exists a high degree of asymmetry in the US economy in terms of the roles that different sectors play as suppliers to others, consistent with the hypothesis that the interplay of sectoral shocks and network effects leads to sizable aggregate fluctuations (p. 2001) and (ii) aggregate volatility decays no faster than $n^{0.15}$ (p. 2002). Thus, they conclude that the intersectoral network of the US economy tends to resemble a 'star network' rather than a 'complete (or symmetric) network' (also see Acemoglu et al. 2010 and Carvalho 2014). Since the latter network corresponds to the case $\mathbf{J} \approx \mathbf{I}$, whereas the former corresponds to the case *rank* $[\mathbf{J}] \approx 1$ and its variants (see Sect. 5.2.1), and since matrix $\mathbf{J}$ accounts for both direct and indirect interconnections, it seems that there is room for combining these two lines of research (towards this direction, also consider Aruka 2015, Chap. 3).

6.5 Concluding Remarks

In his conclusions Bródy (1997) remarks that while one major undertaking in theoretical economies of the twentieth century focuses on the existence of equilibrium,

> [t]he question for the next [twenty-first] century seems to relate to whether the market can be rendered convergent. If not, why; if yes, how? (p. 257)

The results of our analysis for the US economy suggest that the ratio of the modulus of the subdominant eigenvalue to the dominant one increases both with the size of the input-output matrix and, for the same matrix size, over the years lending support to the view of increasing instability (in the sense of Bródy). Thus, it can be concluded that the actual input-output matrices do not share all the properties of random matrices. However, the fact that the majority of the non-dominant eigenvalues of the former matrices concentrates at low values indicates that (i) there are considerable quasi-linear dependencies amongst the technical conditions of production in many vertically integrated industries and (ii) only a few hyper-basic industries are sufficient enough to explain the movement of the aggregate economy in the case of (endogenous or exogenous) disturbances. Hence, future research should use not only flow but also capital stock and joint production data for a number of dissimilar economies and investigate the implications of the eigenvalue distributions for the stability properties of actual economies.

Appendix 1: On the Sraffian Multiplier

The concept of the Sraffian multiplier, for a closed economy of single production with circulating capital, homogeneous labour and two types of income (wages and profits), was introduced by Kurz (1985).[10] This multiplier is an $n \times n$ matrix that depends on the (i) technical conditions of production, (ii) income distribution (and commodity prices), (iii) savings ratios out of wages and profits and (iv) consumption patterns associated with the two types of income. Moreover, it includes, as special versions or limit cases, the usual Keynesian multiplier, the multipliers of the traditional input-output analysis and their Marxian versions.[11]

Although in a quite different algebraic form, the Sraffian multiplier had been essentially introduced by Metcalfe and Steedman (1981) in a model with the following characteristics: open economy of single production with circulating capital, non-competitive imports, homogeneous labour and uniform rates of profits (and growth), propensity to save and composition of consumption. Furthermore, Mariolis (2008b) (i) showed the mathematical equivalence between the Sraffian multiplier(s) derived from Kurz (1985) and Metcalfe and Steedman (1981) and (ii) extended the investigation of the latter to the case of pure joint production.

Assume that there are no non-competitive imports and that the price side of the system can be described by (see Sect. 2.2.3)

$$\mathbf{pB} = \mathbf{w\hat{l}} + \mathbf{pA}\left[\mathbf{I} + \hat{\mathbf{r}}\right] \tag{6.1}$$

where $\mathbf{w}$ ($w_j > 0$) denotes the $1 \times n$ vector of money wage rates, $\hat{\mathbf{l}}$ $(l_j > 0)$ the $n \times n$ diagonal matrix of direct labour coefficients, $\hat{\mathbf{r}}$ ($r_j > -1$ and $\hat{\mathbf{r}} \neq \mathbf{0}$) the $n \times n$ diagonal matrix of the given (and constant) values of the sectoral profit rates and $\mathbf{p}$ is identified with $\mathbf{e}$. Provided that $[\mathbf{B} - \mathbf{A}]$ is non-singular, Eq. 6.1 can be rewritten as

[10] What follows draws on Mariolis (2008a) and Mariolis and Soklis (2014).

[11] For the Keynesian multiplier, see, e.g. Blanchard et al. (2010, Chap. 3); Gnos and Rochon (2008) offer Kaleckian and post-Keynesian explorations of this multiplier. For the multipliers of the traditional input-output analysis, see, e.g. Miller and Blair (2009, Chap. 6) and ten Raa (2005, Chap. 3). Finally, for Marxian versions of the aforesaid multipliers, see, e.g. Lange (1970, Chaps. 2 and 3), Hartwig (2004), Trigg and Philp (2008) and Tsaliki and Tsoulfidis (2015, Chap. 2).

$$\mathbf{p} = \mathbf{w}\mathbf{V_B} + \mathbf{p}\widetilde{\mathbf{H}}_\mathbf{B} \tag{6.2}$$

where $\mathbf{V_B} \equiv \hat{\mathbf{l}}\,[\mathbf{B} - \mathbf{A}]^{-1}$ denotes the matrix of additive labour values, and $\widetilde{\mathbf{H}}_\mathbf{B} \equiv \mathbf{A}\hat{\bar{\mathbf{r}}}\,[\mathbf{B} - \mathbf{A}]^{-1}$.

Also assume that the quantity side of the economy can be described by (consider Sect. 2.2.1.4)

$$\mathbf{B}\mathbf{x}^\mathrm{T} = \mathbf{A}\mathbf{x}^\mathrm{T} + \mathbf{y}^\mathrm{T}$$

or

$$\mathbf{x}^\mathrm{T} = [\mathbf{B} - \mathbf{A}]^{-1}\mathbf{y}^\mathrm{T} \tag{6.3}$$

and

$$\mathbf{y}^\mathrm{T} = \mathbf{f}_w^\mathrm{T} + \mathbf{f}_p^\mathrm{T} - \mathbf{Im}^\mathrm{T} + \mathbf{d}^\mathrm{T}$$

or, setting $\mathbf{Im}^\mathrm{T} = \hat{\mathbf{m}}\,\mathbf{B}\mathbf{x}^\mathrm{T}$,

$$\mathbf{y}^\mathrm{T} = \mathbf{f}_w^\mathrm{T} + \mathbf{f}_p^\mathrm{T} - \hat{\mathbf{m}}\,\mathbf{B}\mathbf{x}^\mathrm{T} + \mathbf{d}^\mathrm{T} \tag{6.4}$$

where $\mathbf{x}^\mathrm{T}$ denotes the activity level vector, $\mathbf{y}^\mathrm{T}$ the vector of effective final demand, $\mathbf{f}_w^\mathrm{T}$ the vector of consumption demand out of wages, $\mathbf{f}_p^\mathrm{T}$ the vector of consumption demand out of profits, $\mathbf{Im}^\mathrm{T}$ the import demand vector, $\mathbf{d}^\mathrm{T}$ the autonomous demand vector (government expenditures, investments and exports) and $\hat{\mathbf{m}}$ the diagonal matrix of imports per unit of gross output of each commodity.

If $\mathbf{f}^\mathrm{T}$ denotes the uniform consumption pattern (associated with the two types of income), s_w denotes the saving ratio out of wages and s_p denotes the saving ratio out of profits, where $0 \leq s_w, s_p \leq 1$ (and s_w and s_p are not both zero and not both unity), then the consumption demands out of wages and out of profits, in physical terms, amount to (see Eqs. 6.2 and 6.3, which imply that $\hat{\mathbf{l}}\,\mathbf{x}^\mathrm{T} = \mathbf{V_B}\,\mathbf{y}^\mathrm{T}$ and $\mathbf{A}\hat{\bar{\mathbf{r}}}\,\mathbf{x}^\mathrm{T} = \widetilde{\mathbf{H}}_\mathbf{B}\,\mathbf{y}^\mathrm{T}$)

$$\mathbf{f}_w^\mathrm{T} = (1 - s_w)\sum_{j=1}^{n}\left(w_j l_j x_j\right)\left(\mathbf{p}\,\mathbf{f}^\mathrm{T}\right)^{-1}\mathbf{f}^\mathrm{T} = (1 - s_w)\left(\mathbf{w}\hat{\mathbf{l}}\,\mathbf{x}^\mathrm{T}\right)\left(\mathbf{p}\,\mathbf{f}^\mathrm{T}\right)^{-1}\mathbf{f}^\mathrm{T}$$

or

$$\mathbf{f}_w^\mathrm{T} = (1 - s_w)\left(\mathbf{w}\mathbf{V_B}\,\mathbf{y}^\mathrm{T}\right)\left(\left(\mathbf{p}\,\mathbf{f}^\mathrm{T}\right)^{-1}\mathbf{f}^\mathrm{T} \tag{6.5}$$

and

$$\mathbf{f}_p^{\mathrm{T}} = (1 - s_p)(\mathbf{pA}\hat{\bar{\mathbf{r}}}\mathbf{x}^{\mathrm{T}})(\mathbf{pf}^{\mathrm{T}})^{-1}\mathbf{f}^{\mathrm{T}} = (1 - s_p)\left(\mathbf{p}\widetilde{\mathbf{H}}_{\mathbf{B}}\mathbf{y}^{\mathrm{T}}\right)(\mathbf{pf}^{\mathrm{T}})^{-1}\mathbf{f}^{\mathrm{T}} \tag{6.6}$$

respectively.

Substituting Eqs. 6.5 and 6.6 into Eq. 6.4 leads to (take into account Eqs. 6.1 and 6.3 and that $(\mathbf{wV_B}\mathbf{y}^{\mathrm{T}})\mathbf{f}^{\mathrm{T}} = (\mathbf{f}^{\mathrm{T}}\mathbf{wV_B})\mathbf{y}^{\mathrm{T}}$, $\left(\mathbf{p}\widetilde{\mathbf{H}}_{\mathbf{B}}\mathbf{y}^{\mathrm{T}}\right)\mathbf{f}^{\mathrm{T}} = \left(\mathbf{f}^{\mathrm{T}}\mathbf{p}\widetilde{\mathbf{H}}_{\mathbf{B}}\right)\mathbf{y}^{\mathrm{T}}$):

$$\mathbf{y}^{\mathrm{T}} = \mathbf{\Lambda}\mathbf{y}^{\mathrm{T}} + \mathbf{d}^{\mathrm{T}} \tag{6.7}$$

where

$$\mathbf{\Lambda} \equiv (\mathbf{pf}^{\mathrm{T}})^{-1}\mathbf{f}^{\mathrm{T}}\left[\mathbf{p} - \left(s_w\mathbf{wV}_B + s_p\,\mathbf{p}\widetilde{\mathbf{H}}_{\mathbf{B}}\right)\right] - \hat{\mathbf{m}}\,\mathbf{B}[\mathbf{B} - \mathbf{A}]^{-1}$$

Provided that $[\mathbf{I} - \mathbf{\Lambda}]$ is non-singular, Eq. 6.7 can be uniquely solved for $\mathbf{y}^{\mathrm{T}}$:

$$\mathbf{y}^{\mathrm{T}} = \mathbf{\Pi}\mathbf{d}^{\mathrm{T}}$$

where $\mathbf{\Pi} \equiv [\mathbf{I} - \mathbf{\Lambda}]^{-1}$ is the Sraffian multiplier linking autonomous demand to net output. Consequently, the change on the money value of net output, Δ_y^i ('output multiplier') induced by the increase of one unit of the autonomous demand for commodity i, is given by

$$\Delta_y^i \equiv \mathbf{p}\mathbf{\Pi}\mathbf{e}_i^{\mathrm{T}}$$

If all the eigenvalues of $\mathbf{\Lambda}$ are less than 1 in modulus, then the dynamic multiplier process defined by (see Chipman 1950)

$$\mathbf{y}_t^{\mathrm{T}} = \mathbf{\Lambda}\mathbf{y}_{t-1}^{\mathrm{T}} + \Delta\mathbf{d}^{\mathrm{T}}, \quad t = 1, 2, \ldots \tag{6.8}$$

is stable (also consider Sect. 2.2.2). In that case, the number $-\log\lambda_{\max}[\mathbf{\Lambda}]$ is called the asymptotic rate of convergence (see, e.g. Berman and Plemmons 1994, Chap. 7) and provides a (rather) simple measure for the convergence rate of $\mathbf{y}_t^{\mathrm{T}}$ to $\mathbf{\Pi}(\Delta\mathbf{d}^{\mathrm{T}})$.

In the hypothetical (or heuristic) case where $\hat{\mathbf{m}} = \mathbf{0}$, $\mathbf{\Lambda}$ reduces to a rank-one matrix, i.e.

$$\mathbf{\Lambda}_0 \equiv (\mathbf{pf}^{\mathrm{T}})^{-1}\mathbf{f}^{\mathrm{T}}\left[\mathbf{p} - \left(s_w\mathbf{wV}_B + s_p\,\mathbf{p}\widetilde{\mathbf{H}}_{\mathbf{B}}\right)\right]$$

the non-zero eigenvalue of which equals

$$1 - (\mathbf{pf}^{\mathrm{T}})^{-1}\left(s_w\mathbf{wV}_B + s_p\,\mathbf{p}\widetilde{\mathbf{H}}_{\mathbf{B}}\right)\mathbf{f}^{\mathrm{T}}$$

or, invoking Eq. 6.2,

$$1-\left[s_w+\left(s_p-s_w\right)\left(\mathbf{p}\,\mathbf{f}^{\mathrm{T}}\right)^{-1}\mathbf{p}\widetilde{\mathbf{H}}_{\mathbf{B}}\,\mathbf{f}^{\mathrm{T}}\right]$$

Thus, the Sraffian multiplier reduces to

$$\boldsymbol{\Pi}_0\equiv\left[\mathbf{I}-\left(\mathbf{p}\,\mathbf{f}^{\mathrm{T}}\right)^{-1}\mathbf{f}^{\mathrm{T}}\left[\mathbf{p}-\left(s_w\mathbf{w}\mathbf{V}_{\mathbf{B}}+s_p\,\mathbf{p}\widetilde{\mathbf{H}}_{\mathbf{B}}\right)\right]\right]^{-1}$$

or, by applying the Sherman-Morrison formula,

$$\boldsymbol{\Pi}_0=\mathbf{I}+\left(\left(s_w\mathbf{w}\mathbf{V}_{\mathbf{B}}+s_p\,\mathbf{p}\widetilde{\mathbf{H}}_{\mathbf{B}}\right)\mathbf{f}^{\mathrm{T}}\right)^{-1}\mathbf{f}^{\mathrm{T}}\left[\mathbf{p}-\left(s_w\mathbf{w}\mathbf{V}_{\mathbf{B}}+s_p\,\mathbf{p}\widetilde{\mathbf{H}}_{\mathbf{B}}\right)\right]\tag{6.9}$$

It then follows that (i) $\mathbf{y}^{\mathrm{T}}$ is not uniquely determined when

$$\left(s_w\mathbf{w}\mathbf{V}_{\mathbf{B}}+s_p\,\mathbf{p}\widetilde{\mathbf{H}}_{\mathbf{B}}\right)\mathbf{f}^{\mathrm{T}}=0\tag{6.9a}$$

and (ii) one eigenvalue of $\boldsymbol{\Pi}_0$ equals

$$\left[s_w+\left(s_p-s_w\right)\left(\mathbf{p}\,\mathbf{f}^{\mathrm{T}}\right)^{-1}\mathbf{p}\widetilde{\mathbf{H}}_{\mathbf{B}}\,\mathbf{f}^{\mathrm{T}}\right]^{-1}$$

while all the other eigenvalues equal 1. The former eigenvalue corresponds to a Kaldorian multiplier (see Kaldor 1955–1956) and could be conceived of as *the* system's multiplier (associated with the case $\hat{\mathbf{m}}=\mathbf{0}$). Furthermore, from Eqs. 6.2 and 6.9, it follows that when both $\mathbf{w}\mathbf{V}_{\mathbf{B}}$ and $\mathbf{p}\widetilde{\mathbf{H}}_{\mathbf{B}}$ are semi-positive, (i) $\boldsymbol{\Pi}_0$ is semi-positive, (ii) its diagonal elements are greater than or equal to 1 and (iii) its elements are non-increasing functions of s_w and s_p (as in the single production case; see Kurz 1985, pp. 133 and 135–136). For $s_w=s_p=s$ (and $\mathbf{p}=\mathbf{e}$), each column of $\boldsymbol{\Pi}_0$ sums to s^{-1}. In the case of homogeneous labour and for $s_w=0$ and $s_p=1$, $\boldsymbol{\Pi}_0$ reduces to a Marxian multiplier defined by Trigg and Philp (2008).

Finally, it seems that only little can be said, a priori, for the case where $\hat{\mathbf{m}}\geq\mathbf{0}$ (also consider Mariolis 2008b). For instance, the application of the previous analysis to the SUT of the Greek economy for the year 2010 ($n=63$) gives the following results[12]:

[12] For the available input-output data as well as the construction of the relevant variables, see Mariolis and Soklis (2014, Appendix I). Furthermore, Mariolis and Soklis (2014) provide detailed results on the output, import $\left(\mathbf{p}\hat{\mathbf{m}}\,\mathbf{B}[\mathbf{B}-\mathbf{A}]^{-1}\boldsymbol{\Pi}\mathbf{e}_i^{\mathrm{T}}\right)$ and employment ($\mathbf{e}\mathbf{V}_{\mathbf{B}}\boldsymbol{\Pi}\mathbf{e}_i^{\mathrm{T}}$) multipliers, and discuss some of their policy implications for the recession-ridden Greek economy, especially for the post-2010 years which are characterized by serious fiscal and external imbalances along with negative net national savings (with the exception of the year 2001, they were negative in each year of the period 2000–2013), negative net investment and exceptionally high unemployment rates (also see Mariolis 2011; Tsoulfidis and Tsaliki 2014).

(i) The matrix $[\mathbf{B} - \mathbf{A}]^{-1}$ (and, therefore, $\mathbf{V_B}$) contains negative elements. Consequently, the system under consideration is not 'all-productive', and, therefore, it does not have the properties of a single-product system.

(ii) The matrix $\hat{\mathbf{r}}$ contains one negative element. The matrix $\widetilde{\mathbf{H}}_{\mathbf{B}}$ contains negative elements, although some of its columns are positive. The vector $\mathbf{p}\widetilde{\mathbf{H}}_{\mathbf{B}}\left(=\mathbf{e}\widetilde{\mathbf{H}}_{\mathbf{B}}\right)$ contains one negative element, while all of its remaining elements are semi-positive and less than 1 (see Eq. 6.2). It then follows that there exist values of s_w, s_p, for which $\mathbf{\Pi}_0$ is not semi-positive (see Eq. 6.9).

(iii) For every value of s_w, s_p, it holds $\left(s_w\mathbf{w}\mathbf{V_B} + s_p\mathbf{p}\widetilde{\mathbf{H}}_{\mathbf{B}}\right)\mathbf{f}^{\mathrm{T}} > 0$ (see Eq. 6.9a). Hence, the dynamic multiplier process defined by $\mathbf{\Lambda}_0$ is stable, $\mathbf{\Pi}_0$ is uniquely determined, and the eigenvalue of $\mathbf{\Pi}_0$ that differs from 1 is approximately equal to $\left[s_w + (s_p - s_w)0.655\right]^{-1}(> 1)$. For instance, for $s_w = 0$ and $s_p = 1$, $\mathbf{\Pi}_0$ is semi-positive, its diagonal elements are in the range of 1–1.059, that eigenvalue is 1.527, and the arithmetic mean of the output multipliers, Δ_y^i, is 1.707. By contrast, the largest eigenvalue of $\mathbf{\Lambda}$ is -18.555 and its dominant eigenvalue ratio is 0.911 ($rank[\mathbf{\Lambda}] = 50$). Matrix $\mathbf{\Pi}$ is not semi-positive, while its diagonal elements are all positive and in the range of 0.051–1.037. The dominant eigenvalue of $\mathbf{\Pi}$ is 1.219, the arithmetic mean of the moduli of its eigenvalues is 0.791, and that of Δ_y^i is 1.032. It can therefore be stated that the foreign sector plays a key role in the Sraffian multiplier for the Greek economy.

Appendix 2: Price Effects of Currency Devaluation

In what follows, let us assume that there are no non-competitive imports and that the price side of the system can be described by

$$\mathbf{p} = \mathbf{p}\mathbf{A} + \mathbf{s} \tag{6.10}$$

or

$$\mathbf{p} = \mathbf{p}\mathbf{A}^{\mathrm{d}} + \varepsilon\mathbf{p}^{\mathrm{m}}\mathbf{A}^{\mathrm{m}} + \mathbf{s} \tag{6.10a}$$

where $\mathbf{p}$ $(= \mathbf{e})$ denotes the stationary price vector of domestically produced commodities; $\mathbf{A}^{\mathrm{d}}$, $\mathbf{A}^{\mathrm{m}}$ the irreducible and primitive matrices of domestic and imported input-output coefficients, respectively; $\mathbf{A} \equiv \mathbf{A}^{\mathrm{d}} + \mathbf{A}^{\mathrm{m}}$, with $\lambda_{\mathbf{A}1} < 1$; ε the nominal exchange rate; $\mathbf{p}^{\mathrm{m}}$ the given vector of foreign currency prices of the imported commodities; $\mathbf{p} = \varepsilon\mathbf{p}^{\mathrm{m}}$; and $\mathbf{s}$ $(> \mathbf{0})$ the vector of gross values added per unit activity level, which, in national accounts terms, equals the sum of consumption of fixed capital, $\mathbf{s}_{\mathrm{C}}$, net taxes on production, $\mathbf{s}_{\mathrm{T}}$, net operating surplus, $\mathbf{s}_{\mathrm{S}}$, and compensation of employees, $\mathbf{s}_{\mathrm{E}}$, i.e.

$$\mathbf{s} \equiv \mathbf{s}_{\mathrm{C}} + \mathbf{s}_{\mathrm{T}} + \mathbf{s}_{\mathrm{S}} + \mathbf{s}_{\mathrm{E}} \tag{6.11}$$

By solving Eqs. 6.10 and 6.10a for $\mathbf{p}$, we obtain

$$\mathbf{p} = \mathbf{s}[\mathbf{I} - \mathbf{A}]^{-1} = (\varepsilon\mathbf{m} + \mathbf{s})\left[\mathbf{I} - \mathbf{A}^{\mathrm{d}}\right]^{-1} \tag{6.12}$$

where $\mathbf{m} \equiv \mathbf{p}^{\mathrm{m}}\mathbf{A}^{\mathrm{m}}$. The price effects of currency devaluation may be represented by the following dynamic version of Eq. 6.10a:

$$\mathbf{p}_{t+1} = \mathbf{p}_t\mathbf{A}^{\mathrm{d}} + \varepsilon_1\mathbf{m} + \mathbf{s}_t, \quad t = 0, 1, \ldots \tag{6.13}$$

where $\varepsilon_1 \equiv \left(1 + \widehat{\varepsilon}\right)\varepsilon_0$, $\widehat{\varepsilon}$ denotes the devaluation rate and

$$\mathbf{p}_0 = (\varepsilon_0\mathbf{m} + \mathbf{s})\left[\mathbf{I} - \mathbf{A}^{\mathrm{d}}\right]^{-1}$$

(see Eq. 6.12). Although there are alternative approaches for modelling the response of sectoral gross value added to currency devaluation, the choice between them should also take into account the input-output data availability. Thus, for the purposes of an indicative estimation, it may be postulated, for instance, that

$$\mathbf{s}_t = \left(\mathbf{p}_t\mathbf{A}^{\mathrm{d}} + \varepsilon_1\mathbf{m} + \mathbf{p}_t\hat{\mathbf{S}}_{\mathrm{CT}}\right)\hat{\boldsymbol{\mu}} + \mathbf{p}_t\hat{\mathbf{S}}_{\mathrm{CT}}$$

where (see Eq. 6.11) $\hat{\mathbf{S}}_{\mathrm{CT}} \equiv [\hat{\mathbf{s}}_{\mathrm{C}} + \hat{\mathbf{s}}_{\mathrm{T}}]\,\hat{\mathbf{p}}_0^{-1}$, $\hat{\boldsymbol{\mu}} \equiv [\hat{\mathbf{s}}_{\mathrm{S}} + \hat{\mathbf{s}}_{\mathrm{E}}]\hat{\mathbf{c}}_0^{-1}$ and

$$\mathbf{c}_0 \equiv \mathbf{p}_0\mathbf{A}^{\mathrm{d}} + \varepsilon_0\mathbf{m} + \mathbf{s}_{\mathrm{C}} + \mathbf{s}_{\mathrm{T}}$$

which imply that Eq. 6.13 becomes

$$\mathbf{p}_{t+1} = \mathbf{p}_t\boldsymbol{\Delta} + \varepsilon_1\mathbf{m}^* \tag{6.14}$$

where $\boldsymbol{\Delta} \equiv \left[\mathbf{A}^{\mathrm{d}} + \hat{\mathbf{S}}_{\mathrm{CT}}\right][\mathbf{I} + \hat{\boldsymbol{\mu}}]$ and $\mathbf{m}^* \equiv \mathbf{m}[\mathbf{I} + \hat{\boldsymbol{\mu}}]$. Then the solution of Eq. 6.14 is

$$\mathbf{p}_t = \mathbf{p}_0\boldsymbol{\Delta}^t + \varepsilon_1\mathbf{m}^*\left[\boldsymbol{\Delta}^{t-1} + \boldsymbol{\Delta}^{t-2} + \ldots + \mathbf{I}\right]$$

and $\mathbf{p}_t$ tends to $\varepsilon_1\mathbf{m}^*[\mathbf{I} - \boldsymbol{\Delta}]^{-1} = (1 + \hat{\varepsilon})\,\mathbf{p}_0$, since $\lambda_{\boldsymbol{\Delta}1} < 1$, while the price movement is governed by

$$\mathbf{m}^*\left[\boldsymbol{\Delta}^{t-1} + \boldsymbol{\Delta}^{t-2} + \ldots + \mathbf{I}\right]$$

which could be conceived of as the series of dated quantities of imported inputs.

In the extreme case where the gross values added are 'insensitive' to devaluation, i.e. $\mathbf{s}_t = \mathbf{s}$, $\boldsymbol{\Delta}$ should be replaced by $\mathbf{A}^{\mathrm{d}}$, $\mathbf{m}^*$ should be replaced by $\mathbf{m} + \varepsilon_1^{-1}\mathbf{s}$, and $\mathbf{p}_t$ tends to $(\varepsilon_1\mathbf{m} + \mathbf{s})\left[\mathbf{I} - \mathbf{A}^{\mathrm{d}}\right]^{-1} < (1 + \hat{\varepsilon})\,\mathbf{p}_0$. Finally, in the 'intermediate' case where $\mathbf{s}_t = \mathbf{p}_t\hat{\mathbf{s}}\,\hat{\mathbf{p}}_0^{-1}$, $\boldsymbol{\Delta}$ should be replaced by $\mathbf{A}^{\mathrm{d}} + \hat{\mathbf{s}}\,\hat{\mathbf{p}}_0^{-1}$, $\mathbf{m}^*$ should be replaced by $\mathbf{m}$, and $\mathbf{p}_t$ tends to $(1 + \hat{\varepsilon})\,\mathbf{p}_0$.[13]

Empirical evidence from the SIOT of the Greek economy for the year 2005 shows that (Katsinos and Mariolis 2012):

(i) The P-F eigenvalue of $\mathbf{A}^{\mathrm{d}}$ is 0.321 and the damping ratio is 1.290.
(ii) The P-F eigenvalue of $\mathbf{A}^{\mathrm{d}} + \hat{\mathbf{s}}\,\hat{\mathbf{p}}_0^{-1}$ is 0.949 and the damping ratio is 1.045.
(iii) The P-F eigenvalue of $\left[\mathbf{A}^{\mathrm{d}} + \hat{\mathbf{S}}_{\mathrm{CT}}\right][\mathbf{I} + \hat{\boldsymbol{\mu}}]$ is 0.893 and the damping ratio is 1.248.[14]
(iv) For $\hat{\varepsilon} = 50\%$, the cost-inflation rate (as measured by the gross value of domestic production) at $t = 1$ is 9.3 % (is 5.3 %), and the arithmetic mean of commodity prices associated with matrix $\left[\mathbf{A}^{\mathrm{d}} + \hat{\mathbf{S}}_{\mathrm{CT}}\right][\mathbf{I} + \hat{\boldsymbol{\mu}}]$ (with matrix $\mathbf{A}^{\mathrm{d}} + \hat{\mathbf{s}}\,\hat{\mathbf{p}}_0^{-1}$) reaches approximately 95 % of its asymptotic value at $t = 14$ (at $t = 30$).

These figures seem to be consistent with the finding that (other things constant) even 'large' devaluations would not imply great inflationary 'pressures'.[15]

References

Acemoglu, D., Ozdaglar, A., & Tahbaz-Salehi, A. (2010). *Cascades in networks and aggregate volatility*. National Bureau of Economic Research, Working Paper No. 16516. http://www.nber.org/papers/w16516. Accessed 20 Apr 2015.

---

[13] This kind of models is open to serious criticism (see Steedman 2000); the appropriate theoretical framework for dealing with the issue is described in Sects. 2.2.3 and 2.2.4. The above model has been formulated and applied by Mariolis et al. (1997), and the findings were consistent with empirical evidence on the rate of imported cost-inflation in the first year after the last drachma devaluation (by 14 % versus ECU) in March 1998 (the estimated values were in the range of 1.16–1.75 %, while the 'actual' one was not considerably greater than 1.2 %; see Bank of Greece 1999, Chap. 4).

[14] For the year 1988, the P-F eigenvalues of these matrices are 0.381, 0.939 and 0.821, respectively (Mariolis et al. 1997).

[15] A detailed study of nine large post-1990 devaluations (i.e. in excess of 38 % vs. US dollar) shows that the rate of inflation, measured by the consumer price index, is very low relative to the exchange rate devaluation (Burstein et al. 2002). For a combination of the price model (6.14) with Thirlwall's (1979, 2011) extended model of balance of payments constrained growth, and its application to the Greek economy, for the years 2011–2012, see Mariolis (2014): the findings of that (hypothetical) exercise lend support to the view that a rather large nominal devaluation, i.e. in excess of 57 %–60 %, is a necessary condition for the recovery of the economy.

Acemoglu, D., Carvalho, V. M., Ozdaglar, A., & Tahbaz-Salehi, A. (2012). The network origins of aggregate fluctuations. *Econometrica, 80*(5), 1977–2016.
Aruka, Y. (2015). *Evolutionary foundations of economic science. How can scientists study evolving economic doctrines from the last centuries?* Tokyo: Springer.
Bank of Greece. (1999). *Annual report for the year 1998 (in Greek)*. Athens: Bank of Greece.
Berman, A., & Plemmons, R. J. (1994). *Nonnegative matrices in the mathematical sciences*. Philadelphia: Society for Industrial and Applied Mathematics.
Białas, S., & Gurgul, H. (1998). On hypothesis about the second eigenvalue of the Leontief matrix. *Economic Systems Research, 10*(3), 285–289.
Bidard, C., & Schatteman, T. (2001). The spectrum of random matrices. *Economic Systems Research, 13*(3), 289–298.
Blanchard, O., Amighini, A., & Giavazzi, F. (2010). *Macroeconomics: A European perspective*. London: Prentice Hall.
Bródy, A. (1997). The second eigenvalue of the Leontief matrix. *Economic Systems Research, 9* (3), 253–258.
Bródy, A. (2000a). A wave matrix. *Structural Change and Economic Dynamics, 11*(1–2), 157–166.
Bródy, A. (2000b). The monetary multiplier. *Economic Systems Research, 12*(2), 215–218.
Burstein, A., Eichenbaum, M., & Rebelo, S. (2002). *Why are rates of inflation so low after large devaluations?* National Bureau of Economic Research, Working Paper No. 8748. http://www.nber.org/papers/w8748.pdf. Accessed 12 Dec 2014.
Carvalho, V. M. (2014). From micro to macro via production networks. *Journal of Economics Perspectives, 28*(4), 23–48.
Chipman, J. S. (1950). The multi-sector multiplier. *Econometrica, 18*(4), 355–374.
Duménil, G., & Lévy, D. (1989). The competition process in a fixed capital environment: A classical view. *The Manchester School, 57*(1), 34–57.
Dupor, B. (1999). Aggregation and irrelevance in multi-sector models. *Journal of Monetary Economics, 43*(2), 391–409.
Egidi, M. (1975). Stability and instability in Sraffian models. In L. L. Pasinetti (Ed.), *Italian economic papers* (Vol. 1, pp. 215–250). Oxford: Oxford University Press.
Flaschel, P. (2010). *Topics in classical micro- and macroeconomics. Elements of a critique of Neoricardian theory*. Heidelberg: Springer.
Gnos, C., & Rochon, L.-P. (Eds.). (2008). *The Keynesian multiplier*. London: Routledge.
Goldberg, G., & Neumann, M. (2003). Distribution of subdominant eigenvalues of matrices with random rows. *Society for Industrial and Applied Mathematics Journal on Matrix Analysis and Applications, 24*(3), 747–761.
Goldberg, G., Okunev, P., Neumann, M., & Schneider, H. (2000). Distribution of subdominant eigenvalues of random matrices. *Methodology and Computing in Applied Probability, 2*(2), 137–151.
Goodwin, R. M. (1970). *Elementary economics from the higher standpoint*. Cambridge: Cambridge University Press.
Gurgul, H., & Wójtowicz, T. (2015). On the economic interpretation of the Bródy conjecture. *Economic Systems Research, 27*(1), 122–131.
Halpern, L., & Molnár, G. (1997). Equilibrium and disequilibrium in a disaggregated classical model. In A. Simonovits & A. E. Stenge (Eds.), *Prices, growth and cycles. Essays in honour of András Bródy* (pp. 149–160). London: Macmillan.
Hartwig, J. (2004). Keynes's multiplier in a two-sectoral framework. *Review of Political Economy, 16*(3), 309–334.
Horvath, M. (1998). Cyclicality and sectoral linkages: Aggregate fluctuations from independent sectoral shocks. *Review of Economic Dynamics, 1*(4), 781–808.
Horvath, M. (2000). Sectoral shocks and aggregate fluctuations. *Journal of Monetary Economics, 45*(1), 69–106.

Hua, L.-K. (1984). On the mathematical theory of globally optimal planned economic systems. *Proceedings of the National Academy of Sciences of the United States of America, 81*(20), 6549–6553.

Kaldor, N. (1955–1956). Alternative theories of distribution. *The Review of Economic Studies*, 23 (2), 83–100.

Katsinos, A., & Mariolis, T. (2012). Switch to devalued drachma and cost-push inflation: A simple input-output approach to the Greek case. *Modern Economy, 3*(2), 164–170.

Kurz, H. D. (1985). Effective demand in a 'classical' model of value and distribution: The multiplier in a Sraffian framework. *The Manchester School, 53*(2), 121–137.

Lange, O. (1967). The computer and the market. In C. H. Feinstein (Ed.), *Socialism, capitalism and economic growth: Essays presented to Maurice Dobb* (pp. 158–161). Cambridge: Cambridge University Press.

Lange, O. (1970). *Introduction to economic cybernetics*. Oxford: Pergamon Press.

Leontief, W., & Bródy, A. (1993). Money-flow computations. *Economic Systems Research, 5*(3), 225–233.

Long, J. B., Jr., & Plosser, C. I. (1983). Real business cycles. *Journal of Political Economy, 91*(1), 39–69.

Lucas, R. E. (1977). Understanding business cycles. *Carnegie-Rochester Conference Series on Public Policy, 5*(1), 7–29.

Mariolis, T. (2008a). *The Sraffian multiplier: Theory and application*. Internal Report of the Study Group on Sraffian Economics, 12 Nov 2008 (in Greek). Athens: Department of Public Administration, Panteion University.

Mariolis, T. (2008b). Pure joint production, income distribution, employment and the exchange rate. *Metroeconomica, 59*(4), 656–665.

Mariolis, T. (2011). The wages-profits-growth relationships and the peculiar case of the Greek economy. In T. Mariolis (Ed.) (2016), *Essays on the work of Dimitris Batsis* (forthcoming).

Mariolis, T. (2014). Modelling the devaluation of the Greek currency. *Business Perspectives, 13* (1), 1–5.

Mariolis, T., & Soklis, G. (2014). *The Sraffian multiplier for the Greek economy: Evidence from the supply and use table for the year 2010*. MPRA Paper No 6253. http://mpra.ub.uni-muenchen.de/60253/. Accessed 12 Dec 2014.

Mariolis, T., & Tsoulfidis, L. (2014). On Bródy's conjecture: Theory, facts and figures about instability of the US economy. *Economic Systems Research, 26*(2), 209–223.

Mariolis, T., Economidis, C., Stamatis, G., & Fousteris, N. (1997). *Quantitative evaluation of the effects of devaluation on the cost of production (in Greek)*. Athens: Kritiki.

Metcalfe, J. S., & Steedman, I. (1981). Some long-run theory of employment, income distribution and the exchange rate. *The Manchester School, 49*(1), 1–20.

Miller, R. E., & Blair, P. D. (2009). *Input-output analysis: Foundations and extensions*. Cambridge: Cambridge University Press.

Molnár, G., & Simonovits, A. (1998). The subdominant eigenvalue of a large stochastic matrix. *Economic Systems Research, 10*(1), 79–82.

Samuelson, P. A. (1970). Law of conservation of the capital-output ratio. *Proceedings of the National Academy of Sciences of the United States of America, 67*(3), 1477–1479.

Steedman, I. (1984). Natural prices, differential profit rates and the classical competitive process. *The Manchester School, 52*(2), 123–140.

Steedman, I. (2000). Income distribution, foreign trade and the value-added vector. *Economic Systems Research, 12*(2), 221–230.

Sun, G.-Z. (2008). The first two eigenvalues of large random matrices and Brody's hypothesis on the stability of large input-output systems. *Economic Systems Research, 20*(4), 429–432.

ten Raa, T. (2005). *The economics of input-output analysis*. Cambridge: Cambridge University Press.

Thirlwall, A. P. (1979). The balance of payments constraint as an explanation of international growth rate differences. *Banca Nazionale del Lavoro Quarterly Review, 32*(128), 45–53.

Thirlwall, A. P. (2011). Balance of payments constrained growth models: History and overview. *PSL Quarterly Review, 64*(259), 307–351.

Trigg, A. B., & Philp, B. (2008). *Value magnitudes and the Kahn employment multiplier*. Paper presented to Developing Quantitative Marxism, Bristol, 3–5 Apr 2008. http://carecon.org.uk/QM/Conference%202008/Papers/Trigg.pdf. Accessed 12 Dec 2014.

Tsaliki, P., & Tsoulfidis, L. (2015). *Essays on political economy (in Greek)*. Thessaloniki: Tziolas.

Tsoulfidis, L., & Tsaliki, P. (2014). Unproductive labour, capital accumulation and profitability crisis in the Greek economy. *International Review of Applied Economics, 28*(5), 562–585.

Index

© Springer Japan 2016

T. Mariolis, L. Tsoulfidis, *Modern Classical Economics and Reality*, Evolutionary Economics and Social Complexity Science 2, DOI 10.1007/978-4-431-55004-4

MIX
Papier aus verantwortungsvollen Quellen
Paper from responsible sources
FSC® C105338

If you have any concerns about our products,
you can contact us on
ProductSafety@springernature.com

In case Publisher is established outside the EU,
the EU authorized representative is:
Springer Nature Customer Service Center GmbH
Europaplatz 3, 69115 Heidelberg, Germany

Printed by Libri Plureos GmbH
in Hamburg, Germany